# NORTHERN
# LIGHTS

## THE AGE OF
## SCOTTISH LIGHTHOUSES

# Scotland's Lighthouses 1636-2010

Muckle Flugga

Eshaness • • Firths Voe
• Out Skerries

• Bressay

• Sumburgh Head

Fair Isle
North & South

Noup Head • • North Ronaldsay
• Start Point

Sule Skerry • Brough of Birsay
Auskerry •
Hoy High & Low • Helliar Holm
• Copinsay
• Cantick Head
Cape Wrath • Dunnet Head • Stroma • Pentland Skerries
• Duncansby Head
Butt of Lewis • Strathy Holburn
Point Head • Noss Head
Flannan Islands • Tiumpan Head • Clythness
• Stoer Head
Arnish Point •

Eilean Glas •
Rubh Re •
Monach • Rona • Tarbat Ness
Neist Covesea Skerries
Point • Cromarty • Kinnaird Head
Ushenish • Chanonry • Rattray Head
Kyleakin • • Buchan Ness
• Ornsay
Hyskeir • • Girdle Ness
Barra Head • • Tod Head
Ardnamurchan • Corran Point • Scurdie Ness
Rubha Nan Gall •
Lismore • Tay Leading Lights
Skerryvore • • Bell Rock
Fladda •
Dubh Artach • • Isle of May
Ruvaal • Fidra • Bass Rock
Skervuile • Cloch Oxcars • • Inchkeith • Barns Ness
Loch Indaal • McArthur's Toward Point • St Abbs Head
Rinns of Islay • Head • Little Cumbrae **Glasgow** **Edinburgh**

Davaar • Holy Island Inner
& Outer
Mull of Kintyre • Pladda
Sanda • • Turnberry
Ailsa Craig

Corsewall • • Loch Ryan
Killantringan • • Southerness
Crammag Head • • Little Ross
• Mull of Galloway

Point of Ayre
• Maughold Head
**Douglas**
• Douglas Head
Calf of Man • • Langness
Chicken Rock

# NORTHERN
# LIGHTS

## THE AGE OF
## SCOTTISH LIGHTHOUSES

A. D. MORRISON-LOW

National Museums Scotland

First published in 2010 by
NMS Enterprises Limited – Publishing
a division of NMS Enterprises Limited
National Museums Scotland
Chambers Street, Edinburgh EH1 1JF

in conjunction with
The Royal Scottish Society of Arts

Reprinted in 2014

www.nms.ac.uk
www.rssa.org.uk

British Library Cataloguing in
Publication Data
A catalogue record for this book
is available from the British Library.

ISBN: 978 1 905267 47 7 (pbk)
ISBN: 978 1 905267 57 6 (hbk)

Cover design: Mark Blackadder
Cover image: Oil painting of the Bell Rock
    Lighthouse by A. Macdonald of Arbroath in 1820,
    one which, according to Robert Stevenson, helped
    form the basis of J. M. W. Turner's watercolour.
    Presented by the Trustees of D. Alan Stevenson.
    (NMS T.2009.108)
Publication format:
    NMS Enterprises Limited – Publishing
Printed and bound in the United Kingdom
    by Bell & Bain Limited, Glasgow.

Published by National Museums Scotland as one
of a number of titles based on museum scholarship
and partnership.

For a full listing of NMS Enterprises Limited –
Publishing titles and related merchandise:

www.nms.ac.uk/books

# Contents

Credits and Permissions . . . . . . . . . . . . . . . . . . . . . . . . . . . . . vi

Acknowledgements . . . . . . . . . . . . . . . . . . . . . . . . . . . . . . . vii

Foreword by
*Jane Carmichael*, National Museums Scotland . . . . . . . . . . . . . . xi

Preface by
*Sir Andrew Cubie*, Northern Lighthouse Board . . . . . . . . . . . . xiii

The Royal Scottish Society of Arts . . . . . . . . . . . . . . . . . . . . . . xv

Introduction: Scottish Lighthouses . . . . . . . . . . . . . . . . . . . . . xvii

CHAPTER 1:  In the Beginning . . . . . . . . . . . . . . . . . . . . . . . . 1

CHAPTER 2:  The Eddystone . . . . . . . . . . . . . . . . . . . . . . . . . 31

CHAPTER 3:  Scottish Lights before the Bell Rock . . . . . . . . . . . . 75

CHAPTER 4:  Building the Bell Rock . . . . . . . . . . . . . . . . . . . . 115

CHAPTER 5:  Lighthouses in Scotland after the Bell Rock . . . . . . 143

CHAPTER 6:  Stevenson Exports and Later Work . . . . . . . . . . . . 187

CHAPTER 7:  Modern Times . . . . . . . . . . . . . . . . . . . . . . . . . 219

Glossary . . . . . . . . . . . . . . . . . . . . . . . . . . . . . . . . . . . . . . 237

Family Tree: The Stevenson Family of Engineers . . . . . . . . . . . 239

Bibliography and References . . . . . . . . . . . . . . . . . . . . . . . . . 240

Selective Index . . . . . . . . . . . . . . . . . . . . . . . . . . . . . . . . . . 254

# Credits and Permissions

*The following listings contain acknowledgements for use of source material within this publication. No reproduction of material in copyright is permitted without prior contact with the publisher or with original sources.*

CAMBRIDGE UNIVERSITY PRESS
for permission to reproduce an extract from Hubert Lamb and Knud Frydendahl: *Historic Storms of the North Sea, British Isles and Northwest Europe* (© Cambridge University Press, 1991)

*COUNTRY LIFE*
for permission to reproduce an extract from Douglas Hague: 'Lighthouse of a Scottish Island' (19 August 1965)

JULIA ELTON
for permission to produce extracts from her paper 'A Light to Lighten Our Darkness', from *International Journal for the History of Engineering and Technology*.

PENNY FIELDING
for assistance in researching the literary estate of Robert Louis Stevenson

HARPERCOLLINS
for permission to produce an extract from Bella Bathurst: *The Lighthouse Stevensons: The Extraordinary Story of the Building of the Scottish Lighthouses by the Ancestors of Robert Louis Stevenson* (© HarperCollins)

JEAN MUNRO
for permission to produce extracts from R. W. Munro, *Scottish Lighthouses* (Thule Press, 1979)

NORTHERN LIGHTHOUSE BOARD
for permission to reproduce extracts from the *Northern Lighthouse Board Journal*

*THE SHETLAND TIMES*
for permission to quote from the 1998 article by Mike Grundon

R. Q. C. STEVENSON
for permission to reproduce quotes from D. Alan Stevenson: *The World's Lighthouses before 1820* (Oxford University Press), and *The World's Lighthouses from Ancient Times to 1820* (Dover)

UNIVERSITY OF CHICAGO PRESS
for permission to produce extracts from P. D. A. Harvey: *Maps in Tudor England* (© University of Chicago Press, 1993), and R. H. Coase: 'The Lighthouse in Economics' from *Journal of Law and Economics*

The author sourced text from Margaret Maria, Lady Verney (editor): *Verney Letters of the Eighteenth Century from the MSS at Claydon House* (© Ernest Benn).
These papers are now held in CAMBRIDGE UNIVERSITY LIBRARY who gave this publisher permission to reproduce extracts from the manuscripts

With additional thanks to Orion Publishing Group, Anova Books, Gomer Press, Hachette UK and Constable & Robinson.

*Every effort has been made to trace and contact the owners of the text reproduced in this book. The Publisher would like to apologise for any inadvertent errors and will be pleased to made the necessary amendments in future editions or reprints if contacted in writing by the copyright holders. Copyright rests with all those authors and holding institutions named in this publication.*

# Acknowledgements

MY EARLIEST MEMORIES of this wonderful collection come from childhood, when my younger sister and I stayed with an elderly cousin during the school holidays in order to acquaint us with the cultural riches of Edinburgh. Each time we stayed with her, we insisted that we must visit the 'Chambers Street Museum', where the Shipping Hall and Lighthouse Gallery above it were my first choice of destination. My favourite piece was, of course, the lead pellet recovered from the unfortunate Henry Hall's stomach, demonstrating I was as ghoulish as the next child. Little did I anticipate that, one day, I would be responsible for the care and maintenance of this material; and, as it has been in store for some twenty years, it has been a delight to reacquaint myself with it all again, and – I hope – to make some useful additions.

It is always a pleasure to record my thanks to friends and colleagues who have helped in a project as large as this one, extending their professional skills often beyond the ordinary call of duty. Members of my department have been truly supportive: Jane Carmichael, Alex Hayward, Dr Tacye Phillipson, Maryanne Millar, Julie Orford, Maureen Kerr; and former colleagues, including Dr Allen Simpson, who made great sense of the files before they became my responsibility. He also was jointly responsible for an earlier version of chapter 3, which was prepared in a somewhat different guise for a conference at Middleburg in 1998. Other colleagues have helped: Dr Philippa Hubbard researched some of the Eddystone printed material, and Dr Godfrey Evans helped me with the Egyptian influences. As ever, NMS Library staff, labouring under the pressure of temporary closure, have provided extraordinary support: Mark Glancy, Ines Castellano-Colmenero, Emma Robinson, Morven Donald, Andy McDougall, Ross Anderson and Alison Lonie. Neil McLean, Joyce Smith and Leslie Florence of NMS Photography have again pulled out all the stops on what must have seemed an endless project. Dorothy Kidd of the Scottish Life Archive has provided many of the images. On the documentation side,

I would like to thank Pam Babes; and for the publication, Maggie Wilson, Kate Blackadder, Lynne Reilly and Lesley Taylor. Members of the Conservation staff have, as always, been friendly and helpful: Dr Jim Tate, Stuart McDonald, Chris Cockburn, Sarah Gerrish, Darren Cox and Alex Walton. Also Lisa Cumming and Tizzy Main. Thanks are due to staff in the stores: Brian Cuthbert, Frank Butler and his team; and to the Exhibition team, especially Sarah Teale; also Alison Cromarty, Elaine Macintyre, Kerryn Fraser, Stephen Allen, Charlotte Hirst, Jan Dawson, Yvonne Brown and Vicky Evans.

Externally, the impetus for appropriate celebration of the bicentenary of the Bell Rock Lighthouse has been building up over some years, thanks mainly to persistent pressure from Peter Mackay CB, former Chief Commissioner of the Northern Lighthouse Board. This led to the formation of a committee under the chairmanship of Professor John R. Hume OBE (Royal Commission on the Ancient and Historical Monuments of Scotland), including Neil Gregory (RCAHMS), Kirsty Lingstadt (RCAHMS), Veronica Fraser (RCAHMS), Helen Foster (SCRAN), Sheila Mackenzie (National Library of Scotland), Valerie Hunter (National Galleries of Scotland), Linda McClelland (NGS), Dr Tristram Clarke (National Archives of Scotland), Professor Roland Paxton MBE, FRSE (Institution of Civil Engineers), Virginia Mayes-Wright (Museum of Scottish Lighthouses), Norman Atkinson (Angus Museums), and Willie Milne (Angus Museums). John Hume also kindly read this manuscript. A second committee was also set up for celebrations to take place during the week of the anniversary in early February 2011 by the Royal Society of Edinburgh: the members of this were also of immense assistance to me: Sir Andrew Cubie CBE, FRSE, Professor Andrew C. Walker FRSE, Bob Kibble, Róisín Calvert-Elliott and Catriona Blair.

Many thanks are due to our exhibition sponsors: first, the Northern Lighthouse Heritage Trust, which ensures that material relating to the Board's history is not disposed of without due consideration, and indeed goes to appropriate heritage bodies. The Trust consists of The Rt Hon Lord Boyd of Duncansby QC, Peter Mackay CB, Robert Quayle, Sheriff Principal Edward Bowen CBE TD QC, Sheriff Principal Bruce Kerr QC, James Will WS, Douglas Gorman, Roger Lockwood CB and Karen Charleson. Second, the long-established Fife and Edinburgh legal partnership, Pagan Osborne, has also generously sponsored the exhibition, which has great relevance to their geographical base. Equally large measures of gratitude are given to the sponsors of this book, the Royal Scottish Society of Arts, whose history plays no small part in the history unfolding within these pages: the President, Robin Harper MSP, the Secretary, Jane Ridder-Patrick, and the Council, which saw my appli-

viii

cation for funding as both appropriate and opportune – long may these cordial relations between the Museum and the Society continue.

I would also like to thank, for allowing me to bother them at inappropriate and inconvenient times, Roger Lockwood CB, Moray Waddell and Lorna Hunter, all of the Northern Lighthouse Board; and James Taylor OBE, previously of the Northern Lighthouse Board and now Chairman of the Board of the Museum of Scottish Lighthouses, for an unforgettable day on the Bell Rock ('Alison, you *shall* go to the Bell'); also Dr Andrew Cook for an illuminating discussion on sea-marking; Dr Anita McConnell for general support and helpful criticism; Alison Barnes for many perceptive conversations about Henry Winstanley; Maureen Attrill of Plymouth City Museum & Art Gallery; Dr Gloria Clifton and Dr Richard Dunn at the National Maritime Museum, Greenwich; Professor Frank A. J. L. James of the Royal Institution, London; Robert Hollingdale and Martin Lawrence from RIN, who helped with sea-marks; Susan Ciccatelli for sharing her ancestor's story with us; Donald Johnson of Cape Bonavista for information about the reflectors there; Sean Hignett for his help; Mrs Alma Howarth-Loomes for the photograph of the 1862 Exhibition material; Dr Joan Schwartz of Queen's University, Kingston, Ontario, who insisted that we visit Ardnamurchan lighthouse on an unexpectedly glorious April day, and providing me with recent references to Canadian lighthouse history; James Lawson of the North Queensferry Heritage Trust for the visit to Inchkeith; the Morrison-Lows for the trip from Anstruther to the Isle of May; and my father for letting me drag him, more or less willingly, to Arbroath.

Once again, my immediate family and friends have had to put up with me endlessly boring on about a project I have enjoyed investigating enormously: my thanks and love, as always, to them.

Alison Morrison-Low
EDINBURGH 2010

# Foreword

## Jane Carmichael

DIRECTOR OF COLLECTIONS
### National Museums Scotland

WE ARE DELIGHTED to have the opportunity to mount an exhibition showcasing our lighthouse collection and to publish this book. Neither would have been possible without the happy conjunction of the anniversary of the lighting of the Bell Rock and the determination of the bi-centennial committee to mark it appropriately. Originally suggested by Peter Mackay CB, former Chief Commissioner of the Northern Lighthouse Board, the notion of the exhibition and the publication was taken forward to become an important part of the celebrations. As a member of the bi-centennial committee, National Museums Scotland would like to thank all its fellow members: the Northern Lighthouse Board, National Galleries of Scotland, National Library of Scotland, National Archives of Scotland, the Institution of Civil Engineers, the Museum of Scottish Lighthouses, Angus Museums and the Royal Commission on the Ancient and Historical Monuments of Scotland, for their contributions. We would particularly like to thank the Chair of the Committee, Professor John R. Hume OBE, and the Chairman of the Northern Lighthouse Board, Sir Andrew Cubie CBE.

The collection of lighthouse material held by National Museums Scotland has been in store during the Royal Museum Project, our major redevelopment of our Victorian building, due for completion next year. This has given us the opportunity to reassess the collection, known to be one of the finest in any museum. Much new information has been found, not only about our collection, but about its relationship to the history of lighthouses in general and Scotland in particular. Our curator and author, Dr Alison Morrison-Low is to be congratulated on the success of her efforts.

We are very grateful to our sponsors – Pagan Osborne and the Northern Lighthouse Heritage Trust – who contributed to the exhibition, and to the Royal Scottish Society of Arts who have supported this publication. Such help is always appreciated, but particularly in the present economic climate.

OPPOSITE PAGE

Edinburgh Museum of Science and Art. The Main Hall from the first floor balcony by an unknown photographer, c.1867.

(National Museums Scotland)

# Preface

## Sir Andrew Cubie CBE, FRSE

### CHAIRMAN
### Northern Lighthouse Board

NATIONAL MUSEUMS SCOTLAND and the Royal Scottish Society of Arts deserve considerable praise for their publication of this book. Their support and encouragement of Alison Morrison-Low has been timely and has enabled Alison to offer us a quite excellent account of Scottish lighthouses, with particular focus on the Bell Rock. Her research and attribution is both detailed and authoritative, and her prose style is a delight.

Inevitably, grand projects from centuries gone by, which bequeath a legacy of international significance, will be both well documented and reviewed. This is, of course, true of the endeavours of the Stevenson family in relation to Scottish lighthouses, and in particular the remarkable achievement in Robert Stevenson's construction of the Bell Rock. Many might have thought that there was little to be added to these narratives, but Alison, in the way in which she has assembled her material and the style in which it is presented, gives any reader additional information.

She takes us on a journey from the early light on the island of Pharos at Alexandria in the 3rd century BC to the impact of dGPS and e-Loran today, entwining from the last two and a quarter centuries the history of the Northern Lighthouse Board and the Stevenson family. Iconic in that account has been the planning, construction and operation of the Bell Rock for two hundred years. Alexander Lindsay, writing in the sixteenth century, stated that 'betuixt Fyvisnes and the Read Head 12 milis est southest of the said Read Head lyethe a daunger called Inchcope'. Unmarked, the Inchcape reef would remain just as dangerous today. Alison properly records the manner in which the Inchcape reef became identified with the noise of a bell, and I am not alone in recalling from early school days in Scotland some sixty years ago, the poem which begins:

OPPOSITE PAGE

Group-flashing apparatus with Stevenson's equi-angular refractor showing three flashes every twenty seconds, designed by David A. Stevenson, constructed by Chance Brothers, Birmingham and James Dove & Co., Edinburgh, for Eilean Glas on the Isle of Harris, in use from 1907 until 1978. The apparatus made three revolutions in one minute. The optic originally revolved on a mercury bath. Presented by the Northern Lighthouse Board.

(NMS T.1978.96)

*The worthy abbot of Aberbrothok*
*had placed that bell on the Inchcape rock ...*

I have a personal connection in relation to that worthy abbot, as the first reference to any Cubie in Scotland is to one who was in the fourteenth century the Abbot of Arbroath. I claim, however, no dynastic connection to the reef!

Without the stalwart Bell Rock, first lit on 1st February 1811, the Inchcape rocks would, over succeeding decades, have continued to take life and generate enormous economic loss. In the ten-year period before its construction began, not only was HMS *York* – a 64-gun man-of-war – lost with all her crew, but in one fateful storm in 1797 it is reckoned that as many as seventy ships were lost in a few days on the Inchcape reef, many blown north from as far south as Yarmouth.

Today, in another age, the abiding risk of weather and hidden hazards to mariners around the 6200 miles of our Scottish coastline has not altered, but the management of them most certainly has in our hands. The Northern Lighthouse Board, in its contemporary form, remains as dedicated as ever to ensuring the safety of all at sea around Scotland and the Isle of Man. We continue to meet our exacting statutory responsibilities with the active engagement of shipowners, mariners and governments and will continue to do so in the years ahead. As Alison correctly notes towards the end of her book, gone are the days of our building lights such as the Bell Rock, Skerryvore or Dubh Artach, and our construction techniques now include the use of 'flatpack', aluminium lattice modular lighthouses, of which a certain Swedish furniture company would be proud!

In her writing, Alison encourages our respect for the past, demonstrates what we can learn from an extraordinary inheritance, and concludes that we remain in an age of Scottish lighthouses. With that view, I entirely agree.

# The Royal Scottish Society of Arts

THE ROYAL SCOTTISH Society of Arts (RSSA) was founded in 1821 as 'The Society for the Encouragement of the Useful Arts in Scotland' and incorporated by Royal Charter in 1841. The Society was established by the great Scottish physicist and natural philosopher, Sir David Brewster, in 1821 as an 'improving society', dedicated to the promotion of invention and enterprise. Its original name showed that it was concerned with the fields that we would now describe as science, technology, engineering and manufacture, but which were then known as the useful arts, as opposed to the fine arts.

For many years, the promotion of invention and improvements of all sorts was the main business of the Society, and its meetings were the focus of a large and active cross-section of Edinburgh society, including academics, gentry, professionals such as civil engineers and lawyers, and skilled craftsmen such as instrument makers, engravers and printers. The Society's published *Transactions* provide a fascinating record of changes in technology, and the Society's extensive archive – accessible in the National Library of Scotland – is a valuable resource used by researchers.

In more recent times, the Society's meeting programme has been based on lectures given by expert and often distinguished speakers. The lectures cover a wide range of scientific and technical topics, but still with the original aim of keeping the membership informed about current concerns in science, engineering, medicine – often with a topical edge. Meetings of the Society are held monthly, at 7 pm on Monday evenings, from October or November to May or June. In addition, organised visits are made each year to a research, manufacturing or industrial establishment. Most meetings are held in Edinburgh's city centre.

The Society was incorporated in 1841 by Royal Charter and was granted a Coat of Arms in 1978.

# Scottish Lighthouses

THE AGE OF Scottish lighthouses began in post-Union Britain with influential Scots lobbying the Westminster Parliament to create their own authority in the north to oversee the safe passage of ships and their cargoes around Scotland's extremely hazardous coasts. The man at Westminster at the sharp end of this was George Dempster (1732-1818), Member of Parliament for Forfar and Fife Burghs. On his advice, a Commons committee was set up, and in due course it recommended that a Bill be prepared to set up a board of trustees, or Commissioners, with the authority to build lights in the recommended positions and to levy dues on every British and foreign ship that passed any of the lights. This is how the modern lighthouse service in Scotland is still funded: the ordinary tax-payer gets this service free. The Board still maintains that careful post-Union phrasing of its name – 'North Britain' as opposed to 'Scotland' – to neutralise any memories of that unfortunate episode in 1745.

The Bill was presented to the House of Commons on 31 May 1786, and became law almost immediately. The early Board was made up of members of the legal profession, with a number of burgh officials. The Board – initially named as 'the Commissioners for Northern Lights' – met for the first time on 1 August 1786 to discuss the building of their first four lighthouses. Unlike their counterpart in England, founded during the reign of Henry VIII as 'The Trinity House of Deptford Strond', which had spent the intervening years farming out its monopoly on lighthouse-construction, the Northern Lighthouse Board began its programme of building sea-marks with an almost clean slate. With the exception of the Isle of May (1636), the lights at Buddon Ness (1687), the lighthouse at Southerness (1749), and the Isle of Cumbrae (1757), all lights in Scotland were new; the older ones were renovated or replaced by the Northern Lighthouse Board in due course.

The Board continues to meet, as it has done now for the past two and a quarter centuries, to debate policy and implement new technologies to ensure that now it is not only ships and cargoes that have safe

OPPOSITE PAGE

Stereoscopic photograph of the 1862 International Exhibition, London, showing the display from the Northern Lighthouse Board, by the London Stereoscopic Company. See page xix for full version.

(© From the Howarth-Loomes Collection at National Museums Scotland)

passage: '*In Salutem Omnium*' means 'For the Safety of All', and the Northern Lighthouse Board, through the many changes that two centuries have brought, takes this motto extremely seriously.[1] We still live in the age of Scottish lighthouses, although we are perhaps less aware of it than ever before. As an island, almost all our raw materials are brought in by ship: our foodstuffs, our consumables, our luxuries. As the United Kingdom has moved from being a primary producer (almost all our goods are now manufactured in China), and her great ships are no longer built, nor ply up and down the Clyde – labour is cheaper in Korea – so her people's awareness of the oceans has diminished. But our lighthouses still shine brightly at night, for the differing classes of user: the Royal Navy, the Merchant Navy, and the smaller but essential benefactors of fishermen and sailors of leisure craft. Using charts, sailing directions and land profiles, and now the more modern navigational aids such as radio and GPS, all are seeking safe havens in rough seas.

There has been a long and fruitful relationship between the Northern Lighthouse Board and National Museums Scotland, as can be seen in three mid-Victorian photographs. The first shows material exhibited as cutting-edge technology by the Northern Lighthouse Board at the 1862 International Exhibition in London; and the same objects are photographed on display shortly afterwards in the semi-completed Main Hall in the Edinburgh Museum of Science and Art, one of National Museums Scotland's precursors, at Chambers Street. This first photograph is undated, but the second has been given a date of about 1867, and shows, I believe, the same scene, but taken from the first floor balcony. It dates from after the opening of the Museum in 1866, but before the second and more westerly part of the building had been put up: the half-completed Main Hall is boarded across what is now the middle.

Over the next half century or so, items relating to lighthouse technology were displayed at many of the major trade exhibitions held in the western world, and on being brought back to Edinburgh were deposited with the Museum. In the 1920s a new wing was added to the main galleries of what had become the Royal Scottish Museum in Chambers Street, and the first floor of this was almost entirely devoted to showing the history of sea-marking. Although this long-term display was dismantled in 1992 to enable building works connected to the new Museum of Scotland next door, through exhibition and publication this collection tells the story of lighthouse technology and history, and is used here to celebrate the bi-centenary of the lighting of the Bell Rock, the world's oldest surviving rock lighthouse, the anniversary of which falls on 1 February 2011.

This anniversary has provided an opportunity to pull together

information about this outstanding collection and its context, a main strand of which has come from the Northern Lighthouse Board, the quasi-government authority – now under the umbrella of the Department for Transport – which maintains sea-marks in Scotland and the Isle of Man. However, this is only part of the story. The family of Engineers to the Board, most recently and successfully discussed by Bella Bathurst in her 1999 book, *The Lighthouse Stevensons*, has also ensured that many items which belonged to them, rather than the Board, have been placed in the care of the Museum, and are thus accessible to the public. Other items, too – from a variety of sources – have found their way to form valuable additions to this collection.

The earliest pieces relating to lighthouse technology to be acquired by National Museums Scotland were a number of important eighteenth-century artefacts connected with the Eddystone Rock in the English Channel. It may seem perverse that items significant to the history of a series of lights built on a rock so far distant from Scottish jurisdiction should end up in her national museum, but any discussion of the provenance of this group demonstrates that this is not as peculiar as it might initially appear. This material, as Charles Waterston relates, was presented by the widowed Susan, Countess of Morton, to the Royal Society of Edinburgh in 1828.[2] Its transfer was noted in the *Gentleman's Magazine*:

> The Countess of Morton has presented to the Royal Society [of Edinburgh] a variety of models, formerly the property of Smeaton, the engineer, together with several drawings and plans of the celebrated Eddystone. Among other curiosities accompanying this

donation, is the mass of lead which was taken from the stomach of the poor man who swallowed it in a fluid state, during the conflagration of the wooden structure which preceded Smeaton's far-famed light-house. This man lived some time, but died in consequence of the accident in Exeter Infirmary [*sic*], when the production of the lead convinced his medical attendants that his story was correct.[3]

The collection was assembled by Robert Weston, manager of the syndicate that purchased the lease of the Eddystone Lighthouse in 1716 and held it until its expiry in 1807; control of the family's majority share passed to his son Robert Harcourt Weston after the father's death. The items connected with John Rudyerd (fl.1703-09) were already in his possession when John Smeaton (1724-92) first met him; and the Smeaton items were acquired by Weston from the engineer. Indeed, Weston wrote to Smeaton in January 1757 about his collection:

Though I take great pleasure in contemplating the powers and arts of human invention, and should like to have draughts and models of all their designs in my museum; yet I will not now insist on the gimlet or the plane, provided you promise to furnish me at leisure with the more common contrivances. ...[4]

Black and white mezzotint engraving of the Eddystone Lighthouse entitled: 'The Edystone Light House' drawn by J. M. W. Turner, engraved by T. Lupton and published by W. B. Cooke, London 1829. Presented by the Trustees of D. Alan Stevenson.

(NMS T.1998.229.15)

Robert Harcourt Weston subsequently presented the collection to George Douglas, 16th Earl of Morton (1761-1827), as he had assisted the younger Weston in his attempts to obtain a pension to help recompense the financial burden placed on his family by the Smeaton rebuilding and the end of the private Eddystone lease in 1804.[5] The collection was subsequently donated by the Royal Society of Edinburgh to another forerunner of National Museums Scotland, the Industrial Museum of Scotland, shortly after its inception, in 1859.[6] Its importance for us lies in the undeniable influence of John Smeaton's design of the third Eddystone Lighthouse, built entirely in stone on the fearsome rock in the English Channel, on Robert Stevenson's subsequent lighthouse at the Bell Rock, the equally fearsome rock off the east coast of Scotland. Stevenson visited this twice, in 1813 and 1818, during his tours around English lighthouses.[7]

Another major source of material for this rich collection relating to lighthouse technology, as indicated above, has been provided by descendants of Thomas Smith (1752-1815) and his stepson and son-in-law, Robert Stevenson (1782-1850). The mid-twentieth century authority on this subject was Robert Stevenson's great-grandson, D. Alan Stevenson (1891-1971), who had planned a book on the history of the Eddystone lights.[8] Although he had gathered material, in particular images of the various lighthouses, for this work – projected on a scale similar to his magisterial *The World's Lighthouses before 1820* published in 1959 – it was never realised. The Trustees of D. Alan Stevenson presented this collection to National Museums Scotland in 1998, and it complements the 1859 material extremely well, adding to our picture of how this dangerous sea-mark was viewed over the centuries.[9]

The Stevenson family has been generous in bestowing their treasures to the nation: material is now lodged in the major repositories of the National Library of Scotland, the National Galleries of Scotland, as well as National Museums Scotland.[10] Over the years, D. Alan Stevenson, followed by other members of his family, presented items to the National Museums Scotland relating to the various engineering endeavours of the Stevensons; many of these, too, are discussed in this volume.

The most outstanding recent history of Scottish lighthouses was that written by the late R. W. 'Billy' Munro (1914-2003), a Scottish journalist with a deep love of history. Once retired, he became a well-known author of books on Scottish history, often together with his wife Jean. *Scottish Lighthouses* was published in 1979, and was compiled in conjunction with his official bi-centenary history of the Northern Lighthouse Board, *The Northern Lighthouses: a short historical account of the development of lighthouses in Scotland and the Isle of Man* (Edinburgh, 1976). This meticulously-researched volume, focussing on the legislative framework behind the Northern Lighthouse Board's activities, was produced without references, but in a typically generous gesture he presented National Museums Scotland with not only a fully-annotated copy of this, but also his research notes on individual Scottish lighthouses, together with a complete set of the Northern Lighthouse Board's house journal. It is clear from these that he had a lifelong love of lighthouses. All of the above have proved indispensable resources for this project.

The Northern Lighthouse Board first lent material to the Museum in 1867. This consisted of items that had been on display at the Great Exhibition of 1851 and the 1862 Exhibition, both held in London. Other international exhibitions held in the latter part of the nineteenth century – in London and Paris, and closer to home, in Edinburgh, Glasgow and Tynemouth – saw the Northern Lighthouse Board displaying material in order to advertise new developments in marine safety, and to win customers from all over the world. Once returned to Edinburgh, these items were displayed – often for fairly short periods – to a more local audience; but after the convulsions of the First World War, these exhibitions ceased, and the collection found a new longer-term exhibition space, the 'Civil Engineering Gallery', on the first floor of a new wing of the Royal Scottish Museum, completed in 1928.[11] For the duration of the Second World War, collections – including the lighthouse material – were removed for safety to Borthwick Castle in Midlothian, well away from the threat of urban bombing. Items were returned to display in 1945.[12]

After the turn of the twentieth century, items for museum display were selected usually for their technological significance for the national collection (social history was a construction of the future) by succeeding Keepers of the Department of Technology from the Northern Lighthouse Board's Depot at Granton, where redundant material was kept. This in turn closed at around the time of lighthouse automation, in 1998. Much of the material which remained there at that date was sent to Fraserburgh, to the recently-opened Museum of Scottish Lighthouses, which was formed in 1995 after an earlier gestation period of about five or six years.[13] The collection at National Museums Scotland, which had been taken off display after the closure of the gallery in 1992, was sent to Fraserburgh, but was returned the following year when the Northern Lighthouse Board transferred its legal ownership to National Museums Scotland. At the time of automation, my former colleague Dr Allen Simpson took the opportunity of acquiring a number of substantial items for the national collections: the optic

and revolving mechanism manufactured by Chance Brothers of Birmingham and James Dove & Co.,
Edinburgh, from the site of one of
the Board's first four lights – the
1907 optic – together with its revolving mechanism originally turning in
a mercury bath, from Eilean Glas; the
remarkable group-flashing hyper-
radiant optic – designed by David A.
Stevenson and constructed in 1895
by Barbier & Bénard, Paris, and
Steven & Struthers of Glasgow –
from Scotland's most remote rock
lighthouse, Sule Skerry; and the
optic from Inchkeith in the Firth of
Forth, made by Chance Brothers; the

'A Not So Lighthouse'
from the *Edinburgh
Evening News*,
6 September 1945.
(© Scotsman Publications
Ltd)

1889 successor to the 1835 seven-lens optic made by Isaac Cookson of
Newcastle, which had already come into the collection in 1890; and the
foghorn from the same site, dating from 1899. The 1833 lantern originally from Girdleness, outside Aberdeen, had been moved to Inchkeith
by Robert Stevenson to test lighthouse optics in the 1840s. This was
kindly donated to the Museum in 1985 by Tom Farmer, who by then
owned the island. In addition to these, further manuscript collections
relating to the Northern Lighthouse Board's work – complementing
material in National Museums Scotland – are held in the Royal Commission on the Ancient and Historical Monuments of Scotland, and
in the National Archives of Scotland.[14] These rich holdings from such
varied sources together tell the history of the sea-marking of one of
the world's most dangerous coastlines; and although this account has
been drawn mainly from published sources, so abundant is the information available that there is still the opportunity for yet another re-
telling in the future.

As with all museum objects, the curator's main concern is with
provenance: and with most of the items in what is known familiarly as
'the lighthouse collection' in National Museums Scotland, the provenance is exceptional. Without a doubt, as this work will demonstrate,
National Museums Scotland possesses, thanks to these kind benefactors and others, one of the finest and most internationally significant
collections of artefacts relating to the history of sea-marking of any
nation. The first chapter sketches the beginnings of sea-marking and
lighthouse history, and looks at lighting methods from coal beacons to

oil lamps; it examines first attempts at focussing the beams, by reflectors and lenses. The second chapter backtracks a little, looking at the various attempts at the building of the Eddystone lighthouse, which ultimately proved to be such an inspiration for the Bell Rock; and this is followed by a return to the north, discussing the background leading up to the formation of the Northern Lighthouse Board, and the Board's lights before the Bell Rock. Chapter 4 is the centrepiece of the story, the epic of the building of the Bell Rock lighthouse, and is followed by chapters demonstrating the later work of the Stevensons, and how they managed to export this technology to far-flung corners of the globe. A final chapter brings the story up-to-date, covering the automation of Scottish lighthouses and looking forward to new, less labour-intensive technologies adopted by the Northern Lighthouse Board which help to bring safety to mariners at sea. This book examines the material culture in Scotland's national lighthouse collection, and it demonstrates that this truly is a continuing age of Scottish lighthouses.

## Notes to Introduction

1   See http://www.nlb.org.uk/theboard/aim.htm
2   Rowatt (1924-25); Waterston (1997), 68-69, 169-70. Other Smeaton material relating to the building of the Eddystone Lighthouse is held by the Royal Society.
3   *Gentleman's Magazine*, 97 (1827), 446.
4   Weston (1811), 133.
5   Coase (1974), 366.
6   For a history of Scotland's national museums, see Anderson (1989), although he dates the 'greatest strength of the technological collections [which] has always been the lighthouse collection, deposited over the years by the Commissioners of the Northern Lighthouses from 1875 [sic]'.
7   Stevenson (1946), 31-38, 51-55.
8   For biographical details of the Stevensons and Smith, see Paxton (2004). Notes relating to D. Alan Stevenson's unpublished work on the Eddystone have been presented to National Museums Scotland.
9   The main collections of images and artefacts relating to the Eddystone Reef remain, as is proper, with Plymouth City Museum & Art Gallery. See chapter 2.
10  Stevenson papers are held by the National Library of Scotland [NLS] Acc. 4215 and Acc. 10706, Records of Robert Stevenson & Sons, Civil Engineers. Portraits of Robert Stevenson [PG 657] and Thomas Stevenson [PG 568] are in the collections of the National Galleries of Scotland. The watercolour by J. M. W. Turner of the 'Bell Rock in a Storm', discussed in chapter 4, was acquired for the nation, together with Turner's letter to Stevenson, with assistance from the National Heritage Memorial Fund and the Pilgrim Trust in 1989, and is to be found in the collections of the National Galleries of Scotland [D 5181A and B]: see Hamilton (1998), 89-91; Campbell (1999), 91-92.
11  'Royal Scottish Museum: Two New Galleries', *Scotsman*, 30 March 1928, p. 8.
12  'A Not So Light-House', *Edinburgh Evening News*, 6 September 1945.
13  http://www.lighthousemuseum. org.uk/
14  For RCAHMS, see http://www.rcahms.gov.uk/ For NAS, NLC1-NLC111, see: http://www.nas.gov.uk/guides/lighthouses.asp

# LIGHTHOUSE.

## PLATE CCCXLVII.

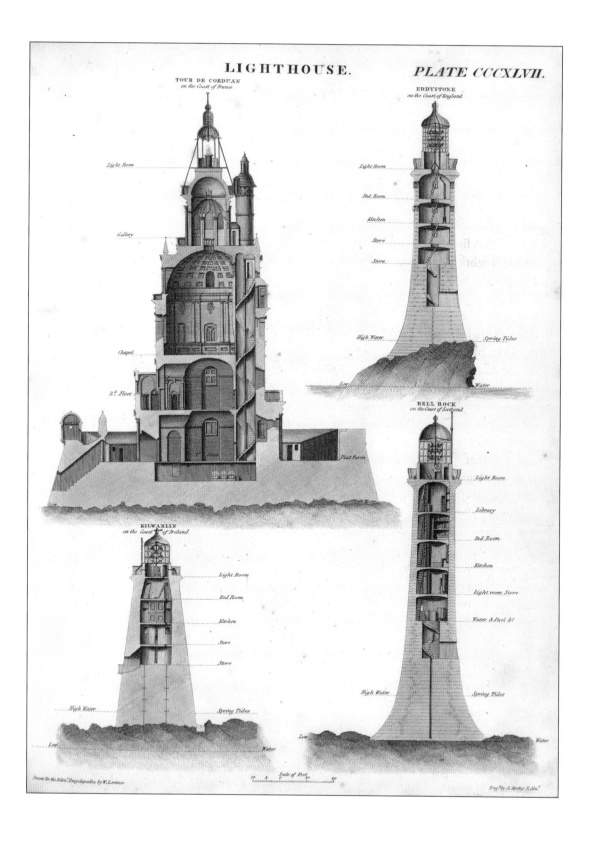

**TOUR DE CORDUAN**
*on the Coast of France*

- Light Room
- Gallery
- Chapel
- 2.ᵈ Floor
- Platform

**EDDYSTONE**
*on the Coast of England*

- Light Room
- Bed Room
- Kitchen
- Store
- Store
- High Water
- Spring Tides
- Low
- Water

**BELL ROCK**
*on the Coast of Scotland*

- Light Room
- Library
- Bed Room
- Kitchen
- Light room Store
- Water & Fuel &.ᶜ
- High Water
- Spring Tides
- Low
- Water

**KILWARLIN**
*on the Coast of Ireland*

- Light Room
- Bed Room
- Kitchen
- Store
- Store
- High Water
- Spring Tides
- Low
- Water

Scale of Feet

*Drawn for the Edin.ʳ Encyclopædia, by W. Lorimer.*

*Eng.ᵈ by J. Moffat Edin.ʳ*

# CHAPTER 1

# In the Beginning

WHAT IS A lighthouse? The first sentence of Robert Stevenson's 1818 article 'Lighthouse', anonymously contributed to David Brewster's *Edinburgh Encyclopaedia*, gives the definition: 'By the term lighthouse is understood, an establishment set apart for exhibiting a light as a landmark for the use of the mariner', and most subsequent definitions follow this.[1] The lighthouse can be regarded as the culmination of physical sea-marking: by day, a recognisable presence, whatever its characteristics, for the mariner to work out a safe passage for his vessel; and by night, identifiable through its own individual light signature, for the same purposes. Yet lighthouses have had a relatively short history in terms of seafaring, and celebrated their coming of age at a time when Western nations were most concerned about maximising trade in terms of profit and loss: that is, during the nineteenth century.

In the beginning, of course, there were no lights. Nonetheless, navigation across the seas out of sight of land has taken place since antiquity, although the vast bulk of sea traffic presumably took place in daylight hours and must have stayed well within sight of the coastline. As the historian of navigation E. G. R. Taylor pointed out, coastal sailing has its own fearsome hazards. Sailors kept well off-shore in order to avoid being driven on to a lee-shore, or being wrecked on hidden rocks or sandbanks, or caught in unexpected rip-tides – all features of inshore waters.[2]

The navigators of antiquity used the knowledge gained by experience and passed through the generations as a craft skill, and were able to use the movements of the heavens, the patterns of the main winds and weather, and an approximation of the distance to be travelled between destinations to assist their safe passage. Yet it still comes as a surprise that the earliest known sailing instructions date from the fourth century BC.[3] Taylor points out that just as modern inshore sailors have little need of compass or charts in clear weather, navigating from landmarks or sea-marks, so for their counterparts in antiquity the pillars and

OPPOSITE PAGE

Top part of Plate 347, 'Lighthouse', from the *Edinburgh Encyclopaedia* (1818), showing light-houses at Corduan (1611), Eddystone (1756), Kilwarlin (1797) and the Bell Rock (1811).

(National Museums Scotland)

temples that sailors set up on strange shores served them also as land-marks.[4]

Coastal navigation calls for different skills to those used by deep-sea mariners out of sight of land. Once a coastline is reached, local knowledge is called for, to enable vessels to find safe havens. The Seven Wonders of the Ancient World in modern reckoning comprised two sculptures, two mausoleums, a shrine, a roof-garden, and a lighthouse, and it is with this final monument and its successors that we are concerned.[5] The flat and monotonous shoreline along the North African coast meant that it was difficult to steer a course for the harbour and port of Alexandria. Thus the tower on the island of Pharos at the harbour entrance could act both as a day-marker and a guide at night. Indeed, whether the tower had a beacon or not remains a matter for discussion.[6] The Pharos at Alexandria may not have been the world's earliest lighthouse, but it is of considerable antiquity. It probably dates from the third century BC, although much of what we know about it comes from the encyclopaedist Pliny the Elder (Gaius Plinius Secundus), who wrote in his *Natural History*, just after discussion of the pyramids of Egypt, which also rank as one of the Seven Wonders, that

> … another tower built by a king also received praise. This is on the island of Pharos, and commands the harbour of Alexandria. … King Ptolemy, in a spirit of generosity, allowed the name of the architect, Sostratus of Cnidus, to be inscribed on the building itself. Its purpose is to provide a beacon for ships sailing by night, to warn them of shallows and to mark the entrance to the harbour. Similar beacons now burn brightly in several places, for example at Ostia and Ravenna.[7]

Pliny wrote his encyclopaedic account of the state of Roman scientific knowledge in the first century AD after his return to Rome in AD 75. Ironically, his intense scientific curiosity led to his untimely death, when he lingered too long observing the eruption of Vesuvius in AD 79.

After Pliny, the effectiveness of the lighthouse at Pharos – the place has given its name in many European languages to meaning 'lighthouse' – was estimated at anything between 34 to 100 miles. In fact, this last estimate does not take into account limitations imposed by the curvature of the Earth, and to be visible at 34 miles the tower would have had to have been 665 feet high, and been equipped with an incredibly powerful light. Modern estimates put its height at around 350 feet, an approximation that is derived from a twelfth-century eye-witness account written by an Arab historian, Ibn al-Shaikh. This information only became available to Western scholars in the early twentieth century, and it inspired an authoritative account published in Spain in the 1930s. According to this, the tower was built in three ascending sections: the lowest, a truncated pyramid, was about 220 feet high; the middle part, a pyramidal octagon, was about 100 feet high; and the uppermost section was cylindrical, just under 30 feet, with the lantern on the top.[8] This astonishing building lasted some 1500 years, until it finally disintegrated through war and earthquake: ancient pieces continue to be recovered from the harbour at Alexandria to this day.[9]

As Pliny indicated, the Romans imitated the success of the lighthouse at Pharos at various places around the Mediterranean, and as their influence increased such towers were put up on the Atlantic seaboard and in the Black Sea. The eminent lighthouse historian D. Alan Stevenson (1891-1971) reckoned that 'some thirty lighthouses are known definitely to have been in service before AD 400 , that is, before the Roman Empire began to decline'.[10] By the Middle Ages, after the void of the so-called Dark Ages between about AD 400 and 1100, at least 30 lights had been noted around Europe – not necessarily at the same 30 places identified before AD 400 – allowing coastal trade to be undertaken in some safety; and after 1500, examples occur in travellers' accounts, pilotage directions and sea-charts. For instance, the Lanterna of Genoa dates from before 1161; the great tower of Corunna from around 1500; that at Boulogne fell into the sea in 1644 but was clearly of some antiquity; and most famously, the lighthouse at Corduan was already ancient by 1550. According to a charter of 1409, a chapel and tower, containing equipment 'necessary for the safety of ships', had been erected on the island in the mouth of the River Gironde by Edward, the English Black Prince, in about 1379; and its upkeep was paid for by a tax levied on all passing vessels carrying wine from Bordeaux.[11] Douglas Hague explains that although it appears now to be a rock lighthouse, this is the result of centuries of river displacement, and the erosion happened very slowly.[12] Around England, among other seamarks, there had been early warning lights at Dover (but by the sixteenth century these were 'long-disused'[13]), St Catherine's on the Isle of Wight (lit by 1314, but probably decayed before the Reformation[14]), and on the Northumberland coast at the mouth of the Tyne, established after 1540, which Stevenson describes as 'the earliest British lighthouse with any pretension to serve coastal navigation'.[15]

### Sea-marking and unlit beacons

It seems that the marking and lighting of coastal Scotland came much later than in England; the first lighthouses being the result of private endeavour as they were in the south, but fewer and further apart along a more dangerous but less inhabited coastline. Even so, lighthouse historians are agreed that the first established lighthouse was built as late as 1636 on the Isle of May in the busy Firth of Forth.[16] Nonetheless, beacons marking the entrance to both Leith and Aberdeen Harbours were recorded earlier, in 1553 and 1566 respectively.[17] It is also possible that lights shining from other suitably-placed buildings may have acted as markers; one such has been suggested as being placed in a window in the 'aumbry' of Dunyvaig Castle on the island of Islay. Now ruined, the castle dates mainly from the sixteenth century.[18] Sea-marks were not solely lights: in the River Tay, navigable to Perth, a small folly on an island off the south bank was named the Lucky Scaup and used as a marker from the mid-nineteenth century until it was finally demolished in 1979.[19] Older landmarks were often ecclesiastical buildings,

frequently taller than surrounding houses: John Adair's *Description* (and his accompanying chart) emphasise the parish church at Crail: 'Creil is built upon a Height right above the Shoar, the Church, with a high pointed Steeple, makes it very remarkable ...'.[20] At a later date Moonzie Parish Church, famous perhaps for being an ancient place of worship in Scotland's smallest parish in north-east Fife, was described thus: 'From its elevated position, it forms a conspicuous object from the Newburgh road, and enjoys the name of the Visible Kirk, from being a landmark to mariners entering the Tay.'[21]

Navigation was becoming more important on Scotland's west coast from the seventeenth century onwards, as transatlantic trade and population settlements grew there. The Solway Firth became a navigable waterway where local authorities became interested in

Wreck of the *Travencore* at Spo Ness, Westray, Orkney Islands, 27 February 1871.
(© Orkney Photographic Archive. Licensor www.scran.ac.uk)

4

the safety of vessels; and although Dumfries today may seem well inland, its position on the River Nith made it for a time a considerable port. Dumfries Town Council commissioned a local stonemason to build a 'beaken' at the entrance to the Nith in 1748, but initially it may have been a stone marker without lights.[22]

Harbour lights around the Scottish coast appear mainly to date from after the formation of the Northern Lighthouse Board in 1786, and in all their guises the current survivors have been well-surveyed. Indeed, one designed by Robert Stevenson and put up in 1817 has recently been renovated with a replica chromed copper reflector and Argand lamp at North Queensferry.[23] However, there are earlier examples. The remains of a pair of beacons, built of rubble, with dressed stone caps, and once lime-washed for visibility to mark the entrance to Montrose Harbour at Scurdie Ness, are still to be seen. John Hume believes that these are eighteenth-century in origin.[24] Sailing directions published in 1809 stated that 'to run into Montrose, you must have plenty of sail. The marks for entering in are, two stone beacons on the south shore in one.'[25] A later *North Sea Pilot* illustrates them, explaining that 'upon the brae side, 500 yards within the ness, are two white stone beacons, which were used for leading into the river before the lighthouses were built; but now they are of little service'.[26] R. W. Munro discusses the rapid actions of the Clyde Trustees in dealing with 'beacons perches and bowies [buoys]' in disrepair along the river in the late eighteenth century.[27] Douglas Hague describes the refuge-beacon built on Horse Isle at the entrance to Ardrossan Harbour as being the earliest of this type – for mariners cast ashore – to be built in the British Isles. Dating from around 1810, it was built by Hugh Montgomerie, 12th Earl of Eglinton, as earlier civic petitioning of the Commissioners of the Northern Lights had not produced the hoped-for lighthouse.[28] The North Carr Rocks off the coast of Fife were marked by the first Northern Lighthouse Board buoy in 1809. Between then and 1818, Robert Stevenson built a beacon based on six columns of cast iron clamped to a masonry support and surmounted by a hollow ribbed ball about 25 feet above mean sea-level. It still survives, but was always considered both 'blind' and 'dumb', emitting neither a light nor a sound signal. As it was thought impossible to build a lighthouse at the site, successive light-vessels (named the *North Carr*) were moored off the rocks from 1887. These were replaced by an automatic buoy in 1975, when a new lighthouse was built on Fife Ness.[29]

Even in the earliest days of the Northern Lighthouse Board's jurisdiction, unlit day-marks were constructed for navigation: a masonry tower was placed on the Start Point of Sanday in Orkney in 1802 (and was, a few years later, lit as the Northern Lighthouse Board's first revolving light), and a cast-iron beacon was placed on Oxcars Rock in the Firth of Forth in 1804 (it was originally to have formed a leading light with that put up the same year on Inchkeith).[30] In the Moray Firth, a dangerous group of rocks known as Halliman's Reef, or Covesea Skerries, off Lossiemouth, was marked by a beacon designed by Alan Stevenson in 1845:

> Beacons … are used to point out those dangers which, either owing to the difficulty and expense that would attend the placing of more efficient marks to serve by night as well as by day, are necessarily left without lights, or which, from the peculiarity of their position, in passages too intricate for navigation by night, are, in practice, considered to be sufficiently indicated by day-marks alone. Beacons … in situations difficult of access and in which works of uncompleted masonry could not be safely left during the winter season, an open framework of cast-iron pipes, firmly trussed and braced, and secured to the rock with strong louis-bats, is preferred.

Stevenson believed that such an iron beacon would cost £640, and in places where it could be secured by filling the base with concrete, it could be put up for about £400.[31] At the same time, a lighthouse with a revolving light had been constructed on the mainland, at a cost of £11,514.[32]

> COVESEA SKERRIES LIGHTHOUSE: Edinburgh, April 10th, 1846 – Notice to Mariners. This lighthouse has been built upon the Point of Craighead, in the County of Elgin, the light of which will be exhibited on the night of the 15th of May 1846, and every night thereafter, from sun-set to sun-rise: and a beacon has been placed on that part of the Covesea Skerries, called Halliman's Scars, which lies off Craighead. The beacon bears from the lighthouse E.N.E. ¼ E., and consists of a frame-work of iron, surmounted by a cylindrical cage, and a cross, 48 feet above high water. There are steps leading from the rock to the cage, in which a temporary shelter may be found, in the event of shipwreck on the rock.[33]

An eighth-size scale model of this, constructed by James Milne & Son, Edinburgh (the contractors who produced the full-size beacon), was displayed at the Paris Universal Exhibition of 1867.[34]

Sea-marking is an important part of the story of lighthouses, possibly seen as a minor ingredient today by the non-seafaring part of the population, whose imagination is fired by tales of epic engineering skills under severe conditions. In these circumstances, men in puny little open

boats are exposed to the wrath of the elements, while they attempt to build sturdy masonry towers in near-impossible conditions. Thus most of the recent extensive secondary literature about lighthouses has emphasised the isolation of the keepers' lives and the extraordinary feats of heroism involved in construction on remote and dangerous locations, perhaps to the point of losing sight of the purpose of a lighthouse – to provide a warning light for mariners. Indeed, what were these lights, how were they fuelled, and just how did they develop?

### Early lighting: wood and coal beacons

In 1848 the Scottish lighthouse engineer Alan Stevenson (1807-65) wrote:

It now seems strange to hear that so lately as the year 1816, when the Isle of May light, in the Frith of Forth, was assumed by the Commissioners of the Northern Lights, it was of that rude description, and had shewn a coal fire for 181 years since 1635; and even in England, the art of illumination had made so little progress that the magnificent Tower of the Eddystone, for about forty years after it came from the hands of [John] Smeaton, could boast of no better light than that derived from a few miserable tallow candles; nay, so lately as the year 1801, the light at Harwick [*sic*], in addition to the coal-fire had a flat plate of rough brass on the landward side, to serve as a reflector![35]

In fact, most of the successful developments and improvements in both the sources of illumination for lights, and their focussing,

7

direction and methods of distinction, occurred during the nineteenth century, and these will be looked at later. Here, the basic forms are outlined.

'Down to a very late period,' Alan Stevenson noted, 'the only mode of illumination adopted in the lighthouses, even of the most civilised nations of Europe, was the combustion of wood or coal in chauffers, on the tops of high towers or hills.'[36] Some authors claim that the Pharos at Alexandria used mirrors, in that the fire was closer to the ground than to the top of the structure. The smoke was extracted by a flue, while the light beam from the fire was reflected up to and out of the top of the tower through a series of mirror reflections: possibly (if true), the earliest catoptric system.[37] Historians Asin and Otera, perhaps wisely, did not address the illumination system of the Pharos, and Alan Stevenson's great-nephew, the lighthouse historian D. Alan Stevenson, disagreed strongly with this mirror theory.[38] He explained that wood-burning lights gave way to coal fires, simply because of the enormous amount of fuel that was necessary to keep the light going. Indeed, the Isle of May was ideally placed, from the point of view of its light power source, on top of the Forth coalfield. Large quantities of fuel were shipped across and dragged over the island, up to the two-storied beacon-tower. Built in 1636, this had an internal spiral stair and a flat roof surrounded by a parapet. The large open grate stood on top, but only after 1786 was a rope-and-pulley windlass used to haul the pans of coal up on to the roof. Astonishingly, this beacon was not replaced until a few years after the building of the Bell Rock lighthouse (when the upper storey was removed to allow the beam from the new lighthouse to shine uninterrupted), so that for a century and a half the fire – consuming a ton of coal each night, or sometimes up to three times as much during severe winter storms – was kept burning by the keeper and his family.[39]

The dreadful story of the death in January 1791 of the keeper, George Anderson, who together with his wife and five of their eight children, was suffocated by the fumes from the partly-burnt ashes which were allowed to accumulate around the base of the beacon, was recounted in the *Statistical Account of Scotland* by the local minister. In fact, so horrified was the local populace by this story that it was repeated by the minister of a neighbouring parish.[40] Only the youngest

*Profile of the Isle of May with smoking lighthouse from Greenvile Collins's Great Britain's Coasting Pilot. Being a new and exact survey of the Sea coast of England and Scotland from the river of Thames to the westward and northward with the Islands of Scilly and from thence to Carlisle, 1776; first published in 1680.*

8

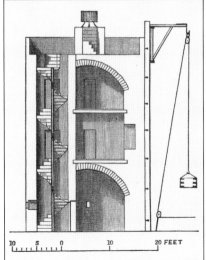

child, Lucy Anderson, survived the tragedy, growing up to marry one of her rescuers, Henry Dowie, and emigrating with him to the United States. Indeed, after a successful life together in the butter trade and having produced twelve children, she now lies buried outside New York. The owner of the island, Miss Henrietta Scott of Scotstarvit, paid for the orphan's education and upbringing. Two assistant keepers were found unconscious, but later revived; Lucy's eldest brother and sister, who 'providentially' were not on the island at the time, were also cared for by Miss Scott.[41]

Even places far removed from the coalfields of the British Isles were fuelled by coal from the early seventeenth century, when mining produced more than five times the total recovered by the rest of Europe. D. Alan Stevenson noted that its use in lighthouses 'met with favour as being a more compact fuel or illuminant than wood, as burning longer in rainy weather, and as requiring less attention by the keepers'.[42] He also observed that 'the number of coal beacons compared with other forms of navigation lights in England and Scotland increased from 1 out of 1 before 1600, to 12 out of 15 in 1700, and to 21 out of 26 in 1760, exclusive of the Eddystone lighthouse and the two English lightships which necessarily were lit by candles or oil lamps'.[43] The sole surviving cast-iron grate from a British lighthouse, that for the lighthouse of St Agnes in the Scilly Isles, possibly made locally in about 1680, is over four feet high; it may give some idea of the

9

cressets used at the Isle of May and elsewhere. (Stevenson gives its size as diameters at base 2 foot 9 inches, tapering to 2 feet and spreading to 2 feet 11½ inches at the top; the heights of the lower and upper portions are 3 feet 6 inches and 1 foot; the cast iron is 1 inch thick, and there is an aperture in the side for raking out the ashes.[44]) It is now to be found at the Tresco Abbey Gardens, Isles of Scilly. Douglas Hague suggests that the grate was removed when the St Agnes lighthouse was converted to oil power in 1809, and that it is one of a succession of many, as such grates would have had a limited lifespan.[45]

It was not until over a century after the Isle of May lighthouse was built that the growth of shipping in the Firth of Clyde led to a move by Glasgow authorities to increase the safety of vessels using the river to the growing city. Little Cumbrae, the island that splits the river into two navigable channels at the entrance to the Firth, was also lit by a coal fire from 1757: this was placed on top of a circular stone tower built at the island's summit. Not until Thomas Smith's new lighthouse, constructed under the auspices of the Northern Lighthouse Board to replace this in 1793, was another form of lighting used, although there had long been concern about the efficiency (or lack of it) of the coal beacon.[46]

Open wood or coal fires proved problematic because they were difficult to control: they could not be kept at a given intensity; they required constant tending; and coal fires in particular were susceptible to weather conditions. With an onshore wind, the land would be lit, leaving a shadow to seaward; and with strong prevailing winds, one side of the fire would leave the fuel unconsumed. Perhaps most dangerous of all, they could be confused

Cresset for the St Agnes lighthouse, Scilly Isles, first lit in c.1680. This was the last cresset used there before the light was converted to oil in 1809; now in Tresco Gardens.

(© Andrew Lawson)

Little Cumbrae lighthouse, coal-lit from 1757 and disused from 1793.

with other domestic or industrial flames, leading to mistaken identification along a hazardous shoreline.[47]

### Early lighting: candles and oil lamps

Some considerable time after the Isle of May was lit – 'Here is Fire Continually kept For a Beacon to ships in the Night', as it states on Richard Cooper's 1730 engraving of Adair's map of the 'River and Frith of Forth' – others began to consider lighting small parts of the coast for their own ends. These lights – warning or guiding – tended to be in the great estuaries of Lowland Scotland, where most of the people and markets were based. Trade with the Scots' nearest neighbours tended to be across the North Sea, to the towns around the Low Countries and the Baltic; and, with dangers of poor roads, bad weather and possible banditry, much of the trade with England was also undertaken by sail.

In 1687 the Scots Privy Council extended to the Fraternity of Masters and Seamen in Dundee the authority to levy dues to put up lights for navigational purposes:

> Whereas the River and Firth of Tay, having a narrow entry betwixt two dangerous Banks, has in all time by-past been Unnavigate and without the assistance of Lights of beacons, to the great prejudice of Trade, Ruin and Loss of Mens Lives. … And now there being an exacte Plate and accurate Description of the said River and Forth, by John Adair Geographer, who is actually Navigate the same, whereby it may be entered without hazard in Day-Light, but under Night, the best experienced Seamen not daring to attempt the same, are ofttimes put to sea, or constrained to turn all Night with great

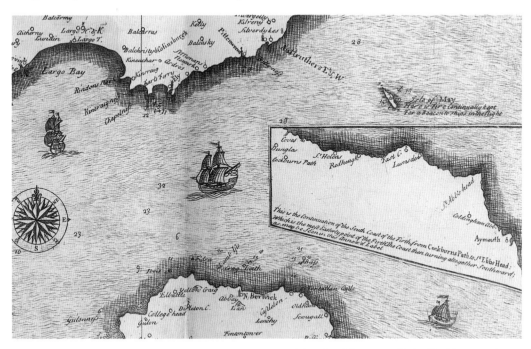

John Adair, 'The river and frith of Forth', engraved by Richard Cooper, 1730; detail of the Isle of May.
(NMS T.2003.309.249)

hazard in the outward Bay (Strangers ordinarily running Ashore and losing all:)

Which great hazard and loss may be altogether prevented by erecting One Light or Two upon the Button Ness. ... The LORDS of his MAJESTIE'S Privy Council, having fully Heard and Considered the foresaid Representation ... by the said Magistrates and Council of Dundee: and finding, that the erecting of the said Lights and beacons will bee of great advantage as is above mentioned Do hereby Warrant and allow the said Fraternity of Masters and Seamen of Dundee, to erect the said Lights and Beacons And impowers them or Authorizes them or their Box-Master [treasurer] or Box-Masters, to exact and uplift upon the account of the said Lights and Beacons, the said Twelve Pennies Scots each Voyage for each Tun, in outcoming or incoming, for all the Ships, Barks, or other Vessels, coming into the said Firth or River of Tay, viz. Betwixt Fifeness and the Reid-Head, inclusive, Foreigners paying double of the said Duty of Twelve Pennies Scots, being Two-Pence Scots for each Tun, as said is.[48]

Surviving accounts show that the Fraternity – which exists to this day – paid a number of people from 1687 to 1689 for fitting up the lights on the north bank of the estuary at Buddon Ness. This is the modern name, and it appears over the years as Button-ness, Bottanais, Buttness, and eventually as Buddon Ness. Unlike the warning fire on the Isle of May, the lights on Buddon Ness were guiding lights: by aligning the two lights, one apparently over the other, the skipper could navigate his vessel from the open sea into the estuary, taking it past the dangerous and shifting sandbanks at the river mouth. As the sandbanks moved, the lower lighthouse was constructed so that it could also be moved and the lights continue to be used safely. It seems that the lights initially used oil (although R. W. Munro suggests that originally the lights were coal-fired); and as the Dundee whaling fleet grew and prospered, its products appear to have been the source for illumination.[49] D. Alan Stevenson states that between 1700 and 1720 the front light consumed one barrel of oil a year, with the rear light burning 8 stones of candles; after 1720, both lights burned oil in 16 domestic iron lamps (or 'cruisies'). Before 1740, the lights were lit only in winter.[50] With the growth of whaling in the ports of Dundee and Peterhead from the mid-eighteenth century, the main form of lighting in Scottish lighthouses generally changed to oil lamps.[51]

No comprehensive account of the use of oil lamps in lighthouses is possible, as D. Alan Stevenson observed, because there was no stand-ard type in even one country. Wicks came in all forms, as did reser-voirs.[52] However, the links between lighting the towns and lighting the seas seem to be strong in Scotland, where the tinsmith-turned-lighting engineer Thomas Smith (1752-1815) became responsible for lights in the north. Smith was born apparently in Ferryport-on-Craig (as he was baptised there in December 1752), a small town across the river from the growing port of Dundee. Much of what we know about him comes from the pen of that reluctant engineer, his great-grandson Robert Louis Stevenson (1850-94), in his tribute to his mechanically-minded relations, *Records of a Family of Engineers*. Louis wrote:

> … the generations of the Smiths present no conceivable interest even to a descendant; and Thomas, of Edinburgh, was the first to issue from respectable obscurity. His father, a skipper out of Broughty Ferry, was drowned at sea while Thomas was still young. He seems to have owned a ship or two—whalers, I suppose, or coasters—and to have been a member of the Dundee Trinity House, whatever that implies. On his death the widow remained in Broughty, and the son came to push his future in Edinburgh. … he appears as a man ardent, passionate, practical, designed for affairs and prospering in them far beyond the average. He founded a solid business in lamps and oils, and was the sole proprietor of a concern called the Greenside Company's Works— 'a multifarious concern it was,' writes my cousin, Professor Swan, 'of tinsmiths, coppersmiths, brass-founders, blacksmiths, and japanners'. He was also, it seems, a shipowner and underwriter. He built himself 'a land'—Nos. 1 and 2 Baxter's Place, then no such unfashionable neighbourhood—and died, leaving his only son in easy circumstances, and giving to his three surviving daughters portions of five thousand pounds and upwards. There is no standard of success in life; but in one of its meanings, this is to succeed.[53]

There appears to be no reference to Thomas Smith's father – also named Thomas Smith – in the surviving records of the Fraternity of Seamen of Dundee.[54] According to parish registers, the elder Thomas Smith had married Mary Kay in April 1749, with Thomas their sole offspring. The younger Thomas Smith's own death notice, announcing that he died on 21 June 1815 in the 62nd year of his age, confirms his birth as during 1752.[55] Smith, as Stevenson family tradition has it, was apprenticed to a Dundee metalworker named Cairns in 1764, and by 1770 had learned enough to leave for Edinburgh.[56] As Craig Mair has pointed out, this was the period of Edinburgh's great expansion, when the crowded tenements of the ancient city were expanding into the classically-designed New Town to the north, where the trade of tinsmith was much in demand. At this time only the Carron Iron Works, at Falkirk in Stirlingshire, was of any great size, and even it could not supply the greatly increased requirement for metalware, ranging from doorknobs to cooking ranges, that the creation of Edinburgh's New Town generated. Smith's products were thus in constant demand.[57]

In Edinburgh's earliest directories he was noted as a tinsmith, located in Bristo Street in 1781, while nine years later he had moved to Blair Street. With the growth of the city, the Town Council grasped that street-lighting – a problem last broached in 1550 – would have to be tackled. An Act of Parliament in 1785 authorised the building of a new bridge with street-lights linking the Old and New Towns. This provided the opportunity to set up two commissions to deal with this – one for the Old Town and the other for the New – each empowered to levy annual rates from house owners. After the original contractor was dismissed, Thomas Smith offered a tender to light the Old Town for 6d per lamp per week. This tender was accepted and sites for 594 lamps were approved. In 1804, by which time Thomas Smith was also providing lights for the New Town, his income from lighting was over £1000 a year.[58]

Thomas Smith's oil-lamp business became closely involved with lighthouses for a while (of which more, below), but the original enterprise also continued for much of the nineteenth century, carried on by the offspring of his first marriage, as this contemporary account states:

> To Mr Smith and his sons who succeeded him (Smiths & Co.) was given the mechanical work of the system, and the furnishing of the oil, which was for a long time train or whale oil, and the wicks and other material for the lights. This business, along with the contract which the firm held from the city for many years for lighting the town, was a large business, and there was no better known house in Edinburgh than Smiths & Co., Blair Street, and no better known man than Thomas Smith, who from his connection with the lighting of the city was commonly called 'Leerie Smith'.
>
> I have often heard old people telling of the daily parade of the lamplighters in Hunter Square, to receive the oil and wicks to fill the cruises, and to have these in order for burning, and the flambeaux, which were tin tubes like policemen's batons, stuffed with tow, and saturated at the top with oil, which they used to light the lamps. The Leeries used the very same flambeaux in our day to light the gas-lamps, until they were provided with little lanthorns with an opening at the bottom.
>
> … But gas took the place of train oil in lighting the streets, and even threatened to take the place of lamps and candles in lighting the shops and private houses, notwithstanding the lamentations of many old ladies, who wondered what was to become of the poor whales; and 'Leerie Smith's' vocation was gone forever, so far as the lamp-lighters were concerned, and the Leeries' parade in Hunter Square was no longer to be witnessed, and the consumpt of train oil in Edinburgh, which had been confined to the dwellings of the lower classes, and the kitchens of the better classes, was greatly curtailed.

Oil and oil-lamps, except in the kitchens, were little known among the middling classes. Candles were the universal light, and families thought themselves well off when, to the light of one moulded 'long six', the mother did her darning, and the children learned their lessons. There was always another candle on the sideboard to be lit if company came in, and there was an oil lamp in the lobby, only to be used on great occasions.

All this was changed when gas came into regular use, which was by no means very fast, for the experience of well-nigh every house in town was that gas was first introduced into the lobbies and kitchens, then when no evil effects followed after a time, into the dining-rooms and parlours, and at length with fear and trembling into the bedrooms. The effect of all of this was that Smiths & Co.'s business became almost exclusively confined to the better class of country people, who burned wax candles, and stately lamps with olive and afterwards rape oil called colza.

By this time two generations of Smiths had passed away, and the third was passing, and though the Blair Street business was still a large and lucrative one, it showed symptoms of requiring a change to more convenient premises for their aristocratic customers, and, like other old businesses on the South Side, they had to follow the fashion, and take up new quarters in George Street, where, under charge of the fourth generation, Smiths & Co., Limited, maintain the family name and the family prestige with lamps of a very different sort, and oil of another kind altogether from the days of the Leeries and Hunter Square.[59]

Thomas Smith died in 1815. From 1808 the lighting firm was carried on by his son, James Smith (1783-1820), who had married Jean Baxter in 1805: they had eight sons, not all of whom survived to adulthood. Their son Thomas, who was named after his grandfather, was appointed 'purveyor and lamp-maker to his Majesty [George IV] in Scotland' in 1822.[60] As the 'Heirs of Mr James Smith', the firm showed themselves to be at the forefront of tinsmithing technology: they displayed a new model of a 'shower machine, for flower beds or fruit bushes' at Lawson's Agricultural Museum in 1840, and at the same venue the following year 'a specimen of Oil of Rape'.[61] As Smiths & Co. they designed a table lamp in 1840, registered a design for 'the economic wick elevator' in March 1850, and exhibited a series of new lamp designs for the railways at the Great Exhibition of 1851.[62] Sadly, no examples of street lamps or even domestic lights from the Smiths' business appear to survive. However, those of us brought up on *A Child's Garden of Verses* find the idea of oil lighting in Edinburgh's New Town unforgettable:

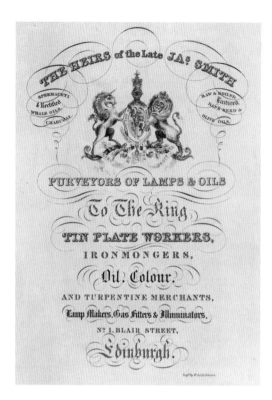

ABOVE: Section of an Argand lamp from Stevenson's *Account*; detail from Plate XX.

LEFT: Handbill for The Heirs of the Late Jas. Smith, Purveyors of Lamps & Oils to the King, Tin Plate Workers, Ironmongers, Oil, Colour and Turpentine Merchants Lamp Makers, Gas Fitters, 1 Blair Street, c.1830.
(NMS W.MS.1995.13.3)

*For we are very lucky, with a lamp before*
    *the door,*
*And Leerie stops to light it as he lights so*
    *many more;*
*And O! Before you hurry by with ladder*
    *and with light,*
*O Leerie, see a little child and nod to him*
    *tonight!*[63]

Smith clearly knew about oil lamps, and he was able to benefit from the tremendous technical innovations which took place in their design in the 1780s. Ami Argand (1750-1803) was the son of a successful and wealthy Swiss watchmaker, whose studies took him from Geneva to Paris in 1775. His developments in distillation techniques attracted great attention, including that of the French King, and took him to the vineyards of Languedoc. In the new industrial environment, distillation needed to go on around the clock and better illumina-

tion was required. So Argand devised a new form of lamp in 1780, which had a tubular oil-burner which held a cylindrical cotton wick and a cylindrical metal chimney. These first metal chimneys were held a few inches above the flame, allowing the light to shine out unimpeded.[64] Unlike previous oil lamps, it was virtually smokeless. Air passed inside as well as outside the wick, and this double air current ensured an even temperature and a good fuel combustion. Argand became involved with the Montgolfier brothers and their famous balloon ascent at Versailles in September 1783, but in investigating how his own lamp design might be manufactured in Paris he allowed others to see and plagiarise it. Fortunately, a visit to London at the end of 1783 enabled him to form a partnership with the leading domestic glass supplier, William Parker of Fleet Street, under the name of Argand's

Patent Lamp & Co., and with the agreement of Matthew Boulton – the Birmingham-based business partner of the famous James Watt – to manufacture the metal parts.[65] A London instrument maker, also of Swiss extraction, Johann Heinrich Hurter (1734-99), devised and fitted a flint-glass chimney to Argand's lamp at his instruction in January 1784. A recent biography of Argand explains that his lamp's efficiency depended on how closely the glass chimney encircled the wick. It was crucial that there was a flow of air across the flame, which ensured good combustion and thus a bright light. However, eighteenth-century glass was incapable of withstanding the rapid and restricted heat of the burner, and usually cracked; flint glass was better than most, but still liable to shatter.[66]

The English patent, no. 1425, was dated 15 March 1784, but as in France it almost immediately ran into problems as others realised the benefits that would accrue from extending daylight hours (witness, for example, the letter from Professor John Robison of the University of Edinburgh to James Watt, Matthew Boulton's partner, dated 11 August 1785, which begins: 'I trouble you at the request of Mr Kier. ... He has invented a form for the Cylindric Wick'd Lamp so much superior to that of Mr Argand that there is little doubt of its supplanting the other').[67] Watt's reply, dated 18 August 1785, states:

> Mr B. has only a small share in the lamp business I believe only ¼. The rest belongs to Mr Parker and to Mr Argand the Inventor who is a most worthy and ingenious man. ...
>
> Mr A. has made two sorts of his lamps which have the flame at top as you describe [one of which is in sale] ... the oil in it is raised by a pump about once in ½ an hour. ... Mr Argand[']s patent is not for any form of a lamp but for the Cylindrical wick and the Glass chimney, so that I apprehend any body using either of these improvements would lye within the patent.[68]

However, Argand's English patent was overturned in a patent trial in December 1785, principally on the testimony of one João Jacinto de Magalhães (1722-90), a Portuguese living in London who had semi-anglicised his name to Jean Hyacinthe de Magellan, but who had close relations with the French.[69] Argand retreated to France, whereupon his workshops were destroyed in the French Revolution of 1789. He later retired to Geneva, and despite petitions organised in London to obtain him a pension, these were unsuccessful. Argand died in penury, his lamp designs, particularly in France, continuing to sell in large numbers, but unacknowledged as his and bringing him no remuneration.[70]

According to D. Alan Stevenson, Trinity House, the English lighthouse authority, was the first to install Argand lights in lighthouses, at Portland in 1789, 'and by 1820 they had been installed at some 50 coastal lighthouses in Britain and Ireland, but at few lighthouses elsewhere'.[71] He goes on to list the combination of Argand lamps and metal parabolic reflectors installed in eleven English lighthouses between 1789 and 1799, 'making the south and south-east coasts of England the best-lighted in the world'.[72] However, it was not until 1804 that a Scottish lighthouse – the new 'substantial' Inchkeith lighthouse in the Firth of Forth – was lit with spermaceti oil in Argand burners, using the new silver-plated copper parabolic reflectors.[73]

In the domestic sphere and in the streets of Europe's growing cities, the success of these Argand lamps – they were of course known by other names in France – enormously increased the demand for sperm oil (oil from the sperm whale, although other unfortunate sea mammals were also hunted for their oil and other products). However, the Revolution and subsequent wars with Britain with her superior sea-power meant that France was effectively cut off from this raw commodity. The French thus turned to colza oil, a vegetable by-product more recently encountered in Britain as rape-seed oil: this produces less sooty deposits and provides a brighter flame. It required a thicker wick in the Argand lamp than that used for sperm oil, and was widely used in British lighthouses from about 1847.[74]

Other oils – olive, seal, even herring – were also tried; all were thick and in cold weather, as Douglas Hague remarks, 'reluctant to flow or respond to the capillary attraction of the wick'.[75] In about 1810, Robert Stevenson devised a 'frost lamp', which was hung below the oil-tube.[76] His son, Alan, described how these Argand burners and the silver-plated copper parabolic reflectors were constructed, improved and assembled for the Northern Lighthouse Board, in considerable detail and with copious illustrations (including how much they cost), first in his *Account of the Skerryvore Lighthouse*, and subsequently in his *Rudimentary Treatise on … Lighthouses*.[77]

This second volume – very much derived from the first for 'students and the practical engineer' – contains a touching introduction from Alan Stevenson:

TO MONSIEUR LÉONOR FRESNEL, INSPECTEUR DIVISION-NAIRE DES PONTS ET CHAUSSÉES SECRÉTAIRE ÉMÉRITE DE LA COMMISSION DES PHARES &c. &c. &c. MY DEAR MR FRESNEL, There is no one to whom I can dedicate this Volume so properly as to you. Much of what it contains is founded on information which I owe to your generosity and friendship. A great part of it, also, is devoted to a description of the beautiful system of Lighthouse Illumination

18

invented by your late distinguished Brother, AUGUSTIN FRESNEL; who, to the high intellectual endowments which have extended his fame over the whole scientific world, united, in a remarkable degree, these amiable qualities which endeared him much to all who knew him, and most to those who knew him best; and from whom, when in early youth I accompanied my Father to Paris, I experienced much consideration and kindness.[78]

A 'great Lamp', discussed by Alan Stevenson and used at Skerryvore, was a development of the Argand lamp, and in its largest state contained four concentric wicks. 'Fresnel himself,' wrote Stevenson, 'has modestly attributed much of the merit of the invention of this lamp to M. Arago; but that gentleman, with great candour, gives the whole credit to his deceased friend …'.[79] Arago and Fresnel had devised and published their improvements to the Argand lamp in 1821, and it was reported in the British scientific press, a full translation appearing the following year.[80]

Used with a first order Fresnel optic (the largest size), this four-wick mechanical lamp, 'in which the oil is kept continually overflowing by the means of pumps, which raise it from the cistern below; the rapid carbonization of the wicks which would be caused by the great heat is thus avoided'. Shown at the Great Exhibition of 1851, the description of its workings explained that 'the flames of the lamp reach their best effect in three hours after lighting, i.e. after the whole of the oil in the cistern, by passing and repassing over the wicks repeatedly, has reached its maximum temperature. After this the lamp often burns 14 hours without sensible diminution of the light, and then rapidly falls. The light varies from 16 to 20 times that of the Argand flame of an inch in diameter; and the quantity of oil consumed by it is greater nearly in the same proportion.'[81] Stevenson's description makes no bones about the lamp's French derivation: 'I have seen the large lamp at the Tour de Corduan burn for seven hours without being snuffed or even having the wicks raised … in the Scotch Lighthouses, it often, with Colza oil, maintains, untouched, a full flame for no less a period than seventeen hours.'[82]

Interestingly, the lamp as manufactured by James Milne & Son, the Edinburgh brass founders who under-

took much of the work for the Northern Lighthouse Board, has a design apparently derived from the famous designer Thomas Hope (1769-1831), complete with a frieze around the top of the cistern, with lions' masks and acanthus flowers, the clockwork mechanism being carried on three satyrs' cloven feet.[83] We shall see in chapter 5 some possible reasons for these manifestations of an Egyptian influence appearing in Scotland as late as the mid-nineteenth century.

Lighting methods changed as the nineteenth century wore on, with colza oil giving way to paraffin, a mineral-based oil, and experiments being made with the new unseen 'fluid', electricity. Such alternative fuels, and their introduction in Scottish lights, will be discussed in chapter 6. For during this earlier period, other devices had been introduced to magnify the effect of the puny flame of the candle and oil lamp.

### Reflectors, mirrors, catoptrics

Following experiments in Sweden in 1757, successful parabolic reflectors with the oil flames focussed into parallel beams were introduced to the lighthouse at Körso by Jonas Norberg. Spherical reflectors at this date were inefficient, and flat plates of the type so excoriated by Alan Stevenson do very little to help enhance the beam.[84] In England, according to Liverpool Council minutes, the Liverpool dockmaster William Hutchinson (1715-1801) set up the first parabolic reflectors behind oil lamps at the Bidston Hill signal station in 1763 at the spot where the first Bidston lighthouse was built in 1771.[85] Liverpool's growth as a port at this time had led to an increase in its methods of sea-marking, and Hutchinson's chart of the Liverpool and Wirral anchorages shows a number of newly-established leading lights, as well as buoys and other markers. Hutchinson's reflectors were initially made from sheets of tin soldered together and lined with pieces of mirror glass. Subsequently, he had larger reflectors constructed.[86] These were wooden bowls, lined with mirror rectangles set into plaster.[87]

> These reflectors are made, as near can be, to the parabolic curve. …
> We have made, and in use here, at Liverpool, reflectors of one, two,
> and three feet focus; and three, five and a half, seven and a half, and
> twelve feet diameter; the three smallest being made of tin plates,
> soldered together; and the largest of wood, covered with plates of
> looking glass … the lamp or cistern part is of copper, for the oil and
> wick behind the reflector, so that nothing stands before the reflector,
> to intercept the blaze from acting upon it.[88]

Robert Stevenson, Thomas Smith's son-in-law and business partner, visited Bidston Hill in 1801 on the first of his English lighthouse tours (undertaken with the agreement of both the Northern Lighthouse Board and Trinity House), and recorded in his diary somewhat critically that

> … the light from Bidston Hill is from oil with one reflector of silvered glass, which is no less than thirteen and a half feet diameter and its focus four feet. This immense reflector is illuminated by one large cotton wick which consumes one gallon of oil in four hours. This lighthouse is remarkably well taken care of – being in every respect clean and in good order. I cannot see any good reason for expending such a quantity of oil for one reflector as the same quantity would answer for thirty reflectors of twenty inches diameter, and I am confident that seven such reflectors would give an equal if not a superior light.[89]

The publication of Hutchinson's *Treatise on Practical Seamanship* in 1777 had promoted the wider adoption of parabolic reflectors. However, he was not alone in developing and experimenting with trying to provide a safe and powerful light source with a concentrated beam. A gentleman scientific amateur, Ezekiel Walker (1741-1834) of Lynn in Norfolk, wrote a number of papers on lights, illumination and instrumentation. He was particularly incensed by the anonymous contribution to the 1801 *Supplement* to the third edition of the *Encyclopaedia Britannica*. Under the article 'Reflector', this stated that 'Mr Thomas Smith, tin-plate-worker, Edinburgh, seems to have conceived the idea of illuminating light-houses by means of lamps and reflectors, instead of coal-fires, without knowing that something of the same kind had been long used in France; he has therefore all the merit of an inventor, and what he invented, he has carried to a high degree of perfection'.[90] Walker complained that 'the writer of this article has certainly been misinformed, for reflectors, such as he describes were invented by me; they were also made, and fixed up, under my direction, in a light-house on the coast of Norfolk, in the year 1779. And, in the year 1787, at the request of the trustees appointed by Act of Parliament for erecting four light-houses on the northern parts of Great Britain, I instructed the above-mentioned Mr Thomas Smith, in the method of constructing light-houses.'[91] Ezekiel Walker was acknowledged in the fourth edition of *Britannica*.[92] However, it has been suggested that as he had not described his reflector in any of his publications, he was possibly 'not unaware' of Hutchinson's developments in Liverpool.[93]

In Scotland the Northern Lighthouse Board, the first lighthouse authority with a national responsibility for lighting the coasts of Scotland, was established by Act of Parliament in 1786. Its initial purpose was 'for erecting four lighthouses in the northern parts of Great Britain, at Kinnaird's Head, Island of North Ranilsha [Ronaldsay],

Point of Scalpa [Eilean Glas], and Mull of Kintyre'.[94] At the first meeting, on 1 August 1786, the Commissioners appointed their Engineer, Thomas Smith, 'tin-plate worker in Edinburgh'.[95] The Board carefully considered the existing lighthouses in the Forth, Tay and Clyde, and they looked at the published work of William Hutchinson, dockmaster at Liverpool. After some correspondence with Ezekiel Walker, they dispatched Smith to Lynn to be instructed by him. On his return, the Board instructed Smith to acquire copper-covered iron lanterns and sheets of mirror glass in Glasgow. The mirror glass was to make into reflectors back in Edinburgh, a mould for which he was already constructing. He was also to manufacture the lamps. As Smith's great-great-grandson wrote:

> The resemblance between Smith's early reflectors and a reflector which Walker constructed in 1795 is very close but it is impossible to say whether Smith departed greatly from Walker's original design. But he certainly improved the lamps, so that they could be withdrawn from the reflectors, and he introduced metal pipes which separated each wick from the others and obtained small smokeless flames.[96]

All four original northern lighthouses displayed fixed lights; that they were an improvement on the previous darkness is demonstrated by the immediate clamour for more of the same by shipowners and sailors.

Using his mirror-faceted parabolic reflectors, illuminated with simple oil lamps, Thomas Smith built the first four lighthouses at the four corners of Scotland, the last of which was completed in 1789. By then, another was being constructed on Pladda, an island off the southeast corner of the larger island of Arran. This was lit in October 1790, but was close enough to those on the Mull of Kintyre, Cumbrae, at the entrance to the Clyde, and Copeland on the Irish coast, to require some means of distinction. This was done by displaying at Pladda a lower light from a small lantern 20 feet below the main light, in effect a double light.[97] Another double light, even more substantial, was constructed in 1794 on the Pentland Skerries at the eastern entrance to that most dangerous tidal stream, the Pentland Firth, where the Atlantic Ocean meets the North Sea between Scotland's north coast and Orkney. The old coal-fired light on Little Cumbrae was so high that its glow was often hidden by cloud, and Thomas Smith was asked by the Cumbrae Trustees to build a new light with a lantern at a lower level overlooking the main channel. This was built under Robert Stevenson's supervision and lit first in October 1793. With Glasgow's ever-increasing shipping, another light was mooted at Toward Point, but instead it was decided in 1795 to build one at Cloch Point. This was lit in August 1797. Smith had by now supplied oil lamps and reflectors to the pair of towers at Buddon Ness.[98] He also provided one of the lighthouses at Leith Harbour with reflectors and oil lamps in 1788, and the following year, after a fire, five faceted reflectors and oil lamps to Portpatrick Harbour, which remained in use until 1834.[99]

The most venerable of Scottish lights, that on the Isle of May, was still coal-fired, and still privately-owned. Estimates for the owner, by now Lord Titchfield, heir to the Duke of Portland, who was married to the Scott of Scotstarvit heiress, showed at least 450,000 tons of shipping by now annually passed the light, so that the revenue from light dues was double the rent. With this increase in traffic in the Forth, local shipowners wished to have the lighthouse managed in a manner similar to that undertaken by the Northern Lighthouse Board, but their petitions went unregarded. Inevitably legal proceedings ensued, and these dragged on into the new century.[100]

The neighbouring island of Inchkeith also posed a threat to shipping coming into the estuary, and in 1801 the

ABOVE
Faceted reflector, with simple oil lamp, to Thomas Smith's design.
(NMS T.1993.164)

smack *Aberdeen* had been wrecked on the Fife coast trying to avoid the island. Unlike previous towers, the lighthouse on Inchkeith was built 'in the most substantial manner, and more like the buildings of a permanent National Establishment'. Also, 'an entire change took place at this period upon the construction of the Light-rooms and the reflecting apparatus, as well as in the extension and enlargement of the accommodation for the light-keepers'.[101] This was the first lighthouse in Scotland to be fitted with the new silver-plated copper parabolic reflectors – 16 in total – combined with Argand lamps using spermaceti oil, and at this point the light was stationary. It was first lit on 1 September 1804.[102]

By now it was felt that the original light placed on Orkney at North Ronaldsay was not in the right place, and the light was transferred in 1806 to Start Point some eight miles

away.[103] This became the Board's first revolving light: Stevenson had been impressed by the examples he had seen on his 1801 tour at St Agnes in the Scilly Isles, and at Cromer:

> The lighthouse is upon the Island of St Agnes and the light was formerly from coal, but a considerable time ago was altered by the Trinity Board to an oil light with argand burners and reflectors, and in order to distinguish it from the Eddystone light (for which it was sometimes mistaken by mariners making the land after long voyages) the reflectors were made to revolve upon an axis once in a minute – three bright flashes of light and three intervals of a faint light. This beautiful and characteristic effect is produced by means of a triangular frame on which the reflectors are fixed. This is turned by machinery, strong and simple in construction, which is acted upon by a weight and the motion of the whole regulated by means of a fly. There are twenty-one reflectors of silvered copper fixed upon this frame, seven of which are ranged on each side of the triangle. … The machinery which gives motion to the reflectors will go seventeen hours without requiring to be touched, and the fountain which supplies each burner is made to hold a quantity of oil equal to its consumption during that period, so that neither the motion of the machinery nor the light meets with any interruption throughout the longest night. The lantern is constructed chiefly of copper, and when altered from a coal light cost £1,250. The annual expense of maintaining the light is £480.[104]

His remarks about Cromer were far briefer:

> Since its alteration from a stationary to a revolving light it is perhaps the most useful upon the east coast, preventing many mistakes made at Yarmouth roads by vessels coming both from sea and coast ways. The light is from argand burners with fifteen

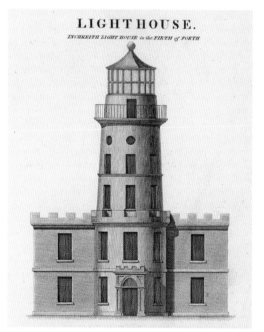

'Inchkeith Light House in the Firth of Forth', engraving from Plate 349, 'Lighthouse', from the *Edinburgh Encyclopaedia* (1818).

reflectors, the same as those at Milford, and they are fixed five upon each side of a triangle frame and made to revolve with machinery in the same manner as at the Scilly lighthouse.[105]

Robert Stevenson was by now equipped with information and full of ideas about the practicalities of lighting he might use in the toughest assignment of his career, lighting the Bell Rock. The building of a tower on such a difficult rock will be looked at later, as will the resistance he met on the way.

## Lenses, prisms, refractors and dioptrics

The introduction of optics into lighthouses became mired in controversy especially in Scotland, thanks to the irascibility of one of her most prominent scientists, David Brewster (1781-1868). His intemperate words, published in scientific periodicals and subsequently in widely-read popular magazines, deeply offended the Stevenson family, and were only put behind them after his death – long after the earlier deaths of Robert Stevenson and his son Alan.[106] Most of this story took place after the lighting of the Bell Rock lighthouse in 1811, but the early parts of the tale are worth telling here.

Thanks to the wars with France for much of the later eighteenth century and up until the defeat of Napoleon at Waterloo in 1815, scientific discussion between Britain and France was, at best, intermittent. Optical science, in particular, appears to have been undertaken in each country in some isolation to developments in the other. In Scotland the young David Brewster left the University of Edinburgh in 1800 with a degree in divinity but a passion for optical science. However, unable to become a minister of the Kirk due to poor public-speaking skills, he turned his hand to journalism in a city full of literary endeavour and publishing houses.[107] From 1808 Brewster became the editor of a new encyclopaedia – competing with the Edinburgh-based *Britannica* – named the *Edinburgh Encyclopaedia*.[108] It was within an early article for this work – sequential parts were gathered up at completion into 18 volumes, with two volumes of plates, as late as 1830 – entitled 'Burning Instruments', which appeared in 1812,

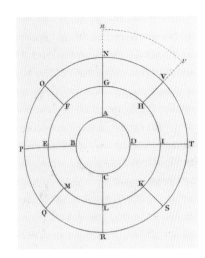

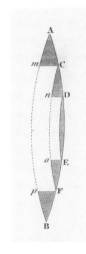

Brewster's Polyzonal lens as illustrated in the *Transactions of the Royal Society of Edinburgh*, 11 (1831), Plate III.

that Brewster based his claims for priority of invention for the device subsequently known as the Fresnel lens.[109]

As it had, like all articles in this encyclopaedia, been unsigned, Brewster included part of the article, that which discussed the construction of a burning lens in segments, in a book he published under his own name the following year.[110]

Burning lenses were known to have had a long history, and had been discussed in classical texts. The quality of the finished product of both mirror-making and glass production has long been felt to have been inferior to the claims made by some authors up until after the Renaissance, and this is supported by those artefacts that do survive.[111] The main use of burning lenses or mirrors was to experiment on minerals and chemical compounds – to analyse their make-up, something which engaged Brewster for many years.

However, before the end of the eighteenth century there had been some early experiments using lenses in lighthouses in England. These were reported in 1791 by the Liverpool dockmaster, William Hutchinson:

We tried the effect of small lenses with small reflectors … but could not get large lenses of solid glass made here, but got some blown in the form of a plano convex, like a bottle, and filled with strong brine to prevent their being broke by frost, which answered the purpose to magnify the light, but the heat of the blaze of the lamp and reflector broke them.[112]

Hutchinson explained that Trinity House had built a temporary lighthouse for optical trials on Blackheath, then outside London, and had subsequently 'advertised liberty to any other people to try experiments for this important purpose'. Thomas Rogers, who was in the glass trade, 'got reflectors blown in one piece of glass to their form, and by a new method silvered over the convex side without quicksilver, made them very bright good reflectors, and had what I call a large circular patent lamp three inches in diameter, consequently the wick nine inches round, stands at the focus of the reflector, and before it a plain convex lens of solid glass twenty one inches diameter and five inches and a half thick in the focus, which makes the light answer the principle of the Magic lantern upon an enlarged scale'. Rogers put lenses into the lighthouse at Portland, before going to Dublin and working for the lighthouse authority there.[113] Robert Stevenson reported that these were still there on his tour of 1801: 'Before each reflector there is placed a large lens not with a view to increase the light but the better to distinguish the lighthouse [from those nearby].'[114]

Meanwhile, across the Channel in France, work on the nature of light had also been undertaken. Discussing the Portland lighthouse experiment in his biography of Augustin Fresnel (1788-1827), the eminent French scientist François Arago (1786-1853) wrote that 'in fact a lighthouse with lenses has been long ago executed in England under the idea, at first sight very plausible, that it would be much more brilliant than lighthouses with reflectors. Yet it was found in practice that mirrors … direct to the horizon a more intense beam of light. Lenses were therefore abandoned.'[115] As Arago – who greatly admired his late colleague – described how

… in occupying himself with the same problem, Fresnel with his habitual penetration, perceived at the first glance where the difficulty lay. He saw that the lenticular lighthouses could only become superior to those with reflectors, by increasing considerably the intensity of the flame which supplied the illumination; or by giving to the lenses enormous dimensions which seemed to surpass all that any ordinary work could accomplish. He observed also that the lenses must have a very short focal length; that, in making them according to the usual forms, they had too great a thickness, too small a transparency; and that their weights were considerable, and pressed too much on the machinery for making them rotate, so as speedily to bring on its destruction.[116]

Such lenses had been devised earlier, for experiments by Georges Buffon (1707-88) using a similar glass shape but for a different purpose, as burning glasses: these are lenses by steps, 'lentilles à échelons', which were built up in small pieces, a plan inspired by another man of science, Jean Condorcet (1743-94). Arago firmly asserts that Fresnel's scheme was thought out without any knowledge of either of these predecessors, or indeed anyone else's proposals; and in any case 'could never have led to any useful result if it had not been combined with suitable modifications of the lamp'.[117] As we have seen, Arago and Fresnel had worked on this end of the problem too, providing a successful outcome in 1821.

Fresnel's compound lenses used reflecting prisms and refracting lenses to focus the beam of light, and the young scientist was swiftly appointed to the newly-formed Commission des Phares in Paris in 1819.[118] His new apparatus was installed as rapidly as the French Government could arrange in France's most venerable lighthouse at the mouth of the River Gironde, at Corduan in 1823.[119] With the establishment of the first lighthouse using Fresnel's apparatus, a new era dawned in lighthouse technology, overtaking the lighting systems used in all British lighthouses at that date. How Scotland adjusted to this new technology, and how her lighthouse authority's engineers incurred the wrath of her pre-eminent optical scientist shall be told in chapter 5. First, some civil engineering problems need to be addressed, and for that we should look beyond Scotland's dangerous coastline, to the busy navigation seaways of the English Channel.

Thin section through glass elements of a condensing lens, with central Fresnel lens and outer annular prisms, dated 1860. Presented by the Northern Lighthouse Board.

(NMS T.1993.147)

## Notes to Chapter 1

1. Stevenson (1818), 1. For Ken Trethewey's 2003 definition, see: http://www.pharology.eu/Lighthouses/WhatIsALighthouse/DT_Definition_of_a_lighthouse.htm
2. Taylor (1971), 4.
3. Ibid., 47-53.
4. Ibid., 62.
5. Clayton and Rice (1988), 1.
6. Sprague de Camp (1965), 423-27.
7. Pliny (1991), 353.
8. Asin and Otero (1933).
9. Hague and Christie (1975), 64; see Empereur (1998). Also Frost (1975).
10. Stevenson (1959), 11.
11. Ibid., 5-28; Dreyer and Fichou (2005), 247-50.
12. Hague and Christie (1975), 119-20.
13. Stevenson (1959), 21.
14. Ibid., 22; Hague and Christie (1975), 16-17.
15. Ibid., 22-23; Hague and Christie (1975), 76-77.
16. Ibid., 37-38; Hague (1965); Munro (1979), 25-38.
17. Munro (1979), 22-23.
18. Gilkes (1991), 102-105.
19. Robertson (2006), 322; and http://www.follies.org.uk/pdf/Foll-e%2013.pdf
20. Adair (1703), 12.
21. Kidd (1845), 796.
22. Munro (1979), 43; Stell (1984).
23. Hume (1997); for North Queensferry, where a replica of NMS 1993.149 was installed in 2010: see http://www.nqht.org/projects/the_lighttower/
24. Hume (1977), 128.
25. *New Seaman's Guide …* (1809), 157.
26. *North Sea Pilot …* (1868), 135.
27. Munro (1979), 49.
28. Bryce (1845), 192; Hague and Christie (1975), 211-12.
29. Allardyce and Hood (1986), 41-42; Munro (1979), 84; Martin (n.d.).
30. Stevenson (1824), 26; Munro (1979), 62-63; Wilson (1994), 6-7.
31. Stevenson (1850), part III, 185-87.
32. Munro (1979), 122; Groome (1894), II, 290.
33. Norie (1846), 100.
34. NMS T.1993.133; see Close (1868), 681.
35. Stevenson (1850), 60.
36. Ibid., 60.
37. Chance and Williams (2008), 22-23.
38. Stevenson (1959), 8-9.
39. Eggeling (1960) 33-46; Hague (1965).
40. Forrester (1792), 85 and Ball (1793), 449.
41. See http://www.taighsolais.com/isle_of_may_archives.htm
    *Courier and Advertiser*, 22 December 2009, p. 8 'Tragic story of island family'; our thanks to Susan Ciccatelli for her help with this. Interestingly, Lucy Anderson's gravestone marks the family tragedy as occurring in 1789.
42. Stevenson (1959), 272.
43. Ibid., 273.
44. Stevenson (1959), 276.
45. Hague (1975), 141-43.
46. Munro (1979), 43-50; Blake (1956), 1-24.
47. Boyle (1996a), 10-11.
48. Quoted in Robertson (2006), 262-63.
49. Robertson (2006), 52; Munro (1979), 42-43.
50. Stevenson (1959), 163.
51. Munro (1979), 42-43; Sutherland (1993); Watson (2003).
52. Stevenson (1959), 277; Bruce Peebles (1891) gives a survey of oil lighting in Scotland.
53. Stevenson (1912a), 16-18.
54. Robertson (2006).
55. Obituary (1815).
56. Mair (1978), 10-11; Bathurst (1999), 18-19; Leslie and Paxton (1999), 13; Paxton (2004).
57. Ibid., 11.
58. Ibid., 13.
59. [Livingston] (1894), 36-40.
60. *Scots Magazine*, new series, 9 (1822), 390.
61. *Quarterly Journal of Agriculture*, 5 (1835), 446; Lawson (1836), 203-204.
62. *Edinburgh New Philosophical Journal*, 29 (1840), 409; *London Journal of Arts, Sciences and Manufactures*, and *Repository of Inventions*, 36 (1850), 207; *Catalogue …* (1851), II, 648, item 452.
63. Stevenson, 'Leerie the Lamp-Lighter', quoted by Harman (2006), 3.
64. Wolfe (1999), 2-3. See also Stevenson (1959), 61-62.
65. Ibid., 3-20.
66. Ibid., 20.
67. Robinson and McKie (1970), 148. Peter Kier's subsequent lamp activities are discussed by Wolfe (1999), 101-105.
68. Robinson and McKie (1970), 150.
69. Wolfe (1999), 68-70; for Magellan, see Home (2004); Betts (2003-07). Schrøder (1969), 167-68 suggests that Magellan's testimony resulted in Argand becoming 'a victim of a miscarriage of justice'.
70. Stevenson (1959), 62; Wolfe (1999), 133-42.
71. Ibid., 63.
72. Ibid., 68.
73. Munro (1979), 62-63.
74. Stevenson (1959), 62.
75. Hague and Christie (1975), 154.
76. Mair (1978), 87.

77  Stevenson (1848), 181-349; Stevenson (1850),
    Part I, 75-131.
78  Stevenson (1850), v-vi.
79  Ibid., Part II, 92-93.
80  Arago and Fresnel (1821) and (1822); the note
    appeared in the *Quarterly Journal of Science,
    Literature, and the Arts*, 9 (1821), 381.
81  *Catalogue …* (1851), I, 320, item 99.
82  Stevenson (1850), Part II, 92-101, quotation p. 93.
83  Hope (1807), plate XIX, fig. 1.
84  Chance and Williams (2008), 24.
85  McConnell (2004);
    www.pol.ac.uk/home/history/hutch.html
86  One of these dating from about 1800, one of three
    used at Walney Island lighthouse, survives at the
    London Science Museum, NMSI 1958-101,
    presented by D. Alan Stevenson.
87  Naish (1985), 100-102; Robinson (2007), 44-46.
88  Hutchinson (1777), 149; Hutchinson (1791), 194.
89  Stevenson (1946), 16; quoted by Robinson (2007),
    49-50.
90  Anon (1801).
91  Walker (1801).
92  'Nautilus' (1831).
93  Stevenson (1959), 54.
94  26 Geo III c 101.
95  Munro (1979), 54.
96  Stevenson (1959), 159.
97  Munro (1979), 59.
98  Ibid., 59-65.
99  Stevenson (1959), 163.
100 Eggeling (1960), 37-39; Munro (1979), 62.
101 Stevenson (1824), 27.
102 Stevenson (1817), 11; Stevenson (1824), 26-30.
103 Stevenson (1824), 30-33; Wilson (1994), 6-7.
104 Stevenson (1946), 21-22.
105 Ibid., 25.
106 Munro (1979), 99-102; Bathurst (1999), 137-44.
107 Brock (1984).
108 Gordon (1869), 65.
109 Brewster (1812). For dating of individual articles in
    the *Edinburgh Encyclopaedia*, see Sherborn (1937).
    This claim was also reiterated by Brewster (1823),
    165, Brewster (1831) 40-44, [Brewster] (1833),
    183, [Brewster] (1835), 235, these last the three
    papers which gave such offence to the Stevensons;
    and again by [Brewster] (1859), 520 and (1860),
    497.
110 Brewster (1813), 399, note.
111 Schechner (2005). For a discussion of eighteenth
    and nineteenth century burning lenses, see
    Smeaton (1987); and for an exhibition containing
    many surviving examples, see Plaßmeyer and Siebel
    (2001).
112 Hutchinson (1791), 199.
113 Ibid., 200.
114 Stevenson (1946), 25.
115 Arago (1859), 268.
116 Ibid., 269.
117 Ibid., 270.
118 Naish (1985), 117; Silliman (1972); Rosmorduc and
    Dutour (2004), 83-96.
119 Dreyer and Fichou (2005), 247-50. The original
    revolving apparatus is to be seen at the Musée des
    Phares d'Ouessant; Fresnel's first panel, installed in
    1823, is held by the Musée des Phares de Trocadero
    in Paris.

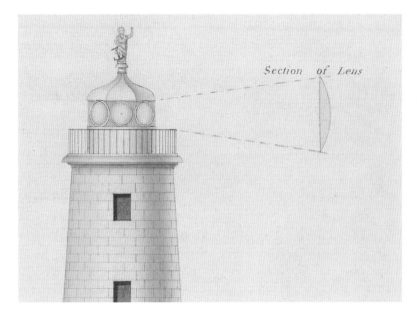

Section of Lens

Robert Stevenson,
*Portland High Lighthouse
in 1801*, drawing with
colour wash; detail show-
ing the first attempt to
use lenses in a lighthouse.
Made of glass by Thomas
Rogers in 1792, they
measured 5½ inches at
the centre.

29

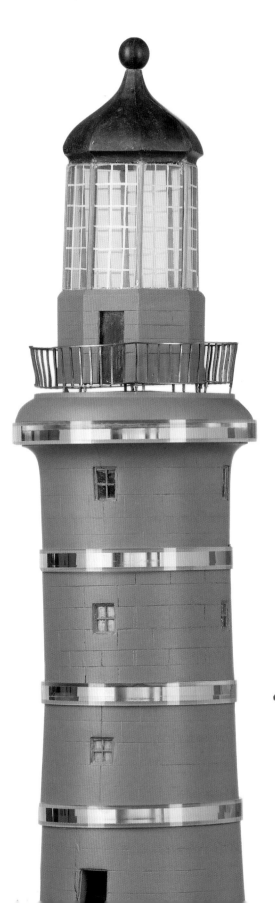
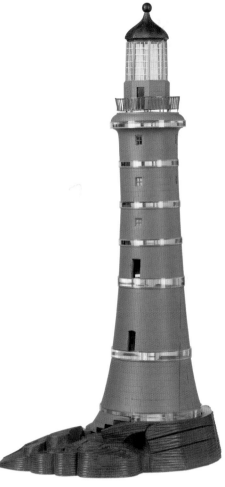

Model in painted wood of Smeaton's Eddystone
lighthouse in ten parts, made by Josiah Jessop
after drawings by John Smeaton, 1763. Presented
by the Royal Society of Edinburgh

(NMS T.1859.414.C.6)

# CHAPTER 2

# The Eddystone

IT MAY SEEM contrary in a book celebrating the building of the Bell Rock lighthouse to devote a chapter to a series of rock lighthouses in another country, 500 miles away to the south. However, the experience of the construction of the four successive lighthouses on the Eddystone Rock, especially that of the third Eddystone, built by the eminent eighteenth-century civil engineer John Smeaton (1724-92), had such a profound influence on such structures produced thereafter (particularly upon Robert Stevenson at the Inchcape Reef) that it is appropriate to devote some consideration to events in the English Channel.[1] Perhaps unexpectedly, National Museums Scotland also has in its collections early and important material relating to these early English lighthouses, and so it is fitting to discuss here how they complement items in the collections relating to Scottish sea-marking.[2]

Britain's geography has made her a maritime nation; however, her shores are surrounded by dangerous natural hazards and these, together with her notoriously changeable weather, have made safety at sea perilous for navigators. Any map of the island will demonstrate the narrow strait between France and the south of England is bound to be a busy channel for shipping, and among the most risky obstacles in it are the treacherous Eddystone Rocks, lying some 14 nautical miles south-southwest off Plymouth. The name, according to Smeaton, means what it says: the submerged rocks disturbing the change of tides into 'eddies', which occur even in the calmest weather.[3] The problem is that they sit in exactly the wrong place for wind-driven vessels coming up the

BELOW

Detail from a chart of the English Channel, showing the location of the Eddystone Rock, from John Smeaton, *A Narrative of the Building, and a Description of the Construction, of the Edystone Light-house with Stone* (London, 1793), Plate 1. Presented by the Royal Society of Edinburgh.

Channel from the west, after a long sea voyage either from the Mediterranean, around the Cape, or, from Tudor times, across the Atlantic, seeking a safe port in the natural harbour at Plymouth. Smeaton wrote:

> It is to be observed, that the soundings of the sea from the southwest-ward towards the Edystone, are from 80 fathoms to 40, and every where till you come near the Edystone, the sea is full 30 fathoms in depth; so that all the heavy seas from the south-west, come uncontrouled [*sic*] upon the Edystone Rocks, and break thereon with the utmost fury.[4]

The rocks are made of a particular form of moorstone granite: 'The most similar to it that I have seen,' wrote Smeaton, 'was in Scotland, yet that varied in some degree from it.'[5] He continued:

> This stone is also in a considerable degree elastic ... especially in endeavouring to divide it with the grain, which lies according to the stiving [sloping] of the rocks; and is nearly one foot dip to the westward, in two feet horizontal, that is, in an angle of about 26 degrees with the horizon. The kind of work which can the most easily be done upon this rock is in boring or drilling holes into it, crossways of the grain, ... every thing else goes on with much labour, and difficulty, except that of splitting it in the direction of the grain.[6]

Most of what we know about the earlier lighthouses on the Eddystone Rock, as well as his own design, comes directly or indirectly from Smeaton's *Narrative of the Building, and a Description of the Construction, of the Edystone Light-house with Stone*, which (as his successor, Robert Stevenson, realised with the Bell Rock lighthouse) he found more of a trial writing than building:

> In truth I have found much more difficulty in writing, than I did in building; as well as a greater length of time, and application of mind, to be required. I am indeed now older by 35 years, than I was when I first entered upon the enterprize ... but when I consider that I have been employed full seven years, at every opportunity, in forwarding this book ... and that the production of these original materials, as well as the building itself, were dispatched in half that time, I am almost tempted to subscribe to the sentiment adopted by Mr Pope, that 'Nature's chief masterpiece is writing well'.[7]

Part of the problem associated with histories of the Eddystone lighthouses concerns the lack of adequate documentation from official sources. Trinity House experienced a number of catastrophic fires that effectively destroyed many of the records pertinent to the constructions at the Eddystone. The first of these was the Fire of London in 1666; the second occurred in 1714; and the third was the Blitz of 1940.[8] 'But,' wrote John Smeaton in the 1793 revision of his account of the lighthouses on the Eddystone Rock, 'whether Mr Winstanley was a proprietor or sharer of the undertaking under the Trinity House, or only the directing engineer, employed in the execution, does not now appear. This will be cleared up in the Addenda by a communication of Sir William Musgrave.'[9]

Trinity House – or to give this ancient guild its more correct name, the Trinity House of Deptford Strond – was an association of mariners, long based on the Thames, which had gained a Royal Charter under Henry VIII, mainly to look after the families of brother mariners lost at sea. Under a statute of Elizabeth I they were empowered 'to erect and set up beacons, marks and signs for the sea, needful for avoiding the dangers; and to renew, continue and maintain the same'. In practice, Trinity House ran this as a monopoly, leasing out the privilege of lighthouse construction to private speculators. These leaseholders then built the edifices at their own expense, were obliged to collect the rents ('light dues') at the harbour side, and were then expected to provide Trinity House with a cut of the profits (if any), before the structure and its rents reverted to Trinity House entirely, at a time stipulated in the lease.[10]

There had been other, earlier English lights; but the Eddystone was the first rock lighthouse to be considered, and thus presented new and different challenges.[11] Civil engineering was not a career as such at this date, and the problems involved were new and testing. Who could be found to rise to such a challenge?

### The first Eddystone lighthouses: Henry Winstanley's towers

As a builder of lighthouses, Henry Winstanley (1644-1703) has had a poor press, historically speaking, and much of what has been written about him is either untrue or very partial.[12] He was born at Saffron Walden in Essex in March 1644, eldest son of a landowning mercer (or dealer in luxury textiles) also named Henry Winstanley, and his wife Anne Gamage. Through his extended family, Winstanley had connections with London and the court. His uncle Nicholas Gamage was a wealthy London stationer, and Alison Barnes suggests that he introduced the young Henry to engravings of buildings abroad, which later inspired him to produce etchings of English country houses.[13] More significant, perhaps, was the role played by Winstanley's father. Between 1652 and 1656, while the boy Henry was still at school, his father acted as bailiff to James Howard, 3rd Earl of Suffolk, at nearby Audley End.

Audley End as it survives today is only a remnant of the Jacobean palace built between 1605 and 1614 on the site of a medieval monastery by Thomas Howard, 1st Earl of Suffolk and Lord Treasurer to James VI and I. It was then the largest private house in England – 'too big for a king', James is supposed to have remarked, somewhat dourly, on a visit in 1614, 'but it might do for a Lord Treasurer.'[14] In fact, the building and maintenance of such a place, together with the expense of bringing up, and providing for, Suffolk's eleven children, left his heirs so burdened with debt (he himself was sent to the Tower for embezzlement at one point) that they were eventually forced to sell up after the Restoration to Charles II in 1669. Subsequently, much of this magnificent building was pulled down during the eighteenth century.[15]

In its heyday the building had inspired the young Henry Winstanley, and he obtained employment in the 3rd Earl of Suffolk's estate office from 1660 to 1669.[16] He then set off on the Grand Tour until 1674 to study European architecture. Winstanley later became Clerk of Works at Audley End from 1679 to 1701, and held a similar position at Newmarket Palace between 1701 and 1703. Thus he became a servant of the crown, and would have encountered those who moved in court circles when the King came to Audley End two or three times a year for the racing at nearby Newmarket. Not only was Winstanley making contacts in the highest echelons of society, but through his job as Clerk of Works he began to understand buildings and how they operate. Perhaps his best-known work as an engraver is the set of 25 plates with plans and views of *The Royal Palace of Audley End*, one of which is dated 1676. The advertisement on his engraving of his home in Littlebury demonstrates his desire to undertake more engraving, and he also published a set of engraved geographical playing cards in 1677.[17] Winstanley was, despite his yeoman origins, someone who had managed to secure royal patronage and was respected for his dealings in architecture. At a time when there was no profession of civil engineer, it is not perhaps so surprising that someone with his sort of background and abilities should take up the challenge of building a lighthouse – also a fairly novel concept – on the dangerous Eddystone Rock.

It helped that, with a change of regime in 1688, the Stuart monarchy was embodied in a Dutchman who was intensely interested in naval matters: William III, Protestant husband of Queen Mary (daughter of the deposed Roman Catholic James II; William's mother was a daughter of Charles I) had a lifelong mission to subdue the French, and sharing his wife's throne certainly helped him in this calling. He was welcomed ashore at Brixham (the wind was in the wrong direction for landing at

Dartmouth), and as Michael Oppenheim noted: 'By the ironic sequence of events the citadel erected to safeguard the hold of the Stuarts in the west was the first fortified place to open its gates to William of Orange. … The Revolution was followed by war with France, and squadrons were frequently in Plymouth Sound.'[18] Plymouth Dockyard was developed by William III from 1690,[19] and thus the need for lighting the dangerous rock obstructing the entrance to the harbour became more critical, even though 'it was in the middle of the furious war with France, and a guardship lay off the Eddystone while the men were working'.[20]

Henry Winstanley had married in 1683, and he and his wife set up home in Littlebury House, near Saffron Waldon. Winstanley had a mechanical turn of mind and was able to dream up and construct a number of unexpected and amusing gadgets. It was subsequently observed by John Smeaton, who constructed the third lighthouse on the Eddystone Rock, that '[Winstanley] had distinguished himself in a certain branch of mechanics, the tendency of which is to raise wonderment and surprize. … [He] is said to have been a man of some property: but it is at least certain, that he established a place of public exhibition at Hyde Park Corner, called Winstanley's Waterworks, which were shewn at stated times, at one shilling each person …'.[21]

The Piccadilly Water Theatre is often referred to by contemporaries. Diarist John Evelyn noted that, on 20 June 1696, 'I made my Lord Cheney a visit at Chelsea, and saw those ingenious water-works invented by Mr Winstanley, wherein were some things very surprizing and extraordinary'[22]; and the essayist Richard Steele mentioned it in both the *Tatler* and *Spectator*, while an advertisement appeared in the *Evening Post* in 1714.[23] By this time of course Winstanley was long dead, but Alison Barnes makes the point that the theatre and its marvels were set up in order to help fund the building of the lighthouse, and it was subsequently run for his widow's benefit until her death in 1721.[24]

In the same way, Littlebury House, Essex, where the Winstanleys lived while Henry Winstanley worked at nearby Audley End, and for which an engraving exists in two states – with and without an advertisement – was run partly as a house of mechanical entertainments. The independent traveller, Celia Fiennes (1662-1741), visited Littlebury in 1697, 'where is a house with abundance of fine Curiosityes all performed by Clockwork and such like which appears very strange to the beholders'.[25] Unfortunately, Winstanley was not at home, so she saw little of its marvels. After his death, it too continued to be run as a financial enterprise for his widow.[26]

As early as 1692, Winstanley's business manager, Walter Whitfield put forward a proposal in which he was to build a lighthouse on the

Eddystone Rock. He and Trinity House would divide equally any profit made; but as events transpired, Whitfield did not undertake the construction. His rights were transferred to Winstanley, and after due negotiation the agreement made in 1696 allowed Winstanley the first five years' profits, after which these would be shared with Trinity House for a further 50 years, before the lighthouse reverted entirely to the control of Trinity House: Winstanley would bear the costs of construction.[27]

Winstanley outlined his own 'Narrative of the Building' of his lighthouse at the Eddystone Rock on his later engraving showing his completed improved 1699 structure. A description appears in the top left-hand corner, and is quoted by Smeaton who owned this example:

> This Light-house was begun to be Built in the Year 1696 and was more than four Years in building, not for ye Greatness of ye Work but for ye Difficulty & Danger of getting backward & forward to the Place, nothing being or could be left safe there for ye first 2 Years, but what was most thoroughly affixed to ye Rock or ye Work at very extraordinary charge & tho' nothing could be attempted to be done but in ye Summer Season, yet ye weather then at times would prove so bad yet for 10, or 14 days together ye Sea would be so Raging about these Rocks caused by out Winds & ye running of ye ground Seas coming from ye main Ocean, that altho' ye weather should seem & be most calm in other Places, yet here it would mount & fly more than 200 foot, as has been so found since there was lodgement upon ye Place, and therefore all our Works were constantly buried at those times & exposed to ye Mercy of ye Seas and no Power was able to come near to make good, or help anything as I have often experienced with my Workmen in a Boat in great danger, only having ye satisfaction to see my Work imperfectly at times as ye Seas fell from it & at a mile or two distance, & this at ye prime of ye Year & no Wind or appearance of bad Weather; Yet trusting in Gods assistance for his blessing on this undertaking, being for a general good & receiving most unexpressable Deliverances I proceeded as following.
>
> The first summer was spent in making twelve holes in ye Rock and fastening twelve great irons to hold ye Work yt was to be done afterwards, the Rock being so hard & ye time so short to stay by reason of Tides or Weather, & ye distance from ye shore and ye many Journeys left yt there could be no landing at all, and many times glad to land at our return at places yt if weather permitted, would take up ye next day to get to Plymouth again.
>
> The next Summer [1697] was spent in making a solid Body, or kind of round Pillar twelve foot high and fourteen foot Diamiter, and then we had more time to Work at the Place and a little better landing, having some small shelter from the Work and something to hold by, but we

had great trouble to carry off and land so many Materials, and be forced to secure all things as aforesaid every night and time we left work, or return them again in the Boats.[28]

Tactfully, Winstanley makes no mention of his adventure in the summer of 1697, when he was captured by a French privateer. Britain was at war with France during the time he began construction work in 1696. The Admiralty instructed the resident commissioner at Plymouth Dockyard, Captain George St Lo (1658-1718), to help him through the use of the guardship *Terrible*, not only for transporting the engineer and his men between the Rock and Plymouth, but also to prevent any attempts by the French to obstruct the building work.[29] In 1689, St Lo – who had seen considerable active service against the French – had been taken prisoner, after losing his ship in a seven-hour engagement. His treatment at the hands of the French left him embittered, although he was exchanged after about a year and, once back in England, wrote and published two pamphlets reflecting on his experience, proposing improvements in the management of the fleet.[30]

Work seems to have been discontinued from August 1696 until June 1697: the log of the *Terrible* mentions this beginning on 14 June. Before it started, the Admiralty repeated the 'Instructions' to St Lo from the previous year. But on 25 June St Lo came on board and sailed to join the fleet elsewhere in the Channel, leaving just a boat with Winstanley and his men, while fog prevented his return for several days. A 'small French Challope' (privateer) sent her boat on about 25 June to the Rock with 30 armed men, and carried Winstanley off to France. The workmen were stripped and turned adrift in their boat. Fortunately the Admiralty moved quickly and Winstanley was rapidly released and exchanged.[31]

Corroboration of these events comes from Narcissus Luttrell (1657-1732), sometime MP for Saltash, Cornwall, who noted in his diary:

*Tuesday 29 June 1697*
    A French privateer has seiz'd Mr Winstanley the engineer, together with his workmen, as they were erecting a light house at Eddystone Rock, off Plymouth, and carried him to France, destroy'd his work, but left his men behind them. ...
*Saturday 3 July*
    The lords of the admiralty have sent to France to have Mr Winstanley, the engineer (who was taken off Edistone rock, near Plymouth,) exchanged according to the cartel [the official exchange of prisoners of war between England and France]. ...
*Tuesday 13 July*
    Mr Winstanley, the Engineer, who was carried to France, is come back, being exchanged according to the cartel.[32]

In acknowledging St Lo's account of the affair, the Admiralty expressed their surprise at the occurrence and directed him 'that you doe let them know how it comes to pass that these people had not a sufficient strength to defend them from the enemy according to the said orders, and you having been short in the relation of this unhappy accident, the Board would have you inform yourself as well as possibly you can, how this whole matter happened and give them a particular account thereof'.[33] By an exchange of prisoners – the 'cartel' – Winstanley was back at work on the Rock on 6 July, guarded by the *Terrible*, and a new system of working was arranged by which the party returned to the warship each night and sailed to Plymouth. The season's work ended with the completion of a stone pillar.[34]

Winstanley's 'Narrative' continued, describing the third year's work, for 1698:

> The third Year, the aforesaid Pillar or Work was made good at the Foundation from the Rock to sixteen foot Diamiter and all the Work was raised which to ye Vane was Eighty foot, being all finished, with the Lanthorn and all the Roomes that was then in it. We ventured to lodge there soon after Midsummer for greater dispatch of this Work, but ye first Night ye weather came bad, & so continued, that it was eleven days before any Boat could come near us again, & not be acquainted with the hight of the seas rising, we were almost all ye time neer drowned with wet, & all our Provision in as bad a condition, tho' we worked night & day as much as possible to make shelter for ourselves. In this storm we lost some of our Materials altho' we did what we could to save them.
>
> But the Boat then returning we all left the House to be refreshed on shore, and as soon as ye Weather did permit, we returned again, and finished all, and put up the light on the 14th of November 1698 [William III's birthday]. Which being so late in the Year, it was three days before Christmas before we had a relief to get ashore again & were almost at the last Extreamity for want of Provisions, but by Good Providence then two Boats came with Provisions, and ye family that was to take care of the Light, and so ended this years Work.[35]

The engraving made of the early design of lighthouse exists in a number of forms. One – which appears contemporary – is entitled 'A PROSPECT of EDDYSTONE LIGHT-HOUSE near PLYMOUTH Being 80 Foot High. Erected & contrivd By HENRY WINSTANLEY of LITTLE-BURY in ye County of Essex Gent. Drawn at ye Rock by Jaaziell Johnston Painter'. It was engraved by John Sturt (1658-1730). Sturt was a London engraver, who later worked with another – Bernard Lens the younger – from about 1697. The original drawing by Johnston appears lost, but recently the historian Alison Barnes has located two contemporary plans, with illustrations of the lighthouse, executed by an unnamed Admiralty draughtsman and dated August 1698. These verify in general, but also add detail to, the Johnston-Sturt engraving.[36] An entry in the *Calendar of Treasury Papers* (7 January 1702), also uncovered by Barnes, refers to two other prints of the Eddystone lighthouse. A man named Thomas Baston, 'by the King's order, through Major Gen Trelawney, … made a draught of the lighthouse on the Eddystone near Plymouth, which the King then had at Kensington … [Afterwards], by his express orders, a second draught of the same, much larger, and according to the new alterations, which were then made, in that lighthouse, together with the draughts of several of the King's ships of war, which after much pains and six months labour, he performed to general satisfaction,

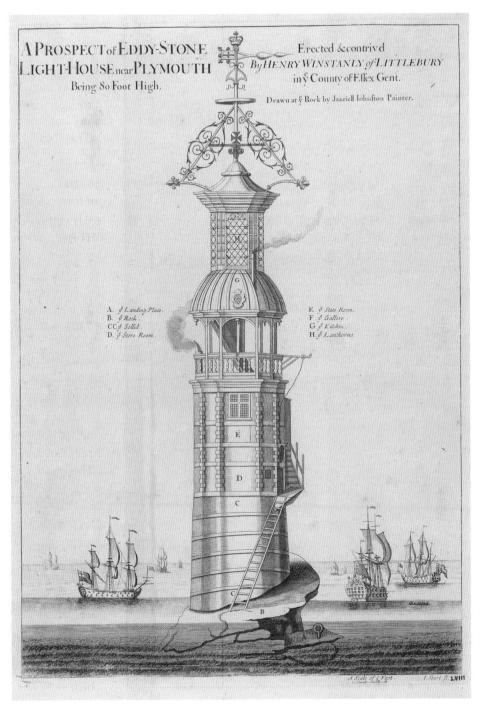

A PROSPECT of EDDY-STONE
LIGHT-HOUSE near PLYMOUTH
Being 80 Foot High.

Erected & contriv'd
By HENRY WINSTANLY of LITTLEBURY
in y.e County of Essex Gent.

Drawn at y.e Rock by Jaaziell Iohnston Painter.

A. y.e Landing Place.
B. y.e Rock.
CC y.e Sollid.
D. y.e Store Room.

E. y.e State Room.
F. y.e Gallery.
G. y.e Kitchin.
H. y.e Lanthorns.

A Scale of 5 Feet    I. Sturt fc. LVIII

Engraving of Winstanley's Eddystone Lighthouse, after a
drawing by Jaaziell Johnston, engraved by I. [John] Sturt,
c.1698. Presented by the Trustees of D. Alan Stevenson.

(NMS T.1998.229.1)

and delivered to the King at Hampton Court'.[37] John Smeaton had the image re-engraved by Henry Roberts for his *Narrative* in 1791, in which the letterpress is under the image, and the ships have been removed from the sea.[38] However, there is little doubt that Winstanley himself would have made drawings, and possibly models, of his great project – but these appear to have been lost.

Another source for knowledge about the probable appearance of Winstanley's first unmodified design can be derived from the appearance of the Eddystone Lighthouse Salt, now among the collections of Plymouth City Museum and Art Gallery.[39] This impressive piece of provincial English silverware can be used to verify how the lighthouse looked at the end of 1698, as it was probably commissioned by the grateful people of Plymouth for Winstanley. The architect of the first English rock lighthouse would have ensured the details of his masterpiece in silver miniature at the time that he felt the enterprise had come to a successful conclusion, not realising he would have second thoughts.

Eddystone standing salt, by Peter Rowe of Plymouth, *c*.1698. A condiment compendium, composed of six stacking sections and two removable elements and a detachable ladder.

Presented by the National Art-Collections Fund in 1942.

(Collection: Plymouth City Museum & Art Gallery ©)

This is corroborated by a description by William and John Blathwayt of Dryham Park, and their tutor, who visited Littlebury in 1703. They found:

> The eighth [curiosity], is the model of the lighthouse that one sees out at sea a few miles from Plymouth, which is built of bricks in the garden, with all the measurements reduced to a small scale in height and circumference. One sees yet another model of this same lighthouse in one of the rooms of the house wrought in silver; we were assured that this work had cost more than ninety pieces.[40]

The intrepid Celia Fiennes undertook what she called 'my Great Journey to Newcastle and to Cornwall' in 1698, and describing in some detail her thoughts about Plymouth ('… the streets are good and clean, there is a great many tho' some are but narrow; they are mostly inhabited with seamen and those which have affaires on the sea …'). From the arsenal she looked out:

> … walking round I had the view of all the town and alsoe part off the main Ocean in which are some islands: … there you can just discover a light house which is building on a meer rock in the middle of the sea; this is 7 leagues off it will be of great advantage for the guide of the shipps that pass that way.[41]

After the successful lighting of the Eddystone in November, Trinity House placed a somewhat self-congratulatory notice in the *London Gazette* on 17 December 1698 to alert shipowners and mariners:

40

The Masters, Wardens and Assistants of Trinity House having at the request of navigation, with great difficulty, hazard and expence, erected a lighthouse upon a dangerous rock called the Eddiston, lying at the mouth of Plymouth Sound, as well for the avoiding the said rock as for the better directing of ships thro' the channel and in and out of the harbour aforesaid. They doe hereby give notice that the said light hath been kindled for some time; and that being discernible in the night at the distance of some leagues, it gives entire satisfaction to all masters of ships that have come within sight thereof.[42]

Unfortunately, there seems to be no contemporary details of just what that lighting was, but given the 60 candles of Winstanley's subsequent modified lighthouse, it seems probable that this original structure was also candle-lit.

Nevertheless, at the end of this initial winter season Winstanley was not happy with his tower in this first incarnation; he could see that it was not high enough to withstand the huge waves that were flung up in the conflicting tidal race around the rocks, and he determined to enlarge and strengthen the edifice. Winstanley's 'Narrative' continues, explaining why and how his original design was modified:

The fourth Year [1699] finding in ye Winter ye effects the Sea had on this house, and Burying the lanthorn at times, altho' more than sixty Foot high, early in the Spring I encompassed ye aforesaid Building with a new Work of four foot thickness from ye foundation, making all solid near 20 foot high, and taking down the upper part of the first Building and enlarging every part in its proportion, I raised it 40 foot higher than it was at first, and made it as now it appears and yet the Sea in time of Storms flies, in appearance, 100 foot above ye Vane & at time doth cover half the side of the House and the Lanthorn as if it were under Water.[43]

This is illustrated in a second engraving (see page 42), dated 1699 (on the inscription above the door, and also above the gallery). Inscribed below the image: 'This Draught was made & Engraven by Henry Winstanley of Littlebury Gent and is Sold at his Waterworks: where also is to be Seen at any time ye Modle of ye said Building & principal Roomes for six pence a Peice.' In the top right corner of the engraving of the lighthouse, there is represented an open book, with clasps, resembling a bible. Perhaps the reader is expected to treat the 'Advertisement' as gospel truth. In the print formerly owned by Smeaton, now in National Museums Scotland, the blank verso page has been annotated: 'Mr Smeaton's scale 6 ft to an Inch This to be drawn by ...', but the space for a name has been left blank. In slightly later examples, presumably sold

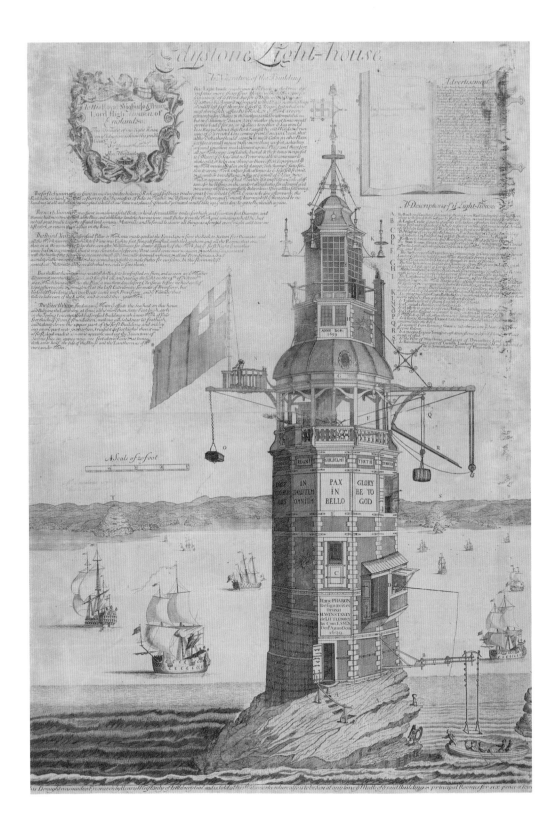

# Edystone Light-house.

after late 1703, such as that in the collection at Plymouth City Museum and Art Gallery, this 'page' has been additionally engraved: 'The Light House thus built, stood until that Dreadfull Storm, of the 27th of November 1703: which destroyed both it and its Ingenious Projector Henry Winstanley Gent Many delightfull Curiosityes of his Invention Severall Drawings and Engravings of Copper Plates, he has left which are Preserved. This Fatall Piece which was his last Work, may Serve for his Monument the House being his Tomb the sea his Grave.'[44]

The recto 'page' in both states of the engraving delivers his 'Advertisement':

> This Light-house bears from Plymouth (or the entrance of the Sound) S. and by W. and from Ramehead S, and half a point Eastwardly & is distant from ye Anchoring in ye foresaid Sound 4 leagues; and from Ramepoint about 3 leagues & a half, which is ye nearest Shore from ye said House: And ye Ile of Maystone bears from ye Lighthouse about N.E. and is also four leagues distant, So, all Ships coming from ye East or West have much ye same advantage of ye light that are bound for Plymouth. All ye Rocks near this House are on ye Eastwardly side, and stretching North but most Southerdly & all are cover'd at high water; but on the West Side any Ship may sail close by ye House, there being 12 or 13 fathom water & no hidden Rock. But towards ye E & by N about a quartr of a mile distant from ye House lies a hidden Rock yt never appears but at low spring Tides, & therefore (not so well known) is ye more dangerous. The Sea Ebs & Flows at this Rock on Spring Tides 19 foot; and yn at high Water all ye rocks are cover'd, tho' a smooth sea; and it is high Water at ye same time as at Plymouth but it runs Tide & half tide so yt it runs East 3 hours after it is high water and yet ye Sea falls lower, & it runs West 3 hours after it is low water; & yet ye sea riseth. At low Tide (especially spring Tide) 3 great ranges of Rocks appear very high & lie almost parrallel, streething [sic] towards ye S.E. & N.W. The House standing ye most West of all. The forementioned hidden Rock is a full Cable-length from all these Rocks & lies as aforesaid.[45]

Below this 'Advertisement' is given 'A Description of ye Light-house', detailing specific points from A to T. Perhaps the most interesting statement is that which accompanies item I:

> The Lanthorn yt hold ye light is 8 square, 11 foot Diameter, & 15 foot high in ye upright Wall: having 8 great Glass windows, and ground Plates for squares & conveniency to burn 60 candles at a time, besides a great hanging Lamp. There is [a] door to go into ye Gallery, that is all round to cleanse ye glass of ye Lanthorn wch often dim'd by salt water yt washeth it in Storms.

OPPOSITE PAGE

Engraved perspective view of Henry Winstanley's second Eddystone lighthouse, 1699. Presented by the Royal Society of Edinburgh

(NMS T.1859.414.A)

Even so, 60 candles and a lamp would have produced a much brighter light than that which shone from from the two towers that came later. As with the earlier print of Winstanley's initial design, this was re-engraved with crucial differences for John Smeaton's *Narrative* in 1791 by Henry Roberts.

It was Winstanley's lack of the 'Good Providence' which had come to his rescue in late 1698, but was to fail him on the night of 26 November 1703, that he and his lighthouse were to experience 'the worst storm in British history'.[46] Perhaps the most well-known contemporary account of that terrifying natural event was that produced by Daniel Defoe (1660-1731), author and probable Government spy. Defoe had just emerged from Newgate Prison, into which he had been immured for sedition. He had published a pamphlet critical of political opponents of his patron, William III, and with the King's death found himself exposed. During the week before the storm of 26-27 November 1703, 'as many as five or six separate depressions, with their origins in the Atlantic waters off the coasts of France and Spain, coalesced over the British Isles, forming what the historical meteorologist Hubert Lamb described as "an increasingly vigorous cyclonic situation focussed over Britain".'[47] Defoe placed advertisements in the then-embryonic national press, and pulled together such eyewitness accounts as he considered true. In a short section – 'short but terrible' – Defoe outlined the extent 'Of Damage to the Navy', including:

> The loss of the Light-House, call'd the Eddystone at Plymouth, is another Article, of which we never heard any particulars other than this; that at Night it was standing, and in the Morning all the upper part from the Gallery was blown down, and all the People in it perished, and by a particular Misfortune, Mr Winstanly, the Contriver of it, a Person whose loss is very much regretted by such as knew him, as a very useful Man to his Country: The loss of that Light-House is also a considerable Damage, as 'tis very doubtful whether it will be ever attempted again, and as it was a great Security to the Sailors, many a good Ship having been lost there in former Times.
>
> It was very remarkable, that, as we are inform'd, at the same time the Light-House abovesaid was blown down, the Model of it in Mr Winstanly's House at Littlebury in Essex, above 200 Miles from the Light-House, fell down, and was broken to pieces.[48]

Defoe subsequently visited Plymouth in 1705, gathering copy for the eventual publication of his *Tour through the Whole Island of Great Britain*, which was ultimately published in three volumes between 1724 and 1726. In this, he remarked:

Upon this rock, which was called the Eddystone, from its situation, the famous Mr Winstanley undertook to build a light-house for the direction of sailors, and with great art, and expedition finished it; which work considering its height, the magnitude of its building, and the little hold there was, by which it was possible to fasten it to the rock, stood to admiration, and bore out many a bitter storm.

Mr Winstanley often visited, and frequently strengthened the building, by new works, and was so confident of its firmness, and stability, that he usually said, he only desired to be in it when a storm should happen for many people had told him, it would certainly fall, if it came to blow a little harder than ordinary.

But he happened at last to be in it once too often; namely, when that dreadful tempest blew, Nov. the 27, 1703. This tempest began on the Wednesday before, and blew with such violence, and shook the light-house so much, that as they told me there, Mr Winstanley would fain have been on shore, and made signals for help, but no boats durst go off to him; and to finish the tragedy, on the Friday, Nov. 26, when the tempest was so redoubled, that it became a terror to the whole nation; the first sight there seaward, that the people of Plymouth, were presented with in the morning after the storm, was the bare Eddystone, the light-house being gone; in which Mr Winstanley, and all that were with him perished, and were never seen, or heard of since.[49]

It is perhaps significant that the eminent mid-twentieth century historian of lighthouses, D. Alan Stevenson, wrote that 'of all works connected with the sea, the erection of this tower was one of the most daring and original ever to be attempted, and Winstanley must be honoured for his decision to build it on these wave-swept Rocks and for his ingenuity and his unflagging resolution to carry out his plan – thus flaunting [sic] the universal qualified opinion as to its impracticability'.[50] Despite many commentators deriding the decoration as impracticable, and the construction as too flimsy, perhaps Winstanley's widow's additional lines to his engraving of the improved 1699 lighthouse should remain his epitaph: 'This Fatall Piece which was his last Work, may serve for his Monument the House being his Tomb the sea his Grave.'

More can perhaps be deduced about the structure of Winstanley's two towers by examining other contemporary artists' representations of his edifices. However, as these are not represented in National Museums Scotland's collections, they are not considered here.[51]

The loss of the lighthouse – and of her husband – came as a great blow to Winstanley's widow, Elizabeth. Most of his capital had been tied up in this enterprise, and up to the date of its destruction he had spent £6,814 7s 6d on building and maintenance for which there was documentary evidence, and had received from dues £4,721 19s 3d.

This left him at least £2000 out of pocket. In addition, over £1000 – for which vouchers had disappeared with the lighthouse – had been paid by Winstanley, so his estate suffered a net loss of over £3000 – a substantial amount of money in those days. Mrs Winstanley petitioned the Crown for a pension, and in January 1704/05 her petition was referred to the Lord High Treasurer, who in turn sent it in March of that year to Trinity House for advice from the Brethren.[52] After much delay, Mrs Winstanley was awarded a donation of £200, and a pension of £100 a year. It was no wonder that she continued to run Littlebury House and the Piccadilly Water Theatre as commercial concerns until just before her own death in 1721.[53]

Within days of the Great Storm the merchant ship *Winchelsea* was wrecked on the Eddystone Rock, and over the next few years many vessels met a similar fate. Trinity House came under pressure from the Admiralty and other interested parties to replace Winstanley's structure.[54] This was, however, delayed while an Act of Parliament was pushed through in early 1706 empowering Trinity House to rebuild the lighthouse, by using the duties payable by shipping passing the Eddystone, enabling them to lease this right to an appropriate leaseholder.

### The second Eddystone lighthouse: Rudyerd's tower

A proposal for a new lighthouse came from an Irish Member of Parliament, Colonel John Lovett (d.1710), who was backing as architect one John Rudyerd (or Rudyard) (fl.1703-09). Smeaton was unable to find out much about Rudyerd:

> … it does not appear that Mr Rudyerd was bred to any mechanical
> business, or scientific profession, being at that time a Silk Mercer
> [dealer] who kept a shop upon Ludgate Hill, London; nor do we find
> that in any other instance he had distinguished himself by any mech-
> anical performance before or after. … However, Mr Rudyerd's want
> of personal experience, was in a degree assisted by Mr Smith and Mr
> Norcutt, both shipwrights from the king's yard at Woolwich; who
> worked with him the whole time he was building the lighthouse.[55]

Rudyerd has recently emerged as a more probable figure as a lighthouse designer than in the past, as it has been discovered that his connections in the City of London may indeed have had more to do with patronage than with trade.[56] More, however, is known about Lovett. His father, Christopher Lovett, the second son of Sir Robert Lovett of Liscombe in Buckinghamshire, had moved to Ireland and become Alderman, and in 1676, Lord Mayor of Dublin. By 1703 his son John was a colonel in the Buckinghamshire militia and Member of Parliament for Phillipstown, County Dublin, in the Irish Parliament. That year he entered into a second marriage (he was a widower) with Mary Verney, also from an old Buckinghamshire gentry family. Mary Verney's dowry was £5000, and Colonel Lovett put this towards the construction of a new lighthouse at the Eddystone Rock in succession to that of Winstanley.[57] As R. H Coase commented, the renegotiated lease was now more in favour of the leaseholders: 'A 99 year lease at an annual rent of £100 with 100 per cent of the profits going to the builders.'[58]

In 1705 Lovett persuaded his new father-in-law, Sir John Verney (1640-1717) – who was created Viscount Fermanagh and Baron Verney of Belturbet, Ireland, on 16 June 1703 by Queen Anne, and who, by right of his Irish peerage, was also a MP at Westminster – to promote there a bill for the creation of another lighthouse on the Eddystone Rock. Lovett also petitioned the Brethren of Trinity House:

> A proposall of John Lovett Esq was this day brought to the Court setting forth his Pretention and Title to the Eddiston Lighthouse and his loss through its being blown down in the great storm in Nov'br 1703. That there were severall Persons who had Interests therein, w'ch could not be settled, by reason the Originall Deeds were burnt in the Fire at the Temple [lawyers' offices in London] and that therefore he design'd to Peticon the Parliam. for leave to bring in a Bill for Rebuilding the sd Lighthouse, and pray'd the Corp'o would Join with him in promoting such Intended Act; After Reading whereof the sd Mr Lovett was called in and acquainted that the Court would take his Case & Proposall into their Consideration and give an answer thereto on the Wednesday following; Upon w'ch Mr Lovett being withdrawn the Court Debated this matter, especially in relation to the Act of Parliam. propos'd and appearing to be a thing of great Moment in regard the Corp'o have already Authority p'r Act of 8th of Elizabeth to Erect all Lighthouses &c. It was resolved to advise wth Councell [a barrister] whether a New Act would not Prejudice the Corporation's power beforementioned; and Ordered that Mr Noyes [secretary to the Court] to draw up a case w'th proper Querys, and wait on Mr Cowper [the counsel] for his Opinion thereon, before the Corporation give their Answer to Mr Lovett on his sd proposall.[59]

Two weeks later, the Court reconvened to discuss the matter: 'Mr Lovet, and also Mr Weston his Attorney, attending without, they were call'd in', so that the Parliamentary petition could be examined so that it 'might in every respect be consistent with the honour and Interest of this House, and conveyed nothing Prejudiciall to the rights of the Corp'o'.[60] The Act of Parliament was formally passed in spring 1706.[61]

The architect selected to rebuild the Eddystone was apparently an old friend of Colonel Lovett, John Rudyerd. He was – according to John Smeaton, who never knew him – born in Cornwall, where his father was described as 'the lowest rank of day-labourers', and his brothers 'a worthless set of ragged beggars'.[62] Apparently, he was in the service of a gentleman, who caused him to be educated, and thus escape his unprepossessing origins. This eighteenth-century hearsay may or may not be true, and Mike Palmer has recently suggested that Rudyerd may have come from a much more respectable family based in Staffordshire.[63] By the beginning of the eighteenth century he was established as a silk mercer on Ludgate Hill, London, and John Lovett apparently knew him well. A letter from Lovett to Sir John Verney

describes John Rudyerd as 'my friend of long acquaintance, and to risk a penyworth he would neither advise nor suffer me'.[64] It is unclear where Rudyerd gained the knowledge to construct such an edifice as the one proposed for the Eddystone. However, he earned the warm approbation of Smeaton:

> It is not very material now in what way this gentleman became qualified for the execution of this work; it is sufficient that he directed the performance thereof in a masterly manner, and so as perfectly to answer the end for which it was intended. He saw the errors in the former building and avoided them; instead of a polygon he chose a circle for the outline of his building, and carried up the elevation in that form. His principal aim appears to have been use and simplicity; and indeed, in a building so situated, the former could hardly be acquired in its full extent, without the latter.[65]

Drawing of elevation and section of Rudyerd's design for a lighthouse at the Eddystone Rock, 1704-1708. Presented by the Royal Society of Edinburgh.

(NMS T.1859.414.B.1)

The principal feature of Rudyerd's plan was that its form – a truncated cone in shape – offered the least possible resistance to the waves and avoided the open galleries and projections of Winstanley's design. His method of securing the building to the rock was to cut dovetailed holes in the rock to which strong iron bolts (or 'branches') were keyed. It consisted of a solid granite base, about 28 feet high and 24 feet in diameter. This was topped by a timber superstructure, clinker-built (overlapping planks, as used in boat construction), caulked and pitch-covered like a ship, with Cornish moorstone for ballast, through which ran a tall square-sectioned 'mast'. The granite base was anchored to the rock by 36 large bolts, and 200 smaller ones, the holes filled with tallow, replaced by molten pewter to anchor the structure to the rock. It was the timber which proved to be the structure's

Achilles heel, and which proved eventually the ruin of an otherwise brilliant achievement. Interestingly, Smeaton commented:

> In like manner as Mr Winstanley; Mr Rudyerd also, after the completion of his work, published a print entituled [*sic*] a Prospect and Section of the Lighthouse on the Edystone Rock off of Plymouth; and he dedicated it to Thomas Earl of Pembroke, then Lord High Admiral of Great Britain and Ireland; with this motto, *Furit natura coercet ars*. The drawing by B. Lens, the engraving by I. Sturt, both eminent artists of their time. This print I suppose to be very scarce, not having seen any other but the single copy I have in my own possession.[66]

In late 1707, Rudyerd wrote to Lovett to say that such of his work which could be done on shore had been completed, and that he 'has had the help of a Guard-ship all the summer which has been very serviceable, and the sea Commander and others are very satisfied with the progress of the work'.[67] After Winstanley's experience in 1697, his relief must have been a very real one. Work began again the following year after stopping during the period of short daylight and poor weather of the winter. Lovett wrote from London in March that 'Mr Rudyerd has been on the Rock and found everything as he left them, and all this winter has not done him a Penny damadge; his man of war is ready at his command, and he has had his orders to have what men and stores he

ABOVE

Model of Rudyerd's wooden lighthouse of 1709-53. Presented by the Royal Society of Edinburgh.

(NMS T.1859.414.B.3)

LEFT

Model of the interior stonework of Rudyerd's wooden lighthouse of 1709-53. Presented by the Royal Society of Edinburgh.

(NMS T.1859.414.B.4)

49

needs out of Her Majties. Yard, at Plymouth, soe that he wants nothing but good weather'.[68] Rudyerd seems to have been granted his wish, for by early May Colonel Lovett was able to write: 'Thank God all things goes well at the Eddystone, and if Mr Rudyerd has 8 or 10 days more good weather, you will see it [the light] in the *Gazett*'. Lovett adds that he intends to give the Commissioners of the Revenue 'a Dish of Meate', because he is to have from them a letter to all the Collectors around the coast which would, he says, be 'of Servis'.[69] This refers to his intended ride around the south coast to the various ports in order to arrange for the collection of his tolls from home-coming ships.

By mid-June 1708, Rudyerd reported to Lovett that 'he has finished all the Sollid part, which is now 42 foote high, which is 36 above High Water Marck'.[70] Lovett was able to write within the month that '… all Affaires goes on well and hope next Saturday seven night to have the Light up and good habitations to live there. … Mr Rudyerd writes to me, my Lord Dursley, Sir George Byng and Sir John Jennings hee dines with. They are to be with him this week, and well pleased, and when it's up it will be a great Sattisfaction to your Lordship's Obedient Son and Servant John Lovett.'[71]

[Dursley, Byng and Jennings were all prominent naval officers: Dursley was James Berkeley, later 3rd Earl of Berkeley (1680-1736), who had witnessed the destruction of Sir Cloudesley Shovell's squadron on the Isles of Scilly on 22 October 1707, but who had himself survived; Byng (1663-1733) was subsequently Dursley's commanding officer off the east coast of Scotland; and Jennings was considered to be one of the greatest mariners of his generation, despite having few opportunities to distinguish himself in action.]

Then, at the end of the month, Lovett wrote:

> I thank God the Lanthorne is sett and all provision, Bedding, candles etcetera, went off to the Person who was to live in it; bad weather forced them back, but by Mr Rudyerd's letter yesterday after the storme, all things was very well, and only staid for 8 hours good weather to lodge the men and everything they should want for six months.[72]

Lovett then dined with, and took his leave of, the Corporation of Trinity House, 'who has promised to do everything I shall ask of them'. Before he left London a letter to his father-in-law stated:

Receipt for the payment of lighthouse dues for the Eddystone Lighthouse, 1734. Presented by the Trustees of D. Alan Stevenson. (NMS T.2009.193)

It's with great Sattisfaction I send your Lordship the good news that
the Light was put up this day 7 night (being the 28th of last month), and
will be in tomorrow's *Gazett* in due forme. I have sent your Lordship
a picture which I beg you acceptance of. One more I will give to the
Prince as Ld. High Admerall, and one to the Corporation of Trinity
House, and one goes for Ireland. In it is the 4 Men of Warr that Atended
on the Worck – viz. – the Roebuck, the Charles Gally, The Albrough,
and Swallow. ...[73]

This is evocative of the contemporary engraving (see page 52) by
Bernard Lens the younger (1630/31-1707/08) and John Sturt which
is elaborately filled with scrolling and legends, and also shows the
ships, as mentioned in this letter. Sturt, it will be recalled, also engraved
Winstanley's first lighthouse after Jaaziell Johnston's early drawing. In
1697 Lens and Sturt opened a drawing school in St Paul's Churchyard,
London, one of the first such in England. Perhaps more significantly,
in 1705 Lens was appointed drawing master at Christ's Hospital, a
charity school where vocational drawing was taught for use in
mapping or navigation.[74] The engraving of Rudyerd's lighthouse is
entitled 'A Prospect and Section of the LIGHT-HOUSE on the EDY-
STONE ROCK off of PLYMOUTH. Rebuilt pursuant to an Act of Parliament made ye 4th & 5th Years of ye reign of Her Sacred MAJTY QUEEN
ANNE. The Lights put up therein ye 28th July 1708.' Beside the image
of the exterior, it states: 'This Light-house [V]. was Designed and Built
by Jon. Rudyerd Gent.' The naval escort was not forgotten and the four
ships were named and described: the *Roebuck*, *Charles Gally*, *Albrough*,
and the *Swallow*.

The dedication is to Thomas Herbert, 8th Earl of Pembroke and
5th Earl of Montgomery (1656/57-1733), Lord High Admiral of Great
Britain and Ireland from 25 November 1708, after the death of Prince
George, and the explanation of the lettered plan is followed by a short
description, which is more factual and less discursive than the one
provided by Winstanley.[75] Rudyerd has had inscribed:

This EDYSTONE-ROCK lyeth 3 Leagues SE and NW of Ram-head
and 4 Leagues from Plymouth. The Building was begun in July 1706, a
Light put up therein and made usefull the 18th of July 1708, completely
finished in 1709 and appears as at V. The Rock Stives from E to W 10
foot 11 inches in 24 foot, which is the Diameter of the Foundation; 25 f
6 Inc is ye largest Circle can be drawn on ye Rock. The Face of ye Rock
is divided into 7 equal ascents. There are 36 holes cut into the Rock
from 20 to 30 Inches deep, 6 Inch square at ye top, narrowing to 5 Inch
at 6 Inch deep, from thence spreading and sloping to 9 by 3 at ye bot-
tom, they are all cut smooth within and wth great dispatch (tho' the

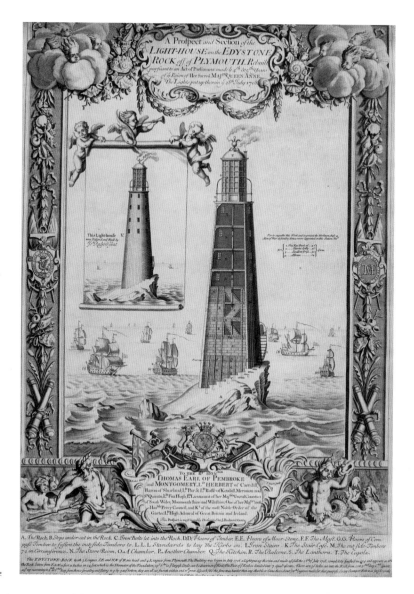

'A Prospect and Section of the Lighthouse on the Eddystone Rock', Rudyerd's lighthouse, engraving by I. Sturt, after Bernard Lens, 1780. Presented by the Trustees of D. Alan Stevenson.

(NMS T.1998.229.2)

Stone was harder than any Marble or Stone thereabouts) wth Engines made for that purpose. Every Cramp or Bolt was forg'd exactly to the bigness of the hole design'd for, they weighing from 200 to 500 wt according to their different lengths and substances. These Bolts serv'd to tye the Solid to the Rock.

A notice alerting shipowners to the newly-lit lighthouse, and thus the impending collections of dues, was placed in the *London Gazette* for 2 August 1708:

… And the Duties granted by the Said Act of Parliament for new Erecting, and constantly keeping and maintaining The Said Lighthouse, being paid from and after the Kindling or placing a Light Therein: All Masters of Ships, Hoys and barks, passing by the same are accordingly asked to take Notice, That the said Duties commence, and are payable from the 28th Day of July last past as aforesaid.[76]

Smeaton's *Narrative* spends some pages discussing the probable structure of the lighthouse tower, and how it was secured to the rock: 'According to Mr Rudyerd's print, the inclined surface of the rock was intended to have been reduced to a set of regular steps', because the hardness and its tendency to splinter would not allow the workmen to reduce it to a level, and although 'the stepping of the rock, has been but imperfectly performed, though in a degree that sufficed'.[77]

Using iron 'branches' wider at the base than further up, these were placed into the holes and the space filled with melted tallow and molten pewter, to seal it from the effects of salt water. 'Mr Rudyerd's method, therefore, of keying and securing, must be considered a material accession to the practical part of Engineering; as it furnishes us with a secure method of fixing ring-bolts and eye-bolts, stanchions, etc. not only into rocks of any known hardness; but into piers, moles, etc.'[78] Using best-quality 'solid squared oak timber', Rudyerd made a 'solid basement ... but in addition to the above methods, he judiciously laid hold of the great principle of Enginery, that weight is the most naturally and effectually resisted by weight'.[79] A model survives, described in 1924 as:

> A third model [of Rudyerd's lighthouse], scale ½ inch to 1 foot shows principally the positions of the 'trees' or iron bolts let into the rock to hold down the lighthouse. These 'trees' were evidently planted where the rock was suitable as they were most irregularly spaced. Unfortunately, some well-meaning but mis-directed enthusiast has repainted this model.[80]

Rudyerd placed a course of moorstone between each wooden course or layer, five of moorstone in all (despite the Lens print showing six courses: Smeaton thinks that this is because the print was made from designs created in advance of the lighthouse's construction), each one foot thick 'to introduce as much weight as possible, into the space to contain them; they were however laid without any cement'.[81]

The large parallel pieces of timber were fastened to the uprights by what Smeaton termed 'Jag-bolts' – these were 'such as with a chissel [*sic*] have a beard raised upon their angles, somewhat like that of a fish-hook, so that when driven forcibly into the wood, those beards, by laying hold, oppose their being drawn out again'.[82] By building up the tower in layers of seasoned timber and moorstone, and binding these securely to the upright timbers and iron branches fixed securely into the rock itself, the weight of this attached structure was to adhere it to the rock to which it was attached. The building was solid to eight feet above the highest part of the rock:

The solid being in this manner completed, the upper part of the building comprehending four rooms, one above the other, was chiefly formed by the outside upright timbers; having one Kirb or circle of compass timber at each floor, to which the upright timbers were screwed and connected; and upon which the floor timbers were rested. The uprights were also jag-bolted and trenailed to one another, and in this manner, the work was carried on to the height of 34 feet above the store-room floor; and there terminated by a planking of three inches thick, which composed the roof of the main column, as well as served for the floor of the lantern, and of the balcony round it.[83]

Smeaton clearly admired his predecessor's work, learning from it lessons to be applied in his own structure: 'Thus the main column of this building consisted of one simple figure, being an elegant Frustrum of a cone, unbroken by any projecting ornament, or any thing whereon the violence of the storms could lay hold. … The whole of the building was indeed a piece of Shipwrightery.'[84]

Smeaton mentions at a slightly later stage in his *Narrative* that the proprietors of the Eddystone lease had an apparently relevant group of plans and models, but

> … I found upon further enquiry, that neither the models, drawings or prints were coeval with the structures they were intended to represent, except the print of Mr Winstanley's Lighthouse published by himself in the year 1699, before referred to; for as to the models, &c. relative to Mr Rudyerd's, save a few original drawings, that shewed how some of the courses of stone were laid … they were all of a late date, chiefly since the year 1734; and rather useful for repairing than rebuilding the house; exhibiting no more of the inside work, than what was discovered by the openings that were made at the time such repairs were carried out, so that at best those could afford but very defective information, as to the particular original design; though they had been necessary for conducting the repairs of that building.[85]

Some 14 of these models showing the internal structure of Rudyerd's tower survive, and all have a square hole in the middle for the 'mast' and are of varying sizes. Unhappily, as Thomas Rowatt observes:

> Some of the most interesting models in the collection refer to Rudyerd's lighthouse, commenced in 1706. The courses of the stone-work are represented by a series of circular oak boards which average 9 in. diam. x ¼ in. thick. The number of the course represented by each 'model' is on the back, and each stone is numbered on the front. On the back of each is a slip of paper with instructions, thus in the case of course No.

Models of Rudyerd's wooden lighthouse, showing 14 courses of stonework, and one wooden course. Presented by the Royal Society of Edinburgh.

(NMS T.1859.414.B.6)

14, 'Stand in the centre and read the figure to the right and join No. 19 and 1 together on the middle of No. 1 underneath and observe the figures and characters of the draught'. These draughts are mentioned by Smeaton where he refers to a plan of the moorstone courses 'compiled from old working draughts, that appear to have been given out by Mr Rudyerd during the course of the work, for forming and fixing these courses'. Unfortunately, some methodical person has evidently scraped the instructions off the back, rewritten them on neat pieces of paper and stuck them on. Authorities on handwriting tell me that the figures on the front of the draughts date from about 1700 while the writing on the paper on the back is about 1800, which points to the probability that the new labels were put on when Mr Weston cleaned up the models before he gave them to the Earl of Morton.

Lovett died a few years later in 1710, and the lease of the Eddystone light came to his widow as part of her settlement, but it proved to be an unsatisfactory possession. The letters to her father are full of laments concerning the treachery and duplicity of her agents and collectors. Eventually her lease was put up for auction. A syndicate, of which lawyer Robert Weston was a member, bought it for £8000, and the money was paid on Lady Day 1716. The widowed Mary Lovett thought the purchasers had 'a great bargain', but she was 'glad to be rid of it'.[86] She survived until 1769, and thus heard of the replacement, third lighthouse, by John Smeaton. As for Rudyerd, he is not heard of beyond the engraving by Lens, dated 1709. John Smeaton believed that he died shortly after the completion of his masterpiece, and he notes that the Lens engraving did not relate to the completed design, from which 'I therefore must conclude, that … Mr Rudyerd's application must have been slackened by want of health'.[87]

Rudyerd's lighthouse captured the public imagination sufficiently for a number of engravings to be made of it. One such image is a reproduction and simplified version of another original print, designed by Isaac Sailmaker (c.1633-1721) and engraved by Henry Hulsbergh [Hulsberg] (d.1729). This latter is entitled: 'EDYSTONE LIGHTHOUSE BEING 90 FOOT HIGH, 1713', and was originally published by Henry Overton in 1713. It contained a labelled key to guide readers through the main points of the lighthouse construction, although the version on page 56 lacks the key.

## ABOVE

Hand-coloured line engraving of Rudyerd's Eddystone lighthouse, unsigned and undated, a reproduction and simplified version of an original print, designed by Isaac Sailmaker (c.1633-1721) and engraved by Henry Hulsbergh [Hulsberg] (d.1729). Presented by the Trustees of D. Alan Stevenson.

(NMS T.1998.229.3)

## RIGHT

Print from a pencil and grey wash drawing of Rudyerd's 'Edystone Light-house', by Edward Spragge, c.1721, also derived from that of Henry Hulsbergh. Presented by the Trustees of D. Alan Stevenson.

(NMS T.1998.229.4)

EDYSTONE LIGHT-HOUSE
being 90 feet high; Drawn Nov. 1721

56

Both appear to be based on work by Isaac Sailmaker, who had been commissioned in 1708 by Colonel John Lovett to paint Rudyerd's lighthouse; and of his four versions, three survive today.[88] Later engravings, dating from just before the destruction of the lighthouse, show that it remained a popular public icon: for example, the line engraving of Rudyerd's Eddystone lighthouse, drawn by C. Lempriere, engraved by W. H. Toms and sold by John Boydell, London, c.1754.[89]

Rudyerd's lighthouse was completed in 1709 and continued in service for the next 46 years. However, as it was made of wood it was attacked by sea-worms. Smeaton mentions that this decay was first spotted in 1723, and so the proprietors of the lease (Robert Weston who owned three-eighths, Richard Noyes two-eighths, and a Mr Cheetham of Dublin three-eighths) appointed John Holland, 'then a foreman shipwright in his Majesty's dock-yard at Plymouth, to survey and direct the repairs; which he very judiciously did, from time to time'.[90] Holland was promoted to Woolwich, but continued to give advice to work at the Eddystone, which was undertaken by 'a creditable shipwright at Plymouth dock'. However, 'some considerable repairs being necessary in the year 1734, Mr Holland, by leave of the Lords Commissioners of the Admiralty, was sent down to Plymouth to construct the same'. A better understanding of the structure and the defects to which it was prone began at about this date, thanks to Holland's careful work:

> In this year [i.e. 1734] Mr Holland made a very curious draught of the Lighthouse [see page 58], in which every one of the outside upright timbers was distinctly represented; so that every one of them could numerically be referred to; and the places and nature of the scarfing or joinings distinguished. ... the figure thus formed would become a kind of Evolute of the surface of the whole building. ... this draught distinctly represents the kant at the bottom; and hereby it was first known, that the real number of uprights was 71; and not 72 as had been before imagined.[91]

An attempt to prevent the effects of the marine worms by using copper on the outside of the uprights of the lighthouse, analogous to copper-bottoming of naval vessels at this time, proved to be unsuccessful. At the end of 1744, after the running repairs were completed, there was a tremendous storm from the east, which

> ... tore away no less than 30 pieces of the uprights all together; which in part made an opening in the store-room: this disaster however, by great exertion, was entirely repaired by the 14th December following, under the inspection and direction of Mr Josiah Jessop, then (and

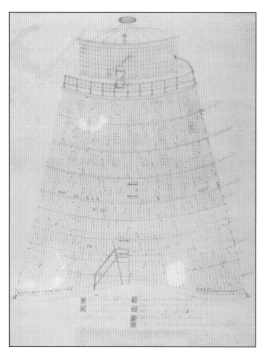

Ink-developed elevation of Rudyerd's lighthouse, unsigned, but probably by John Holland, 1734. Presented by the Royal Society of Edinburgh.

(NMS T.1859.414.B.2a)

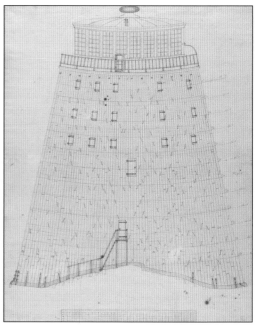

Ink-developed elevation of Rudyerd's lighthouse, unsigned but probably by Josiah Jessop, 1744. Presented by the Royal Society of Edinburgh.

(NMS T.1859.414.B.2b)

indeed until his death) no more than that species of foreman shipwright, called a Quarter-man in Plymouth dock. This person, whose modesty and ingenuity caused him to be deservedly respected by many, Mr Holland recommended to the proprietors to be their overseer, which they still rank among the eminent services he did them.[92]

In a footnote, Smeaton observed:

After the appointment of Mr Jessop, and in consequence of the number of uprights torn away in the storm of 1744, which enabled him to see further into the construction of the solid than had been known before; he made a still more accurate Evolute, and also a model of the Lighthouse, and it is principally from the measures of this Evolute, that I have compiled the present draught Plate No 6.[93]

58

'We now come to the last awful scene, containing the fatal catastrophe of this celebrated building,' wrote Smeaton, possibly with some enjoyment: this part of his *Narrative* may have been easier to write than others. Annual running repairs had been completed by 2 August 1755, and the boat had brought stores (as it had done regularly all summer and autumn) as recently as 1 December. Everything appeared normal. On the evening of 2 December, for some unaccountable reason, the lighthouse caught fire. Smeaton suggests that since the entire building was made of wood, the heat from the candles would have been 'considerable'. He writes that '24 candles [were] burning at once, five whereof weighed two pounds; and it was usual to go into the lantern to snuff them every half hour'.[94] He also suggests that many years of the candles burning below the wood ceiling supporting the lead cupola, had made this tinder-dry. At two o'clock in the morning a keeper routinely went to snuff the candles and discovered the light-room full of smoke. Unable at first to rouse his two colleagues, he found leather buckets to throw sea-water brought up from 70 feet below.

> Meanwhile, the flames were gathering strength every moment, and the poor man, though making use of every exertion, having the water to throw full four yards higher than his own head, to be of any service; we must by no means be surprised, that under all these difficulties, the fire, instead of being soon extinguished, would increase; and what put a sudden stop to further exertions, was the following most remarkable circumstance.
>
> As he was looking upward with the utmost attention, to see the direction and success of the water thrown; on which occasion, as physiognomists tell us, the mouth is a little open; a quantity of lead, dissolved by the heat of the flames, suddenly rushed like a torrent from the roof, and fell, not only upon the man's head, face and shoulders, but over his cloaths; and a part of it made its way through his shirt collar, and very much burnt his neck and shoulders: from this moment he had a violent internal sensation, and imagined that a quantity of this lead had passed his throat, and got into his body. Under this violence of pain and anxiety, as every attempt proved ineffectual, and the rage of the flames was increasing, it is not to be wondered that the terror and dismay of the three men increased in proportion; so that they all found themselves intimidated, and glad to make their retreat from that immediate scene of horror, into one of the rooms below. ...[95]

And so they retreated, room by room, as the fire advanced, until they were standing on the rock itself.

The blaze could be seen from the shore, and a fishing boat set out, arriving at the rock at ten o'clock the following morning, after the fire had been raging a full eight hours. The keepers were by now 'found sitting ... under the iron ladder, almost in a state of stupefaction; it being then low water'.[96]

Fortunately, the wind was not too strong, although blowing in an awkward direction. With difficulty, the keepers were taken off and taken to Plymouth for assistance. Yet, 'no sooner however were they set on shore, than one of them made off, and has never since been heard of'. His panic, reasoned Smeaton, had driven him to do the opposite of what he meant to do. 'But the man already described to have suffered so much by the melted lead, was sent to his own house at Stonehouse, a village near the place where they landed.'[97] As the news reached Plymouth, the collector of the duties, Mr Alderman Tolcher, and his son Joseph Tolcher, went out to inspect the damage. They were unable to land as the building was still burning with incredible ferocity, and it was clearly going to consume itself entirely. One of the naval vessels in Plymouth Sound sent out a sloop 'with a boat and an engine [fire pump] therein', but the sea was too rough to deploy this, and they were unable to land; the wind got up from the wrong quarter and fanned the blaze to total destruction.

Smeaton continues the grisly tale:

We will now return to the poor unfortunate man, who had received so peculiar an injury by the melted lead. His name was Henry Hall of Stonehouse near Plymouth, and though aged 94 years, being of a good constitution, he was remarkably active considering his time of life: he had invariably told the surgeon who had attended him (Mr Spry, now Dr Spry of Plymouth, who constantly administered the proper remedies to such burns and hurts as could be perceived) that if he could do any thing effectual to his recovery, he must relieve his stomach from the lead, which he was sure was within him: and this he not only told Dr Spry, but those about him, though in a very hoarse voice; and he also said the same thing to Mr Jessop, who went to see him several times during his illness, and who gave me this information. ... the twelfth day being seized with cold sweats and spasms, he soon afterwards expired.

Mr Jessop was desired by Dr Spry to attend the opening of the body; but being averse to sights of that kind, he excused himself from seeing the operation; as did also the daughter of the deceased, and another woman who was in the house. On opening the stomach, Dr Spry found therein, a solid piece of lead of a flat oval form, which weighed Seven Ounces and five drachms, and this he immediately shewed to the two women and afterwards to Mr Jessop. I have also seen the piece of lead since in the hands of Mr Tolcher, and it appeared to me, as if a part of the coat of the stomach firmly adhered to the convex side thereof.[98]

Piece of lead taken from the stomach of a keeper after the fire of 1755. Presented by the Royal Society of Edinburgh.

(NMS T.1859.414.B.7)

Smeaton goes on to discuss Spry's letter to the Royal Society about this entire episode, which was subsequently published in the *Philosophical Transactions*. Spry then went on to test the effects of molten lead on various species of animals and birds; and, unsurprisingly, was censured for cruelty to animals.[99] Another account, as reported by the elder Mr Tolcher to Robert Weston, writing on 4 December, was subsequently published by Robert Harcourt Weston, and runs along very much the same lines as that of John Smeaton.[100] A few days later, Josiah Jessop wrote to Weston:

The account they give of the fire happening is as follows: Roger Short having the first watch went up into the lanthorn at 8½ [8.30 pm] to snuff the candles, and then returned to Richard Hall in the cook room, Thomas Strout was in bed. Richard Hall at nine o'clock went up into the lanthorn, and to his great surprise found it full of smoke; but saw no fire until he had opened the lanthorn door and went outside the lanthorn, where he found the upright of the lanthorn next to the copper funnel, all on fire. He called to Short and Strout to bring him water and come to his assistance, for the lanthorn was on fire. They brought him water to the foot of the lanthorn stairs in a bucket, but would not go up into the lanthorn to his assistance: he made use of all the water in the lanthorn … about half a hogshead. The fire increased to that degree that it melted the lead on the top of the cupola, and burnt his face and hands so that he was forced to go down into the cook room. They had not continued long there, but they were forced to go from room to room, and at last to the coal-pit, where they continued until break of day, and ultimately they were obliged to go on the rock. A piece of upright fell down upon Richard Hall and bruised him very much, so that they thought him dead for some time; another fell down upon Thomas Strout, and put his shoulder bone out and bruised him very much. Roger Short received no damage. At 1½ PM a fishing boat took them off from the rock with a small rope, and fastening it round their waists they were drawn through the water one by one. They are all living; Richard Hall and Thomas Strout are in a miserable condition.[101]

Hall's first name is given here as 'Richard', by Smeaton as 'Henry', and in a further document as 'William': at 94 years of age he was presumably known widely merely as 'Mr Hall'. A contemporary label, removed from the lead in 1930, reads: '… [?] the Lead Dr Spry / found in the body of Wm Hall / Edystone Lt Keeper / Dec 1755 8oz 13 [?].'[102]

Thus the proprietors of the lease, after almost 50 years of successfully lighting the notorious rock, still had over 50 years of leasehold left to run, and so 'immediately applied themselves in the most strenuous manner towards the erecting of another Lighthouse in the place of that which had been, both for themselves and the public, so unfortunately destroyed'. Who could they now turn to as an appropriate designer of a rock lighthouse?

### The third Eddystone lighthouse: John Smeaton's stone tower

First, the proprietors needed to reorganise themselves. The three families who had shares had in the intervening 30 years passed these on into many divisions. Fortunately, Robert Weston had retained his shares (three-eighths), but also 'had the utmost trust and confidence reposed in him by the whole body of the proprietors'.[103] Weston contacted the President of the Royal Society, George Parker FRS, 2nd Earl of Macclesfield (*c*.1695-1764), who gave an unstinting recommendation for the young Yorkshireman, John Smeaton. At this point, Smeaton had only left his career as a scientific instrument-maker some three years previously, and even in the slowly-evolving profession of civil engineering, a rock lighthouse was a new departure. As the structural engineer Rowland Mainstone has observed, it was a daunting commission that could not be measured against other contemporary civil engineering projects such as bridges, roads, canals, or even fen drainage, docks or harbour works. The main difficulties were rooted in the location of the Rock and its extreme exposure to the wrath of wind or waves.[104]

Smeaton himself was at this point, early January 1756, in the north of England on other business:

> I had at that time, but barely heard that the Edystone Lighthouse was destroyed by Fire; and having seen a popular print of it, I understood that it was a building very critically placed out at sea, upon a single rock: but as I had no doubt that its foundation part at least, was built with Stone, though its upper works had the appearance of timber, I could not readily conceive how it could be totally destroyed. I concluded therefore, that the object was to repair or restore the Upper Works: and therefore I received the call without joy. …[105]

However, realising from a friend that 'it was a total demolition', Smeaton excused himself from his work in the north, and in modern parlance 'cleared his desk'. Arriving in London in late February,

Stipple engraving of John Smeaton, engraved by R. Woodman, published by Charles Knight, Pall Mall, London, *c*.1830. Presented by the Trustees of D. Alan Stevenson.

(NMS T.1998.229.22)

… the next day, agreeable to a message I had received for that purpose, waited on Robert Weston, Esq; till then totally unknown to me. The hours spent in this interview, were taken up in my attention to a relation of the nature of the structure of the former Lighthouses of Mr. Winstanley and Mr Rudyerd; and in examining several plans, models, and drawings in Mr Weston's possession that referred thereto. …

The models and drawings having been sent to me, I endeavoured by a full consideration of them, to investigate the particular plan of the respective architects; but could not trace out that of either of them to my perfect satisfaction. They afforded me just so much light as to enable me to discern the want of more information … after all I could glean from the drawings and models, as well as every insight into the nature of the work, that Mr Weston from several interviews could give me; I was naturally led to consider what could be done by an erection entirely of Stone. ...[106]

Smeaton's thoughts about a possible new structure first ran along the lines of how Rudyerd's lighthouse had needed more weight, as well as strength, and that a stone building would be more expensive but need fewer repairs. The shape seemed generally good, but required a larger base 'which from the models before me appeared to be practicable'.[107]

His ideas turned to 'the natural figure of the waist or bole of a large spreading Oak, [which] presented itself to my imagination. ... Connected with its roots, which lie below the ground, it rises from the surface thereof with a large swelling base, which at the height of one diameter is generally reduced by an elegant curve, concave to the eye, to a diameter less by at least one-third, and sometimes to half of its original base.' Being a hands-on mechanic,

> I immediately rough-turned a piece of wood, with a small degree of tapering above; and leaving matter enough below, I fitted it to the oblique surface of a block of wood, somewhat resembling the sloping surface of the Edystone Rock; and soon found, that by reconciling Curves, I could adapt every part of the base upon the rock to the regularly turned tapering body, and so as to make a figure not ungraceful; and at the same time carrying the idea of great firmness and solidity.[108]

This model does not appear to survive, whereas the next problem – considering 'how the blocks of stone could be bonded to the rock, and to one another' – led him to recognise that any mortar would be washed away by the sea, and that 'Mr Winstanley had found the fixing 12 great irons, and Mr Rudyerd 35, attended with such a consumption of time' that a different solution would have to be sought.[109] He considered cutting the steps made by Rudyerd into dovetails, ensuring that 'the foundation stones of every course were engrafted into, or rather rooted in the rock; which would not only keep all the stones on one course together; but prevent the courses themselves (as one stone) from moving or sliding upon each other'. He also saw that cement would have to be used to bind the structure together and to the rock.[110]

Arriving in Plymouth in late March 1756, Smeaton met up with Josiah Jessop, 'who besides being an approved workman in his branch as a shipwright, I found a competent draughtsman and an excellent modeller, in which last he was accurate to a great degree'.[111] They made several trips out to survey the rock, and toured the vicinity looking for a work base, choosing Mill Bay, about a mile west of Plymouth. He then inspected possible quarries, finding a source for moorstone – 'which in reality is the true Granite' – about 15 miles upriver from Plymouth. Smeaton was shown Portland stone, used to line the King's Docks, and he was alarmed to see that it had been drilled with holes made by some kind of marine worm, and decided 'therefore that Portland stone ought not to be used for the outside of the Edystone Lighthouse, especially of the lower works: though it might be used with great advantage for the works within, on account of the greater ease with which it might be wrought'.[112] He thus concluded that it could be used for the interior, as cutting it would save time, and therefore money.

Smeaton returned to London via Portland, visiting the quarry there, passing Weymouth, where 'I did not fail to visit the Lighthouses, built nearly on the highest part of the island; but as they are built upon the dry Land, and burnt coals, I found they contained nothing singular, or material to my present purpose'.[113] In London he persuaded the proprietors of the lease to rebuild the Eddystone lighthouse in stone, by showing them his plans and models:

> My models and preparatory matters were now so far brought forward, that Tuesday the 13th of July [1756] was duly appointed by the Proprietors for receiving my explanation of what I had to lay before them. I accordingly attended, and submitted to their inspection a complete model of the house-rock, in the state in which I had found it; and representing all the iron branches broken and whole, of which model, Plate No 7 contains a reduced plan and elevation: and this was accompanied with another model of the same rock, cut to the intended shape for receiving the building; and therewith connected, a model of the building itself; shewing distinctly how the work was to be adapted to each separate step in the ascent of the rock, as high as I proposed to continue it; and particularly exhibiting the construction of the first entire course, after rising to the level of the upper surface of the rock; to which a solid being fitted, this model shewed the external form of the whole building, including the lantern; and by a complete section of this on paper, to the same scale, the rooms and conveniences on the inside were fully expressed … .[114]

Having convinced the proprietors, '… they were pleased … to declare unanimously, their entire approbation of, and satisfaction in the whole of my proposition; and therefore desired me to shew my models and draughts, and explain my scheme to the lords commissioners of the Admiralty, and to the corporation of the Trinity House … .[115]

The Admiralty replied favourably after seeing and hearing Smeaton; but nothing was heard from Trinity House. Smeaton decided, as time was pressing, to return to Plymouth. In fact, their verbal message requesting him to present his case was delayed, and the proprietors had felt that he should return.

The models that were prepared and exhibited as above related still remain in my hands ... Plate No 7 is, as already mentioned, taken therefrom; for being professedly an exact representation of the rock, in the condition I first found it; this admits of no change: but the other model and section, containing the design for the Lighthouse (which as I have before hinted, was subject to some change in entering on the detail of the work at large) no longer remains an exact model of what was executed: nor at the completion thereof, had I any perfect design of it in that finished state; but having taken memorandums of the alterations, I have been able to make out a due representation of the work as it now stands: and as the original models, &c. served very well for many years to explain the nature of the work that had been done; the difference not being very considerable, in like manner the present representations of the work as really executed, will equally explain, what was formerly exhibited; first to the Proprietors themselves, then to the lords of the Admiralty, and afterwards to the honourable board of Trinity House; who to my great satisfaction entirely approved thereof.[116]

Smeaton's *Narrative*, closely emulated by Robert Stevenson's 1824 *Account*, gives a day-by-day detailed chronicle of the construction, beginning with 'I arrived at Plymouth on Friday the 23rd of July 1756 ...'.[117] There is no doubt that Stevenson learned much from his eminent predecessor who, after gleaning as much as possible from his own forerunners at the Eddystone Rock, was attempting something radically new and never tried before.[118] Smeaton had tried to obtain a temporary floating-light from Trinity House, but initially this proved impossible, although one was later deployed; but more positively, workmen (masons and Cornish tin miners) were hired. Construction then began, and while one party was out at the site levelling the 'steps', others were employed at the Mill Bay workyard in dressing stones. By the end of October the weather was turning nasty, and Smeaton wrote, 'I now considered, that nothing remained to be done of this season's work, that could possibly hinder the beginning to set the foundation courses, at the commencement of the next season; as the top of the rock could be brought to a regular floor, and the dovetails in the upper steps corrected, in the intervals that would necessarily happen, while the lower courses were setting'.[119] And so he turned his attention to 'the completion of the workyard, with its machinery, and conveniences, as also the channel up to the Jetty Head, so as to be ready to receive the Portland vessels'. Various shears and tackle were tested, 'and now the workyard was ready for receiving the stone'.[120]

Smeaton pioneered the use of 'hydraulic lime', a form of lime-based natural concrete that will set under water, and his work on the chemical constituents of the perfect cement took up much of his account.[121] He

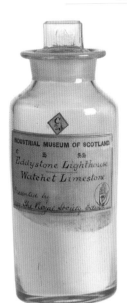

developed a technique of securing the granite blocks together using
dovetail joints on each course, and marble dowels between each course.
Each course was drawn out, the stones were scaled up, and then placed on
a platform in the workyard to ensure that they fitted snugly together
before taking them out to the Rock:

> On Saturday the 11th of June [1757] the first course of stone was put
> on board the Edystone boat, ... with all the necessary stores, tools, and
> utensils. ... We landed at eight on Sunday morning the 12th of June,
> and before noon had got the first stone into its place, being that
> upon which the date of the year 1757 is inscribed in deep charac-
> ters; and the tide coming upon us, we secured it with chains to
> the old stancheons [sic], and then quitted the rock till the evening
> tide, when it was fitted, bedded in mortar, trenailed down, and
> completely fixed; and all the outward joints covered over with
> Plaster of Paris, to prevent the imminent wash of the sea upon the
> mortar. This stone, according to its dimensions, weighed 2¼ tons.
> – The weather serving at intervals, it was at the evening of Monday
> the 13th that the first course, consisting of four stones, was fini-
> shed; and which, as they all presented some part of their faces to
> the sea, were all of Moorstone.[122]

By September, the structure – with its courses of dovetailed
stones, wooden trenails and square marble joggles, each offset
against the next – had risen to the seventh course:

> September the 5th the seventh circle was finished and the eighth
> begun; ... being the first circular course: I therefore went ... on
> board the Edystone boat, which was loaded with the center [sic],
> and its surrounding stones, of Course VIII. ... Course VII was
> completely closed, pointed and grouted; and that the top of the
> work, where it was needed, had been levelled, and every irregu-
> larity in the face of the work rectified.[123]

A model of this course, and that above it, was constructed
by Jessop to Smeaton's instruction for Weston in March 1757:
'... Tomorrow morning will be forwarded to you a box, containing Mr Jessop's model of the platform, and course seven
thereon, with so much of course eight as is necessary to show
the relation between the two courses.'[124]

Many other such models of details of courses and construction features were made either by or for Smeaton; in particular
there is a model in painted wood of his Eddystone Lighthouse in
ten parts, made by Josiah Jessop after drawings by Smeaton. As
already noted, Smeaton used model-making to solve problems as

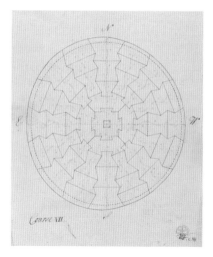

he encountered them. The lowest part of the model shows the exposed portion of the central reef at low spring tide with the sloping surface of the granite cut into steps dovetailed to take the lower courses of masonry; the next two parts show the six incomplete courses of stone at the base of the tower and the seven complete courses up to the main entrance level, all coloured to distinguish the outer moorstone granite casing from the inner Portland limestone and the interconnecting marble joggles. Five sections show successively the internal staircase, lower store-room, upper store-room, kitchen, and bedroom, this last depicted with a chain set in the wall head to take the spreading load of the floor; and finally the balcony, glazed iron lantern and cupola. (The cupola is in wood, as are the glazing bars.) It is incised on the external wood to indicate stonework courses and joints, and painted dark grey to show the moorstone granite courses. The inner Portland limestone is painted a paler grey, with cubes that represent marble joggles painted black.[125]

After four years intensive work, and some dramatic adventures – to say nothing of the

appalling weather, but happily no mortalities – the work was completed, with the final stone being set over the door of the lantern on the east side on 24 August 1759. Then some time was spent fitting up the lantern and putting up a lightning conductor.[126] The lighting was delayed by bad weather, and the 24-candle chandelier was first lit on 16 October 1759. While in use, Smeaton's lighthouse was 72 feet high, and had a diameter at the base of 26 feet, and at the top of 17 feet. It had cost £16,000, while a wooden one would have come in at about £12,000. Savings in maintenance, however, were more than enough for the leaseholders.

Trinity House then behaved badly. Indeed, it had already been behaving badly over the floating-light, which had broken away from her moorings eight times and was off her station for 50 weeks out of the three and half years she was in service – by taking the leaseholders to court. The case was eventually proved for the leaseholders, who were awarded the dues owed to them, as well as the costs of the case.[127]

The chandelier was replaced by an array of 24 Argand lamps and reflectors in 1811; and these in turn were superseded in 1845 by a Fresnel lens system with a four-wick lamp, visible for over 13 miles.[128] Smeaton's stone tower remained in use until 1877, when it was discovered that the rock upon which it stood was becoming eroded: each time a large wave hit the lighthouse, it shook from side to side. After considerable discussion it was decided to build on another part of the reef. The upper part of Smeaton's tower was dismantled and rebuilt as a memorial to Smeaton on a new base on Plymouth Hoe in 1882, replacing the triangular obelisk that had been built there by Trinity House as a navigation aid in the early 19th century. It was opened to the public by the Mayor of Plymouth on 24 September 1884.[129]

The foundations and stub of the old tower still remain on the Eddystone Rocks, close to the current lighthouse; the foundations proved too strong to be dismantled, so the Victorians left them where they stood. It is ironic that although the previous two lighthouses were destroyed by the elements, Smeaton's stone lighthouse proved to be stronger than the rock upon which it was built and could not be intentionally dismantled.

The new Eddystone, designed and built by Sir James Douglass, was begun in 1878 and completed in 1882; it cost £80,000. At 168 feet high, it differs from Smeaton's in that it stands on a vertical cylindrical base. The exterior was, again, cased in granite, some from a local Cornish quarry at De Lank on Bodmin; other material came from Dalbeattie, Kirkcudbrightshire. The oil-powered lamp of Douglass's tower was

replaced first by a paraffin burner, then by electric illumination in 1956; and, more drastically, a helipad was built on the top of the strengthened lantern in 1980. This was the first part in a modernisation programme, leading to automation, on 18 May 1982, exactly one hundred years after the light was first lit at the top of the replacement tower.[130]

The achievement of John Smeaton, which was to be so influential on the young Robert Stevenson, should not be underrated. The effect on the national consciousness was generally fairly widespread, and could be seen, for instance, by a representation of the Eddystone lighthouse on the back of the pre-decimal penny from 1859. Victorian historian Samuel Smiles was to write about it in his own inimitable way:

> Many a heart has leapt with gladness at the cry of 'The Eddystone in sight!' sung out from the maintop. Homeward-bound ships, from far-off ports, no longer avoid the dreaded rock, but eagerly run for its light as the harbinger of safety. It might even seem as if Providence had placed the reef so far out at sea as the foundation for a beacon such as this, leaving it to man's skill and labour to finish His work. On entering the English Channel from the west and the south, the cautious navigator feels his way by early soundings on the great bank which extends from the Channel into the Atlantic, and these are repeated at fixed intervals until land is in sight. Every fathom nearer shore increases a ship's risks, especially in nights when, to use the seaman's phrase, it is 'as dark as a pocket'. The men are on the look-out, peering anxiously into the dark, straining the eye to catch the glimmer of a light, and when it is known that 'The Eddystone is in sight!' a thrill runs through the ship, which can only be appreciated by those who have felt or witnessed it after long months of weary voyaging. Its gleam across the waters has thus been a source of joy and given a sense of deep relief to thousands; for the beaming of a clear light from one known and fixed spot is infallible in its truthfulness, and a safer guide for the seaman than the bearings of many hazy and ill-defined headlands.[131]

### Notes to Chapter 2

1   How the successive structures on the Eddystone Rock are numbered seems to depend on how you decide to do it. I have chosen to count both Winstanley's structures as the first (although strictly speaking, his altered tower was almost a total rebuild); Rudyerd's as the second; Smeaton's the third and Douglass's as the fourth, principally because this is what most of the historical literature does.

2   This discussion is based on the work by Rowatt (1924-

25); Waterston (1997), 68-69, 169-70; and Millon (1999), 554-55.

3   Smeaton (1793), 9.

4   Ibid., 10. A fathom is six feet.

5   Ibid., 12.

6   Ibid.

7   Ibid., v.

8   Majdalany (1959), 14. The account of Oppenheim (1968) uses national archives based in London, and

as it was written at the start of the twentieth century, it uses material subsequently caught up in the Blitz. However, he did not use Trinity House manuscripts.

9 Smeaton (1793), and 13 note. Unfortunately, this Addenda is not included. The Trinity House manuscripts relating to this period do not survive.

10 Majdalany (1959), 11-22; Coase (1974); Taylor (2001).

11 Stevenson (1959), 21-24; 97-109; 133-51.

12 However, the updated online version of Waterhouse and Chrimes (2004) takes into account much recent research; see also Barnes (2003).

13 These include Wimbledon House, Surrey, 1678; Pycote House, Oxfordshire, 1680 and Tythorp, Buckinghamshire, 1680. See also Winstanley (1686), Barnes (2003), 2 and 6, and Everett (2006).

14 Drury (1980), 22.

15 Drury and Gow (1984), esp. pp. 40-57.

16 Waterhouse and Chrimes (2004).

17 Griffiths (1998), 245-50; Wayland (1967).

18 Oppenheim (1968), 71.

19 Ibid., 74-96.

20 Ibid., 97.

21 Smeaton (1791), 13; Smeaton (1793), 13. See also Altick (1978), 78-79.

22 Bray (1879), III, 131-32.

23 Steele (1709), (1711); *Evening Post* (1714), illustrated in Barnes (2003), 15, and Barnes (2008b), 9; see also Lewer (1918).

24 Barnes (2008b).

25 Fiennes (1947), 64.

26 Advertisement in the *Post Boy*, 18 December 1712, quoted in Lewer (1918), 166 and Majdalany (1959), 67-68.

27 Coase (1974), 365.

28 Winstanley (1699); Smeaton (1791), 14-16; Smeaton (1793), 14-16.

29 Oppenheim (1968), 97; Semmens (1998), 36.

30 Merriman (1945); MacDougall (2004).

31 Merriman (1945); Majdalany (1959), 45-46.

32 Luttrell (1857), 245, 247 and 251, and quoted by Majdalany (1959).

33 Quoted in Semmens (1998), 40.

34 Majdalany (1959), 47; Semmens (1998), 41.

35 Winstanley (1699); Smeaton (1793), 14-15.

36 Barnes (2005c); original drawing in the Bodleian Library, Gough Maps 5 (but not by Baston, whose drawings are lost).

37 *Calendar of Treasury Papers*, vol. 77 (1889), 6, entry for 7 January 1702, quoted by Harrison-Wallace (2004).

38 Smeaton (1791), Plate No. 4; Smeaton (1793), Plate No. 4.

39 Acquired by Plymouth Museum, inv. no. 1942.47, its history is discussed by Morgan (1878) and O'Riordan (1982). See: http://www.plymouth.gov.uk/museumobjectmonth2?objid=139882

40 Hardwick (1977), 7, quoted by O'Riordan (1982). A 'piece' was equal to a pound at this time.

41 Fiennes (1947), 252-54.

42 *London Gazette*, 17 December 1698.

43 Winstanley (1699); NMS T.1859.414.A, where the engraving was presented to the Industrial Museum of Scotland (a forerunner of National Museums Scotland) by the Royal Society of Edinburgh in 1859; presented to them by Susan, Countess of Morton in 1829; acquired by George Douglas, the 16th Earl of Morton (1761-1827) from Robert Harcourt Weston, son of Robert Weston, one of the original lessees of the Eddystone Lighthouse, who obtained it from John Smeaton. Smeaton (1791), 15; Smeaton (1793), 15.

44 Plymouth Museum, inv. no. ZP890, and reproduced by the Western Litho Company of Plymouth, 1982, with an example held at NMS T.1998.229.21; contemporary examples also held at the British Museum (inv. no. P&D.1862,0614.1451); Science Museum, London (NMSI 1982-0270); National Maritime Museum, Greenwich (PAH9777 and PAI7109).

45 Winstanley (1699); Smeaton (1791), 15-16; Smeaton (1793), 15-16.

46 Hamblyn, 'Introduction' to Defoe (2005), x.

47 Lamb and Frydendahl (1991), 62, quoted by Hamblyn, 'Introduction' to Defoe (2005), xi.

48 Defoe (2005), 148-49, quoted by Smeaton (1793), 17.

49 Defoe (1971), 223-24.

50 Stevenson (1959), 116.

51 See Harrison-Wallace (2004) for a discussion of the paintings by Peter Monamy and a sketch attributed to van der Velde the Younger. The paintings were almost certainly produced after the destruction of the lighthouse and are thus not done from life.

52 Trinity House Manuscripts: Court Minutes, 27 September 1705, p. 16.

53 Stevenson (1959), 116-17. Barnes (2008b) explains that the lease on the Piccadilly property expired in 1720.

54 Smeaton (1793), 17, quoting Defoe (2005).

55 Ibid., 19.

56 Palmer (2005), 29-30.

57 Much of the background to the Verneys and their association with the Eddystone is discussed in Verney (1930). The Lovett family is discussed by Lovett (1941).

58 Coase (1974), 366.

59 Trinity House Manuscripts: Court Minutes, 7 November 1705, p. 19.

60 Ibid., 21 November 1705, pp. 20-21.

61 4 and 5 Anne Cap 20: An Act for the better Enabling the Master, Wardens and Assistants of Trinity-House, to Rebuild the Light-house on the Edystone Rock.

62 Smeaton (1793), 19, note.

63 Palmer (2005), 30, 134-35.

64   Verney mss. Letter from Lovett to Sir John Verney, 13 April 1703: Verney (1930), I, 129-30.
65   Smeaton (1793), 19.
66   Smeaton (1793), 19; the example in National Museums Scotland came from the collection of the late D. Alan Stevenson.
67   Verney mss. Letter from Lovett to Lord Fermanagh, 7 September 1707; Verney (1930), I, 201.
68   Ibid., 25 March 1708: Verney (1930), I, 201.
69   Ibid., 1 May 1708: Verney (1930), I, 201-202.
70   Ibid., 22 June 1708: Verney (1930), I, 202.
71   Ibid., 1 July 1708: Verney (1930), I, 203.
72   Ibid., 29 July 1708: Verney (1930), I, 204.
73   Ibid., 4 August 1708: Verney (1930), I, 205.
74   Coombs (2004). The engraving by Lens (NMS T.1998.229.2) and the original drawing by Rudyerd from which it differs (T.1859.414.B.1) are both illustrated and described by Millon (1999), 336, 554-55.
75   Besides the example NMS T.1998.229.2, which came from D. Alan Stevenson, and appears to be based on the drawing owned by Smeaton T.1859.414.B.1, other examples in public collections include NMSI 1982-0271, and British Museum P&D 1862-6-14-1452 and 1862-6-14-1454, all of which, including a drawing after these by an unknown artist (P&D 1862.0614.1282), lack the 'prospect' and the three supporting putti. Also at the National Maritime Museum, PAH 9778.
76   Quoted in Palmer (2005), 37.
77   Smeaton (1793), 21.
78   Ibid., 22.
79   Ibid.
80   Rowatt (1924-25), 18.
81   Smeaton (1793), 23.
82   Ibid., 23 note.
83   Ibid., 25.
84   Ibid.
85   Ibid., 40.
86   Verney mss., quoted by Verney (1930), I, 362.
87   Smeaton (1793), 20; Nicholson (1995), 28, reckons he died in 1713; Palmer (2005), 135, believes he died 20 November 1718, and his widow in May 1719.
88   http://www.nmm.ac.uk/collections/explore/object.cfm?ID=BHC1796
89   NMS T.1998.229.6, from the collection of D. Alan Stevenson; A copy of this print, described as: 'Eddystone Lighthouse with shipping beyond', dated 1 June 1738, survives in the National Maritime Museum (PAF 4979). The Museum also owns several other prints in the series by Lempriere and Toms from 1738. These are similarly characterised by shipping scenes surrounded by frames in the ornamental style of the period.
90   Smeaton (1793), 29.
91   Ibid., 29 note; the drawing is discussed by Rowatt (1924-25), 18; illustrated by Stevenson (1959), 121; and Palmer (1998), 58, and Palmer (2005), 52.
92   Smeaton (1793), 30.
93   Ibid., 30 and note; discussed by Rowatt (1924-25), 18; illustrated by Waterston (1997), 68.
94   Ibid., 31 and note.
95   Ibid., 32.
96   Ibid., 33.
97   Ibid., 33.
98   Ibid., 34-35.
99   Ibid., 35; see Spry (1756). Also recounted in the London Magazine or Gentleman's Monthly Intelligencer, 26 (1757), 446-48. For Spry, see Munck (1878), 281-83.
100  Weston (1811), 40.
101  Ibid., 46-47.
102  Hague and Christie (1975), 250-52, Appendix D, 'Light-Keepers', transcript of a letter, now destroyed, about the incident, from Frederick Rogers, Superintendent of Plymouth Dockyard, 12 December 1775: in this, Hall is identified as 'Wm Hall'; (label NMS T.1930.74).
103  Smeaton (1793), 37.
104  Mainstone (1981), 83.
105  Smeaton (1793), 38.
106  Ibid., 39-40.
107  Ibid., 41.
108  Ibid., 42.
109  Ibid., 42-43.
110  Ibid., 43-44. A wooden model showing how the lowest layers of the lighthouse fit into the rock is in Leeds Museum; http://secretlivesofobjects.blogspot.com/2010/04/john-smeatons-model-for-foundation-of.html
111  Ibid., 45.
112  Ibid., 52.
113  Ibid., 63.
114  Ibid., 71-72.
115  Ibid., 72.
116  Ibid., 73.
117  Ibid., 74.
118  Stevenson tried to visit the lighthouse in 1801, but was thwarted by foul weather; managed to land in 1813 and again in 1818: Stevenson (1946), 24-25; 31-38 and 51-55.
119  Smeaton (1793), 86.
120  Ibid., 87.
121  Ibid., 97, 99, 102-23.
122  Ibid., 125.
123  Ibid., 138.
124  Weston (1811), 140; Rowatt (1924-25), 19; Millon (1999), 554.
125  Rowatt (1924-25), 19; Millon (1999), 339, 554.
126  Smeaton (1793), 168-69.
127  Oppenheim (1968), 101-102.
128  Nicholson (1995), 37.
129  Kitton (1892); Barnes (2005a).
130  Nicholson (1995), 44-47.
131  Smiles (1862), 45-46.

Woodcut of the Smeaton and Douglass Eddystone
lighthouses, standing side by side, unsigned, c.1882.
Presented by the Trustees of D. Alan Stevenson.

(NMS T.1998.229.19)

C. Stralhat

Rofose

Lawernes

C. Terhat

Dornok

I. S. Martin

Vuffe

Norne

I. Hiplant

C de Hobrunt

Finderne

Hoeck van Elgin

Culane

Dunketh

Denet

Barradul

Spea fluin.

Mandenpaupes

Catenelfe

Nois head

Olde wijck

Banfe

Dungifke

Pitslantschare

Slaves

Pichlantsc.

Douem

Pefage

Speylaont.

Spi.

Boekenelfe

Boekenelse

# CHAPTER 3

# Scottish Lights before the Bell Rock

SCOTLAND IS A maritime country, and her people have always been aware of their proximity to the sea. This has brought many blessings: fishing and shipbuilding have been, until recently, important staple industries, but, conversely, the sea also brings its own particular hazards. It is perhaps a truism to state that Scottish geography has influenced her history more than most countries. The comparative fertility of her eastern shores meant that these were the first to be settled, while the inhospitable rugged mountains to the west, where the wild Atlantic onshore winds scoured less friendly regions, were more sparsely populated. In medieval times, trade in Scotland was concentrated on her eastern seaboard. Here, the royal burghs were located and traded between themselves, up and down the coast. It was also from here that her exports were sent to Europe, and, in reciprocation, from the Continent that various luxuries and other goods were sent by sea to her royal burghs. Scotland faced towards Europe, but even the North Sea did not lack its own hidden dangers. This chapter will take a few steps back from chapters 1 and 2, and provide an overview of how developments in cartography, navigation instrumentation and practical sea-marking combined to help the mariner find his way through Scottish waters to a safe haven, through the storm and darkness from early times until the lighting of the first of the Northern Lighthouse Board's new lights, at Kinnaird Head, in 1787. This will be followed by a brief résumé of the new lights before the building of the Bell Rock lighthouse, now the oldest surviving rock lighthouse in the world.

In an apposite opening paragraph entitled 'A Coast in Darkness', R. W. Munro sketched the basic problems facing mariners in Scottish waters – those of darkness and danger:

> Northabout round Scotland from Berwick to the Solway, the track of a ship circling the Scottish mainland and all but the remotest isles would run to nearly a thousand miles, and the actual coastline would extend

OPPOSITE PAGE

Detail of 'De kuften van Schotlandt van Donde tot de Eylaneti Orcanesse' ['The east coast of Scotland from Dundee to the Orkney Isles'], 17th century. With sailing instructions in Dutch and headland profiles on the reverse.

(NMS T.2003.309.153)

to more than four times that length. Before they were lighted, the seas to be navigated and the coasts to be shunned were among the most dangerous in Europe, and they can still bring anxiety and disaster to those whose business takes them there.[1]

Severe storms have pounded Scottish shores since antiquity, and though many tempests have gone unrecorded, others have been marked by historic wrecks: *El Gran Grifón* on Fair Isle, 27 September 1588; the *Swan* in the Sound of Mull, 22 September 1653; the *Dartmouth*, again in the Sound of Mull, 9 September 1690; the *Kennemerland* in December 1664 on Shetland; and the *Adelaar*, 25 March 1728, on Barra, are among the best known because of investigations by marine archaeologists.[2] Some storms have been memorialised in poetry: for example, the eighteenth-century 'Ballad of Sir Patrick Spens'. Other wrecks are

noted in local administrative records. The burgh records of Aberdeen, for example, contain a brief and early reference to an unidentified vessel that ran aground and broke up close to the town in the summer of 1444.[3] This was not an isolated incident, as demonstrated by a guidebook of 1837, discussing the entrance to Aberdeen Harbour:

We were speedily past the Breakwater and the Bruntscalies, and opposite to the small bay called the Greyhope, which, about four-and-twenty years ago, was the scene of one of the most calamitous shipwrecks that ever happened in the neighbourhood of Aberdeen. On the first of April, 1813, the *Oscar*, Greenlandman, was driven among the rocks by a most tempestuous gale of wind from the north-east, and dashed to pieces, when upwards of forty seamen lost their lives. No calamity of equal magnitude had happened

William Easton, 'Wreck of the *Oceanic* at St Monance, Fife', 1912.

in this quarter from the year 1637, when four vessels were driven from the harbour by a great flood in the river; and the wind being from the south-east, they were cast on shore upon the sands and wrecked.[4]

Although those living by the sea could on occasion assist unfortunate seafarers that were wrecked upon their doorstep, there was no form of national lifeboat service until the early nineteenth century.[5] Those who were washed up on Scottish shores were very much at the mercy of the efforts of the local population. The wreck of the English ship *Edward Bonaventure*, west of Fraserburgh in November 1556, can stand as an all-too-typical example for the Medieval and early modern period. She had embarked from Russia for London with a cargo of furs and other luxury goods valued at £20,000 sterling (a huge sum), in the company of three other English vessels in July, but had become separated from the others in bad weather in the North Sea. On board were the Russian ambassador and his entourage, and the ship was under the command of Richard Chancellor, one of the great English Tudor navigators. Of the hundred souls aboard, most were drowned, including Chancellor, although the Russian ambassador survived. Furthermore, the cargo washed ashore was 'by the rude and ravenous people of the Country thereunto adjoining, rifled, spoyled and carried away ...'.[6]

In the early Medieval period, Scotland's external trade had been largely restricted to coastal traffic, which had looked south to English ports. As the historian Alexander Stevenson stressed, it was only in the late thirteenth century that improved merchant ship design made direct trade across the North Sea to the Low Countries and Germany more reliable.[7] It has been argued that the disruption to trade caused by the wars with England was severe, and that Scotland's overseas trade never fully recovered. This was indeed a dangerous time for mariners, when ships' cargoes were at risk of being seized, and profits were to be made by Continental merchants running English goods to Scottish ports.[8]

## Ships and shipping

How did Scots traders get their goods to market at this early period? Internal communications – roads and tracks, such as there were – were often impassable in bad weather. The sea and the estuaries remained the main highways for freight and transport until well into the seventeenth century. There were essentially two main groups of mariners using the coastal thoroughfares along the Scottish East Coast: inshore traffic, made up of indigenous people who knew the coastlines and local dangers; and those, who from the late thirteenth century, were prepared to cross the North Sea, usually, but not exclusively, for economic reasons. These latter led to local people who knew their native shores well becoming pilots for the 'foreigners', helping to guide vessels into port past hidden dangers.

There were three principal types of vessel to be found in the early Medieval northern seas, all clinker-built (with overlapping longitudinal planks): the 'keel', 'hulk' and the 'cog'.[9] As time went on, shipbuilding technology was influenced by contact with other seafaring peoples from further south and from the Mediterranean. Although there was clearly great diversity to be found in the variety of European vessels in the later Middle Ages, it is hard to match the individual names to a particular design.[10] The technological breakthrough came with the evolution of the three-masted, full-rigged ship, capable of long, open-ended journeys of exploration, indeed global circumnavigation, as well as instilling confidence into its crew that they would be able to venture into unknown seas and return safely home.[11] Essentially, by combining the characteristics from the northern cog adapted by shipbuilders of the Mediterranean, together with elements of both the keel and the hulk, a new and improved vessel was developed.[12] The hull was made larger, there was an internal skeleton, and steering was controlled by a stern-post rudder, which evolved into the whipstaff (and the man steering the vessel was able to watch carefully how the sails were set, and accordingly make adjustments). But it was the rigging, incorporating features from square-rigged and lateen-rigged models, which enabled better propulsion and much tighter control of the ship's course.[13]

The peoples who were involved in transforming the ship from a small inshore carrier of goods into an efficient instrument, displaying military power and economic muscle, were those creating their own nation-states at approximately the same time. The Portuguese, Spanish, English and other northern Europeans were jostling for a position on a much larger stage than had previously been available. The Scots had ambitions in this area, too, especially under their late Medieval King who had most pretensions to making his mark in Europe – James IV.

Norman Macdougall has characterised James IV's interest in his Navy as a 'royal obsession'.[14] The main centres for shipbuilding were Leith, Edinburgh's port, on Scotland's east coast; and Dumbarton on the west coast. Dissatisfied with existing facilities, the King developed the 'new haven', west of Leith in 1504, and another dockyard eight miles east of Stirling, at Pool of Airth, constructed by 1506.[15] Besides the royal ships paid for out of royal revenues, there were also the ships hired from shipmasters such as Sir Andrew Wood of Largo, and Andrew and John Barton of Leith. Elsewhere, Macdougall writes:

Contemporary records leave us in no doubt that James IV considered himself first and foremost a warrior. His expenditure on warfare ... is remarkable by any standards, and quite astonishing for the ruler of a small and remote European kingdom. Over the entire period of the reign, the cost of buying, building, outfitting and maintaining a Scottish navy, and paying the crews to man it, cannot have come to less than £100,000 Scots – and it may have totalled substantially more. The showpiece of the fleet, the 'great' *Michael*, an enormous capital ship with a crew of 300, costing over £30,000 and launched in 1511, was immediately copied by the young Henry VIII of England ... who built the *Henri Grace à Dieu* to more or less the same specifications in 1512.[16]

Two years later James lay dead after the battle of Flodden, and shortly afterwards the *Great Michael* was sold to Louis XII of France to be absorbed into the French Navy as *La Grande Nef d'Ecosse*.[17] With her went Scotland's pretensions as a great European naval power, but not her involvement in maritime affairs.

During the minority of James's son and successor, James V, there was little maritime activity from the administration, which had other concerns. However, by 1536 the King was able to set sail for France to bring back a wife (after two decades of diplomacy concerning most of Europe's eligible princesses), in a fleet of seven ships carrying 500 men for protection. (His first attempt to reach France by sailing around the north of Scotland was abandoned when storms scattered the Scottish fleet.) The ill-health of James's bride, Madeleine of France, delayed the marriage, but the young couple returned to Scotland with a French escort in May 1537. Madeleine died on 7 July.[18]

Yet by 1540 James was ready to take to the sea again to make an important expedition around his kingdom in a convoy of 16 ships. One of the reasons for maintaining some sort of Navy was the requirement by the Scottish Kings to control the semi-independent clan chieftains of the Western Isles. James IV had made a few such expeditions, starting from ports in the Clyde, and these must indicate local navigational knowledge, especially in narrow and dangerous waters. It was another period

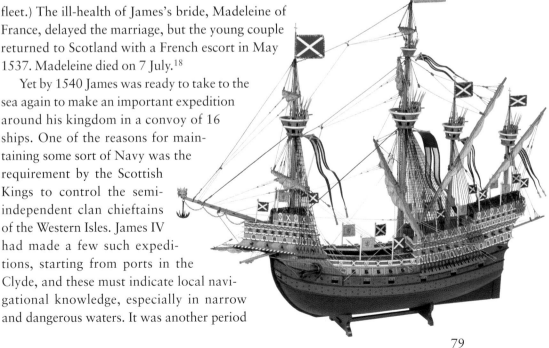

Early 20th-century model of the *Great Michael*. (NMS T.1926.20)

79

D. O. Hill and Robert Adamson, 'Newhaven fishing boat with crew', early photograph, 1843-48.

(© Edinburgh City Libraries. Licensor www.scran.ac.uk)

of unrest in the west that was the excuse for James V's 1540 voyage.[19]

A very full account of the circumstances of this voyage has been given by historian A. B. Taylor in his work discussing the six surviving manuscripts which outline the sea route.[20] This is the earliest surviving set of maritime instructions describing coastal features for Scottish waters, known as a 'rutter' (French: *routier*), and attributed to one Alexander Lindsay.[21] Indeed, scholarship has suggested that Lindsay put the rutter together from a series of earlier compilations and instructions – the fact that there are several alternative courses and sailing instructions helps to support this – but no other original rutters survive.[22] A French translation of this, published in 1583 by Nicolas de Nicolay, mentioned a chart in association with the rutter directions. This chart is known to have been used by the French fleet in the siege of St Andrews Castle in 1547, although it seems to have been lost subsequently.[23] However, a version of the chart was also published by Nicolay, and it is significant that this sea chart, originating with Lindsay, represents the outline of Scotland more accurately than many later maps produced during the next three hundred years.

Apart from the large ships of the Navy – which were extremely few and unusual – there were also the smaller craft used for Scottish inshore traffic, for local trading and fishing. Much less is known about this. Writing in the 1930s, Peter Anson commented that 'until the latter part of the Middle Ages we really know very little about the fisheries on the [east] coast of Scotland. According to certain authorities Scotland was doing a trade in herring with the Netherlands over nine hundred years ago … during the fourteenth century, Flemish, Dutch, and German boats were fishing off the Scottish coast.'[24] Up until about 1880, when steam fishing boats were introduced, 'fishing on the east coast of Scotland was carried on by small open boats … their scope and capacity were limited. They could only fish in certain weathers and required skilful handling, and their effective area of operation was restricted by the necessity for bringing the catch ashore as fresh as possible.'[25]

By the later Medieval period, trade between Scotland and Scandinavian countries had opened up, with timber being one of the main Scottish imports which continued into the mid-sixteenth century.[26] In an

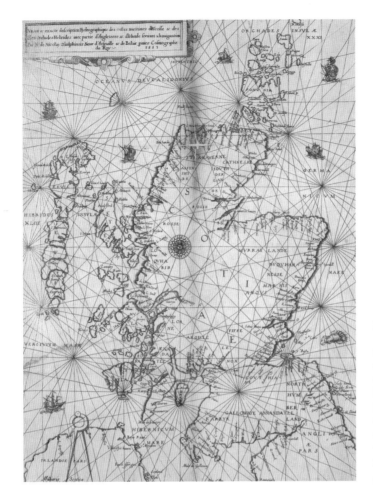

First chart of Scotland, 'Vraye & exacte description hydrographique des costes maritimes d'Escosse, Isles Orchades Hebrides … la navigation, par N. de Nicolay d'Arfeville …', 1583.

illuminating essay looking at the Sound Toll Registers kept at Copenhagen, Thomas Riis found that Scottish skippers – the number varied from one burgh to another – were engaged in taking a variety of commodities in either direction; some were involved in a triangular trade between Scotland and two foreign ports.[27] Merchant trading continued with the Low Countries and France from this time, but was strongest with the Baltic States, in particular the Danish Empire. There was a series of royal marriages between Stuart monarchs and the Danish royal house, including those of James III, James VI and Anne: James VI in particular was keen to emulate Christian IV in architecture and the humanities.

## Navigation instruments

Mariners depended upon knowledge and skill to guide their vessels safely from one place to another, and from ancient times this meant knowledge of weather patterns, the changing nature of the sky at night, as well as the force and nature of the tides, and such natural hazards as rocks or shifting sandbanks. From an early date, particular instruments evolved to assist the safe conduct of boats from place to place. With the frequency of cloudy nights obscuring the northern skies, to say nothing of the sea-fog – still known today locally on the east coast of Scotland as the 'haar' – the first navigation instruments to be used in the seas off Scotland could not look often to the northern heavens for reliable assistance.

The instruments needed for making and then using a rutter, such as that compiled by Alexander Lindsay, would have been a magnetic compass (for directions), a sandglass (for timings), a lead and line (for soundings), and possibly a traverse board (which was used to crudely record distance and direction).[28] However, examples of these somewhat mundane instruments, and with a Scottish provenance of this date, do not appear to have survived, although later instances of rather more sophisticated devices have been recorded. In addition, Scottish gravestones and other pictorial representations go some way to demonstrate that these instruments were not unknown to Scottish mariners, and were presumably acquired on voyages abroad.[29]

The purchase of marine instruments was listed in early sixteenth-century Scottish records: for example, in 1512 there is a document of the import to Leith from Flanders of 'twa kase compase … four utheris compas, tua nichtglassis … and ane creile [basket] to pak thame in'. Purchases of compasses for the Scottish royal ships are also recorded in 1504-06, 1533 and 1538.[30] Nevertheless, with no tradition of continuous instrument-making to be found in Scotland until the eighteenth-century Enlightenment (and then in her university towns rather than her ports) most of the navigation instrumentation must have been acquired by mariners on the Continent.[31]

The invention of the magnetic compass and its introduction to Mediterranean and Atlantic coast shipping is obscure, but it seems to have been in use by the twelfth century.[32] In fact, the earliest survival in the British Isles was that famously found on the English ship, the *Mary Rose*, which sank in the Solent in 1545.[33] Apparently, native English instrument-makers were producing compasses for sundial compendia and other land-based instruments from the earliest days that the trade had stabilised in London, and a compass may be found in appropriate surviving instruments dating from 1575 onwards.[34] Pocket sundials with coloured compass cards were found during marine archaeological work on the wrecks of the Dutch East Indiamen, the *Lastdrager*, lost off Yell in Shetland in 1652, and the *Kennemerland*, also wrecked in Shetland waters in 1664. It has been speculated that because these would only work properly at the latitude for which they were designed – in central Europe – and thus useless and inaccurate elsewhere, they were probably a speculative (although illegal) venture by an enterprising crew member for sale to Batavian natives.[35] The steering compass of the Cromwellian warship, the *Swan*, was recovered by marine archaeologists; the vessel sank in the Sound of Mull in 1653. Other instrumentation found on wrecks in Scottish waters appears to be almost entirely post-Medieval, including sounding leads, single-handed chart dividers, and the instruments developed from the late sixteenth-century: the cross-staff, back-staff and the Davis quadrant.[36] Even the astrolabe – or rather, its maritime relative – does not appear to have been developed until 1481, with the earliest survivor dated 1540. The only example known with a Scottish provenance may date from the mid-sixteenth century, but it was made in the Iberian peninsula, and its use in Scottish waters can only be dated from the 1680s.[37]

The sandglass, which would measure time elapsed on board ship, was probably developed in the western Mediterranean in the thirteenth century, but again there seem to be no early Scottish examples which survive, possibly because of the fragility of the item.[38] However, the sandglass is mentioned in Scottish records, probably for maritime use, from the early sixteenth century: in 1506 'tua sandglasses for the King, 4s. 8d', and later that year '3 sandglasses … quhen the King was in schip'.[39] Examples found in museum collections today are usually later relics used in church to time the sermon.[40]

With the sandglass and the compass, the master of the ship could use a traverse board, on which he could peg or mark the distance and direction made in successive courses each half-hour of consecutive watches, thus keeping a reasonable estimate of the distance the vessel had travelled. A late example of a traverse board (probably European in origin) was found on the island of Barra in 1844, and is now in the National Maritime Museum, London.[41] Even so, these items are notoriously difficult to date; most examples found in public collections, lacking provenance, have been ascribed tentatively to the nineteenth century and appear to be of Continental origin.

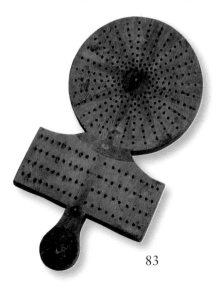

The earliest item describing the Scottish coasts was the rutter apparently compiled by Alexander Lindsay for the 'daunting of the Western Isles' by James V in 1540, and mentioned above. Its contents, when produced, were highly confidential, and meant for the King's (or his captains') eyes only. The original now-lost compilation would have been in Scots; of the six surviving early copies, three are in English translation, and three in French. A. B. Taylor outlines the histories of each of these, demonstrating that the knowledge contained in the rutter was regarded as a military secret, despite its eventual French publication by Nicolas de Nicolay d'Arfeville in Paris in 1583.[42] This particular translation was also accompanied by an engraved and printed chart showing 'VRAYE & exacte description Hydrographique des costes d'Escosse & des Isles Orchades Hebrides ...'. Although none of the rutter manuscripts now has an accompanying chart, the published chart of Nicolas de Nicolay – credited by him to Alexander Lindsay – has been described as 'a much better outline of Scotland than any previous map ... in fact more accurate than any later maps of the seventeenth century'.[43] How could this be possible?

An essay by Peter Barber on the theme of cartography as a Government tool explains in some depth the flurry of map-making activity under Henry VIII of England: among the groups of scholars who produced maps in England were some Scots who were working at the English court. Some of these men may have been connected with Lindsay, for it is apparent that charts of the Scottish coasts were available south of the border and, Barber suggests, may have contributed to English military successes in Scotland between 1544 and 1547, the period known as the 'Rough Wooing'.[44] Lindsay – about whom few personal details are known, although there was a man of that name on the *Great Michael* in 1513 – may well have been associated with one or a number of those sources.[45] Nicolay describes Lindsay as an 'excellent Pilote Escossois', and it is possible that someone who had been a seaman in 1513 had become an experienced ship's pilot by 1540.[46]

Among sixteenth-century map-makers who may have been in contact with Lindsay was John Elder (fl.1533-65), a well-educated native of Caithness and member of the court of James V. However, having converted to Protestantism, he was forced into exile by 1543. In England he prepared various memoranda for Henry VIII, including a detailed manuscript map (now lost) of Scotland, including 'the situacion of all the principally yles ... called Orknay and Schetland, and of the out yles, commonly namede the Sky and the Lewys; ... the cost [coast] of the same; the dangers lying therby, with every port, river, loigh, creke, and haven ther …'. Another map-maker was London-born George Lily (d.1559), who produced a map of the British Isles, published in Rome in 1546, with further editions until 1589, in which representations of the west coast of Scotland began to resemble the modern outline. A third map-maker was the Scot, John Leslie, Bishop of Ross (1527-96), who compiled two maps while in exile in Italy and France, which were published in Rome in about 1578. A fourth may have been the Oxford-educated antiquary and traveller Laurence Nowell (1530-c.70), known to be the compiler of two manuscript maps of Scotland of around 1561 and 1566, with text describing some of the Western Isles.[47]

The picture is unclear, but at this date all map and chart-makers were pulling together knowledge gleaned from earlier compilations: and it is the enigmatic John Elder who appears to have been the closest in time and place to Lindsay, and may have known him personally. Taylor suggests that Lindsay borrowed Elder's first-hand knowledge of parts of Scotland with which the (probable) Lowland pilot would have been unfamiliar.[48] In support of this, there is Elder's statement:

> I was born in Caitnes … educatt, and brought up, not onely in the West yles … namede the Sky and the Lewys, wher I have bene often tymes with my frendis, in ther longe galeis, arriving to dyvers and syndrie places in Scotland, wher they had a do; but also, beinge a scholar and a student in the southe parts of it, called Sanctandrois, Abirdene and Glasgow, for the space of XIIth yeares wher I have travailed, as well by see as by Land, dyvers times. …[49]

In contrast John Leslie, spy and churchman, seems to have had very limited first-hand knowledge of the highlands and islands that Elder claimed to know so well (despite having held his diocese in Ross).[50] However, it remains uncertain in what order various details might have been absorbed from whose compilations; and of course many of the manuscripts and intermediate charts have been lost since they were made in the mid-sixteenth century.

Meantime in Europe, map-making was coming out of its late Medieval cocoon of secrecy. The humanist climate of the Renaissance no longer allowed knowledge to be the restricted powerful tool of princes, but was shared amongst scholars, antiquarians and mathematicians, and from them disseminated to a wider public. P. D. A. Harvey describes this as 'a cartographic revolution'; and although discussing the English case, he demonstrates that from 1500, when 'maps were little understood or used[,] By 1600 they were familiar objects of everyday life'.[51] By the end of the sixteenth century, maps – and charts – were drawn to scale and had conventional signs well-understood by their users; and the introduction of the printed map further popularised the use of such schematic diagrams to a larger audience.

One of the first printed maps of Scotland by itself – 'Scotiae Tabula' – was published by Abraham Ortelius (1527-98) in Antwerp in 1573. The outline in turn had been copied from a large map engraved by his friend and mentor Gerard Mercator (1512-94) at Duisberg in 1564. Mercator has been characterised as:

… a humble man of universal vision. Where his contemporaries had adopted a piecemeal approach to cartography, Mercator sought to wrap the world in overlapping, uniform maps. … He participated in the naming and the mapping of America, and he devised a new method – a 'projection' – of converting the spherical world into a two-dimensional map. He constructed the two most impor-

tant globes of the sixteenth century, and the title of his pioneering 'modern geography', the Atlas, became the standard term for a book of maps.[52]

In effect, Mercator was the principal European figure in Harvey's sixteenth-century cartographic revolution. In an illuminating essay, Peter Barber has closely examined Mercator's sources for the mapping of the British Isles, which he portrayed at least seven times during his long life of 82 years.[53] Understanding what the sources were for his eight-sheet map of Britain, published in 1564, is vital to grasping how the topographical knowledge of such difficult terrain as the highlands and islands of Scotland could reach a map compiler who had never crossed the North Sea. For the purposes of this chapter, these sources would explain how Mercator managed to delineate the coasts so much more accurately than his predecessors.

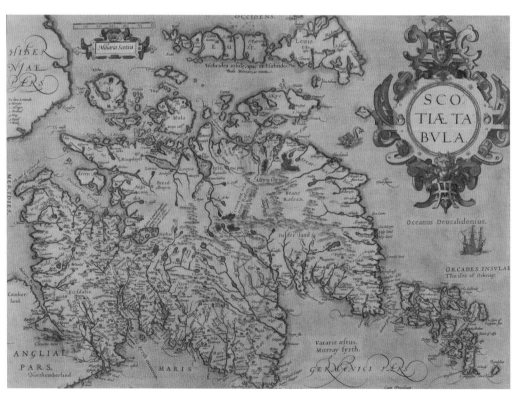

Barber's assessment is that the representation of Scotland on Mercator's map of the British Isles (dated 1564) was a great advance on all earlier published maps. In his opinion it showed the first reasonably realistic illustration of the west coast, and the Inner and the Outer Hebrides.[54] He agrees with Moir's earlier opinion that much of the material must have originated with John Elder, the Scot who defected to Henry VIII and supplied him with a (no longer extant) map of Scotland in 1543.[55] But how had this reached Mercator, based in Duisberg in the Rhineland, especially as there seems to have been no direct link between Mercator and Elder? Mercator engraved text on the map itself, explaining that a friend offered him a manuscript map of the British Isles and asked him to engrave it; unwilling to offend this friend, he did so without alteration. This is confirmed by Mercator's biographer, his contemporary Walter Ghim, who wrote that an eminent friend from England – again, unnamed – produced the manuscript map.[56] Moir suggests that the friend might be John Dee, mathematician, astrologer and antiquary at the English court; Barber examines the case for Dee, but dismisses him on the map's internal evidence, namely that it was designed from a Scots, Catholic and anti-Elizabethan perspective. Barber goes on to consider other possible figures, including Laurence Nowell, George Lily, and Lily's patron Cardinal Reginald Pole. Barber concludes, however, that it seems most likely that Elder was the one who sent it from France shortly before he left the country in 1561, and it may even have been associated with a note of approval from Elder's powerful ally and paymaster, the Cardinal de Lorraine.[57] Intriguingly, another name has been put forward by another Mercator biographer, Nicholas Crane, who suggests that the link might have been his student friend and contemporary Antoine Perronet de Granvelle, who became Catholic Archbishop of Mechelen, Primate of the Low Countries, and a Cardinal in 1559: he, like the Cardinal of Lorraine and Philip II of Spain, was keen to see again a Catholic British Isles.[58]

At this point, the cartographic revolution took a turn which left the initiative in the hands of the great printing houses of the Low Countries. Dutch cartographers, amongst whom was Abraham Ortelius – author of the first atlas and young friend of Mercator – were skilled in copper-plate engraving.[59] They were able to print multiple copies of maps and charts in such numbers that they came to control the business, both for sea and land maps. The early seventeenth century thus saw the Dutch domination of chart production of the Scottish coasts. The first printed sea-atlas, the *Spieghel der Zeevaerdt*, was published by Lucas Jansz Waghenaer in Leiden in 1583, and contained a chart of the east coast from Bamburgh to Aberdeen. This was followed by a second atlas

OPPOSITE PAGE

Abraham Ortelius, 'Scotiae Tabula' from *Theatrum Orbis Terrarum*; first published in Antwerp in 1573. This is from the third edition of 1579.

(NMS T.1908.64)

in 1592, with three Scottish charts – the east coast (already showing some modifications from practical experiences), the Shetland islands, and the Hebrides. Over the next 80 years or so, these were copied by other publishers, with little or no changes, and atlases of sea-charts became known as 'waggoners', a corruption of the name Waghenaer.[60] These were designed to enable mariners to cross the North Sea and get safely into Scottish (or English) harbours on the east coast. They also showed profiles of the coast, as seen from the approaching vessel, and came with directions. However, they were not particularly representational, and neither did they have particularly fine detail of the many hazards. Clearly, a more systematic form of mapping and surveying was needed – but that would be time-consuming and expensive.

### Mapping and charting: the seventeenth century

This Dutch domination of the sea-chart endeavour became an embarrassment, particularly to the English. (Although the King of Scotland, James VI, had become James I of England upon the death of his cousin Queen Elizabeth in 1603, Scotland and England maintained separate Parliaments, and remained separate countries, for the meantime.) This shame perhaps reached its peak during the Second Anglo-Dutch War, in the reign of James I's grandson, Charles II, when in June 1667 the Dutch – using their charts of English waters – were able to come up the Medway and destroy the English fleet at anchor at Chatham. Although attempts were made by the enterprising London chart publisher John Seller to break into this market with his *English Pilot* of 1671-72, very little of what he published was original, and much was cribbed from Dutch sources.[61] By this time the Admiralty in London was determined to rectify the position. A naval officer called Greenvile Collins (d.1694), who had previously voyaged to the south seas, and in 1676 had been on an unsuccessful attempt to find a north-west passage to China, was given a royal appointment to undertake a survey of the coasts around Britain.[62] With funds administered by Trinity House, Collins began his survey in 1681 as commander of the yacht, *Merlin*, beginning on England's vulnerable south coast. Over the next seven years, from a number of different vessels, Collins undertook practical coastal survey work, although he 'probably used existing charts and seamen's sketches and notes, as well as his own observations in this remarkably ambitious undertaking'.[63]

One of the seamen's sketches incorporated by Collins – in fact, the only one whose input he acknowledged – was subsequently published in his *Great Britain's Coasting Pilot* in 1693. This chart was accredited:

'The Sea coast from Fiffnesse to Montros was Survey'd by Mr Mar an injenious Marriner of Dundee.' Interestingly, a manuscript map of the Firth (or estuary) of the River Tay previously attributed to earlier Scottish mapmaker Timothy Pont has been reassigned to John Marr, who published the first Scottish text on marine navigation, *Navigation in Coasting; or a Sea-man's Instructor*, in 1693. Further printed Dutch maps dating between 1682 and 1720 credit Marr with input, and it has been speculated that he traded fairly regularly between Dundee and the Netherlands, and so he may have dealt directly with the Dutch publishers, as well as with Collins.[64]

Collins's charts were published individually upon completion. At an early stage, his project was well-received by the diarist John Evelyn, who wrote in February 1682/83:

I made my court at St James's, when I saw the sea charts of Capt. Collins; which that industrious man now brought to shew the Duke [of York], having taken all the coasting from the mouth of the Thames, as far as Wales, and exactly measuring every creeke, island, rock, soundings, harbors, sands, and tides, intending next spring to proceed till he had finish'd the whole iland, and that measured by chains and other instruments. A most exact and useful undertaking.[65]

In 1693 the charts were privately published in two parts, covering England and the east coast of Scotland, together with Orkney and Shetland, and some important Irish ports: the proposed third part was for Ireland, but this was never completed. John Moore quotes Samuel Pepys's response, less enthusiastic than the earlier comment of Evelyn, especially

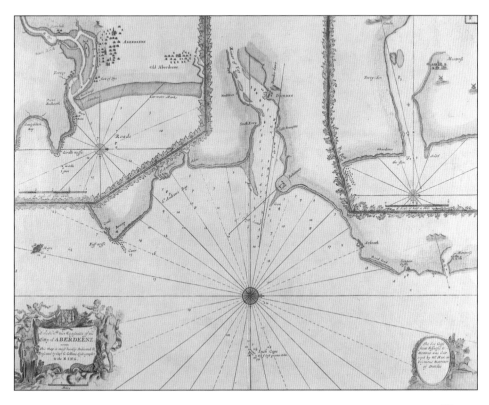

concerning the accuracy of Collins's work.[66] He had surveyed the coast from Harwich to Edinburgh in 1684, and the following year the coast from Edinburgh to Orkney and Shetland: this produced nine charts and one engraving of profiles of the land from the sea. 'I could heartily wish that the West Part of Ireland and Scotland may be hereafter surveyed,' he stated.[67] Although Collins was eventually paid for his work, it had greatly exceeded his original estimate. Nonetheless, *Great Britain's Coasting Pilot* appeared in 20 editions between 1693 and 1792, although not regularly updated by mariners submitting information to Trinity House, as Collins had wished, and thus becoming less reliable.[68]

At about the same time as Collins's seven-year survey, there was a similar exercise being undertaken by a Scotsman for the Scottish coasts. This seemingly unnecessary duplication of effort and expense has been characterised as 'surprising' and 'a mystery' by John Moore, particularly as the Scottish economy was in recession.[69] Perhaps because the Scottish work started as a different project and then transmogrified into a series of sea charts, it was not perceived to be an unnecessary doubling of effort at the time. The Edinburgh-based geographer John Adair (1660-1718) was commissioned by Moses Pitt, a London map and bookseller, to produce maps of Scottish counties for his proposed *Great Atlas*, projected in twelve volumes, of which Pitt had already published two. The genesis of this project was prolonged and complicated, and Adair had been involved in it from about 1676.[70] He petitioned the Scottish Privy Council for support to survey Scotland, offering a completed plan of Clackmannanshire (presumably produced for Pitt) in May 1681 as proof of his ability. He was licensed to do so in May 1681, and given financial and moral support. How-

ever, as Pitt's project slid into financial difficulty and debt – only four of the projected volumes were ever published – another scheme came into being. This was Sir Robert Sibbald's proposed *Scottish Atlas*, an ambitious project which intended to build on part of the ruins of the *Great Atlas*, by supplementing it with antiquarian material and new maps undertaken by Adair.[71] But patronage from Sibbald proved to be a mistake. First, Sibbald was also supporting the efforts of a Dutch artillery officer, John Slezer, who was producing his *Theatrum Scotiae*, a projected volume of views of towns and important buildings, which proved to be overwhelming competition. Second, Adair's relationship with Robert Sibbald bound him between 1683 and 1691

90

to provide his patron with exclusive rights to any maps he produced, for which he was paid only a guinea for each map. And, third, Sibbald was in turn allied with the York (Catholic) party through his own patron, the Earl of Perth; and with the expulsion of the King, James II, formerly the Duke of York, in the Glorious Revolution of 1688, despite subsequently reconverting to Protestantism, Sibbald's credibility, together with his projects, turned to dust.[72]

Adair was funded by the Scots Parliament from 1686 through 'an annual tonnage levy of 1s (Scots) on native ships over 8 tons, and 2s. for foreign ships, to be paid annually for five years'.[73] Slezer also successfully petitioned the Scots Parliament, and his name was added to the beneficiaries of this act, but at a higher rate than Adair. Financial affairs began to dominate Adair's life, and although by the mid-1680s he had completed several surveys of a number of counties, he had by now also embarked on surveys of the Scottish coastline, which arguably would not infringe Sibbald's monopoly. He visited the Netherlands to inspect the map-makers' activities, and on his return, at the Privy Council's request, he brought the engraver James Moxon with him. Although a number of Adair's coastal surveys had already been done, Moxon engraved only one of these charts – a faithful copy of Nicolay's earlier 1583 outline of the Scottish coast, now dated 1688 (see page 81). Moxon left Edinburgh for London, possibly frustrated by Adair's business methods, or lack of them.[74] Eventually James Clark, an engraver who worked at the Scottish Mint, produced the completed Adair charts for publication. They appeared in the first of two proposed volumes as his *Description of the Sea-Coast and Islands of Scotland* in 1703 (see page 92), which comprised five charts of the coast from Holy Island to Aberdeen, and the Moxon version of Nicolay's map.[75] This was accompanied by detailed sailing instructions, as in the case of Collins and, indeed, the earlier rutter compiled by Lindsay, continuing a long maritime tradition.

Adair spent considerable time in the late 1690s surveying the Western Isles, and after the publication of the 1703 book of charts, he carried out a similar exercise in the Shetland and Orkney islands; but ill-health and finally death overtook him in 1718. Although his widow handed over all his maps and surveys to the Government in return for a state pension, these – which would have made up his proposed second volume – were believed to have been destroyed in a fire in 1811.[76] However, a group of manuscript charts by Adair was found in the Admiralty collection at the end of the twentieth century, and appear to be most of these missing items. In the light of this discovery, Moore has expressed the view that as Adair's published atlas covered the major harbours of

OPPOSITE PAGE

Frontispiece to Greenvile Collins's *Great Britain's Coasting Pilot: Being a new and exact survey of the Sea coast of England and Scotland from the river of Thames to the westward and northward with the Islands of Scilly and from thence to Carlisle*, 1776; first published in 1680.

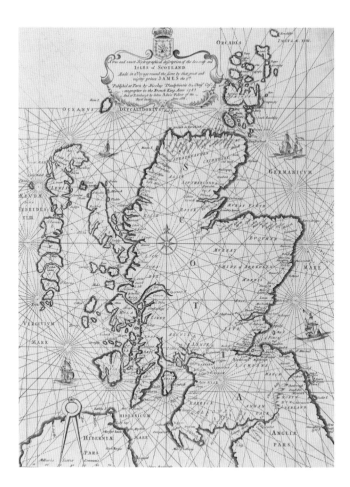

John Adair's chart of Scotland, derived from Nicolay's 1583 chart, now dated 1688.

(NMS T.2003.309.269.1)

the east coast of Scotland (then remaining the most important centres for overseas trade), and nonetheless appeared to have sold in restricted numbers, any attempt on his part to find profit in publishing charts of the more remote areas would seem to have been doomed to further disillusionment.[77]

Unlike Collins's often-republished *Coasting Pilot*, Adair's work appeared in only one edition. Charles Withers summed up Adair's career as failing to make its expected mark, as too much remained in manuscript form, despite his wide-ranging surveys and unrivalled completed maps. In short, as a figure in cartographic history, Adair sadly falls short of his potential.[78]

### Mapping and charting: the eighteenth century

In 1707, for a variety of reasons that need not detain us here, Scotland's Parliament was united with that of England. Broadly speaking, the key to understanding the administration, Government and running of every aspect of Scotland during the eighteenth century, appears to be in the all-enveloping web of patronage which covered positions in all walks of life from the law, through the universities and various agencies, to the encouragement of trade, and of artists and artisans.[79] As we have seen, patronage had been important before the Union; afterwards it remained vital for the achievement of particular projects. Scotland was ostensibly governed from Westminster, where a handful of Scottish nobles were realising their interests and becoming irreversibly Anglicised in the process. However, through the patronage of their political masters, a new class of managers emerged in Scotland, often related to each other through extended family networks, and based mainly in Edinburgh. There, through the Kirk, the Law, and various Government boards, new structures of administration developed during the eighteenth century.

By mid-century, Edinburgh could be seen as a centre of the establishment in Scotland. Her university, founded in 1583, became a focus of what was subsequently termed the Scottish Enlightenment. Scholarly work during the past 20 to 30 years has demonstrated that this was essentially an urban phenomenon, and was centred mainly on the three universities of Aberdeen, Glasgow and Edinburgh.[80] (The fourth, at St Andrews, was based in a town by now too small to provide the urban infrastructure necessary for Enlightenment.) This was no mere local phenomenon, although it has been argued that in its Scottish form, there were distinct characteristics. Throughout the eighteenth century a general spirit of enquiry into the natural and human worlds permeated much of intellectual European thought, and came to be known as the Enlightenment. In Scotland it was marked, among other important philosophical pursuits, by a particular interest on the one hand in antiquarianism, and on the other, amidst a whole range of practical scientific activities, by the quest for increasing precision in science and technology.[81] Many map compilers had antiquarian interests.

One of the ways this manifested itself was through the foundation of societies that investigated these antiquarian and scientific affairs, and the foremost of these was the Philosophical Society of Edinburgh. This had a fairly chequered career, and may have had its roots in earlier societies, one of which was formed in the 1680s by Sir Robert Sibbald. Colin Maclaurin (1698-1746), professor of mathematics at the University of Edinburgh, appears to have been the main intellectual force behind the mid-eighteenth century form of the society. As with many other formal bodies in Scotland at this time, the Philosophical Society of Edinburgh became a vehicle for patronage, in particular for James Douglas, 13th Earl of Morton (1702-68), who from 1737 until his death was its President. Morton had become close friends with Maclaurin after his return to Scotland from a Cambridge education and the Grand Tour. Elected a Fellow of the Royal Society of London in 1733, he observed a solar eclipse in 1737 with, among others, Maclaurin and the Edinburgh telescope-maker James Short. All of those involved in this astronomical soirée went on to become founder members of the Philosophical Society of Edinburgh, and Maclaurin and Short, in particular, were beneficiaries of Morton's patronage. Morton was a Whig representative peer in the Westminster Parliament, Grand Master of England's Grand Masonic Lodge and, after 1764, President of the Royal Society of London.

Another member of the society was the minister, Alexander Bryce (1713-86). This former pupil, and subsequently protégé, of Maclaurin was involved with trigonometric survey work in the early 1740s for the Earl of Morton. (The Earls of Morton had obtained ownership of the Orkney Islands through a mortgage to the Crown in 1707.) Bryce produced his map, dated 1744, and engraved by Richard Cooper (who had also engraved some of Adair's manuscript maps, posthumously in the 1730s) and dedicated it 'to the Right Honble. The Earl of Morton'. Also, in a second cartouche, he stated that his 'Map of the North Coast of Britain' from Assynt in the west to Wick in Caithness in the east 'by a Geometrical Survey with the Harbours, Rocks & and Account of the Tides in the Pentland Firth [was] done at the desire of the Philosophical Society at Edinburgh'. The Earl of Morton subsequently provided Bryce with a church living at Kirknewton, just west of Edinburgh, in 1744.[82]

By the mid-eighteenth century, the Atlantic trade was becoming much more important to Scotland, and there was also a growing exchange between Glasgow and Liverpool, ensuring that mapping of the Clyde and the west coast became priorities. Map historian Diana Smith observes that the wreck of a Swedish East India Company ship off Orkney, with great loss of life and cargo in 1740, prompted public pressure to chart accurately a channel which was the dangerous alternative whenever the English Channel was effectively closed to merchant shipping by war.[83] The most famous marine survey undertaken in the west was by a naval commander named Murdoch Mackenzie. This project was once again prompted by the private interest of the Earl of Morton, who, as before, sought the advice of Colin Maclaurin about a coastal survey of the Orkney Islands. Just as Maclaurin had suggested a former pupil with connections in the Caithness locality – Bryce – to map there, this time he suggested Mackenzie, an Orcadian, who had also learned about triangulation at Maclaurin's mathematics classes. This resulted in a subscription-funded atlas of eight charts of the Orkney Islands and Lewis, *Orcades*, published in 1750, leading to Mackenzie being commissioned by the Admiralty to survey the west coast of Britain and the coast of Ireland.[84] *Orcades* combined its charts showing soundings with profiles of headlands and views of the shoreline as seen from the sea, and also had the written 'directions' alongside. In the years to come, one or other of these forms of maritime signposting was sometimes contained in separate bindings: but mariners really required all of them to be used together. In dangerous waters, one needed all the help available.

Mackenzie's charts were a great improvement in accuracy on existing charts, and his own work was further improved by the efforts of other individuals including James Huddart. However, the founding of the Admiralty Hydrographic Office in 1795 – under Scotsman Alexander Dalrymple – meant that reliability and accuracy, to say nothing of scientific methodology and regular updating, were at last built into charting. From the early nineteenth century, the mariner could rely on the charts of the Scottish coasts during daylight hours at least.[85]

**First lights: dangers in the darkness**

If one had taken a trip around Scotland's edge, examining the sea-marks from the Tweed to the Solway before the advent of the Bell Rock lighthouse, perhaps the most striking aspect would have been how few lights there were. Bearing in mind that a ship's course around the mainland and most of the islands covers

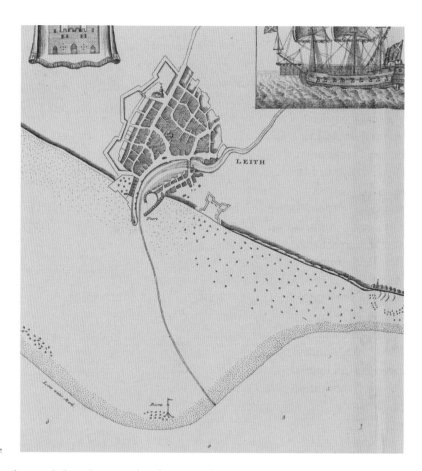

Greenvile Collins's Plate 'O', showing Leith with its beacon, from *Great Britain's Coasting Pilot* ..., 1776; first published in 1680.

almost a thousand miles, and that the actual coastline runs to over six times that amount, even in imagination, this is a long, dark and dangerous route. Leith, as Edinburgh's port – and where James IV had encouraged ship-building – appears to have been the earliest place in Scotland to have some sort of sea-mark. There was both a west and east beacon to the harbour entrance by 1553, when the town treasurer's accounts note payments for ongoing maintenance: '... to sax men that laubourit twa dayis in the redding [repairing] of the bekyn and the casting [heaping] of the stanis [stones] thairto agane, ilk [each] man XXd, [20d] in the day', and 'efter the bekyn being brokin be ane Inglis schip, the maister payit the hale expensis in the upsetting theirof except xxiiijs [24s]'. Subsequently, the total of

£5 18s 8d was paid 'for the making of twa bekinnis on the eist end of the bulwark of Leyth', and a further 5s 8d was paid in 1554 for 'mending of the eister bekin of Leyth'.[86] Clearly this continual preservation was expensive. By the time Greenvile Collins surveyed Leith in 1684-85, he could write that 'Leith is a Tide Haven, where you enter at High Water, leaving the Beacon on the Larboard Side going in', and his Plate 'O' shows Leith Harbour, with its beacon, engraved by 'N. Yeates'. A detail of Plate 'N', 'Edinburgh Firth' also shows a 'Becon' off Leith.[87] John Adair also shows the Leith beacon in his chart 'Frith of Forth from the entry to the Queensferry'.[88]

The first lighthouse – as opposed to a beacon or sea-mark – to be built in Scotland, as seen in chapter 1, was that on the Isle of

May, in the entrance to the Firth of Forth. Lindsay mentioned the 'Yle of May', more as a landmark than a hazard, although it clearly was one. Lighting the Forth was to prove a long and expensive business: first proposals were mooted as early as 1625, and for many years it was debated in the annual Convention of the Royal Burghs, delayed because of the expense, yet seen as a necessity because of the growth in trade, and the development of coal-mining and salt-works. Munro points out that it was 'the stimulation of fishing around the Scottish coasts that made some further warning of points of special danger necessary', leading to the erection of the first Scottish lighthouse.[89]

Eventually, after much debate and a number of political setbacks, three landowners – Alexander and John Cunningham of Barns, father and son, and James Maxwell of Innerwick near Dunbar – obtained a patent from the King in 1636 to put up a lighthouse on the Isle of May. This granted the partners the right to levy a due from all vessels arriving in port across a line drawn from Dunottar Castle in the north to St Abb's Head in the south, set at two shillings Scots per ton if Scottish and four shillings if foreign. The dues were to be fully paid to the partners for 19 years, while they in turn paid the King £1000 Scots annually. Charles I was always short of money, and at this point his troubles were turning towards civil war.[90]

The beacon-stand – for this is what the early light proved to be – appears to have been constructed almost immediately, although no records of the building appear to have survived, and a coal fire was burned in a brazier on the top of the tower between 1636 and 1816. The masonry tower has walls four feet thick and is 24 feet square (7.47 metres), originally standing some 40 feet high (12 m). The ground floor contained the living quarters, the upper the sleeping quarters; and access was obtained to the flat roof surrounded by a parapet by a spiral staircase. On top was a large grate standing on a central pillar, and after 1786, when the Northern Lighthouse Board was established, a rope-and-pulley windlass was installed to haul up pans of coal.[91] Greenvile Collins illustrated the lighthouse most clearly on the chart crediting John Marr – although the island appears in his other relevant charts – and described it thus: 'The Isle of May … is bigger than the Bass, but not so high, on which stands a Light-house, that Ships may know the

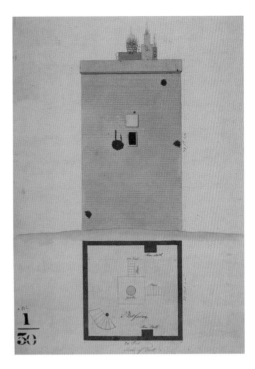

Drawing of the Isle of May lighthouse by Robert Stevenson.

(Trustees of the National Library of Scotland)

97

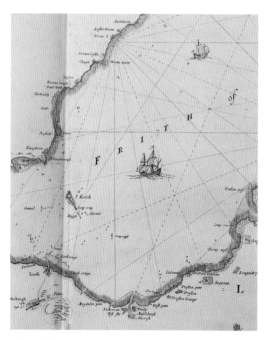

Detail from John Adair's 'Frith of Forth', showing the Leith beacon, from Adair's *Description of the Sea-Coast and Islands of Scotland* (Edinburgh, 1703).

(NMS T.2003.309.259.13)

Frith in the Night, this Light may be seen 6 Leagues off.'[92] John Adair mentioned the Isle of May incidentally, and marks the lighthouse plainly on his chart 'The Frith and River of Tay' in his *Description of the Sea Coast*. In the subsequent (and posthumous) 1730 engraving of his 'The River and Frith of Forth', it is endorsed 'Isle of May Here is Fire Continually kept For a Beacon to ships in the Night'. The coal was supplied locally, and it appears to have consumed most of a ton of coal at night in fair weather, and up to three tons in stormy weather. Douglas Hague conjures up a particularly vivid and unpleasant picture:

Clearly the work of the keeper was cruelly hard; but an island is very different from the cramped quarters on a rock station, and family life of a sort was possible. It needs little imagination to envisage the dreadful conditions facing a keeper's wife, living

beneath a perpetual bonfire, never able to free herself from clinging coal-dust and never able to escape from the smoke and fumes.[93]

The inevitable accident befell the family of the keeper George Anderson in the winter of 1791 (as recounted in chapter 1).

Meanwhile, this privately-owned lighthouse had changed hands from its original owners, the Cunninghams of Barns, as the Isle of May and its light, together with other parts of the Barns estate, was sold in 1714 to another Fife landowning family, the Scotts of Scotstarvit. Light dues, never easy to collect, remained difficult but extremely lucrative as the villages around the Firth grew in prosperity, and although attempts were made to improve the light by enclosing it in some kind of lantern, the fire smoked the glass so much that the light could not be seen. The last individual proprietor of the Isle of May was one Henrietta Scott, eldest daughter of General John Scott of Balcomie, a member of the Scotstarvit family; she later became the wife of William Bentinck (1768-1854), Marquess of Titchfield and later 4th Duke of Portland.[94]

In 1809, while the construction of the Bell Rock lighthouse was underway, Robert Stevenson drew to the attention of the Commissioners of the Northern Lighthouse Board that navigation in the area would still be compromised unless the light on the Isle of May was improved. The Commissioners felt that only the proprietor could address this problem. However, their hand would be forced in December 1810 by the loss of two naval frigates, the *Nymph* and the *Pallas*, wrecked near Dunbar because the lookout believed that the fire from a coastal limekiln was that of the May light. Fortunately, only nine men were lost out of a total of 600, but the vessels cost the Government some £100,000 at a time of war. The outcome was that, after negotiations in 1814, the Isle of May, and its light, was purchased from the Duke of Portland for £60,000, and the same year an Act of Parliament reduced lighthouse duty to one penny a ton for all British ships.[95]

During the 18 months following the acquisition of the island by the Commissioners, a new lighthouse was constructed, and the old beacon shone out for the final time on 31 January 1816. Its two-storied bulk interfered with the path of the beam of the proposed new light – a stationary oil light with lamp and reflectors, visible for about 21 miles – and Robert Stevenson had decided to demolish it.[96] However, in the summer of 1814 the author and antiquary Sir Walter Scott accompanied the Commissioners on their annual tour of inspection of the Northern Lights (although he was Sheriff of Selkirkshire, that county does not have a seaboard, so he was not one of the *ex officio* Commissioners). As he recounted in his *Journal*, after embarking from Leith on Friday 29 July 1814:

> Reached the Isle of May in the evening; went ashore and saw the light – an old tower and much in the form of a border-keep, with a beacon-grate on the top. It is to be abolished for an oil revolving-light, the grate-fire only being ignited upon the leeward side when the wind is very high. (*Quaere* – Might not the grate revolve?). … Mr Stevenson proposed demolishing the old tower, and I recommended *ruining* it *á la picturesque*, i.e., demolishing it partially. The island might be made a delightful residence for sea-bathers.[97]

Stevenson and Scott had long been good friends, first encountering each other through the Edinburgh Volunteers (a war-time armed force, similar to the Home Guard in the Second World War) in 1795, and Scott's presence on this lighthouse tour was at Stevenson's invitation: the single-storey beacon on the Isle of May remains to this day as a mark of Stevenson's respect for his friend, and of Scott's respect for antiquities.[98]

The delay over purchasing the Isle of May meant that the further hazard upstream at the island of Inchkeith impeded vessels seeking shelter in the estuary. In 1801 the smack *Aberdeen* was lost on the Fife shore, with ten of her passengers and crew and £10,000 worth of cargo. The Commissioners of the Northern Lighthouse Board received an application from Trinity House in Leith, and Robert Stevenson and their representatives went to the island. This resulted in a new lighthouse there being lit on 1 September 1804.[99] 'Hitherto,' wrote Stevenson, 'the erections of the Light-house Board had been confirmed simply to two apartments for one light-keeper; and from the infant state of the fund, the first light-houses were more of a temporary nature, to answer the immediate purpose of the shipping.' But Inchkeith was to be different.

> ... the funds being in a more prosperous condition, instead of two small apartments for a single light-keeper, the plan of the houses was now extended to the accommodation of a principal and an assistant light-keeper, who now keep a constant watch, by night, in the light-houses, in the same manner as is done on ship-board, when a vessel is at sea; and the whole establishment is more like the appointment of a public board. The dwelling house at the light-house stations, instead of exposing, as formerly, a long slated roof on a house of one floor, is now built, as at Inchkeith, with two stories, or floors, and covered with a leaden roof. On the same substantial plan the light-houses are constructed; for instead of the roof of the light-room being framed with timber, and the windows glazed with crown-glass, that of Inchkeith is composed of copper, and the windows are glazed with polished plate glass, of much larger dimensions; and the whole premises are, in great measure, rendered fire proof.[100]

Stevenson continued, that on completion in 1804:

> ... it was what seamen call a stationary, or fixed light, and contained 16 reflectors, made upon the parabolic curve, formed of copper, strongly coated or plated with silver, instead of the hollow, or cavity of the reflector being lined with facets of mirror glass as formerly. Inchkeith light remained a stationary light until the year 1815, the period when the light of May was altered from an open coal fire, to a stationary light, with oil and reflectors; and it became necessary to alter the character of the Inchkeith light, from a stationary to a revolving light, agreeably to its present appearance; and, with this alteration, seven reflectors, instead of the former number, are now found perfectly sufficient.

His description of the rotating mechanism is worth repeating, as it was used elsewhere in various lights:

> The machinery for making the light revolve, consists of a movement or piece of strong clock-work, kept in motion by a weight, and curiously fitted with two governors, upon the plan of a steam engine, instead of a fly wheel. The reflectors are ranged upon a horizontal frame, which is made to revolve periodically, upon a perpendicular axis, exhibiting, to a distant observer, the alternate effect of light and darkness, in a very beautiful and simple manner. The reflectors are brought round in succession to the eye of the observer, and the angles, or interstices between them, produces the effect of darkness, by which this light is distinguished from the light of the Isle of May, and also from the numerous surrounding lights on the opposite shores.[101]

100

This 1815 arrangement was to stay in place until 1834, when new lenses, seven in all, revolved around a single burner: but this episode will have to wait until after the story of the building and lighting of the Bell Rock.[102]

As we saw in chapter 1, getting safely into the next great estuary to the north, the Tay, had long been a problem, because of the shifting sandbanks on either side of the river, the Gaa and Barry Sands off Buddon Ness on the north side, and the Abertay or Drumlee on the south. Another of the early east coast sea-marks was put up to guide mariners into Dundee Harbour, and was in the form of double or 'leading' lights, which allowed ships to enter the firth at any time. This was done by the ship's pilot bringing the lights into line, one apparently over the other. These were shown on an early manuscript chart produced by John Marr of Dundee, now dated at about 1666. They also appeared in Greenvile Collins's map 'P' in his *Great Britain's Coasting Pilot*, which credits Marr with having done the survey. Collins wrote: 'On the North Side of the River is a red Sand Hill, called Buchan-nis, or Bottannis, on which stand two Light-houses by the Sea, being a Leading Mark to sail into the River Tay, between two sands ...'.[103] There were two lights on the spit of land on the north side of the river, shown as one near the tip of 'Botannais' (Buddon Ness), and another further inland. In a chart surveyed by Marr and published after his death by Gerard van Keulen of Amsterdam in 1734, these were identified as a 'Small Light' and a 'Great Light'. Adair also illustrates both lights in his chart 'The Frith and River of Tay with all the Rocks, Sands, Shaolls &c.', describing them thus: '... the ordinary mark to sail in, was, to bring the midmost height or Doun at the Buttonness, N. W. half way, but now there are two Light-Houses Built near the Point below the said Douns, which being brought, the one above the other, leeds safely in, both by Night and Day.'[104] The Fraternity of Masters and Seamen of Dundee was empowered by the Scottish Privy Council in 1687 to collect dues from marine traffic to pay for these lights, which were built on land leased from the Earl of Panmure. In time, these were rebuilt, and the poles with candle-lit lanterns replaced by oil lamps, using the whale oil for which Dundee had become famous.[105]

By the end of the eighteenth century these were described as:

Two reflecting lighthouses, reared to direct the vessels trading to Dundee and Perth through the perilous entrance of the Tay. The largest, which is stationary, is a circular building erected on piles; the other a moveable wooden fabric, raised on rollers. When the two lights are seen in one, the pilot may navigate the river without fear.[106]

These two 'stationary leading lights' are illustrated to accompany Robert Stevenson's article 'Lighthouses' in David Brewster's *Edinburgh Encyclopaedia*, and mentioned in the 1867 edition of Charles Lyell's influential work, *Principles of Geology,* as an example of erosion: 'It had become necessary before 1828, to remove the lighthouses at the mouth of the estuary of the Tay, in the same county [Forfarshire, where Lyell was from] at Button Ness, which were built on a tract of blown sand, the sea having encroached for three quarters of a mile.'[107] These lights and the harbour lights further up the Tay were the responsibility of the Fraternity of Masters and Seamen in Dundee, also known as Dundee's Trinity House. By the end of the eighteenth century, these lights had been provided with oil lamps and reflectors by Thomas Smith.[108] In 1816 his partner Robert Stevenson observed the erosion:

> Within the last century the sea has made such an impression upon the sands of Barrey [today's Barry], on the northern side of the Tay, that the light-houses at the entrance to that river, which were formerly erected at the southern extremity of Buttonness, have been from time to time removed about a mile and a quarter further northward, on account of the wasting and shifting of these sandy shores, and that the spot on which the outer light-house stood in the 17th century is now two or three fathoms [12 or 18 feet] under water, and is at least three quarters of a mile within flood-mark. These facts I state from information obligingly communicated to me by George Clark, Esq. master of the Trinity House, Dundee, from the records of that corporation.[109]

By 1844 the lights at Buddon Ness were described as 'stationary, and appear like stars of the first magnitude. When seen in one line they bear from each other N.N.W half W. and S.S.E. half E.' Further upstream:

> A light is erected on the East Pier, and on the starboard hand at the entrance of Dundee harbour, and another on the Middle Pier on the larboard [port] hand in entering the Wet Docks. These lights are of the same height. When seen in one line, they are leading lights for clearing the southern side of the beacon. A stationary light is also exhibited throughout the night at Craig Pier, for the direction of the Ferry boats, and at Newport, on the Fife side of the Ferry, two lights are erected, the one somewhat higher than the other: they are leading lights for clearing the east end of the Middle Bank.[110]

The Trinity House of Dundee called in the firm of D. & T. Stevenson on the next occasion when the Buddon Ness lights needed amendment, which was in 1865: they built two masonry towers, replacing the earlier wooden ones dating from 1753. Thomas Stevenson designed a new condensing light where 'it was found necessary to illuminate an arc of only 45° in azimuth. For this purpose,' he wrote, 'I designed … apparatus, which is remarkable from its employing every kind of lighthouse dioptric agent': this will be further discussed in chapter 5.[111] Such was the rate of movement of the sandbanks in the mouth of the river that David Cunningham (1838-96), who by 1869 had become Engineer to the Dundee Harbour Trust, was entrusted with the task of moving the lower Buddon Ness lighthouse '160 feet north-east of the old site' during May to early June 1885, and this was completed successfully.[112] Nevertheless, the sandbanks in the river mouth continued to move, and in 1943 both higher and lower lighthouses were taken out of service, and the area is now restricted by the Ministry of Defence.[113]

Off the entrance to the Firth of Tay lies the notorious Inchcape reef, and the building of a sea-mark there merits a chapter of its own.

Further northwards, Aberdeen had provided an early sea-mark, shortly after those noted in Leith. In 1566 the Provost and Council decided to re-erect 'ane gryt bowat [hand lantern] or lamp quhair the same wes obefoir, on the east gawill [gable] of Sanct Ninianis cheppell, vpone the Castelhill, with thre gryt flammand lychtis' to burn continually through the winter nights, so that ships coming into harbour or sailing past the coast 'may be the said lamp have

'Leading Lights of Tay', engraving from Plate 348, 'Lighthouse', from the *Edinburgh Encyclopaedia* (1818).

Drawing of a 'Section of the Lower light of Tay, 1813'.
(Trustees of the National Library of Scotland)

103

jugement and experiens quhair thai ar to eschew danger'.[114] However, it was not until 1833, in response to the loss of the whaling ship *Oscar* in 1813, that the Northern Lighthouse Board responded with a permanent light to mark the dangerous entrance to Aberdeen Harbour.[115]

There were also, as mentioned in chapter 1, two early, pre-Northern Lighthouse Board lighthouses in the west, but constructed later than those on the busier east coast. Although Dumfries is no longer considered as a port, in the mid-eighteenth century the volume of water-borne traffic was such that the Town Council felt it was necessary to build a day-mark 30 feet high at Southerness on the Solway Firth. It is not clear what form the original lighting was, but in due course the lighthouse was run by the Nith Navigation Commission and provided with oil lights and reflectors. The tower was constructed in 1749 by a local mason contracted to do so by Dumfries Town Council.[116] The tower was heightened in about 1790, according to the *Statistical Account*, but still had no light at this date.[117] From about 1826 the Nith Navigation Commission found their lighthouse expensive to run, and applied unsuccessfully to both Trinity House and the Northern Lighthouse Board for financial assistance. For the next 25 years, the Nith Navigation Commission tried to persuade the Northern Lighthouse Board to take over responsibility for the lighthouse at Southerness, but the Commissioners felt that it was poorly sited and in ramshackle condition, and the Nith Navigation Commission extinguished the light in 1867. Later in the nineteenth century maritime trade revived and the lighthouse was restored and in use from 1894; it finally ceased operating in 1936.[118]

Further north, the River Clyde upstream of Dumbarton was gradually deepened after 1750, one of the main reasons Glasgow was transformed 'from a small market-town 22 miles distant from salt water … on the banks of a shallow stream meandering through green fields, into a smoky industrial city of nearly two million persons in 1930 on a navigable channel bearing … the world's largest-drafted ocean-liners and battleships'.[119] The Firth of Clyde is 40 miles seawards from the city, but is obstructed by two small islands – Great and Little Cumbrae – which narrow the river at its estuary to just over a mile. Glasgow's Town Council appears to have seized the initiative here, and obtained an Act of Parliament in 1756 which enabled them to form the Cumbrae Lighthouse Trustees. As Hector Mackenzie has pointed out, the Trust was authorised to collect dues to enable it to improve navigation below Greenock – the first body in Britain to be enabled to do so – some 30 years before the formation of the Northern Lighthouse Board, and at a time when Trinity House had the right to erect sea-marks but no power to collect dues for their maintenance.[120] The Trust then authorised a local man, James Ewing, to build a lighthouse on the highest part of Little Cumbrae the following year.[121] This was built by late December 1757, when the minutes of the Trust state that the light was now 'kindled'. The tower itself was 30 feet high, with an iron grate for an open coal fire set on top, to burn during the hours of darkness.[122] Unfortunately, in attempting to guide ships in two parallel channels, mariners found this light was too far from either, and too high, often being obscured by the weather. In 1793 a second light was constructed by Thomas Smith at a lower level for the west channel, while the upper light was retained for the east. Shortly afterwards, at the request of sailors, the Trustees put up another

lighthouse, closer to Glasgow; this was built at Cloch Point in 1797, and the 'old' coal-fire on the summit of the island was abandoned. Cloch lighthouse (see p. 23) was constructed for the Clyde Trustees by Thomas Smith, this time with his stepson and apprentice Robert Stevenson: both lighthouses were lit with oil lamps and reflectors.[123]

### First years of the Northern Lighthouse Board

These early attempts to warn mariners of some of the worst perils along the Scottish coasts had hardly scratched the surface of the problem; and by the 1780s fishing, trade and travel had increased the amount of seaborne traffic.

Southerness lighthouse, Solway Firth, in 1959.

William Daniell, 'Lighthouse on Eilean Glas on Scalpay', from *A voyage round the North and North-West coast of Scotland and the adjacent islands: with a series of views illustrative of their character and most prominent features* (1819).

Munro cites the unremitting bad weather of 1782 which put pressure on Parliament to provide lighthouses at some of the more obvious hazards, such as the Mull of Kintyre (all shipping to and from Glasgow must pass this) and the point of Scalpay on Harris (where traffic from Liverpool must pass on its way across the North Sea to the Baltic or to the Netherlands). This pressure was not exacted through a humanitarian concern for the enormous annual loss of life at sea, but for the economic draught felt by shipowners with their loss of precious cargo. Led by George Dempster (1732-1818), Member of Parliament for Forfar and Fife Burghs, a Bill was prepared to set up a Board of Trustees (or Commissioners) with authority to build lights in four selected Scottish sites and levy dues on all passing ships, British or foreign. This is how the modern British lighthouse service is still funded, with-

out recourse to the tax-payer. It is interesting too that Dempster was a friend of, and related by marriage to, Alexander Dalrymple, and both of them had interests in developing Scottish fisheries and promoting safety at sea.[124]

With remarkable speed this Bill was made law in 1786. The early Board was thus made up of members of the legal profession, with a number of burgh officials. Initially the Trustees comprised the Lord Advocate and the Solicitor General, the Lord Provosts and the Senior Bailies of Edinburgh and Glasgow, the Provosts of Aberdeen, Inverness and Campbeltown, and the Sheriffs of Edinburgh, Lanark, Bute, Argyll, Inverness, Ross, Orkney, Caithness and Aberdeen. The Board met for the first time on 1 August 1786, to discuss the building of their first four lighthouses. The lights were to be built at Kinnaird Head near Fraserburgh, North Ronaldsay in Orkney, Eilean Glas on the Minch, and the Mull of Kintyre. The first of these to be completed was that on top of a redundant castle owned by Lord Saltoun at Kinnaird Head, lit on 1 December 1787. The others were ready under two years later.[125]

These four lights were greeted with immediate and universal praise, so much so that another Act of Parliament was passed in 1789 authorising the Commissioners of the Northern Lights (as they were now named) to put up other lighthouses on the Scottish coasts where they thought fit. Over the next few years, more lighthouses were constructed by the Board's Engineer, Thomas Smith. In 1790 a lighthouse was constructed on the island of Pladda, just off Arran, but almost immediately it had to

have a second, lower light built alongside it 'to distinguish it in the night from those on the Mulls of Kintyre, Galloway and Cumbray', as the local minister observed.[126] The Pentland Skerries lighthouse, Robert Stevenson's first work for the Northern Lighthouse Board, was constructed in 1794, in the hope of opening up the dangerous Pentland Firth, which was 'well-known,' wrote Robert Stevenson in 1818, 'for its tempestuous seas, and cross running tides; and it is only in certain directions of the wind, and a very calm state of the sea, that its lighthouse can be approached with any degree of safety'.[127] This was a shorter route for seaborne traffic than circumnavigating the entire Orkney archipelago, and a double light was

North Ronaldsay, the old beacon, photograph 1964.

The double light on Pladda, off Arran, c.1880.

provided at the eastern entrance to the Pentland Firth with two towers, one 80 feet high, the other 60 feet high and 60 feet apart (it had to be rebuilt in the 1820s).[128] We have already looked at the 'complete establishment' of the lighthouse finished at Inchkeith in the Forth in 1804, and the Board's first revolving light, installed at the new lighthouse on Start Point in Orkney, in 1806: these had input from both the elderly Thomas Smith, and increasingly more from his assistant and stepson, Robert Stevenson.

Thomas Smith had first taken Robert Stevenson as an assistant in about 1791, when the younger man was 19. Robert and his widowed mother had lived next door to the Smith family, and after Smith was left a widower for the second time, with three small children, it was not long before the neighbours married. Mrs Stevenson already knew the Smith children well, and the industrious young Robert Stevenson trained as best he could to become a civil engineer by taking practical classes at the University of Glasgow during the winter for three years, while working on lighthouse projects during the summer in the Blair Street premises. He also attended a variety of scientific classes at the University of Edinburgh. His experiences in Smith's lamp-making business allowed him to be involved in the installation of the lights at Portpatrick Harbour in 1794, and at the new Pentland Skerries lighthouse. Between 1796 and 1802 he served his apprenticeship as a tinsmith with Thomas Smith, but in fact was gaining skills and knowledge on a much broader front.[129]

Thomas Smith stepped down in favour of his apprentice from 1797, formally allowing Stevenson to become Engineer to the Northern Lighthouse Board in 1808, and continued with his business of street-lighting, with which he remained involved until standing aside to make way for his son James Smith, also in 1808. In 1804 he had built a large six-storied house in what is now Baxter's Place, near Calton Hill. Here 'it stood well back from the quiet road that led down to Leith. A ground floor side entrance opened directly into Greenside Lane: both Thomas and Robert were able to conduct the lighthouse business from there for the duration of their partnership. Thomas' manufacturing business continued in Blair Street.'[130] After Thomas Smith's death, his widow, Robert Stevenson's mother, continued to live in the house at Baxter's Place. Robert had married his step-sister Jean Smith in 1799, and they too lived in the house: altogether they had 13 children, of whom only five survived to adulthood: and the business of the family firm, together with much lighthouse work, continued to be carried out from these premises. Smith's lamp business acquired a manufacturing works in Greenside Place, just around the corner.

In the meantime, the Northern Lighthouse Board usually met in the secretary's house in the early years of the nineteenth century. This became inconvenient, and the premises at 84 George Street was first rented and then purchased by the Northern Lighthouse Board in 1832, with the Stevenson engineering firm moving into the floor above their main clients, and remaining there until just before the Second World War.[131]

The Board was not Robert Stevenson's sole patron: his engineering practice was broader than building and maintaining a lighthouse service, although many would have thought that sufficient. As Craig Mair explains, the early nineteenth century saw the growth of the engineering profession through practical expertise based on experience, although the embryonic discipline was not yet taught in the universities. Many of the older practitioners – and there were few enough of them – were based in London, and highly paid for their consultancies. Men of Robert Stevenson's generation, placed outside the metropolis, were able to respond more rapidly, and in Stevenson's case he had valuable local knowledge, especially of the Scottish coastline. As a result he was increasingly called upon to undertake an escalating amount of work across a wide spectrum of activity, including building and repairing harbours, surveying and construction of roads, bridges, canals and railways, river embankments, as well as a variety of tasks that nowadays would be the concern of an architect.[132]

The 1790s saw more extremely stormy weather around the Scottish coastline, and in particular, as Robert Stevenson was to recount,

> … a storm from the south-east, in the month of December 1799. This storm having continued with little intermission for three days; a number of vessels were driven from their moorings in the Downs and Yarmouth Roads; and these, together with all vessels navigating the German Ocean [or North Sea] at this time, were drifted upon the coast of Scotland. … But still, from dread of the Bell Rock, in the one case, and the danger of mistaking the entrance to the Frith of Dornoch for that of Moray, by taking the northern instead of the southern side of Tarbetness, in the other, a great number of vessels were lost. … It has even been reckoned, that seventy sail of ship were either stranded or lost upon the eastern coast of Scotland during that gale, when many of their crews perished.[133]

With a further casualty believed to be the Bell Rock's responsibility (HMS *York*, a 64-gun man-of-war, lost with all hands in January 1804), the Northern Lighthouse Board (as the Commissioners collectively became known) moved rapidly towards constructing a lighthouse in this most difficult and dangerous of places.[134]

Although 1787 can be seen as a significant moment in the marking and mapping of the Scottish seas with the realisation of the Board's first four lighthouses, perhaps the lighting of the Bell Rock, marking the most dangerous Inchcape Reef, can be seen as a pinnacle of engineering triumph. Except in times of war or after catastrophic accidents, the Bell Rock has been continuously lit from 1 February 1811, and it is to the story of that achievement we now turn.

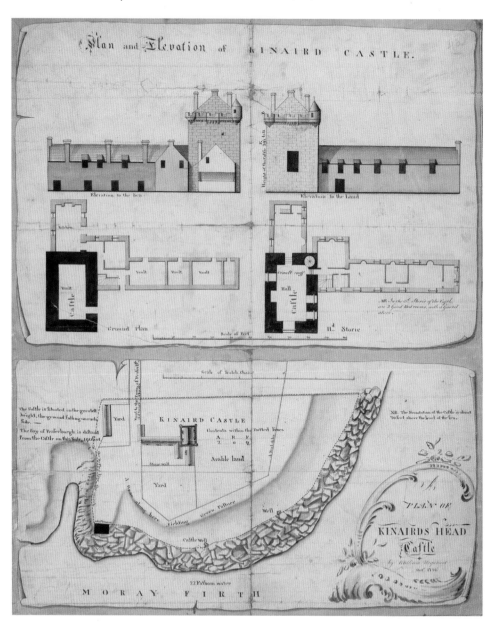

## Notes to Chapter 3

1 Munro (1979), 13.
2 Martin (1998).
3 Quoted in Ferguson (1991), 5.
4 [Duncan] (1835), 2.
5 See, for instance, an overview of the history of the Royal National Lifeboat Institution, Beilby (1992).
6 Hakluyt (1889), quoted by Ferguson (1991), 6; for Chancellor, see Taylor (1954), 170.
7 Stevenson (1988), 184.
8 Ewan (1990), 68-69.
9 Hutchinson (1994), 5-20; Greenhill and Morrison (1995), 216-55.
10 Unger (1980), 203-204.
11 McGowan (1981), 4-5.
12 Unger (1980), 216. See also Parry (1973), 76-95, Landström (1978), 90-111; Greenhill and Morrison (1995), 256-57.
13 Unger (1980), 219; Greenhill and Morrison (1995), 258-73.
14 Macdougall (1997), 223-46.
15 Macdougall (1997), 235.
16 Macdougall (1991a), 33.
17 Macdougall (1991b), 56.
18 Cameron (1996), 122-23; Cameron (1998), 131-33.
19 Cameron (1998), 228-54.
20 Taylor (1980).
21 Taylor (1980), 9.
22 Taylor (1980), 28-29; Moore (1988), 3-4.
23 Ward (2004), 32.
24 Anson (1930), 1.
25 Anson (1930), 2-3.
26 Ditchburn (1990), 84.
27 Riis (1992), 59-75.
28 Taylor (1980), 20.
29 Morrison-Low (1993), 218-31; for gravestones, see Willsher (1990).
30 Taylor (1980), 20, quoting Balfour Paul (1877-1978), IV, 302; III, 91; VI, 164; VIII, 159.
31 Morrison-Low (2002), 23-24.
32 Waters (1958), 211; Hutchinson (1994), 168; Hackmann (1994), 161; Jonkers (2003), 147-53.
33 Rule (1982), 119, 121.
34 Turner (2000), 63-65.
35 Muckleroy (1978), 108-109.
36 Muckleroy (1978), 120-25; Simpson (1990).
37 Hutchinson (1994), 180; Morrison-Low (1993), 219.
38 Hutchinson (1994), 178.
39 Taylor (1980), 21, quoting Balfour Paul (1877-1978), III, 180 and 337.
40 Waters (1958), 308-10; also Waters (1955).
41 Taylor (1980), 21, quoting Waters (1958) plate X; more information on this piece is given in [Waters

et al.], (1970), II, 33, Frontispiece, Item C.60/48-421, now NAV1697.
42 Taylor (1980), 30-35.
43 Moir (1973), I, 19.
44 Barber (1992), 35.
45 Taylor (1980) 9; more recently, a reference to an occasion in 1597 when a man named Robert Lindsay presented a sea chart of Europe, Africa, Asia and America to Aberdeen Council has produced the speculation that this Lindsay might be related to Alexander Lindsay: see Webster (2005), 6-8, quoting Stuart (1848), 158-59.
46 Moir (1973), I, 19.
47 Moir (1973), I, 9-18; see also Merriman (2004); Mayer (2004); Marshall (2004) and Warnicke (2004).
48 Taylor (1980), 38.
49 Moir (1973), I, 13.
50 Taylor (1980), 14-15.
51 Harvey (1993), 7; see also Buisseret (2003).
52 Crane (2002), xi.
53 Barber (1998a), 43; see also Barber (1998b).
54 Barber (1998a), 60.
55 Moir (1973), I, 12-16; Barber (1998a), 60-62.
56 Moir (1973), I, 14-15.
57 Barber (1998a), 66-71.
58 Crane (2002), 174-78 and note 43.
59 For Ortelius, see van den Broeke et al. (1996); Binding (2003).
60 Moir (1973), II, p.1.
61 Verner (1978); Shirley (1995), 4-5.
62 Moore (1995).
63 Baigent (2004).
64 Dated by the National Library of Scotland to c.1666, this map is Adv. MS.70.2.9 (Pont 31). For discussion of Marr and his work, see Laing (2002); see also Riis (1992), 72, 75.
65 Bray (1879), II, 400.
66 Moore (1985), 31-32.
67 Collins (1776), 28.
68 Moore (1985), 30; Moir (1973), II, p. 10.
69 Moore (1985), 30.
70 Simpson (1993), 32-36.
71 Withers (1996), 58-59; Withers (1999), 505-507.
72 For background, see Ouston (1979).
73 Anon. (1836); see also Withers (2004).
74 Moir (1973), I, p.67.
75 For Clark, see Bryden (1998-99), 18.
76 Moir (1973) I, 72-78; Withers (2001), 91-96.
77 Moore (2000), 59.
78 Withers (2004).
79 See Phillipson and Mitchison (1970); Stuart Shaw (1983); Stuart Shaw (1999). For artists, see Holloway (1989). For artisans, the telescope maker

James Short and the clockmaker Alexander Cumming are discussed by Morrison-Low (2002), 17-53.

80    Emerson (1992); Pittock and Carter (1987); Hook and Sher (1995); Daiches, Jones and Jones (1986).

81    For Scottish antiquarianism, see Piggott (1976), 133-59; Brown (1980); and Bell (1981). For Scottish science at this time, see Chitnis (1976), 124-94; Emerson (1988); and Withers and Wood (2002).

82    For Bryce, see Chambers (1835), IV, 488-93; Emerson (1979) and Emerson (1981).

83    Smith (1987), 278.

84    Moir (1973), I, 89-91; Robinson (1981); Webster (1989).

85    Moir (1973) I, 102; Robinson (1958). For Dalrymple, see Cook (2004a).

86    Marwick (1871), 275-76, 289, 295, quoted by Munro (1979), 22-23; Stevenson (1959), 25.

87    Collins (1776), 23.

88    Adair (1703).

89    Munro (1979), 24.

90    Stevenson (1959), 37-38; Eggeling (1960), 33-46; Munro (1979), 25-38.

91    Hague (1965), 465; Hague and Christie (1975), 74-75.

92    Collins (1776), 23.

93    Hague (1965), 466.

94    Munro (1979), 36-38.

95    Eggeling (1960), 37-40; Allan (2002), 25, 40-42.

96    Munro (1979), 82-84.

97    Lockhart (1878), 258; subsequently quoted in Eggeling (1960), 40; Hague and Christie (1975), 74; Munro (1979), 83 and Allan (2002), 42. Robert Stevenson's account of this was written in the year of his death, and subsequently published by his grandson, Robert Louis Stevenson (1893), 495.

98    Leslie and Paxton (1999), 28.

99    Munro (1979), 62.

100    Stevenson (1817), 11.

101    Ibid.

102    Jardine (1845), 820.

103    Collins (1776), 24.

104    Adair (1703), 14.

105    Munro (1979), 39-42.

106    Sim (1792), 243.

107    Lyell (1867), I, 508.

108    Munro (179), 61.

109    Stevenson (1816a), 176.

110    Chambers (1844), I, 115 and 233, quoting Norie (1846), 91 and 93.

111    Stevenson (1868), 543.

112    Cunningham (1885), 349.

113    Munro (1979), 231; and see http://www.scotlandsplaces.gov.uk/search_item/index.php?service=RCAHMS&id=266246

114    Munro (1979), 23, quoting Stuart (1844), 361-2; Stevenson (1959), 24.

115    Munro (1979), 85.

116    Munro (1979), 43; Stell (1984).

117    Neilson (1795), 127-28.

118    Stell (1984).

119    Stevenson (1959), 155.

120    Mackenzie (2006).

121    The Act is summarised by Blake (1956), 7.

122    Blake (1956), 9-10.

123    Stevenson (1959), 155-56; Hague (1977), 78-79; Munro (1979), 43-50.

124    Evans (2005), 145, 160; Evans makes the interesting suggestion (p. 357, ref. 13) that Dempster may have known Thomas Smith, as both were natives of Broughty Ferry.

125    Munro (1979), 51-56; Stevenson (1959), 158-61; Allardyce and Hood (1986), 10-17.

126    Hamilton (1797), 167-68.

127    Stevenson (1818), 15.

128    Munro (1979), 59.

129    Mair (178), 28-42; Leslie and Paxton (1999), 34.

130    Leslie and Paxton (1999), 18.

131    Munro (1979), 94; Leslie and Paxton (1999), 24-25.

132    Mair (1978), 97.

133    Stevenson (1824), 84.

134    Munro (1979), 68.

OPPOSITE PAGE

Chart of the East Coast of Scotland by Captain Greenvile Collins, 1689.

(NMS T.1910.45)

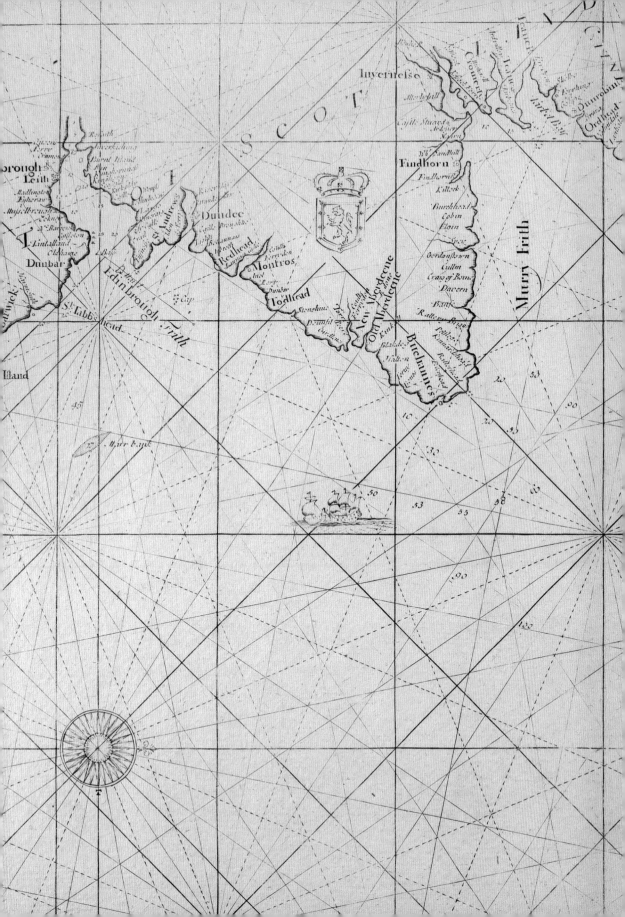

SCOT

Inverness

Findhorn

Murry Frith

Findhornne
Killock
Burghhead
Cobin
Elain
Spey
Gordanstown
Cullin
Craig of Boine
Davern
Banff
Ratterus Shlb
Fraburgh
Rosyth
Inverkithing
Burnt Island
Kinghorn
Kirkadie
Weymis
Disert
Kinkarden

Inverkithing

St Andrews

Dundee
Redhead
Montros
Lodhead
Stonehue
Drumsit

New Aberdeene
Old Aberdene
Kink
Stakake
Walton
Fraburgh
Birchunnes

Madlington
Fysheraw
Iohns
Barbony
Coleton

Linlathland
Oldham
Dunbar

St Tabbs Head

Edinbrough Frith

Cap

Island

Mur bank

45

50
53
55
58

20
30
60
90
100

10
20
30

50

60
90

100

# CHAPTER 4

# Building the Bell Rock

THE ROCKS AT Inch-cope or Inchcape were perhaps among the most feared on the east coast of Scotland, situated as they are off the Firth of Tay and about twelve miles from Arbroath, and in the path of ships crossing the North Sea from the Baltic. The reef is covered at high water to the depth of about twelve feet, and at low water of spring tides, when the ebbs are greatest; the highest point of the rock is not more than four feet above the level of the sea. At the time of the greatest ebbs it is uncovered to the extent of about 430 feet in length by 230 in breadth, but at low water of neap tides, scarcely any part of it is to be seen.[1] The whole length of the reef in a south-western direction, from the highest part, measures more than one thousand feet.[2] The sixteenth-century pilot Alexander Lindsay described it in his 'rutter' as 'betuixt Fyvisnes and the Read Head 12 milis est southest of the said Read Head lyethe a daunger called Inchcope'.[3]

Greenvile Collins marked it with dire warnings on his charts 'N' and 'P'; John Adair similarly advised that 'the Scape or Cape, is the most dangerous Riff of Rocks on all the East Coast of Scotland, and lyes right off the middle of the Entry to this Frith …'.[4]

Legend has it that the Inchcape rocks owe their present name to the pious care of an Abbot of Arbroath who placed a bell upon it, which, being rung by the motion of the wind and waves, warned seamen of the impending danger. There is also a tradition, reinforced by the nineteenth-century poet Robert Southey, of a sea pirate who, having from wantonness or cupidity carried off the bell, was afterwards shipwrecked upon the rock and he perished along with all his crew. At one time all Scottish school children could recite:

> The worthy Abbot of Aberbrothok
> Had placed that bell on the Inchcape Rock;
> On a buoy in the storm it floated and swung,
> And over the waves its warning rung.

OPPOSITE PAGE

Watercolour of the 'Bell Rock lighthouse in a storm' by J. M. W. Turner, commissioned by Robert Stevenson for his book *Account of the Bell Rock Light-House* (1824).

(© Joseph Mallord William Turner/Bell Rock Lighthouse/National Gallery of Scotland, purchased by private treaty sale, 1989, with the aid of funds from the National Heritage Memorial Fund and the Pilgrim Trust)

BELOW

Chart detail for 'The Citty of Aberdeene' showing Greenvile Collins' showing the 'Inch Cape dry of last quarter Ebb'.

(NMS T.2003.309.129)

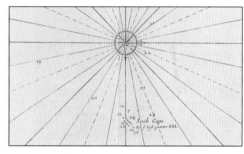

115

When the rock was hid by the surge's swell,
The mariners heard the warning bell;
And then they knew the perilous rock,
And blest the Abbot of Aberbrothok.[5]

The tale was first reported in the early seventeenth century:

> By east the Isle of May, twelve miles from all land, in the Germayne
> seas, lyes a great hidden rocke, called Inchcape, very dangerous for
> navigators, because it is overflowed everie tide. It is reported, in old
> times, upon the said rocke there was a bell fixed upon a tree or timber,
> which rang continually, being moved by the sea, giving notice to the
> saylers of the danger. This bell or clocke was put there, and maintained
> by the abbot of Aberbrothok, and being taken down by a sea pirate, a
> yeare thereafter he perished upon the same rocke with ship and goods,
> in the righteous judgement of God.[6]

Perhaps the point about the legend is that it is immaterial that it may
not be true. The effect of the rock upon the imagination was such that it
was held in superstitious dread by locals and 'foreigners' alike. Thanks
to the legend, the rock is now known as the Bell Rock, and it was here
that one of the most famous of the Northern Lighthouse Board's structures was built, engineered by Robert Stevenson (1772-1850), and
constructed in heroic circumstances from 1807 and lit in 1811.[7]

Engraved portrait of
Robert Stevenson (1772-
1850) after John Syme's
portrait, c.1840.
(NMS T.1993.105)

### Robert Stevenson and the Bell Rock

Stevenson was largely self-taught, as were most
engineers of his generation. He had, according to his
grandson Robert Louis Stevenson, been thinking
about the problem of the Inchcape reef since 1794.
He was encouraged by his friend John Clerk of
Eldin (1728-1812), the naval tactician, who had
known John Smeaton, builder of the Eddystone:

> I was fortified by an expression of my friend Mr
> Clerk in one of our conversations. 'This work',
> said he, 'is unique, and can be little forwarded
> by experience of ordinary masonic operations.
> In this case, Smeaton's "Narrative" must be the
> text-book, and energy and perseverance the
> practique'.[8]

In his own *Account of the Bell Rock Light-house ...*,
he states:

... in the summer of 1794, when on a voyage to the Northern Light-houses, in passing the Bell Rock, he [i.e. the author] directed the vessel to be brought near it, when he had an opportunity of observing the sea breaking heavily upon it. From this period, the difficulties which must attend the erection of a habitation on this rock, appeared in a stronger point of view than they had hitherto done. He, nevertheless, was resolved to embrace every opportunity of forwarding this great object.[9]

It is perhaps worth saying something about the contemporary literature concerning the Bell Rock. Robert's *Account* was dictated to his daughter Jane (later Jane Warden) and took some years to compile. Finally published in 1824, the author was by then aged 52, whereas he was an active 35 when he began construction work.[10] It was for this work, which helped to reinforce Stevenson's reputation as a giant among engineers, that he commissioned the famous watercolour 'Bell Rock in a Storm' by the foremost artist of the day, J. M. W. Turner[11] (see page 114). The frontispiece of his book was an engraving taken from this image by the Scottish artist John Horsburgh.

Stevenson, writing anonymously in the *Edinburgh Philosophical Journal* (but identified as the author of the article in the *Royal Society Catalogue of Scientific Papers*), states that 'we understand that only 240 copies were printed for sale: the circulation must therefore be very limited, and it must speedily become a scarce book'.[12] Robert Louis Stevenson himself was to write later:

I am now for many pages to let my grandfather speak for himself, and tell in his own words the story of his capital achievement. The tall quarto of 533 pages from which the following narrative has been dug out is practically unknown to the general reader, yet good judges have perceived its merit, and it has been named (with flattering wit) 'The Romance of Stone and Lime' and 'The Robinson Crusoe of Civil Engineering'. The tower was but four years in the building; it took Robert Stevenson, in the midst of his many avocations, no less than fourteen to prepare the *Account*.[13]

And Louis's 'true Monument of Robert Stevenson with a little of the moss removed' has been reprinted subsequently, and most recently in 2004.[14] Nevertheless, Robert Stevenson had certainly published earlier, less fully-detailed accounts of what was regarded as the 'Scottish Pharos', including his piece on the 'Bell Rock' issued in 1810, before the lighthouse was lit, in David Brewster's *Edinburgh Encyclopaedia*. This says very little about the creation of the building, possibly because it was still underway.[15] Roland Paxton believes a slightly later unsigned 1813 *Account* was probably his first publication on the subject. In this, the author states that 'a very minute detail seems unnecessary, because there is every reason to expect the speedy publication, by Mr Robert Stevenson, engineer, of a particular account of the whole operation, illustrated by engravings', for which readers still had to wait for over ten years.[16] This was followed by a contribution to the *Supplement to the Encyclopaedia Britannica*, issued as a part and separately in 1816, although the entire volume was not published until 1824.[17] All of these sources, from the horse's mouth as it were, were then précised, quoted, copied and repeated by newspapers, journals and magazines, keen to reflect the epic story of this heroic undertaking.[18] It is a story that continues to be told, and not only in book form: the BBC, for example, produced a docu-drama in 2003, which is frequently broadcast.[19]

The crying need to put a warning light on the Inchcape Rock had been accentuated by the loss of some 70 vessels in a particularly bad storm off the east coast of Scotland in 1799. Resistance to this idea stemmed mainly from the thought of the expense that would be necessary, as the situation was considerably more difficult than the prevailing conditions where other successful stone-built rock lighthouses – the Tour de Corduan, the Eddystone, the South Rock or Kilwarlin lighthouses – had recently been constructed or reconstructed. This resistance was gradually overcome by the undoubted expense of continually losing large amounts of valuable cargo upon a well-known but unmarked rock: and so the Northern Lighthouse Board prepared to face up to raising the costs.[20]

### Preparations, and the first year's work

According to his *Account*, Stevenson had been thinking about the problems of lighting the Bell Rock since his observations of 1794 recounted above. These had resulted in a visit two years later to a rather similar site at Kilwarlin Rock off Newcastle, County Down, in Ireland, and the construction of models – an engineer's three-dimensional way of drafting up proposals.[21] He finally managed to land on the Inchcape Reef itself in 1800:

> ... the crew being unwilling to risk their boat into any of the creeks in the rock, very properly observing that the lives of all depended on her safety, and as we could only remain on the rock for two or three hours at most, we landed upon a shelving part on the south side of the rock ....[22]

Nonetheless, this landing confirmed for him that a stone structure, on the pattern devised by Smeaton at the Eddystone Rock, was the way forward. He estimated that it would cost over £42,000, and prepared a

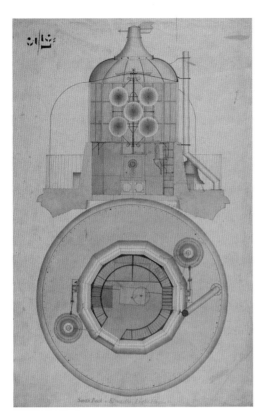

Kilwarlin, or South Rock lantern, a rock lighthouse off the Irish coast, constructed in 1797, but disused since 1877.

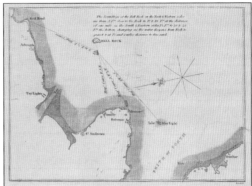

Detail of the 'Notice to Mariners', alerting them to the Floating-Light, shining from 15 September 1807.

new model and plans to persuade the Northern Lighthouse Board.

The Board were not unaware of the menace of the Bell Rock, but in the first years of the nineteenth century their powers to levy such a large sum meant that they had to return to Parliament to obtain a special Act enabling them to do so. They also consulted the most eminent engineer of his generation, John Rennie (1761-1821), whose advice coincided with Stevenson, that a stone building was the answer, along the lines of Smeaton's Eddystone lighthouse. The first attempt to secure the Act in 1803 failed, but a second attempt in 1806 was successful[23] (it became law on 21 July 1806), but it was already too late to start work that year.[24] However, levying the extra cash from mariners could only begin once a 'floating-light' was placed over the reef: for this, Stevenson acquired a Prussian fishing boat, the *Tonge Gerrit*, captured off the Dogger Bank and impounded in Leith (Britain was at war with Napoleonic France and her allies and conquests until after the victory at Waterloo in 1815). Her hull was of shallow draught and flat to allow her to sail over sandbanks, but she had to be entirely re-rigged and equipped as a light-ship, renamed the *Pharos*, for obvious reasons. As light-ships were new to Scotland, Trinity House was involved, giving advice. By July 1807, refitted, and with three lanterns, one at each masthead, she was placed over the reef and strongly anchored there.[25] Stevenson designed lanterns to encircle each mast, which could be lowered for servicing. Each lantern contained a ring of ten small agitable oil lamps, each with a cotton-thread wick, and a tiny parabolic reflector of three-inch focus.[26] A Leith-built sloop was constructed 'expressly for the Bell Rock service, to be employed as a tender for the floating-light, and as a stone-lighter for the use of the

119

work'. Named the *Smeaton*, in honour of the great lighthouse engineer, she was ready by August 1807.[27]

In the winter of 1806, preparations for building began. Material from the granite quarries of Rubislaw, Aberdeenshire, was ordered for the outer casing of the lower and solid first 30 feet of the proposed tower, while blocks of sandstone for the inside and higher parts came from Mylnefield quarry, near Dundee. At the top, the finer sandstone from Craigleith quarry, Edinburgh – from which the New Town of Edinburgh was still being constructed – was obtained. All this diverse stonework was sent to Arbroath, where these stones were cut to size and dressed, before being taken out to the rock. The Arbroath workyard was leased for seven years.[28]

Work began at the rock itself in August 1807. At this point little preparation was put towards the foundations; instead, the priority was to put up a temporary shelter of some sort, partly because most of the workers were landsmen, and staying on the *Pharos*, even in fine weather, was at best uncomfortable, but also partly in case an accident might disable the waiting boats, thus ensuring the safety of the workmen, otherwise stranded on a rock covered at high tide.

> As the work could only be proceeded with at low water of spring tides, and as three hours were considered a good tide's work, it became necessary to embrace every opportunity of favourable weather, as well in the day tides as under night by torch-light, and upon Sundays; for when the flood tide advanced upon the rock, the workmen were obliged to collect their tools and go into the attending boats, which often, not without the utmost difficulty, were rowed to the floating light, where they remained till the rock began to appear next ebb-tide.[29]

Sundays in Scotland at this time were sacrosanct: no work, no play, and depending on one's religion (and everyone had a religion), much of Sunday was spent in contemplation of the Bible. Four of the masons said from the start that they were not prepared to work on Sundays, but those who were ready to do so were rewarded with extra pay. A pep talk was given by Stevenson at the start of the project, in which he explained that he would be working Sundays 'from a conviction that it was his bounden duty, on the strictest principles of morality'. The effectiveness of this led him to comment 'that throughout the whole of the operations, it was observable that the men wrought, if possible, with more keenness upon the Sundays than at other times, from an impression that they were engaged in work of imperious necessity, which required every possible exertion'.[30]

The first year's work ended in October, by which time they had completed the workmen's beacon or barrack. This was constructed from twelve large beams of wood arranged in a 30-foot circle, rising to a 50-foot height. At the top these beams were gathered together in a point, while at their base they were attached strongly to the rock with iron batts and chains. The upper part, which in moderate weather was well above sea-level, consisting of a wooden tower several stories high, was used during working periods as a smithy, a cookhouse, and a shelter for the workmen. As the tide covered the rock, the workmen could retreat there with their tools. As the tower progressed upwards, it was then connected to the barrack by a wooden gangway which helped the workmen to transfer materials across and up inside the building.

This beacon, or temporary house, was used as a barrack for the artificers while the work was in progress, and remained on the rock until the summer of 1812, when it was removed. To the erection of this beacon, the rapidity with which the lighthouse was got up is chiefly to be ascribed; and it is extremely doubtful if it ever would have been accomplished, without some such expedient, certainly not without the loss of many lives; for in a work of this nature, continued for a series of years, it is wonderful that only one life was lost on the rock, by a fall from a rope-ladder when the sea ran high, and another at the mooring-buoys, by the upsetting of a boat.[31]

There was also the trial of landing large blocks of masonry from Arbroath, delivered by the *Smeaton*, and this had resulted in Stevenson devising a plan to place the blocks on arrival onto smaller decked praam-boats, ready to be put into place.[32] As the season wore on, the weather deteriorated. Just towards the end of it, in early October, John Rennie and his son George paid a visit to the Bell Rock.

It being then too late in the tide for landing, they remained on board of the Light-House Yacht all night, when the writer, who had now been secluded from society for several weeks, enjoyed much of Mr Rennie's interesting conversation; both on general topics and professionally upon the progress of the Bell-Rock works, on which he was consulted as chief engineer.[33]

At the end of this first season, Stevenson calculated that actual time spent on the rock, though it seemed much longer, 'amounted to about 180 hours, of which only 133 or about

13½ days, of 10 hours each, could be said to be actively employed'. He was astonished at how much had been achieved in such a short space of time, 'for the artificers wrought at the erection of the Beacon as for life; or somewhat like men stopping a breach in a wall to keep out an over-whelming flood'. By building the framework of the beacon, 'the rock had in a great measure been robbed of its terrors'.[34] Now they had to build a lighthouse.

### Operations in 1808

Stevenson visited the rock in November, checked out the floating-light, and after returning home to Edinburgh in early December ensured that preparations were well underway for 1808.[35] Work began as early as the weather would permit, and an eight-ton brand new schooner was purchased and christened the *Sir Joseph Banks* (named after the recently deceased President of the Royal Society, who had ensured Government money would be made available for the construction of the lighthouse), to take workers back to the floating-light, so they were not too fatigued by rowing through the adverse and tricky currents. 'Thus provided with a place of safety on the rock in the beacon-house, and a tender always ready in case of necessity, the work went forward even in pretty blow-ing weather, and by struggling both during day and night tides.'[36]

Cutting out and levelling the site for the foundation of the tower was extremely difficult and dangerous: there was only a small window be-tween tides for working on the uncovered rock, so nothing could be done in storms or during the winter when, in any case, daylight hours were extremely short. Each day, after the tide had dropped, they had to pump water manually out of the hole they were constructing for the foundations. But overcoming these difficulties mostly with mere muscle-power and a lot of determination – there were no pneumatic drills, no electric pumps – by early July the site of the lighthouse was cut deep into the rock and levelled out. Stevenson decided that the best way of manoeuvring the large blocks (each weighing a ton) from the various landing-places around the site, without damaging them, was to con-struct a cast-iron railway across the rock.[37] The men could thus push or pull the blocks of masonry on little trucks from the water's edge to the growing structure. Various cranes, carts and other lifting devices, also pumps and winches, were taken out to, and put together on, the rock itself. Every stone of every course had to be designed very carefully, as 'each particular stone required to be cut with accuracy, to fit its precise place in the building'.

First, the Clerk of Works drew a plan on a piece of paper, and then this was scaled up to full size and put on a platform. From the enlarged draught, James Slight, the principal mould-maker, would make full-sized moulds for a part of a particular course, which could be repeated within that course, in well-seasoned timber, numbered with oil paint. If any of the stones were lost at sea, they could be replicated in the Arbroath workyard with a minimum of fuss.[38] As with Smeaton's Eddystone, each course was assembled on a platform at the yard, before being taken out to the reef to its final destination.

Considerable thought went into the selection of building materials and mortar for the construction of the tower, and Stevenson followed Smeaton by using a system of 'oaken trenail and wedge … for fixing the stones, till the mortar [bonded], and a superincumbent weight was got upon them to prevent the sea from sweeping them away'.[39] By 4 June, 'this being the birth-day of King George III, who was now entered into the 70th year of his age, and 50th of his reign, a considerable effort was made to get the first entire course of the building laid upon the platform at Arbroath, where it was to be marked and numbered, and made ready for shipping to the Rock'. Sixty stonemasons were busy in the Arbroath workyard, and preparations were being made for building the first three courses of the lighthouse.[40] By 21 June, 58 workmen were landed on the Rock. The lighthouse's foundation stone was laid on 10 July 1808, with some considerable ceremony, some of it appropriately masonic.[41]

They worked throughout the summer, and Stevenson's record, which takes the form of a diary with detailed daily accounts of weather and progress of the works, was generally upbeat. By the end of September the second year's operations were brought to a successful conclusion with the first and heaviest courses of the carefully-dovetailed blocks having been laid, to a height of five feet six inches above the lower bed of the foundation stone. He reckoned 400 blocks weighing about 388 tons of stone had been put in place, with 738 oaken trenails and 1215 pairs of oaken wedges. They had worked about 265 hours on the rock this season, but only 80 were spent on the building. 'It was further highly satisfactory to find, that the apparatus, both in the work-yard at Arbroath, and also the craft and building apparatus at the Rock, were found to answer every purpose much beyond expectation.'[42]

The indefatigable Stevenson then set off on his annual tour of inspection by yacht around the northern lighthouses, returning to the Bell Rock for a critical inspection on 31 October. Everything portable had been removed, and taken back to the Arbroath workyard, for the dark and stormy winter, where the masons continued to prepare blocks for the following year's construction.

## Operations in 1809

In spring 1809 they returned to the reef, and were delighted to find that of the four courses built into the rock, not a single stone had shifted during the course of a long and severe winter. Two new praam-boats had been kitted out especially for work at the rock, and 'every thing being in readiness for commencing the operations, it was fully expected that the solid part would be completed in the course of the ensuing season, and the Light-house thus carried to a height of 30 feet'.[43] Before they could bring anything on to the reef, they had to provide moorings for the increased numbers of tenders and praam-boats, and reassemble the machinery to lift the stone blocks off the boats, and the cranes to take them off the railway and place them on to the building.

> Hitherto the operations of the builders were wholly confined to the low-water work. From the great exertions, however, made by the shipping department, in supplying materials this season, the builders now made rapid progress. On some occasions, no fewer than 50 blocks of stone were brought to the rock in the course of a tide; 30 of which, during the same period, were sometimes laid by the builders.[44]

The builders or artificers, as Stevenson called them, lived in the most uncomfortable circumstances, and shared these to a very large extent with the engineer. Occasionally life in the barrack could turn out to be life-threatening. He took care to mention a joiner named James Glen, who helped keep up the spirits of a damp and cold party stranded in the beacon for over 30 hours:

> In the early part of his life, he had undergone many curious adventures at sea, which he now recounted somewhat after the manner of the Tales of the Arabian Nights. When one observed that the Beacon was a most comfortless lodging, Glen would presently introduce some of his exploits and hardships, in comparison with which, the state of things at the Beacon bore an aspect of comfort and happiness. Looking to their slender stock of provisions, and their perilous and uncertain chance of speedy relief, he would launch out into an account of one of his expeditions in the North Sea, when the vessel being much disabled in a storm, was driven before the wind with the loss of almost all their provisions; and the ship being much infested with rats, the crew hunted these vermin, with great eagerness, to help their scanty allowance. By such means, Glen had the address to make his companions, in some measure, satisfied, or at least passive, with regard to their miserable prospects upon this half-tide rock in the middle of the Ocean. This incident is noticed, more particularly, to shew the effects of such a happy turn of mind, even under the most distressing and ill-fated circumstances.[45]

By early July it was noticed that for the first time the water, which was at neap tide, did not overflow the structure at high tide. Flags were raised, a three-gun salute was fired from the lighthouse yacht at high water, three cheers rang out and 'a glass of rum was then served out to all hands on the Rock, and on board of the respective ships'.[46] The building having now reached the ninth course, the guy-ropes of the ordinary type of beam-crane had become too upright, or 'taunt', and other measures would need to be taken. Stevenson had been considering this for some time, devising 'a new machine, called a Balance-crane, [which] was therefore put in preparation for the use of the works next season; in this, the upright shaft was to be retained in an erect position, by a weight acting on the opposite end of the loaded beam, which was thus to be kept *in equilibrio*'.[47]

The tower was now tall enough so that work could – in moderate weather – last as long as five or six hours, and even an hour or two after the rock itself was submerged by the tide. The beacon house was now fully occupied as a barrack and a smithy, and between this and the rising walls of the lighthouse tower, a rope-ladder connected the two.[48] On 25 August 1809, 45 stones were landed 'which completed the Twenty-fourth course, reckoning above the first entire one, and the twenty-sixth above the Rock. This finished the solid part of the building, and terminated the height of the outward casing of granite, which is 31 feet 6 inches above the Rock … and about 17 feet above high-water of spring-tides.'[49] After this event, marked 'with the usual ceremonies', the workers spent some time tidying away all movables for the winter, motivated in particular by the impending equinoctial gales, which they had experienced in previous years.

Stevenson was by now looking forward to spending the winter perfecting the balance-crane, and experimenting with the lighting. He realised that the Bell Rock's proximity to other lighthouses along the east coast would mean that in some way it should be distinguishable from its neighbours. He had already tried shades of different coloured glass in tests at Inchkeith, the island in the Forth plainly visible from Edinburgh, demonstrating to his own satisfaction that alternating red and white lights were most suitable. In due course, two opposite sides of the rotating light frame contained reflectors covered with red glass, giving the impression of a red-and-white flashing light from the lantern. He set off to inspect those at Flamborough Head, where similar lights had been recently installed, encountering a fearful storm on the way.[50]

## Operations in 1810 and lighting the Bell Rock

As with the preceding year, inspection visits went to the Bell Rock from the Arbroath workyard over the winter. The fourth season began in 1810 as early as possible, because of the difficulty of keeping building materials anywhere on the rock with the narrowing of the diameter of the rising tower, while the landing of stones was still restricted to a few hours of low water at spring tides. It was unclear at the start whether they could raise the building up to the full 70 feet in one season, but they managed to complete this by December 1810.[51] Various materials for the light-room had been ordered and the manufacture of the fittings was also underway:

> ... the sheets of silver-plated copper for the reflectors having been ordered from Messrs Boulton and Watt, – the glass from the British Plate-Glass Company, – the cast-iron sash-frames from Mr John Patterson of the Edinburgh Foundry, – while the construction of the reflectors and reflecting-apparatus, together with the framing of the whole Light-room and its appurtenances, were executed under the immediate directions of Mr Thomas Smith, the writer's predecessor, who had now retired from the more active duties of engineer to the Lighthouse Board.[52]

The rope-ladder connecting the beacon to the tower was to be replaced this season by a timber bridge or gangway, and its strength enabled materials to be brought up on it.[53] By early May the balance-crane parts had arrived at Arbroath, ready to be installed on top of the tower. Stevenson first fixed the position of the entrance door into the tower, at the opposite side to the strongest growth of sea-weed, which indicated the direction of the heaviest seas: so it was placed facing south-west.[54] The balance-crane was assembled, the gangway put in place and loads of stones were brought out to the rock as in previous years. After some repairs, the workers were once again able to lodge in the beacon. By 22 May, the 35th course had been completed. The interior walls of the structure (now standing at 45 feet high) were diminishing from their original seven-feet thickness at the entrance, to the one-foot thickness further up, so that the courses could be completed more rapidly. By 5 June the 38th course was completed, and the walls were three feet two inches thick. As Stevenson explains:

> The floor-courses of the Bell Rock Light-house lay horizontally upon the walls ... they consisted in all of 18 blocks, but only 16 were laid in the first instance, as the centre-stone[s] were necessarily left out, to

allow the shaft of the balance-crane to pass through the several apartments of the building. In the same manner also, the stone which formed the interior side of the man-hole, was not laid till after the centre stone was in its place, and the masonry of the walls completed. ... The floors of the Edystone Light-house, on the contrary, were constructed of an arch-form, and the haunches of the arches bound with chains, to prevent their pressing outward, to the injury of the walls. ... The writer foresaw many advantages that would arise, from having the stones of the floors to form part of the outward walls without introducing the system of arching: in particular, the pressure of the floors upon the walls would thus be perpendicular.[55]

This cantilevered and bonded floor design, rather than the flat-arched floors used by Smeaton, was an innovation subsequently much used in rock lighthouse construction.[56]

By early July the workers had reached the 68th course on the tower, and reduced their numbers to 22 because of lack of space on the top of the building. Stevenson went to Edinburgh to find out how the apparatus for the light-room was progressing, and found that most of it was in a state of 'considerable forwardness', and the bell-founders Thomas Meirs & Son of London stated that they would cast the pair of fog-warning bells at a week's notice.[57] By 16 July the 81st course was laid. This was of twelve stones of Craigleith quarry sandstone, and had a groove for an iron ring set around the edge, to act as added support for the weight of the cornice above it. Despite stormy weather the next nine courses were laid, and on 30 July the final, 90th, course was completed, bringing the height of the tower to 102 feet six inches.[58]

In early August the eight sash-frames of the light-room were placed on the balcony, and the balance-crane was dismantled and taken down. On 29 September the final stone was put in place, with some ceremony. Then the light-room had to be fitted up and a considerable amount of completion works undertaken. On 8 December some final adjustments were made: James Dove, smith, came to put together the frame for the reflectors, 24 in all; James Clark, an eminent Edinburgh clock-maker, had made and was there to regulate the revolving machinery for the lights (this also rang the warning bells in foggy weather); and John Forrest, from the Northern Lighthouse Board, was there to ensure that lamps and reflectors were correctly adjusted.[59] Apparently the Scottish reflectors were plated so thickly that they could afford the loss of silver through cleaning, and thus gave long service. The metallic silver was recovered by collecting and burning the cleaning cloths.[60] They were also set up using a gauge, which ensured that the lamp – and thus the beam – was always set up correctly after cleaning.[61] It is unclear whether many gauges of this type have survived. However, one survival (initially owned by the Stevenson firm, and now in National Museums Scotland) is a device which can set a series of reflectors on a frame for a fixed light (not a revolving light, such as the one at the Bell Rock). 'In fixed lights,' wrote Alan Stevenson, 'it is necessary, in order to approach as near as possible to an equal distribution of the light over the horizon, to place the reflectors, with their axes inclined to each other, at an angle somewhat less than that of the divergence of the reflected cone [of light]'.[62] The instrument is signed by Adie & Son, Edinburgh, and was made for the Stevenson firm.[63]

Clark and Dove left the rock on 27 December, leaving Forrest and four keepers – Reid, Bonnyman, Leask and Fortune – 'in possession of the Light-house'.[64] They were effectively marooned there in bad weather until 29 January, when they were found to be safe and well, and provided with new stores. So the lantern was illuminated for the first time on 1 February 2011. The floating-light vessel was then unmoored and removed.[65] Stevenson reckoned that the flashing light, with its distinctive red and white signature, could be seen from about 35 miles, depending on the state of the atmosphere.[66]

Brass gauge to ensure that reflectors are correctly set at the right angle on a frame, made by Adie & Son, Edinburgh. Presented by D. Alan Stevenson. (NMS T.1958.50)

In background, fig. 41 from Alan Stevenson, *Account of the Skerryvore Lighthouse, with Notes on the Illumination of Lighthouses* (Edinburgh and London, 1848).

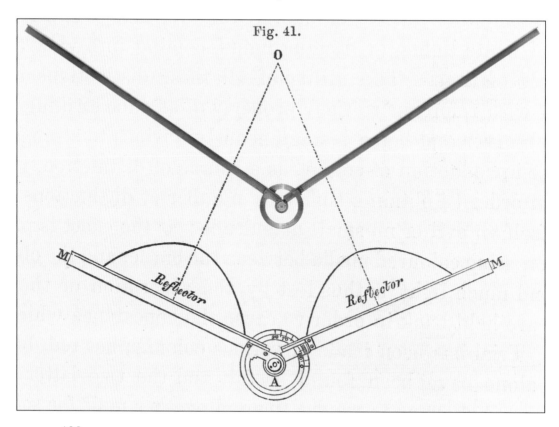

Fig. 41.

128

## The Bell Rock lighthouse, as first constructed

Stevenson's *Account* states on the title page that it was 'drawn up by the desire of the Commissioners of the Northern Light-Houses', and thus it concludes with a number of appendices, demonstrating to a Governmental body that those who paid light dues had obtained (as we might say) 'value for money'. The entire edifice had cost £61,331 9s 2d, perhaps £20,000 more than the original estimates.[67] Nonetheless, the contemporary anonymous contributor to the *Edinburgh Annual Register* was moved to write:

> The expence … is supposed to amount to about fifty-five thousand pounds sterling. Whether, therefore, we consider the magnitude of this most useful work, or the success which has attended the operations, from their commencement in 1807 till their completion in 1810, this work will be found to do equal honour to the spirited exertions of the Hon. Board of Commissioners for Northern Lights, to the talents, activity, and perseverance of the engineer, and to the resources of a country which, while struggling with unparalleled difficulties in the field of war, yet enjoying the most perfect security at home, is able and ready to pursue the works of industry, and to attend to the calls of humanity.[68]

Unlike Smeaton's Eddystone lighthouse, which was stepped into the rock, the Bell Rock lighthouse's foundations are almost on a level with the sea when it is at low water of ordinary spring tides, and thus at high water the building is covered for its first 15 feet. The first two masonry courses are dovetailed and joined to each other, resembling 'nothing so much as the pieces of a dissected map, forming one connected mass from the centre to the circumference. The successive layers of stone are also attached to each other by joggles of stone.'[69] The cement used – based on Smeaton's experience – was a mixture of pozzolano, earth, lime and sand, in equal proportions.

The ground course measures 42 feet in diameter, and as it rises the tower diminishes to a thickness of 13 feet. The masonry stretches up for 100 feet, but including the original light-room, a further 15 feet was added. After the first solid 30 feet, the entrance door was reached by a ladder with wooden steps: 'Strangers are carried up and down by a chair and crane.' (Visitors today wear hard-hats, steel-toe capped boots, and use a harness climbing the vertical iron ladder to the entrance.) At first the walls are seven feet thick, and they diminish further up to a mere foot. Between the entrance doorway to the lantern at the top, there were originally six flats, or single apartments, each reached from the one

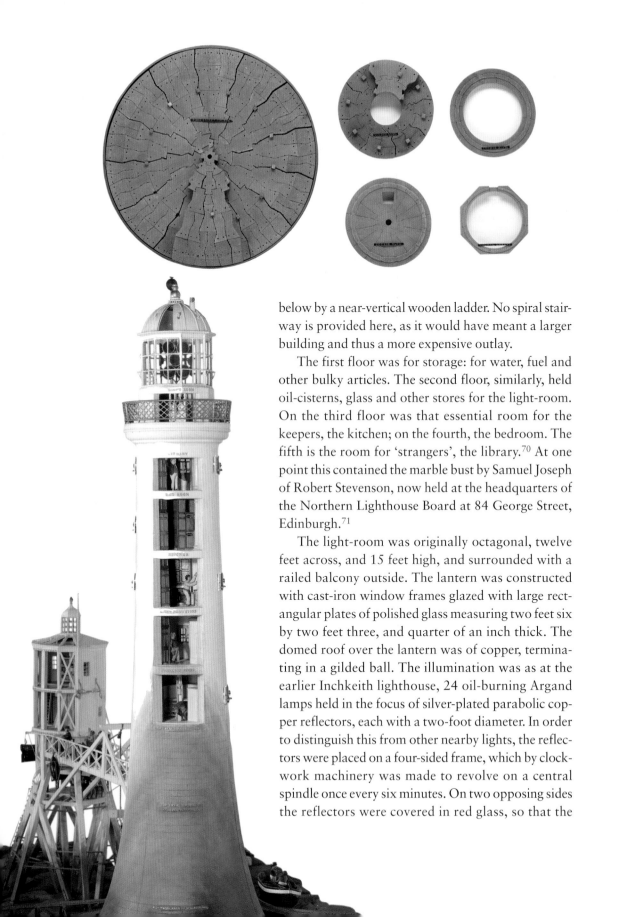

below by a near-vertical wooden ladder. No spiral stair-way is provided here, as it would have meant a larger building and thus a more expensive outlay.

The first floor was for storage: for water, fuel and other bulky articles. The second floor, similarly, held oil-cisterns, glass and other stores for the light-room. On the third floor was that essential room for the keepers, the kitchen; on the fourth, the bedroom. The fifth is the room for 'strangers', the library.[70] At one point this contained the marble bust by Samuel Joseph of Robert Stevenson, now held at the headquarters of the Northern Lighthouse Board at 84 George Street, Edinburgh.[71]

The light-room was originally octagonal, twelve feet across, and 15 feet high, and surrounded with a railed balcony outside. The lantern was constructed with cast-iron window frames glazed with large rect-angular plates of polished glass measuring two feet six by two feet three, and quarter of an inch thick. The domed roof over the lantern was of copper, termina-ting in a gilded ball. The illumination was as at the earlier Inchkeith lighthouse, 24 oil-burning Argand lamps held in the focus of silver-plated parabolic cop-per reflectors, each with a two-foot diameter. In order to distinguish this from other nearby lights, the reflec-tors were placed on a four-sided frame, which by clock-work machinery was made to revolve on a central spindle once every six minutes. On two opposing sides the reflectors were covered in red glass, so that the mariner saw white lights flashing alternately with red ones. In an early attempt to provide warning in foggy weather, two large bells were tolled day and night by the same train of machinery that rotated the lights.[72]

Four men manned the lighthouse: a Principal Lightkeeper, Principal Assistant and two others, three of whom were always at the light, while one was ashore with his family at Arbroath. The reason for these numbers is the ghastly story of an unfortunate early keeper at the Eddystone, as recounted by John Smeaton:

> It seems that for many years after the establishment of this Lighthouse, it was attended by two men only; and indeed the duty required no more; as the principal part of that, besides keeping the windows of the lantern clean (and in general the rooms) was the alternately watching four hours, and four hours, to snuff and renew the candles; each at the conclusion of his watch taking care to call the other and to see him on duty before he himself retired: but it happened, that one of the men was taken ill and died; and notwithstanding the Edystone Flag was hoisted, yet the weather was such for some time, as to prevent any boat from getting so near the rocks as to speak to them. In this dilemma, the living man found himself in an awkward situation; being apprehensive that if he tumbled the dead body into the sea, which was the only way in his power to dispose of it, he might be charged with murder; this induced him for some time to let the dead corpse lie, in hopes that the boat might be able to land and relieve him from the distress he was in. By degrees the body became so offensive, that it was not in his power to get quit of it without help; for it was near a month before the attending boat could effect a landing; and then it was not without the greatest difficulty that it could be done, when they did land. To such a degree was the whole building filled with the stench of the corpse, that it was all they could do to get the dead body disposed of and thrown into the sea; and it was some time after that, before the rooms could be got freed from the noisome stench that was left. This induced the proprietors to employ a third man; so that in case of a future accident of the same nature, or in the sickness of either, there might be constantly one to supply the place.[73]

However, on rock stations cared for by the Northern Lighthouse Board, even three men was not enough.

At Arbroath, a shore station was put up during

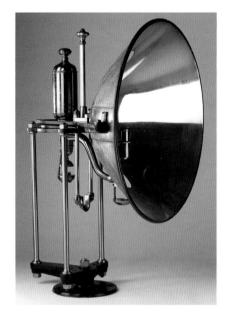

131

1813, fairly close to the workyard and the harbour. Each keeper's family had three rooms, while above it was the signal-tower: in the room at the top, a five-foot achromatic telescope on a stand was placed. A flag-staff with a copper signal ball, 18 inches in diameter, was placed on the roof. With this, and another at the lighthouse, communication was kept with the shore station. The copper ball at the lighthouse was raised between 9 am and 10 am to indicate that all was well (between 1 pm and 2 pm if the early morning haar or sea-mist gave poor visibility). If the ball at the rock remained down, the lighthouse tender immediately put to sea, to find out if a keeper had been taken ill, or some crucial part of the provisions

had run low.[74] The keepers generally spent six weeks on the rock and a fortnight ashore; but during winter months this was dependent on the state of the tides and the weather, and sometimes keepers would be there for a period of three months without relief. On those occasions, carrier pigeons would be released from the lighthouse, with messages attached to their feet.[75]

One of the characters long remembered with some affection was Bassey the horse, owned by the carter James Craw. Using the adapted Woolwich sledge, Craw and his gigantic beast carted the blocks of stone sent from the various quarries up from Arbroath Harbour to the workyard, and then after these had

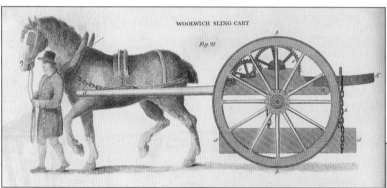

ABOVE: From Stevenson's *Account*, Plate X, 'Certain implements' [detail showing Bassey], fig. 21.

RIGHT: A detail from Stevenson's *Account*, Plate XII, 'Arbroath Harbour and plans and elevation of Signal Tower'.

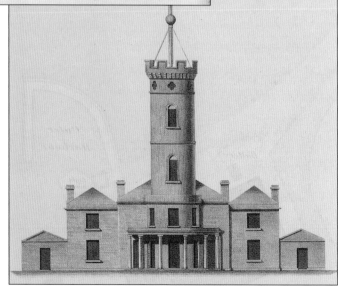

132

been cut to size and shape, and dressed by the stonemasons, took them back down again to the harbour for transporting out to the rock. In July 1810 Craw and Bassey were taken to Edinburgh, where they processed in style through the city and down Leith Walk to the port with the final principal stone for the lighthouse on the cart; both man and beast wearing coloured bows and streamers. The stone was ceremonially taken aboard the *Smeaton*, the entire public relations exercise provoking enormous interest.[76] It was calculated that the horse – an extremely large specimen – had carried the entire weight of the lighthouse at least twice, and after the completion of this mammoth task it was sent to spend the rest of its days in well-earned retirement out to grass on the island of Inchkeith. After Bassey died in 1813, Dr John Barclay (1758-1826), the famous Edinburgh anatomist, prepared and displayed the horse's skeleton in his own personal museum. In 1922 it was transferred to St Andrews University's Bell-Pettigrew Museum, where it can still be seen.[77]

Robert Stevenson's great-grandson, lighthouse historian D. Alan Stevenson, summed up his ancestor's achievement thus:

> The completion of the tower in 4 seasons was due to careful planning, ready improvisation and the continuous employment of comparatively large numbers of men and much shipping. ... This was the last sea-tower erected before steam-vessels were available to transport building materials. Today [1959], unaltered and without having required repair, it stands on the Inchcape Reef, serving its original purpose.[78]

## ... and afterwards

The question which remains, and has to be addressed by all who write about the Bell Rock, is – who was its engineer, Robert Stevenson or John Rennie? While the elder John Rennie was alive (he died in 1821, before Stevenson's *Account* had appeared), nothing was said publicly, although Rennie wrote to Matthew Boulton in Birmingham in March 1814:

> When the Bell Rock Lighthouse was erected, Stevenson was employed to superintend the whole. A regular head mason and carpenter were employed under him. The original plans were made by me, and the work was visited by me from time to time during its progress. When the work was completed, Stevenson considered that he had acquired sufficient knowledge to start as a civil engineer, by writing and applying wherever he thought there was a chance of success.
>
> He assumed the merit of applying coloured glass to lighthouses, of which [Joseph] Huddart was the actual inventor, and I have no doubt that he will also assume the whole merit of planning and erecting the Bell Rock Lighthouse, if he has not already done so. I am told that few weeks pass without a puff or two in his favour in the Edinburgh papers.[79]

Samuel Smiles (1812-1904) from East Lothian, like Rennie, wrote about the Bell Rock in his bestselling series *The Lives of the Engineers* under the achievements of John Rennie:

> Notwithstanding the facts which we have stated, showing that Mr Rennie acted throughout as the chief engineer of the lighthouse – that he settled the design, arranged the details of the building, recommended the kind of materials to be used down even to the mode of mixing the mortar, and from time to time made various alterations and

modifications in the plans of the work during its progress, with the sanction of the Commissioners – his name has not usually been identified with the erection of this structure; the credit having been almost exclusively given to Mr Robert Stevenson, the resident engineer, arising, no doubt, from the circumstance of Mr Rennie being in great measure ignored in the 'Account of the Bell Rock Lighthouse', afterwards published by that gentleman. ...

During Mr Rennie's lifetime various paragraphs were published in the Edinburgh papers, claiming for Mr Stevenson the sole credit of having designed and erected the lighthouse. At this he [Mr Rennie] was naturally annoyed; and the more so when he learnt that Mr Stevenson was about to 'write a book' on the subject. 'I have no wish,' he said, in a letter to a friend, 'to prevent his writing a book. If he details the truth fairly and impartially, I am satisfied. I do not wish to arrogate to myself any more than is justly my due, and I do not want to degrade him. If he writes what is not true, he will only expose himself.' ... The volume, however, was not published until three years after Mr Rennie's death; and it was not, we believe, until the appearance of Sir John's work on Breakwaters, that his father's claims as chief and responsible engineer of the lighthouse were made public.[80]

As Smiles says, it was John Rennie's son, Sir John Rennie (1794-1874), also an engineer, who ignited the long-running controversy in 1848 in his book on the Plymouth Breakwater by stating that his father had 'designed and built' the Bell Rock lighthouse.[81] The argument erupted the following year into the columns of the *Civil Engineer and Architect's Journal* between Rennie's son and the sons of Robert Stevenson, Alan and subsequently David.[82] Later Robert Stevenson's great-grandson devoted an entire appendix to 'The Bell Rock: its Designer and Constructor' to vindicate his ancestor's position. Roland Paxton was to write, '... the issue was still very much alive at the time of D. Alan's death in 1971. On several times both he and the late James Rennie FICE urged the author [Paxton] that if he ever wrote about this matter he should make it very clear that it was their forefather who designed and built the lighthouse!'[83] Paxton, a civil engineer himself, goes on to make the case for both men, and there is much to be said on both sides. Like Craig Mair, he points out that the success of the Bell Rock lighthouse 'enabled Robert, from 1811, to establish within a decade, an indigenous civil engineering practice of sufficient importance to make modest inroads even into the work of the London based practices of Telford and Rennie. The firm which he founded, with changes of partners from time to time, practised continuously until 1952'. Perhaps Robert Stevenson's acute drive and ambition were what was necessary, as Bella Bathurst has suggested. He thought well ahead of events, and he had sufficient confidence in himself to believe that the Bell Rock would make his name, even before the initial survey of the Inchcape Reef. That he was eventually proved correct is commendable, but it does not make him a more congenial character.[84]

In that 1814 lighthouse tour, to which we have already referred, Walter Scott 'watched ... the revolving motion of the now distant Bell Rock light until the wind grew rough, and the landsmen sick. To bed at eleven, and slept sound.' The following day, 30 July, he was

> ... waked at six by the steward; summoned to visit the Bell-Rock, where the beacon is well worthy of attention. Its dimensions are well known; but no description can give the idea of this slight, solitary, round tower, trembling amid the billows, and fifteen miles from Arbroath, the nearest shore. The fitting up within is not only handsome, but elegant. All work of wood (almost) is wainscot; all hammer-work brass; in short, exquisitely fitted up. You enter by a ladder of rope, with wooden steps, about thirty feet from the bottom, where the mason-work ceases to be solid, and admits of round apartments. The lowest is a store-room for the people's provisions, water, &c.; above that as storehouse for the lights, of oil, &c; then the kitchen of the people, three in number; then their sleeping chamber; then the saloon or parlour, a neat little room; above all, the lighthouse; all communicating by oaken ladders, with brass rails, most handsomely and conveniently executed. Break-fasted in the parlour.

Lockhart's footnote at this point states that 'on being requested, while at breakfast, to inscribe his name in the album of the tower, Scott penned immediately the following lines:

> 'PHAROS LOQUITUR
> Far in the bosom of the deep,
> O'er these wild shelves my watch I keep;
> A ruddy gem of changeful light,
> Bound on the dusky brow of night,
> The seaman bids my lustre hail,
> And scorns to strike his timorous sail.'

'On board again at nine,' Scott continues, 'and run down, through a very rough sea, to Aberbrothock. All sick, even Mr Stevenson. God grant that this occur seldom!'[85] Robert Stevenson leaves out this last rather unpleasant novelistic detail, both in his *Account* and in his much later *Reminiscences*, although one wonders what use his grandson might have made of it.[86]

In 1842 new reflecting apparatus was installed where the strength of the red and white beams were equalised, and the original apparatus was sent to Newfoundland, to be placed in a new lighthouse then under construction at Cape Bonavista.[87] This lighthouse, completed in 1843, was the third to be built on the treacherous coast of Newfoundland, and was replaced in 1966, with the original wooden structure now preserved as a historic monument. Its original lights from the Bell Rock were replaced there in 1892 by other carefully-tended, but undoubtedly well-used Scottish reflectors. These had been installed new on the Isle of May, when the Northern Lighthouse Board's building was first completed in 1816, and they were subsequently sent out to Harbour Grace Island in 1837, when Alan Stevenson was experimenting with new dioptric lenses. In all, three sets of Argand burners and parabolic reflectors were sent out to Canada from Scotland in the 1830s and 1840s: those from Inchkeith (1804) went to Cape Spear (1836); those from the Isle of May (1819) to Harbour Grace Island (1837); and those from the Bell Rock (1811) to Cape Bonavista (1843). The emerging Newfoundland lighthouse service, with little enough funding, was prepared to accept the tried and tested Scottish lighting mechanisms as perfectly satisfactory for their needs. The original Bell Rock lights no longer survive, but those from the Isle of May can still be seen at the restored Cape Bonavista lighthouse.[88]

In about 1877 the Bell Rock lighting apparatus was converted to use paraffin instead of colza oil as an illuminant, and in 1890 the two original fog-bells were replaced by a tonite, which was an explosive fog-signal made from gun cotton and barium nitrate. However, this was not without risk: on 5 April that year one of these charges detonated prematurely, damaging the windows of the lantern and the optic itself. The light failed to shine for the next week while it was being repaired: the first time it had not shone since 1811.[89]

In 1902 a new lantern, in D. Alan Stevenson's view 'perhaps unnecessarily large', was set upon the Bell Rock tower to continue the sending of red and white beams of light through the best optical apparatus manufactured at that time: this was one of the hyper-radiant lights devised by the Stevensons, and which is discussed in chapter 6. It had equiangular prisms and a focal distance of 1330 millimetres, and was exhibited at the 1901 Glasgow Exhibition before being installed.[90] Its setting up was discussed by one of the keepers, James Maclean Campbell, who served at the Bell Rock between 1895 and 1904 for a total of eight years and ten-and-a-half months. His passion was natural history, but he happened to witness the installation of the new lens and lighting machinery in July 1902:

On the evening of Sunday 27th our new light was exhibited for the first time, the coveted honour of 'first light' falling in the ordinary routine of duty to the writer. The new apparatus – a bewildering arrangement of massive glass prisms – is in striking contrast with its predecessor, the old reflector system, by the way, now almost obsolete. The following description of the new light is copied from an engraved plate affixed to the new apparatus: – 'Combined hyper-radiant and 1st order apparatus, with equiangular dioptric elements and catadioptric back prisms; power of red flash and white flash equalised. White and red flashing light, showing white and red flashes alternately every half minute, the period being one minute. Designed Messrs Stevenson, Civil Engineers, Edinburgh. Contractors, Messrs Steven & Struthers, Glasgow, and Messrs Société Des Establissements Henry Lepaute, Paris. David A. Stevenson, Engineer to the Board. Apparatus makes one revolution in one minute – 1901.'[91]

Campbell further described the new installation:

The machine – an exaggerated form of clockwork – is driven by a weight of 400 lbs travelling in the centre of the spiral stair of the first flat. The speed of the machine is regulated by adjustable fans; and a speed indicator, furnished with an alarm bell intimates the periods of winding – an operation necessitating two minutes' stiff winding every half-hour. The entire lens, with its supporting carriage, is estimated to weigh about six tons. The lamp ... is placed upon an iron pedestal in the centre of the platform or service table, as it is called, in the interior of the lens. It is fitted with what is known as the stepped Doty burner, and carries six concentric wicks, each slightly elevated above the other towards the centre. The burner is six inches in diameter, and consumes paraffin oil at the rate of eighteen gills per hour. To maintain this supply, a forty gallon tank of polished brass is placed on the light room floor; and a small force pump, with triple plungers, working in conjunction with the revolving machinery, maintains a constant supply of oil, which is kept cool by circulating within an inch of the burning edge of the wicks, the surplus oil returning to the pump-tank. The flash, on being transmitted through the lens, is reckoned to be equal to 60,000 candles; and the characterisation of the light – a red and white flash alternately every half-minute – visible twenty miles distant.[92]

This lens was removed in 1962 and replaced with the 1875 optics from Chicken Rock, Isle of Man, which was being automated. At the same time, the paraffin vapour burner was replaced with a single 3500 watt electric light bulb, producing a single white flash every three seconds that was visible for 28 miles. Part of the hyper-radiant optic is still on display at the Arbroath Signal Tower.

The lights around the United Kingdom were turned out for the duration of both World Wars (see in chapter 7), except when instructions
came from the Admiralty to light the seas for passing Allied convoys.
Keepers were not supposed to report enemy movements, in order to
remain 'neutral'. During the First World War, in October 1915, the
captain of HMS *Argyll*, a Devonshire Class Armoured Cruiser (10,850
tons) radioed a routine request to the Admiral at Rosyth – the main
Scottish naval base – asking that the Bell Rock lighthouse be lit on the
night of 27-28 October for safe passage. Unfortunately, the lighthouse
had no radio at this time (wireless telephone was not installed until
1935), and all messages had to be delivered by boat; heavy seas made
this impossible, so the message was never delivered, and the *Argyll* ran
aground. She sank, but fortunately all of her 655 crew were rescued
without casualty.[93]

During the Second World War, the light was again extinguished for
the duration, but this did not render it immune from enemy action. In
April 1940 an explosive shell was dropped on the rock, close enough to
cause a number of lantern panes to break.[94] At the end of October 1940,
the press reported that the lighthouse had been machine-gunned:
'Following the attack on the lighthouse, people on the mainland saw
what they took to be a "dog-fight" between two heavy bombers – one
British and the other German. The sound of firing was heard and soon
British fighter aircraft joined in the combat, the outcome of which
could not be ascertained from the shore.'[95] This was not the only enemy
attack on the lighthouse – it happened again on 30 March and 5 April
1941 – but fortunately (unlike other stations) there were no fatalities.

This was sadly not the case in December 1955, when there was a
helicopter tragedy at the lighthouse. Training flights from nearby RAF
Leuchars regularly passed the light and had begun – when the weather
was favourable – to drop newspapers and magazines in a friendly though
unofficial gesture. However, on 14 December the weather was sufficiently inclement for the lightkeepers to remain indoors and the air-
men decided to drop their gifts on to the lantern. But something went
wrong, and the helicopter hit the lantern, plunging onto the rock below.
Incredibly, the lightkeepers were unharmed, and scrambled down to
the entrance doorway, 30 feet above the rock. The heavy seas rapidly
claimed the wrecked helicopter which was carried away into deep
water: none of its crew had survived. The lantern was damaged slightly,
and the light extinguished for a week.[96]

In July 1962 it was announced that the paraffin light and cartridge-
operated fog-signal at the Bell Rock lighthouse, the tonite mentioned
above, now the last of its type in Scotland, were to be replaced with

'electrical installations', and at the same time the living quarters were to be 'modernised'. This renovation would take some time, because of the inaccessibility of the situation, but nevertheless 'the light of 392,000 candle-power shows white and red alternately every 60 seconds and is visible for 15 miles'.[97]

A fire in the kitchen towards the top of the lighthouse trapped the three keepers in September 1987, who were below, and unable to get to the extinguishers which were above. The radio melted in the searing heat, and the men went below, sealing the kitchen area off. The Arbroath lifeboat was launched and stood off the rock, but because of the force 6 winds, it was felt safer to winch the men off the rock by helicopter from nearby RAF Leuchars. All three keepers were successfully rescued without injury.[98] This fire was so severe that it delayed plans for automation, which did not occur until October 1988, since when the light has been monitored from the Northern Lighthouse Board headquarters at 84 George Street, Edinburgh. A further conversion process in 1999 included installation of solar panels around the lantern gallery, providing power for batteries for rotating the optics, powering the 'racon' (radar beacon), the radio monitor and the light.

Nonetheless, maintenance inspections occur at least twice a year to ensure that the light will shine regardless, for the Inchcape Reef remains a hazard to shipping. It is not a pleasant place, even on a calm and beautiful day, with the shores of Angus, Fife and East Lothian glowing warmly in the sunshine. Although the Bell Rock lighthouse shines out every night as a friendly warning beacon, as R. W. Munro wrote, with feeling: 'Those who know it most intimately say that the best view of the Bell Rock is over the stern of a ship.'[99]

Bell Rock fog-bell with inscription 'Thomas Mears [*sic*] & Son of London fecit 1810'.

(© Angus Council. Licensor www.scran.ac.uk)

139

1. 'Neap tides' are the minimum tides when the Sun's attraction is pulling contrary to that of the Moon; 'spring tides' are the maximum tides when the Sun's attraction is pulling in conjunction with that of the Moon: *Collins English Dictionary* (1972).
2. Description from Chambers (1844), I, 86; derived from Stevenson (1824), 69-71.
3. Taylor (1980), 48.
4. Collins (1776), 23; Adair (1703), 13.
5. Robert Southey, 'The Inchcape Rock' (1802), vv. 3 and 4, quoted by Allardyce and Hood (1986), 21.
6. Monipennie (1612), 155, quoted in [Duncan] (1835), 65-66.
7. Stevenson (1824); Stevenson (1959), 299-304; Mair (1978), 63-94; Munro (1979), 66-81; Leslie and Paxton (1999), 34-39; Bathurst (1999), 66-105. Much of what is said here is drawn from these sources.
8. Stevenson (1912a), 93, quoted in Munro (1979), 69.
9. Stevenson (1824), 90.
10. Leslie and Paxton (1999), 29; Bathurst (1999), 106-108.
11. Hamilton (1998), 89-91; Campbell (1999), 91-92.
12. Stevenson (1825), 18. The copy in the NMS library was acquired in 1880, and has been rebound, losing the numbering information.
13. Stevenson (1912a), 98. RLS elsewhere cites the *Account* as 'the Robinson Crusoe of engineering', but without naming the source: Stevenson (1893), 494. In fact, it was RLS's boyhood hero, R. M. Ballantyne (1865), 40.
14. Stevenson (1912a), 99; Stamp (2004).
15. Stevenson (c.1810); for dates of publication of the parts of this, see Sherborn (1937).
16. Stevenson (1813), 65.
17. Stevenson (1816a); Leslie and Paxton (1999), 176-77.
18. For example, Anon. (1811); Chambers (1844), I, 86-88; Ballantyne (1865).
19. 'Seven Wonders of the Industrial World – Bell Rock Lighthouse'; the book of the same name was produced at the same time: Cadbury (2003), 63-106.
20. Munro (1979), 66-67.
21. For this lighthouse, disused since 1877, see Hague and Christie (1975), 128.
22. Stevenson (1824), 91.
23. Ibid., 92-106; Munro (1979), 66-67.
24. 46 Geo. III c 57.
25. Stevenson (1824), 107-15.
26. Stevenson (1959), 77.
27. Stevenson (1824), 115-16.
28. Ibid., 115; 196-99.
29. Anon. (1811), 545.
30. Stevenson (1824), 135.
31. Stevenson (1813), 68; Stevenson (1824), 107-84.
32. Stevenson (1824), 143-46.
33. Ibid., 179.
34. Ibid., 180.
35. Ibid., 184.
36. Anon. (1811), 545.
37. Stevenson (1824), 189-90.
38. Ibid., 194-95.
39. Ibid., 196-205.
40. Ibid., 220-21.
41. Ibid., 236-38.
42. Ibid., 254-55.
43. Ibid., 265.
44. Stevenson (1825), 26.
45. Stevenson (1824), 279-80.
46. Ibid., 295.
47. Stevenson (1825), 26-27. Paxton (2004) attributes the invention of the balance crane and the design of the barrack as built to the fireman millwright Francis Watt.
48. Ibid., 27.
49. Stevenson (1824), 309.
50. Ibid., 309-12; 321-22.
51. Stevenson (1825), 27.
52. Stevenson (1824), 321.
53. Ibid., 323-24.
54. Ibid., 323-24.
55. Ibid., 345.
56. Stevenson (1959), 221; Paxton (2004).
57. Stevenson (1824), 366. These were each 5 cwt in weight: Renton (2001), 4. One survives at the Signal Tower Museum, Arbroath (Inv. A1976.36): see http://www.scran.ac.uk/database/record.php?usi=000-000-193-120C&scache=3ma2hlvg1z&searchdb=scran. For the history of the bell-founders, Thomas Meirs & Son, see www.british-history.ac.uk/report.aspx?compid=22170
58. Stevenson (1824), 371-77.
59. Ibid., 387-400.
60. Stevenson (1959), 284.
61. Stevenson (1848), 226.
62. Ibid., 230.
63. Stevenson (1824), 402.
64. Ibid., 402.
65. Ibid., 403-404.
66. Ibid., 527.
67. Ibid., 423 and 475-83.
68. Anon. (1811), 548.
69. Chambers (1844), 87.
70. Ibid., 87.
71. Allardyce (1998), 53.
72. Chambers (1844), 87.
73. Smeaton (1793), 30-31.
74. Stevenson (1824), 417; Hague and Christie (1975),

112-13; Munro (1979), 79. Since 1970 the Signal Tower at Arbroath has served as a local museum, and displays a number of artifacts connected with the Bell Rock Lighthouse.

75 Stevenson (1825), 34.
76 Campbell (1904), 103-105.
77 Stevenson (1824), 498-99 and Plate X; see also http://biology.st-andrews.ac.uk/bellpet/feature_2.aspx
78 Stevenson (1959), 81.
79 Ibid., 81.
80 Smiles (1862), 232-34.
81 Rennie (1848), 29.
82 *Civil Engineer and Architect's Journal*, 12 (1849), 77-79; 136-42; 180; 253; and 25 (1862), 152-53; 215-16.
83 Stevenson (1959), 299-304; Leslie and Paxton (1999), 35.
84 Mair (1978), 97; Leslie and Paxton (1999), 39; Bathurst (1999), 80.
85 Lockhart (1878), 258.

86 Stevenson (1824), 64 and 419; Stevenson (1893), 495-96.
87 Stevenson (1959), 227.
88 Page (1860), 52-54; Tulloch (1983), 49. My thanks to Donald Johnson of the Cape Bonavista Lighthouse: http://www.bonavista.net/lighthouse.php
89 Nicholson (1995), 93-94.
90 Stevenson (1959), 227.
91 Campbell (1904), 51.
92 Ibid., v-vi.
93 Munro (1979), 219-20; see http://canmore.rcahms.gov.uk/en/site/121118/details/hms+argyll+bell+rock+north+sea/
94 Nicholson (1995), 95.
95 *Scotsman*, 1 November 1940.
96 Stevenson (1959), 227; Nicholson (1995), 96; *Scotsman*, 16 December 1955; www.nlb.org.uk/LighthouseLibrary/Lighthouse/Bell-Rock/
97 *Scotsman*, 23 July 1962.
98 *Glasgow Herald*, 4 September 1987.
99 Munro (1979), 81.

General view of the Bell Rock works, oil painting, unsigned and undated, possibly by Alexander Carse.

(© From a private collection)

# CHAPTER 5

# Lighthouses in Scotland after the Bell Rock

JUST AS THE Bell Rock lighthouse was completed, a nasty incident occurred that demonstrated that the Inchcape Reef was not the only danger on Scotland's east coast. Two Royal Navy frigates, HMS *Pallas* and HMS *Nymphe*, were wrecked on the coast of East Lothian, and it was believed that their navigators had mistaken the glow of a limekiln near Dunbar for that of the coal-burning light on the Isle of May.[1] The Duke of Portland, now the island's owner by virtue of his wife's inheritance, suggested that the Northern Lighthouse Board lease and run the lighthouse, bringing it up to date. The Commissioners were not happy with this proposal; however, acquiring the island from the Duke meant another enabling Act of Parliament, and another Treasury loan, which was passed with some considerable opposition in July 1814. R. W. Munro regards this Act as a milestone in Scottish lighthouse history, for as well as allowing a loan of half the Isle of May's purchase price of £60,000, the Commissioners were enabled to improve the lighting system there, and to 'erect and maintain such additional lighthouses upon such other parts of the coast and islands of Scotland as they shall deem necessary'. The ten lighthouses already built were named, and the preamble to this Act produced a wish-list, naming Galloway, Skerryvore, Cape Wrath, Shetland and Tarbat Ness as sites in particular need of lighting.[2] Once again, the costs were to be recouped from lighthouse duties raised from shipping traffic, now reduced to a penny per ton for all British ships.

The new lighthouse on the Isle of May, described in a twentieth-century architectural guide as a Gothic toy fort, with a square tower supporting the lantern, was built in 18 months before being lit on 1 February 1816.[3] It was a substantial stone building, providing a board-room for those away days so beloved of a later and more management-conscious age. It also contained accommodation for three families, all completed to a high level of finish. The stones were dressed in the same workyard at Arbroath that had supplied the masonry blocks for the Bell

Pentland Skerries after the alteration to a single light.

Rock lighthouse, and these were shipped back for construction on the island.[4] Sir Walter Scott's intervention that the old light should be ruined 'à la picturesque' was heeded by his admirer, and the top storey was removed to allow the new beam to shine unobstructed.[5] At first constructed, this was a fixed light with Argand lamps and reflectors, replaced first by a fixed Fresnel optic in 1836, and subsequently by a revolving, but still oil-fuelled, flashing light with Fresnel lenses in 1843.[6]

Meanwhile, the Northern Lighthouse Board was ensuring that lights were going up and illuminating the Scottish coasts: the ten mentioned in the 1814 Act were Kinnaird Head (1787), Mull of Kintyre (1787), North Ronaldsay (1789; discontinued 1809), Eilean Glas (1789), Pladda (1790), Pentland Skerries (1794), Inchkeith (1804), Start Point (1806), Bell Rock (1811) and Isle of May (1816). Coastal traffic was increasing on the south-west of the country, and so much of the Scottish lighthouse dues were collected there. After consultation, a light was put up on Corsewall Point in 1816, marking the Scottish side of the channel between the Rhinns of Galloway and the Irish coast.[7]

The Isle of Man, the large island in the north Irish Sea, with England to the east, Ireland to the west and Scotland to the north, had been considered by Liverpool merchants as a site for warning lights for navigation as early as 1658, but opposed by Trinity House, which had felt that the dues would be expensive and difficult to collect. In 1692 some Whitehaven merchants petitioned the Earl of Derby (their feudal overlord) for permission to build a light, but nothing came of this. There may have been a late medieval beacon on the Calf of Man, but this has not been substantiated; and the Commission of Enquiry of 1792 was petitioned with a suggestion that the Calf, Langness, Douglas Head and Point of Ayre were all suitable locations for lighthouses. Two years later there was an idea to build two leading lights on the Calf to guide shipping past the dangerous Chicken Rock, but this too came to nothing.[8] Robert Stevenson visited the Isle of Man on his 1801 tour of lighthouses, and observed that there was no Parliamentary provision to support Manx lights.[9] By now, the Duke of Atholl had succeeded to the feudal rights over the island, and he was approached by the Northern Lighthouse Board (which had in turn been petitioned by Glasgow shipping interests) for permission to build a light at the Point of Ayre and the Calf of Man. Such structures required new legislation, and as none had previously covered the Isle of Man, this could not be seen as an infringement of the powers of Trinity House.[10] Construction work began in 1817, and both lighthouses were lit on 1 February 1818. The one at the Point of Ayre (1818) still stands, while the Calf of Man light (1818) was discontinued in 1875, replaced by the rock lighthouse at Chicken Rock (1875), which will be discussed below.[11]

Over the next 15 years, ten more lighthouses were put up around the Scottish coast: five in the west, two in the north, and three on the east coast. Robert Stevenson was assisted in their construction by his eldest son Alan in 1830, but even before this he was devising new and ingenious ways of distinguishing these lights from each other: colour, flashing, intermittent, stationary, and all using Argand lamps backed with parabolic reflectors.[12] Even before Alan had joined his father, Robert had turned his attention to the Continent, where remarkable things were being done with lighthouse optics.

## Alan Stevenson's early lighthouse work

Alan (1807-65) was the eldest surviving son of Robert Stevenson. Unlike his father, he received a thorough grounding in classics and mathematics at Edinburgh's High School, and then at the University, after which he expected to go into the ministry. However, in 1823 he decided to go into engineering, perhaps through parental pressure, and became his father's apprentice for the following four years. Even so, in the winter months he attended relevant classes at the University of Edinburgh, graduating in 1826. This was followed by study tours on the Continent and practical experience on dock and canal projects in England. In 1828, with his father's encouragement (and access to his notes), Alan compiled and had published a list of descriptions of British lighthouses, *The British Pharos*, aimed at mariners. A second edition was brought out three years later.[13]

Alan has been regarded as the most intellectual of the Stevensons, and perhaps in a different family he would have moved in another direction; but as his father's eldest son, not only did he work in the family firm as an assistant, he also was appointed Clerk of Works to the Northern Lighthouse Board in 1830 (Robert Stevenson remained the Engineer).[14] Over the following three years he worked on new lighthouses at the Mull of Galloway (1830), Dunnet Head (1831), Douglas Head (1832), Girdleness (1833), Barra Head (also 1833) and Lismore (1833). With his enquiring mind he became interested in improving lighthouse optics, and in the summer of 1834 – with the Commissioners' blessing – he visited lighthouses and workshops in France.[15]

One of the most important changes in Lighthouse apparatus was, unquestionably, the introduction of Revolving Lights at the Tour de Corduan about the year 1780 [Alan wrote in his 'Introduction' to his *Account of the Skerryvore Lighthouse*], by which the means of distinguishing one light from another were greatly extended, and a marked difference in the appearance of contiguous lights was at once simply obtained. The mere variation of the velocity of the revolution is so simple as to afford an obvious source of distinction among lights; and yet it is remarkable, that it was only lately that one of its principle advantages was perceived by my Father, who first applied it in the year 1827 as a means of distinction for the Light at Buchanness.[16]

By revolving the reflector frame more rapidly and giving it more sides or faces, the light appeared to flash, and this innovation was also applied to the Rinns of Islay lighthouse in 1825.[17] Robert Stevenson had also developed what was called 'intermittent light', introduced at

Mull of Galloway (1830), Tarbet Ness (1830) and Barra Head (1833). This 'consists of the apparatus of a fixed Light, in front of which two cylindric shades are alternately shut and opened by a vertical movement, so as to produce a sudden extinction and exhibition of the light', and it was much more rapid than the 'gradual decline and growth of the flash, which is produced in revolving Lights'.[18]

But, as Alan states in his *Account of Skerryvore*, 'the introduction of lenticular apparatus into Lighthouses has been the last great improvement effected in their illumination. So far back as 1823, the attention of the Commissioners was first called by their Engineer to the invention of the late Augustin Fresnel, who had succeeded in building polyzonal lenses of large dimensions, and in adapting to them a lamp of great power, having four concentric wicks supplied by oil by a clock-work movement ...'.[19] This created enormous interest, not only from the Northern Lighthouse Board, but also from the Commissioners of the Irish Lights and from Trinity House. Robert Stevenson, on the Northern Lighthouse Board's behalf, made a visit to France in autumn 1824, in order to meet Augustin Fresnel and to discuss his recent improvements. He ordered two square-framed lens panels from François Soleil (in business 1819-49), the Parisian optician who constructed these stepped echelon lenses to Fresnel's specifications. These were for assessment by the Commissioners and they eventually arrived in Edinburgh in June 1825, having been delayed at Dover while exemption from customs duty on glass was successfully negotiated with the Treasury: they had cost £50 each.[20] A burning lens also made by Soleil, was acquired by Sir John Leslie (1766-1832), Professor of Natural Philosophy at the University of Edinburgh, and reported to the City Council's College Committee in July 1826.[21] Later that year, all these lenses were demonstrated at the University, where to David Brewster's fury they were described as 'French' inventions.[22] As we have already seen, Brewster believed – and as time went on and he rehearsed his arguments increasingly vociferously – he continued to believe passionately, indeed, with adamantine certainty, that he had priority of invention over Fresnel.

In fact Brewster made such a fuss that 'the Commissioners ... allowed me opportunities of explaining to them, both personally and in writing, the construction and advantages of the new apparatus; and I have been authorized to have one of the Polyzonal Lenses constructed under my own superintendence. This work has been entrusted to Messrs Gilbert of London, who are now executing one of these lenses in flint-glass, with a diameter and a focal

Burning lens, made by François Soleil, Paris, c.1825, and acquired by the University of Edinburgh in 1826. Presented by the University of Edinburgh.

(NMS T.1999.351)

147

length of three feet.'[23] However, thanks to another of Brewster's optical projects, these London manufacturers, to whom Stevenson might have turned for practical assistance, went bankrupt in early 1828, and instead he contacted Isaac Cookson, a close business associate who owned a glassworks at Newcastle.[24]

To produce the optically dense, pure, heavy glass for the prisms in a Fresnel lens required specialist plant and an abundance of coal. One of the difficulties encountered in producing good flaw-free optical glass was the necessity of skilled labour-intensive working of the molten glass, and this was not resolved on an industrial scale in Britain until Chance Brothers of Birmingham imported foreign 'know-how' in 1848. The other extremely hampering condition was the excise duty levied on all glass-making – from domestic window-panes and bottles to lighthouse optics. This severely inhibited all enterprise through crippling expense, until the legislation was repealed in 1845.[25] It was hardly surprising that there were no specialist glass manufacturers in Scotland and few in England during the first half of the nineteenth century. The knowledge and skills lay across the Channel.

In the summer of 1834 Alan was sent by the Commissioners to France to investigate their lens system, where he toured various lighthouses on the coast in the company of Léonor Fresnel, Secretary of the Commission des Phares, and brother of the late Augustin Fresnel, who had died in 1827. Stevenson arrived in Paris on 9 June, and did not leave until 14 July:

> During my stay, I was occupied in making drawings of apparatus, and preparing various documents relative to the dioptric system; and, in conjunction with M. Fresnel and his assistants, making experiments on the lamps and lenses. ... Much of my time, too, was spent in the workshops of MM. Soleil, Lepaute, and Bordier-Marcet [all optical craftsmen], and in that belonging to the Commission des Phares ....[26]

Alan Stevenson's *Report* is a masterly summary of the state of lighthouses in Scotland and France in 1835. He explains that although the parabolic reflector worked well, in a fixed light the banks of reflectors provided an uneven coverage for the mariner. Also, 'there are now no fewer than twenty-three lighthouse stations within the district of the Commissioners, though the act of Parliament by which the Board was constituted, contemplated no more than four lights. The difficulty of distinguishing the lights from each other, was of course increased with their number.'[27] He lists and describes the six distinctions: fixed, revolving white, revolving red and white, flashing, intermittent, and leading lights. Then he turns his attention to lenses – commenting on the extremely difficult and successful (and prohibitively expensive) echelon lens ground from the whole by Cookson. Building such lenses in segments, he concedes, was described by Jean Condorcet (in his 'Eloge de Buffon') in 1804, Brewster in 1811, and Augustin Fresnel – 'alike unacquainted with the suggestions of Condorcet, or with the labours of the Scotch philosopher' – in 1822.[28]

Stevenson then reminds the Commissioners of their more recent trials over the past two winters made at Gullane in East Lothian, looking particularly at the costs. Brewster had been present at these, and had been convinced by the trials that lenses were both cheaper and more brilliant than reflectors. Enraged at what he saw as Robert Stevenson's obstruction to new and better technology, he wrote a savage and anonymous article, ostensibly reviewing recent lighthouse literature, in the *Edinburgh Review* in April 1833:

> The Legislature has carefully excluded from [the composition of lighthouse boards in Great Britain] men of science, opticians, and engineers, – the only classes of persons who were pre-eminently qualified for the office; and the Boards themselves, true to the parent spirit which was breathed into them, have, we believe, never on any one occasion called in the aid of theoretical or practical science to assist them in their vast and responsible undertaking. The consequences of this system have been such as might have been predicted. The optical apparatus of British lighthouses displays none of the improvements of modern science; their lights are too feeble to penetrate the hazes and fogs of our murky climate; and the methods by which they are distinguished from each other are of the worst and the most inefficient description.[29]

This public row – Alan Stevenson wrote a detailed response, clearly unaware of the identity of the author – paved the way to a Parliamentary Select Committee Enquiry, chaired by the radical Member of Parliament, Joseph Hume (1777-1855).[30] It sat for 18 days between February and June and the Report is dated 8 August 1834. The main recommendation was, naturally, that all public lights throughout the land should be placed under the authority of a single board, based in London and using one management system. Light dues should be set at a single fixed rate, collected at Custom houses and paid into the Treasury, as with other taxes. Both Stevensons were quizzed about the nature of lights, Robert stating that reflectors and Argand burners were 'most economical', but Alan showing a more forward-looking attitude, and this was the point that he was sent to France to learn more about lenses. The Bill, introduced into Parliament to create a new single board, met considerable opposition and failed; Hume brought in another in 1836, which granted the three boards continued control and management of the lights in their separate jurisdictions; but to bring about management uniformity and a reduction of dues, Trinity House was placed in a supervisory role above the other two. This was passed in August 1836.[31]

Meantime, Cookson had delivered a seven-lens rotating apparatus for the Northern Board's lighthouse on Inchkeith, which was first lit in October 1835 and was the first lighthouse apparatus in Britain to use lenses. This consisted of a seven-lens array – which still survives – encircling a single lamp, with three concentric wicks, and five tiers of curved mirrors ranging one above another (which do not survive). Although it used twice as much oil as the old apparatus, it was considerably more brilliant.[32] The Isle of May lighthouse was converted to become the first British fixed light with lenses, again with an improved form of refractor made by Cookson, and the new light was first shown on 22 September 1836. A committee of the Royal Society of Edinburgh, appointed to co-operate with the Commissioners for Northern Lights, met at Dunbar in October 1836, and was asked to compare the new light to the older one, set up temporarily nearby: the committee was unanimous in pronouncing the effect of the new light, 'which appeared brighter than the old one in the ratio of not less than 4 or 5 to 1'.[33]

These two lights were considered so successful that Trinity House wished to follow suit, and their first Fresnel lens lighthouse was intro-

Central belt of seven panels of built-up stepped lenses, installed in the light for Inchkeith Lighthouse in 1835 and removed from service in 1890, by I. Cookson, Newcastle. This was the first lighthouse optic in the United Kingdom to use Fresnel lenses. The original complete optic had five tiers of curved mirrors above this array, and its lamp had three concentric wicks. Presented by the Northern Lighthouse Board.

(NMS T.1993.154)

duced in 1836, at Start Point, Devon (not to be confused with Start Point on Orkney), to Alan Stevenson's design, and under his supervision. This was also constructed by Cookson of Newcastle.[34]

The availability of reasonably local optical glass of this quality did not mean that the Stevensons abandoned the high-quality wares produced by Parisian firms. Cooksons was by this time in some financial difficulty and went out of business in the mid-1840s; the works were bought by R. W. Swinburne & Co. in 1845 (Robert Swinburne had been a manager, subsequently a partner with Cooksons), but the company did not continue with the making of lighthouse optics. The next major Scottish lighthouse, the remote Skerryvore tower located to the south-west of the island of Tiree, was designed by Robert's son Alan Stevenson, and completed in 1843. This had a first order rotating optic made by Soleil's son, confusingly named François [Soleil] *jeune*, who continued his father's business.[35] National Museums Scotland has a fifth-scale model of the original optical apparatus used there, and this was also displayed at the Great Exhibition of 1851.[36] After the Great Exhibition, the firm of Chance Brothers of Birmingham became the main suppliers of lighthouse optics in the United Kingdom, especially to Trinity House and to the growing needs of an Empire that depended on sea-power and commerce.

The glass-making firm of Chance Brothers & Co. had come into existence in 1834, although family members had been glass-makers in London and Birmingham since the mid-eighteenth century. David Brewster approached the young James Chance in 1845 – the year the excise restrictions were removed – saying, 'I cannot doubt from what I saw at your Works that you could overcome the difficulties which had been insurmountable by them [Cookson's failure to produce echelon lenses for Scottish lighthouses], and that the branch of manufacturing lenses would be both an interesting and a profitable addition to your establishment'.[37] Chance Brothers were able to benefit from the favourable financial climate, and managed to create 'the enormous works at Spon Lane. ... There, intersected by the canal ... and divided by lines of railways, the stupendous range of workshops, forges, and ovens extends over an area of twenty-four acres; while from amidst the separate piles of building there rise a score of shafts and chimneys – the steeples of this great temple devoted to labour and to art.' This enthusiastic report continues:

> It will be some indication of the extent of the business carried on at the Spon Lane works to remember that the glass which covered the Great Exhibition of 1851 was supplied by Messrs. Chance, that this

occupied only the 'sheet-glass' department, and that 300,000 of the panes, 49 inches by 10 inches, were supplied in the course of a few weeks without in any way interfering with the ordinary business.[38]

As a Chance Brothers employee, James Kenward wrote in 1866:

> Messrs. Cookson, after producing several lens apparatus, excellent for that day, were forced to abandon the undertaking with considerable loss. Messrs. Chance ventured on it, with the conviction that such a manufacture ought to be not less English than French, and that the exclusive resources at their command would enable them to occupy at least an equal position with the French.
>
> Totally unsupported by Government, and unaided by Lighthouse Boards, they worked out, *ab initio*, the most important problems and processes, and centralised in their own establishment the fabrication of every part of the apparatus.
>
> They have devoted to the lighthouse branch an area in their works of nearly an acre and a-half, a steam engine of fifty-horse power, a glass house for casting, about forty newly contrived machines for grinding with mathematical exactness, and polishing the lenses and prisms of all forms; as many lathes, planing and other machines, in the fitting shops, where lanterns, lamps, clockwork, and all metallic accessories are prepared; and lastly, a staff of about one hundred workmen; but this, of course, is no measure of the magnitude of an enterprise where machinery plays so large a part.[39]

Despite this successful growth, the Northern Lighthouse Board did not entirely abandon French optics for their lighthouses: the experimental lenses which had been made by the Parisian firm of Soleil were followed by the optic installed at Skerryvore, constructed by the same firm in 1843. Changes in the firm's personnel with the retirement of Soleil *fils* and the splitting of the works into discrete businesses producing instruments and lighthouse optics under Soleil's sons-in-law, meant that superficially the continuity appeared to have been lost, but this was not in fact the case.[40] As Kenward wrote in 1866:

> Soleil, Letourneau, Sautter, Lepaute, are names of deservedly high repute in this branch, all apparently having enjoyed the benefit of working under the immediate auspices of Augustin or Léonor Fresnel. The excellent glass, too, supplied by the St Gobain Company gave for a long time an advantage to the Parisian makers which no other country could share. But, above all, the direct and unwavering patronage accorded to them by their governments, the zealous recommendation of them by the diplomatic staff everywhere, and by the Lighthouse Department at Paris, armed these few makers with a vast monopoly, little calculated to enhance the improvement of dioptric apparatus, or to reduce its cost.[41]

As reflectors were replaced by lenses, and more new lights were built, in the 1840s and 1850s most of the optics for the Northern Lighthouse Board were manufactured by Theodore Letourneau of Paris, the son-in-law of François [Soleil] *jeune*, and installed by Milne & Son of Edinburgh.[42]

After Robert's retirement in 1843 part-way through the Skerryvore project, Alan was appointed his successor as Engineer to the Northern Lighthouse Board, and found himself devoting his time entirely to lighthouses and their construction, leaving the family engineering business very much in the hands of his younger brothers David and Thomas.

### Alan Stevenson and Skerryvore (1844)

'From the great difficulty of access to the inhospitable rock of Skerryvore, which is exposed to the full fury of the Atlantic, and is surrounded by an almost perpetual surf, the erection of a Light on its small and rugged surface has always been regarded as an undertaking of the most formidable kind', remarked Alan Stevenson in his opening comments to his book on his greatest achievement.[43] His father, Robert Stevenson, first landed there in 1804 on his annual voyage around the coast of Scotland, and on the next occasion he was accompanied, as we have already seen, by the novelist Walter Scott, in August 1814. Scott confided in his diary:

> At length, by dint of exertion, come in sight of this long ridge of rocks (chiefly under water) on which the tide breaks in the most tremendous style. There appear a few low broad rocks at one end of the reef, which is about a mile in length. These are never entirely under water, though the surf dashes over them. To go through all the forms, Hamilton, Duff [two of the Commissioners], and I, resolve to land upon these bare rocks in company with Mr Stevenson. Pull through a very heavy swell with great difficulty, and approach a tremendous surf dashing over black pointed rocks. Our rowers, however, get the boat into a quiet creek between two rocks, where we contrive to land well wetted. I saw nothing remarkable in my way excepting several seals, which we might have shot, but, in the doubtful circumstances of the landing, we did not care to bring guns. We took possession of the rock in the name of the Commissioners, and generously bestowed our own great names on its crags and creeks. The rock was carefully measured by Mr S. It will be a most desolate position for a lighthouse – the Bell Rock and Eddystone a joke to it, for the nearest land is the wild island of Tyree, at fourteen miles distance. So much for the Skerry Vhor.[44]

Robert Stevenson's own remarks are more prosaic:

> ... at Skerryvore we found the landing difficult, and the nimblest of
> the sailors found it a task to climb up the sloping face of the rock, and,
> but for their assistance with the help of ropes some of the party must
> have been left in the boat, owing to the glassy smoothness of the rock,
> rendered so from being the resting place of hundreds of seals. Sir Walter
> was much delighted with this landing, the difficulties of which gave
> additional buoyancy to his spirits. In the evening, at our 'Saturday
> night at sea' we had the chorus of a highland song altered to 'O!
> Skerryvore, Skerryvore!'[45]

Provision for building a lighthouse on this extremely dangerous
rock, which threatened the growing amount of shipping to and from
the Clyde and the Mersey passing around the north of Scotland, was
granted in the Act of 1814 (the Isle of May legislation). Although the
topic continuously came before the Commissioners, it was not until July
1834 that action was taken. A survey was begun, but bad weather meant
that it could only be completed the following summer. Soundings, tide-
levels and charting of nearby sunken rocks were all taken, and the
geology of these ascertained. (The name 'skerry mhor', pronounced
'skerry vhor', means 'big rock' in Scottish Gaelic.)

The nearest point of land was at the south-east corner of the
somewhat bleak and windswept neighbouring island of Tiree, home in
1841 to some 4687 souls: Alan Stevenson chose Hynish, twelve miles
across the water from Skerryvore, to be the workyard, harbour and
quarry for the new lighthouse. Fifteen acres was feued from the Duke
of Argyll, the landowner, for a permanent lighthouse establishment,
which would eventually house four lightkeepers' families.[46] However,
it turned out that the local stone on Tiree was unsuitable for the
purpose, there not being enough material of the quality that Stevenson
required.[47]

Alan Stevenson considered a rock tower's vulnerability to nature:

> When it is recollected, that, so far from possessing any accurate infor-
> mation regarding the momentum of the waves, we have little more than
> conjecture to guide us, it will be obvious, that we are not in a situation
> to estimate the power or intensity of those shocks to which Sea Towers
> are subject; and much less can we pretend to deal with the variations
> of these forces which shoals and obstructing rocks produce, or to
> determine the power of the waves as destructive agents.[48]

He cited the work of his youngest brother, Thomas, who had recently
devised a marine dynamometer, an instrument that registered wave

force.[49] However, Alan noted that 'these experiments have not been continued long enough as yet to render them available for the Engineer'. So for stability in his sea tower, he looked to weight rather than strength, and an internal cohesion of the structure (incidentally pointing out the illogicality of John Smeaton's tree analogy in his 1791 *Narrative*). He considered the methods that bound the courses of masonry together at the Eddystone and the Bell Rock, and he 'entirely dispensed with dovetailing and joggles between the courses' because he calculated that the weight and pressure of the masonry would hold the whole structure together (stones were retained by temporary wooden trenails during construction), and this avoided expensive stone dressing. However, Alan 'adopted the ribband-joggle in the higher part of the Tower, where the walls begin to get thin in the very same manner as at the Bell Rock … [and] also ventured to leave out the metallic ties at the cornice, which consisted, at the Eddystone, of chains, and, at the Bell Rock, of copper rings'.[50]

Exposed to the full fury of the Atlantic, the first season's work – along the lines of the Bell Rock experience – saw a wooden workmen's barrack assembled, disassembled and taken out to the reef. Alan's *Account* is full of descriptions of the appalling weather they encountered in 1838, even during the summer months:

> When I looked back upon the works of the season, upon our difficulties, and, I must add, dangers, and the small result of our exertions – for we had only been 165 hours at work on the Rock between 7th August and 11th September – I could see that, in good truth, there were many difficulties before us; but there was also much cause for thankfulness, in the many escapes we had made.[51]

Imagine his feelings when, in November, there was a particularly heavy sea, and Stevenson received a message from the store-keeper at Hynish: 'I am extremely sorry to inform you, that the barrack erected on Skerryvore Rock has totally disappeared.'[52]

Stevenson had to rethink the barrack, and its attachment to the reef. He also had to consider a new source for the sort of stone he required, and after visiting quarries near Oban, and around Morven and Mull, he concluded that the 'great masses of granite' to be found on the Ross of Mull were the most suitable for his purpose. 'Granite, indeed, is a material in many respects superior to sandstone, gneiss, or porphyry,' he thought.[53] This quarry went on to produce the largest granite blocks in Britain, at over 50 feet long, with 15-feet blocks shipped to the United States. Its northern coastal location made it suitable for lighthouse construction, and after Skerryvore its granite was used in lighthouse construction at Ardnamurchan (1849), Dubh Artach (1872), and also Hyskeir (1904) lighthouses.[54]

Alan Stevenson discusses the quarrying and dressing of the stone blocks (this latter operation took place at Hynish) – 'the whole of the materials for the Tower were to be dressed in such a manner as to avoid the necessity of any fitting on the Rock.' This was labour-intensive: 'In dressing one of the outside stones of the first or lowest courses of the Skerryvore Tower, a mason was occupied for eighty-five hours; and in dressing one of the largest of the hearting or inner stones of the same courses, fifty-five hours.'[55] Nevertheless, they managed to start to dig out the foundation in the rock between 6 May and 3 September 1839: 'A more unpromising prospect of success in any work than that which presented itself at the commencement of our labours, I can hardly conceive. … the Rock … is a hard and tough gneiss, and required the expenditure of about four times as much labour and steel for boring as are generally consumed in boring the Aberdeenshire granite.'[56] This disheartening procedure 'occupied 20 men for 217 days in all, where-of 168 days were in the season of 1839 and the rest in the summer of 1840'.[57]

The barrack survived the winter of 1839-40, to everyone's relief, although it was clearly not a comfortable billet. Building the lighthouse tower began on 4 July, and the Duke of Argyll, together with a group of family and friends, arrived in a steamer to perform the ceremony of lay-ing the foundation stone. Building operations were carried out with the assistance of two cranes with moveable jibs: one positioned to bring stone blocks from the landing place to the tower; the second – as at the Bell Rock – fixed on the tower. These helped to lay the stones, rising upwards as the building grew. The mortar was that used by Smeaton at the Eddystone, and Stevenson's father at the Bell Rock.[58]

By 21 July 1842 the masonry was completed. The lantern was landed on the rock on 10 August, 'when my Father, in the course of his annual tour of inspection, as Engineer for the Northern Lights, visited the Rock, two days after the iron work had been landed'.[59] The following year was taken up with fitting the interior of the tower to make it habitable for the four keepers resident there at any given time. A 26-feet high vertical ladder ascended to the way in. The first apartment, at entrance level, was designed for iron water tanks, holding 1251 gallons. The next floor upstairs was for coal, stowed in large iron boxes. The third floor was a workshop, with the fourth as the provisions store, and the fifth was the kitchen. The next two storeys each contained sleeping accommo-dation for two keepers, and over these was the room for any visitors. Upstairs again on the ninth floor was the oil-store, with the light-room on the very top.[60]

The light was first displayed on 1 February 1844, and Stevenson described it as 'revolving, appearing in its brightest state once in every minute of time. It is elevated 150 feet above the sea, and is well seen as far as the curvature of the earth permits; it is also frequently seen as a brilliant light from the high land of Barra, a distance of 38 miles.'[61] Stevenson had developed 'totally reflecting' zones of prisms below the central belt of eight annular lenses, inspired by the 'zones of the small Harbour Light Apparatus of the fourth order, which was also designed by Fresnel'.[62] An

Small Fresnel lens developed as a harbour light, by F. Soleil, Paris, c.1830. Presented by the University of Edinburgh.
(NMS T.1999.355)

example of the fourth order harbour light, also made by Soleil, had recently arrived in Edinburgh, commissioned by the University for classroom demonstration.[63] This example had possibly been examined by Stevenson, who remained on good terms with the French suppliers. In a recent paper Julia Elton points out that small harbour lights of this type appear very complex and compact when measured against contemporary large optics with tiers of mirrors, which lost much of the reflected incidental light. Both Léonor Fresnel and Alan Stevenson realised that if the twin manufacturing problems of weight and correct calculation could be overcome, catadioptric prisms could be successfully applied to large fixed optics.[64]

Thomas Stevenson agreed: 'This [the small harbour light] was not only the first application of total reflection to lighthouses ... leaving in fact no room for improvement; and, accordingly, this beautiful instrument continues till now [1881] in universal use.'[65]

The optical apparatus for Skerryvore was, Alan Stevenson stated, made from 'lenses, mirrors and zones ... from the works of M. François [Soleil *jeune*] of Paris, whose name I shall afterwards have occasion to notice; and ... the machinery was constructed to my entire satisfaction, and in a manner worthy of his reputation as a mechanician, by Mr John Milne of Edinburgh'.[66] National Museums Scotland has a one-fifth scale model of this, originally displayed at the 1851 Great Exhibition, which caused a far more recent author's disparagement when he failed to realise it was *not* the full-size item he was inspecting: 'It may have been the most powerful lamp in the world, but to look at it was disappointingly small – small enough to fit easily into a modern dustbin.'[67]

The task of assembling the delicate but very heavy component lens panels into a com-

Model of a first order 8-beam light, one-fifth scale, by F. Soleil, Paris, for Skerryvore, 1844, with rotation clockwork by James Milne, Edinburgh. Designed by Alan Stevenson, with reflecting prisms below the revolving Fresnel lenses and plane mirrors above. Presented by the Northern Lighthouse Board.

(NMS T.1993.144)

plete rotating optic was complex. The site, high in the lighthouse lantern, was cramped and comparatively inaccessible; and not only did the tall optic have to remain in balance during construction; its shape also had to be adjusted within narrow margins to ensure that the optimum optical performance was achieved. Alan Stevenson's diagrams show how the problem was elegantly resolved, by using specially designed instruments engineered for him by the Edinburgh scientific instrument maker John Adie (1805-57), to align the panels as tension was taken up at their boundaries. The first instrument ensures that the lenses meet at 'the proper horizontal angle, so that their axes shall meet with the proper inclination in the focus'.[68] The second ascertains the verticality of the main lenses, or sets the subsidiary lenses or mirrors at the required angle, with a spirit level; so this is in fact a special clinometer. The third, and final example, is a device which tests the true position of the lamp itself in the context of the lenses. It acts as a radius, with F being the central burner, 'while its point A touches the centres of the lenses. At B is a graduated slide, which allows the radius arm to be lengthened or shortened to suit various different focal distances.' The dotted outline shows the device being moved on to an adjacent lens.[69] Without these scientific instruments, constructed for just this specific purpose, the complex lenses of Skerryvore could not have shone out with clarity over the Atlantic waves.

Once completed, the tower at Skerryvore was 155 feet high, with a diameter at the base of 42 feet, with nine floors one on top of another: it contains 58,580 cubic feet of carefully-cut masonry, weighing 4308 tons. Alan Stevenson's memorial should be regarded as the lighthouse at Skerryvore, just as his father's is that at the Bell Rock. After his death in 1865, the obituary in the journal of his profession, that of the civil engineers, stated:

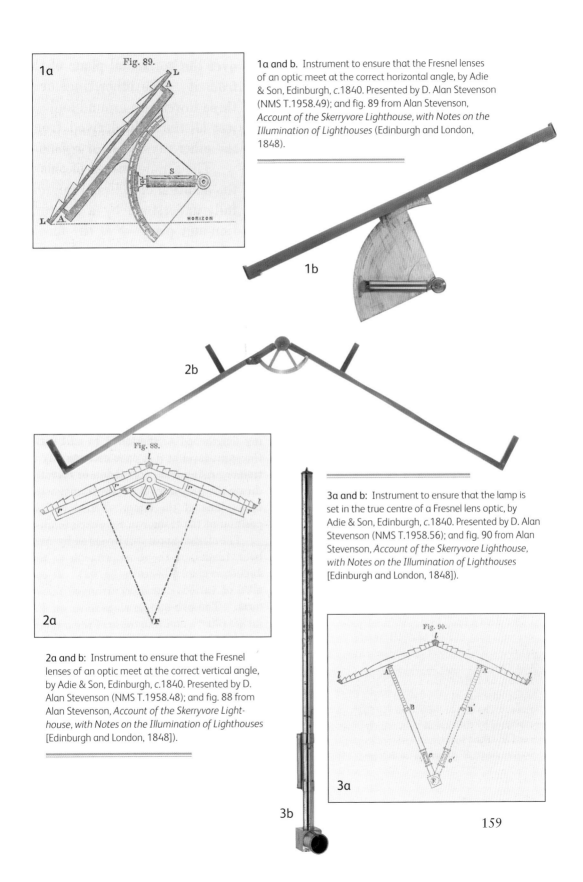

**1a** Fig. 89.

**1a and b.** Instrument to ensure that the Fresnel lenses of an optic meet at the correct horizontal angle, by Adie & Son, Edinburgh, *c*.1840. Presented by D. Alan Stevenson (NMS T.1958.49); and fig. 89 from Alan Stevenson, *Account of the Skerryvore Lighthouse, with Notes on the Illumination of Lighthouses* (Edinburgh and London, 1848).

**1b**

**2b**

**2a** Fig. 88.

**2a and b:** Instrument to ensure that the Fresnel lenses of an optic meet at the correct vertical angle, by Adie & Son, Edinburgh, *c*.1840. Presented by D. Alan Stevenson (NMS T.1958.48); and fig. 88 from Alan Stevenson, *Account of the Skerryvore Lighthouse, with Notes on the Illumination of Lighthouses* [Edinburgh and London, 1848]).

**3a and b:** Instrument to ensure that the lamp is set in the true centre of a Fresnel lens optic, by Adie & Son, Edinburgh, *c*.1840. Presented by D. Alan Stevenson (NMS T.1958.56); and fig. 90 from Alan Stevenson, *Account of the Skerryvore Lighthouse, with Notes on the Illumination of Lighthouses* [Edinburgh and London, 1848]).

**3a** Fig. 90.

**3b**

159

... in personally conducting that great work, during a period of five working seasons, his courage and patience were severely tried, and his abilities as an Engineer were fully tested. They were found equal to the task of successfully accomplishing what will ever be regarded as a triumph of lighthouse engineering, and as perhaps the finest combination of mass with elegance to be met with in architectural or engineering structures. After trying four different curves, the parabolic, the logarithmic, the hyperbolic, and the conchoidal, Mr Alan Stevenson adopted the hyperbolic curve for the tower. ... Alluding to the Bell Rock and Skerryvore Lighthouses, a writer in the *Quarterly Review* says: 'Taken altogether, they are, perhaps, the most perfect specimens of modern architecture which exist. Tall and graceful as the minaret of an Eastern mosque, they possess far more solidity and beauty of construction; and, in addition to this, their form is as appropriate to the purposes for which it was designed as anything ever done by the Greeks, and consequently meets the requirements of good architecture quite as much as a column of the Parthenon.' In proof of the correctness of this criticism, it may suffice to say that the proportions of the Skerryvore tower were adopted by Captain Fraser, R.E., for the Alguada Reef Lighthouse, lately constructed by him for the Indian Government. ...[70]

More will be said about Skerryvore's 'twin' in the Far East in chapter 6.

### After Skerryvore

The most striking element of Alan's architecture and detailed designs is the overt Egyptian influence: this can be observed particularly in the lightkeepers' cottages at Noss Head (1849), those remodelled at Eilean Glas (1847), at Chanonry Point (1846), at Cromarty on the Black Isle (1846), and the lighthouse and keepers' cottages at Ardnamurchan (1849) – to say nothing of the model of the fixed Fresnel lens sent to the Great Exhibition in 1851. This striking piece with its three cast bronze Egyptian statues supporting a fixed optic on their heads is reminiscent of a pair of candlesticks with similar figures, which scholars reckon are derived from a design in Thomas Hope's *Household Furniture*.[71] The optic has the helical joints in the central belt as devised by Alan Stevenson.[72] Douglas Hague, an architectural historian himself, felt that of the entire Stevenson family, Alan showed the most perceptive response towards architecture.[73]

Egyptian influences in design and architecture seem to have grown from two impulses: first, a general post-1750 picturesque movement, which included Chinese pagodas, Greek temples and Gothic ruins; and second, from a response to the more scholarly activities of the French in

Egypt itself. In Britain, the victory of Nelson at the Battle of the Nile in 1798 was reflected in, for example, William Bullock's London Museum (the Egyptian Hall in Piccadilly), and in Thomas Hope's furniture designs.[74] This early nineteenth-century effect can still be seen in the sphinxes at Gosford House, East Lothian, designed between 1792 and 1800 by Robert Adam, and those on the Princes Street building designed by William Playfair between 1822 and 1826 as the Royal Institution, now the Royal Scottish Academy. When, ten years later, this was extended, it was decorated with the biggest family of sphinxes in Scotland.[75]

According to Eric Grant, this later flowering of interest in Egyptian design was particularly Scottish, and any attention had by this time entirely faded away in England. The Edinburgh-born artist David Roberts produced his three-volume book of lithographs of his travels in Egypt and Nubia from 1838, and this was to have widespread effect in the north. Grant believes that in Scotland there was an Enlightenment impetus to find national validation in antiquity, which might help to lay aside the unfortunate Jacobite tendencies of the more recent past with which the country was associated. Egyptian design symbolised sturdiness, durability and dependability, but it was always linked to the secrets of freemasonry (witness the pyramid on the United States dollar bill); and, as Grant suggests, at this time it could be almost guaranteed that every well-known Scots designer, builder, architect, master trades-man or manufacturer was a freemason.[76]

In looking for reasons for the Egyptian influence in Alan Steven-son's designs, he may have been influenced by these prevailing Scottish trends. He was also acquainted with the second Astronomer Royal for Scotland, Charles Piazzi Smyth (1819-1900) – Stevenson had taken a group of eminent astronomers to view a solar eclipse north of Bergen on the annual lighthouse tour of inspection in 1851 – but was not involved in Smyth's activities relating to the Great Pyramid at Giza in the mid-1860s.[77] Of course, the most overt reference in lighthouse detail by Alan Stevenson must be to the Pharos of Alexandria (the George Washington Masonic National Memorial building in Alexandria, Virginia, was built in the 1920s to resemble the original Pharos), but his classical bent meant that he had other interests in the Egyptian past besides freemasonry.

Robert Stevenson had marked the laying of the foundation stone and the topping out ceremony at the Bell Rock with religious rites ('the usual ceremonies observed by the Brotherhood on occasions of this kind'), but there is nothing similar to this mentioned in his eldest son's book.[78] However, in a discussion about the construction of lighthouse towers, Alan Stevenson states:

> It is deserving of notice, as one of the many proofs which the records of antiquity afford of the similarity of the results of human thought in all ages, and of the truth of the Wise Man's saying, that 'there is nothing new under the sun', that the ancient Egyptians appear to have had the same conceptions of the solid of stability that were present to the mind of the modern Engineer of the Eddystone lighthouse. In the admirable work recently published by Sir J. Gardner Wilkinson on the *Manners and Customs of the Ancient Egyptians*, he gives in the first volume of his second series, at page 253, a wood-cut, shewing the figure of the deity Pthah, under the symbol of stability, according to Egyptian conceptions. This symbol is so closely and strikingly resembles the general appearance of the Eddystone, that I willingly give it a place in the text, denuded, however, of the arms and head-dress of the deity whom it shrouds.[79]

Once Alan had embarked on the second part of his book, he gave himself full rein to write a succinct account of the early but 'uncertain' history of lighthouses, quoting (in Greek) from Homer's *Odyssey* and

Model of a lighthouse exterior lantern structure of a first order light, with diagonal astragals, dome and stonework above the parapet floor level, one-fifth scale, as used at Ardnamurchan, 1849. Presented by the Northern Lighthouse Board.

(NMS T.1993.134)

*The Iliad*, and other ancient authorities, discussing in learned footnotes the literary interpretation of various translations, before getting down to the more familiar discussions about the Tour de Corduan, the Eddystone and the Bell Rock lighthouses.[80] Alan's final published work contained some poetry of his own composition, but was mainly a translation of *The Ten Hymns of Synesius, Bishop of Cyrene*, in which the reader discovers that – of course – Synesius was an Egyptian.[81]

Another innovation by Alan was the glazing bars of the lighthouse lantern. Diagonal glazing bars appeared more or less simultaneously in England, but these produced helical or lozenge-shaped panes, whereas those in Scotland were triangular. Skerryvore was one of the last Scottish lighthouses to use rectangular glass lantern panes. The new triangular form gave added strength against the wind; but, more important to Alan Stevenson, who was trying to maximise the available light, vertical bars were more noticeable in a fixed light. Some of the castings were produced by the Carron Iron Company, but others were manufactured by the Edinburgh brass founders, Milne & Son.[82] This improvement was first used at Noss Head (1849), completed just before the most westerly light on the Scottish mainland at Ardnamurchan (1849), and became standard for the Northern Lighthouse Board.[83] The fifth-scale model of the Ardnamurchan lantern was also shown at the Great Exhibition of 1851 Interestingly, inside the lantern at Ardnamurchan itself, the glazing bar intersections are covered by lion masks, reminiscent of the detail (possibly derived from Thomas Hope) on the Argand lamps. The original lens at Ardnamurchan was used until 1988, when it was replaced at automation by a modern halogen installation.[84]

All Robert Stevenson's early towers were topped with glazed lanterns made up of prefabricated cast iron frames with moulded decorative motifs and dolphin handles. Nearly all these lanterns, with their rectangular-paned framed glazing panes were replaced with the new triangular structures introduced by Alan Stevenson when their reflectors gave way to more efficient lenses. When the 1833 lighthouse at Girdleness outside Aberdeen was being modernised in 1847, the upper lantern was not destroyed (the lower one remains, although it was no longer lit). Instead, it was shipped to Inchkeith, where it was set up some distance from the main 1804 lighthouse, its original iron and glass frame being used to shelter experimental optics and lamps from

Girdleness lantern on Inchkeith, as seen in a nineteenth-century engraving, to the right of the lighthouse. From James Grant, *Cassell's Old and New Edinburgh* (1883).

the elements. Here some of Thomas Stevenson's important developments on holophotal glass optics were tested.[85]

Alan Stevenson drove himself as hard as his father, but his constitution was clearly not so robust. As the workload increased after the completion of Skerryvore, the engineer to the Northern Lighthouse Board discovered that he was physically suffering, with occasional catastrophic breakdowns. Bella Bathurst has suggested that Alan Stevenson may have been suffering from multiple sclerosis, a disease not recognised before 1868.[86] Between 1838, when he began his work at Skerryvore, and 1853, when he was forced reluctantly through ill-health to retire, he completed a total of 13 lighthouses: at Little Ross (1843), Isle of May lower (1844), Covesea Skerries (1844), Chanonry (1846), Cromarty (1846), Loch Ryan (1847), Noss Head (1849), Ardnamurchan (1849), Sanda Island (1850), Hoy Sound High and Low (both 1851) and Arnish Point (1853). An outstandingly able and professionally-trained engineer, Alan's most impor-

tant improvement to lighthouse apparatus was the introduction of the 'dioptric system', or Fresnel lenses, to Scottish lighthouses.

### The role of the Royal Scottish Society of Arts

For much of the age of Scottish lighthouse improvement, its technological developments were aired and discussed at an Edinburgh society formed in 1821 and still flourishing – although in a rather different form – today. Surprisingly, this was not Scotland's national academy of science, the Royal Society of Edinburgh, finally established after a series of false starts in 1783.[87] Instead, a new forum for practical mechanics was founded by David Brewster as the 'Society for Promoting the Useful Arts in Scotland'. Its manifesto proclaimed that its objects were: 'To stimulate and reward genius and mechanical industry, and to afford a ready and useful medium of intercourse among men of all ranks, who were engaged either in the pursuits of Science or in the various practical departments of the Arts.'

Its proceedings were reported annually in a journal which at that time was co-edited by Brewster, the *Edinburgh Philosophical Journal*, published by the Edinburgh publisher Constable.

Unfortunately Brewster fell out with the other editor, the eminent natural historian Robert Jameson (1774-1854), and by 1824 Brewster had managed to persuade the publisher Blackwood to support his rival *Edinburgh Journal of Science*, which survived until 1832.[88] From 1824 the Society of Arts' proceedings appeared in this journal, until Jameson presumably relented, and they also were noted from 1837 in the renamed *Edinburgh New Philosophical Journal*.

In 1841 the Society obtained its Royal Charter, and changed its name from the 'Society for Promoting the Useful Arts in Scotland' to the 'Royal Scottish Society of Arts'. That same year it began to publish its own series of *Transactions*, and in the first volume a Preface gives a resumé of its objectives, its meetings, and the prizes and premiums which could be awarded for submissions to the Society. At the end of this first volume there is a copy of the Charter of Incorporation (in both English and Latin), a list of its 440 members, and a summary of its laws. In this and the other volumes that followed, many of the contributions of the Stevenson family can be found, and of their employees and associates, to the improvement of lighthouse technology.

Robert Stevenson, always a believer in education, was a founding member of this society. It is clear from the manuscript memoranda quoted in Alan Stevenson's *Biographical Sketch* that his father's incomplete education merely made him thirst after what he had not obtained:

> I [Robert] was prevented, however, from taking my degree of M.A. by my slender knowledge of Latin, in which my highest book was the orations of Cicero, and by my total want of Greek.[89]

Not only was Robert Stevenson a founding member of the Society for Promoting the Useful Arts in Scotland, 'in addition to his professional exertions, he took an active part in advancing the interests of science, in so far as it lay in his power; and was one of the original promoters of the Astronomical Institution, out of which has grown the present establishment of the Royal Observatory. In 1815 he became a fellow of the Royal Society of Edinburgh; and he afterwards joined the Geological Society of London, and the Wernerian and Antiquarian Societies of Scotland.'[90]

Robert Stevenson wrote a number of academic papers, but the last of these – eleven are listed in the *Royal Society Catalogue of Scientific Papers* – was published in 1833, before the Society of Arts began pub-

Detail of engraved portrait of Robert Stevenson (1772-1850) after John Syme's portrait, c.1840.

(NMS T.1993.105)

Miniature portrait of David Stevenson (1815-86).

(© The Trustees of D. Alan Stevenson)

lishing its *Transactions*.[91] However, he sat on a number of committees examining the 'new Inventions, Models, and Drawings' laid before the members of the Society, including that in 1838 which examined Edward Sang's 'Dioptric Light erected at Kirkcaldy Harbour'. Together with the surveyor William Galbraith and the Edinburgh scientific instrument maker Alexander Adie, Stevenson found Sang's method of 'grinding annular surfaces … novel and ingenious'; and Alan Stevenson, in discussing his innovation of diagonal astragals, mentioned with approval the Kirkcaldy light as being the only one not suffering from interference from vertical astragals.[92]

Robert Stevenson's second surviving son, David FRSE, Civil Engineer, whose lighthouse activities are always (and perhaps unfairly) considered alongside his younger brother Thomas, was elected a Fellow of the Society of Arts in 1838. (Thomas was elected in 1847, a year after their cousin, William Swan.) David served as President in 1854, and again in 1869.[93] Among the papers he published was one concerning improvements to levelling instruments: two examples of these are in the collections of National Museums Scotland, both made by Adie & Son. In an adjacent paper, his brother Thomas also discussed a similar topic.[94]

David Stevenson's first Presidential Address was a 'brief recapitulation of the history of our Society' to 1854. No doubt long-lived Fellows would have put their President right over detail before he came to work up his address for publication, although by this time his father had died. He confirms that David Brewster, and others 'were chiefly instrumental in bringing the proposal [of forming an Institution for the Promotion of the Mechanical Arts in Edinburgh … conceived somewhere about the year 1819] into notice'.[95] But there were difficulties, as glossed over here by David Stevenson. In a complicated episode, teased out by the historian of science Steven Shapin, Brewster appears to have been involved with the businessman and educationalist Leonard Horner (1785-1864) in setting up the Edinburgh School of Arts, the first of the many 'mechanics' institutes' set up for the scientific education of local artisans around the country at this period. This was, as Shapin explains, instantly successful, with more than 450 students enrolled in its first year. Then, in an almost inexplicable move – Shapin suggests that Brewster had somehow convinced himself that Horner's School was merely temporary – Brewster set out in 1822 to establish a similar body, more closely linked to the Society of Arts, with the same name and the same lecturers, and very nearly managed to destroy both. There was a public meeting – explanations were given – but Brewster had formed another implacable enemy.[96]

Finally the Society got underway, and early minutes demonstrate attendance by, among others, David Stevenson's father Robert. David remarks soothingly – Brewster was still alive and actively pursuing his 'lighthouse controversy' in 1853 – that 'one result of these preliminary meetings appears to have been the establishment of the present Edinburgh School of Arts, an institution which has been singularly successful in maintaining a course of instruction for the industrial classes by persons eminently qualified to discharge that duty'.[97] In due course, the Edinburgh School of Arts became, first, the Heriot-Watt College in 1885, and subsequently Heriot-Watt University in 1966.[98] By early 1823 the Society was apparently meeting occasionally, but by the following year there were 'regular evening meetings [held] once a fortnight; and these meetings have, since that date, been continued without intermission'.[99] Naturally, with two World Wars in the twentieth century, this is no longer the case, although the society is still actively concerned with science and education.[100]

Stevenson explains that the constitution had allowed initially for the election of an honorary president, usually a locally-based scientifically-inclined nobleman. By 1836 the fellowship elected to choose a president from amongst their own working cohorts. These eminent people are listed, including the 'vice-presidents under the old system … who were virtually presidents of the Society', and they include Robert Stevenson, who did his turn as vice-president.[101] Stevenson then examines the contents of the Society's *Transactions*, which began at the same time as its name change in 1841 with acquisition of the Royal Charter. He notes the premiums awarded, starting with that 'given to the late distinguished Professor Wallace for his improved Eidograph, a communication which all who know the value of that exceedingly beautiful instrument must admit was worthy of the high approval of our Institution'.[102] The eidograph, a brass copying instrument which had evolved from the more commonly-encountered pantograph, was produced in some numbers by the Edinburgh scientific instrument-making firm of Adie & Son, and an early example was used in the office of D. & T. Stevenson for reproducing drawings and plans: David's admiration for its elegance and utility is apparent.[103]

The end of his history deals with the awarding of the Keith Medal – which at this point was the highest accolade the Society could present: amongst the winners is his brother, Thomas Stevenson, for his 'holophotal system of illuminating lighthouses'.[104] He then does what presidents normally do at their annual general meetings, and gives a brief review of the past year, in which he notes that the fellowship stands at 397, and that amongst others, the Society has lost through death 'the late M. Arago, perpetual secretary of the Institute of France, … elected an honorary member in 1834, shortly after his visit to Edinburgh'.[105]

Alan Stevenson, David's eldest brother, appears to have been the sole male member of his generation in the Stevenson family who did not stand for election, although he addressed at least three papers to the Society (and presum-

Portrait of Alan Stevenson (1807-65).
(© The Trustees of D. Alan Stevenson)

Portrait of Thomas Stevenson (1818-87).
(© The Trustees of D. Alan Stevenson)

ably attended their meetings). He also donated several of his lighthouse reports to the Society. Perhaps he had too much to cram into his curtailed professional life: he was, however, elected a member of the Institution of Civil Engineers (based in London), and a Fellow of the Royal Society of Edinburgh.[106]

Thomas Stevenson, youngest of the Stevenson brothers, was elected a member in 1847 and used its forum for many of his optical papers. A tribute written by his famous son is worth quoting for what it says both about him and the entire family in a professional capacity:

> Two things must be said: and, first, that Thomas Stevenson was no mathematician. Natural shrewdness, a sentiment of optical laws, and a great intensity of consideration led him to just conclusions; but to calculate the necessary formulae for the instruments he had conceived was often beyond him, and he must fall back on the help of others, notable on that of his cousin and life-long intimate friend, *emeritus* Professor Swan, of St Andrews, and his later friend, Professor P. G. Tait. It is a curious enough circumstance, and a great encouragement to others, that a man so ill equipped should have succeeded in one of the most abstract and arduous walks of applied science. The second remark is one that applies to the whole family, and only particularly to Thomas Stevenson from the great number and importance of his inventions: holding as the Stevensons did a Government appointment they regarded their original work as something due already to the nation, and none of them has ever taken out a patent. It is another cause of the comparative obscurity of the name: for a patent not only brings in money, it infallibly spreads reputation; and my father's instruments enter anonymously into a hundred light-rooms, and are passed anonymously over in a hundred reports, where the least considerable patent would stand out and tell its author's story.[107]

Nevertheless, it has been emphasised that Thomas's intuition (as his son might put it) together with his brother David's solid engineering skills made an effective partnership which produced inspired work.

Thomas published a considerable number of papers, many of them read before the Royal Scottish Society of Arts, winning commendations and medals on a number of occasions.[108] Not all were concerned with lighthouses; he was interested in meteorology, harbour engineering, experiments on the force of waves, and other subjects.[109] Thomas was President for 1859-60. After his death, the then President, David Bruce Peebles (1826-1899), recounted Thomas's achievements over four pages, saying:

> This long catalogue of discoveries and inventions, brought before us from time to time in a series of most valuable and admirable papers, shows how much we are indebted to the author, and proves how deeply he had the welfare of the Royal Scottish Society of Arts at heart. I have thought it better to bring his works before you and let them speak. They tell you what he was, and what he did, and are a better eulogy on his character and genius than any words I can offer.[110]

Portrait of William Swan (1818-94). (© Courtesy of the University of St Andrews Library [ALBI-103])

We shall look more closely at Thomas Stevenson's lighthouse optics in due course below.

His first cousin was William Swan (1818-1894), who became a gifted optical worker and had the mathematical skills that Thomas Stevenson lacked. Swan was elected to the Society in 1846. Together he, Thomas Stevenson and the instrument maker John Adie worked on the practical development of prisms and lenses, using the Society as a forum for their activities.[111] Swan's mother Janet Smith (sister to Jane, who married Robert Stevenson), was widowed when her only child was three years old. She was overprotective of Swan, and had him educated at home. Swan apparently led an unhappy and lonely childhood, his only real friend being his close contemporary and first cousin, Thomas Stevenson.[112] However, after studying divinity at the University of Edinburgh, he set up as a tutor of mathematics and physics in Edinburgh, and by 1850 had obtained a school appointment teaching mathematics. Sir David Brewster exercised his influence to obtain him the post of Professor of Natural Philosophy at the University of St Andrews from 1859. Swan made his mark in the new science of spectroscopy by devising a new prism in 1844, predating the Littrow spectroscope of 1863; and by pioneering the use of a collimator in his astronomical spectroscope in 1856.[113] He also made instrumental advances in photometry. Much of his prize-winning lighthouse work was published alongside that of his

J. M. Balfour (1831-69), from F. W. Furket, *Early New Zealand Engineers* (Wellington, 1953).

(© The Trustees of the National Library of Scotland)

Photograph of Robert Louis Stevenson (1850-94), Presented by Mrs Pamela Godfrey (*née* Stevenson).

(NMS H.1996.239)

cousin, Thomas, and he, too, became President of the Royal Scottish Society of Arts for 1882-83.[114]

Thomas Stevenson's brother-in-law, James Melville Balfour (1831-1869), was elected to membership of the Royal Scottish Society of Arts, after publishing in their *Transactions* a series of prize-winning papers, not all of them concerned with lighthouse illumination. His design of a 'Refraction Protractor' for lighthouse use, won the Society's silver medal, as did another of his papers.[115] He was elected a member in December 1857, giving his address as 84 George Street – his business address as a member of the firm of D. & T. Stevenson.[116] In early 1863, the year he left Scotland for a career as an engineer in New Zealand (and this is discussed further in chapter 6), he delivered another medal-winning paper on the 'Description of a simple Improvement on Reflectors for Lighthouses'; it is clear that the Society was greatly impressed with young Mr Balfour.[117]

Thomas's only child, later known to the world as the great writer Robert Louis Stevenson (1850-94) was destined by his father to follow into the family business, but it was not to be. Even more reluctant than his father had been as a youth to apply himself to his books, a recent biographer has judged that Louis' relationship with his father was always powerful, difficult and disturbing. Despite himself, Thomas Stevenson conspired with his son and his attempts at truancy, yet was conversely gripped by the authoritarian ideal of being the responsible Victorian father figure.[118] Rather as Alan had been badgered into taking up engineering at the end of his schooldays, Louis similarly found himself in 1867 enrolled as a student in the arts faculty at the University of Edinburgh (there was no specific science or engineering course at this point), and two years later found himself undertaking courses in mathematics and natural philosophy (or what we would call physics). The following year he continued with these, together with the new engineering classes of Professor Fleeming (pronounced 'Fleming') Jenkin (1833-85), who had just arrived to take up his appointment of the recently-established chair of engineering in 1868.[119] In his memoir of Jenkin, Louis wrote:

I was inclined to regard any professor as a joke, and Fleeming as a particularly good joke, perhaps the broadest in the vast pleasantry of my curriculum. I was not able to follow his lectures; I somehow dared not misconduct myself, as was my customary solace; and I refrained from attending. ... During the year, bad student as I was, he had shown a certain leaning to my society; I had been to his house, he had asked me to take a humble part in his theatricals; I was a master in the art of extracting a certificate even at the cannon's mouth; and I was under no apprehension. But when I approached Fleeming, I found myself in another world; he would have naught of me. 'It is quite useless for YOU to come to me, Mr. Stevenson. There may be doubtful cases, there is no doubt about yours. You have simply NOT attended my class.'

Typically, Stevenson managed to sweet-talk his professor into producing a form of words that would satisfy all parties, including his father – but it left Louis with no sense of triumph, although a deep and lifelong admiration for Jenkin.[120]

In March 1871 Louis gave a paper, 'On a New Form of Intermittent Light for Lighthouses' before the Society; in Roland Paxton estimation this as 'a creditable effort'.[121] After discussion, the paper was sent to a committee which consisted of Professor Jenkin and two others, who in due course awarded it the Society's silver medal – value, three sovereigns.[122] Louis's father was not deceived, however, for, as his biographer relates, about ten days after this engineering success, Thomas took Louis on an evening walk and bluntly asked him about his thoughts for his future. The discussion was distressing for both, for Louis was forced to admit that his sole concern was for literature. Thomas had come to that defining moment where he realised that

his only son had studied for four years at university, spent three summers at the firm's engineering works, and simply was not interested in following in his father's footsteps.[123]

Louis's connection with the Royal Scottish Society of Arts ended in 1871, and his relationship with engineering remained ambivalent: 'I ought to have been able to build lighthouses and write "David Balfours" too.'[124] He also wrote movingly of this ambivalence:

*Say not of me that weakly I declined*
*The labours of my sires, and fled the sea,*
*The towers we founded and the lamps we lit,*
*To play at home with paper like a child.*
*But rather say*: In the afternoon of time
A strenuous family dusted from its hands
The sand of granite, and beholding far
Along the sounding coast its pyramids
And tall memorials catch the dying sun,
Smiled well content, and to this childish task
Around the fire addressed its evening hours.

Louis composed this verse in the 1880s, living in a house in Bournemouth (paid for by his father), named 'Skerryvore' (after his uncle's greatest achievement); and, writes a recent biographer, how cleverly Louis has changed the typeface, from what he thinks will be said about himself to what he would like to have said. Yet the image of his 'strenuous family' and their 'tall memorials' is less arresting than his harsh description of himself 'playing at home with paper like a child'.[125] His public, however, was perhaps better off with the inspired writings of the author of *Treasure Island*, *Kidnapped* and *Dr Jekyll and Mr Hyde* than they would have been with the resultant works of a reluctant engineer.

The 'good little boys', as RLS somewhat unkindly named his first cousins, the sons of David Stevenson – David A. Stevenson (1854-1938) and Charles Stevenson (1855-1950) –

were elected to the Society in 1879 and 1881 respectively.[126] Both graduated as engineers from the University of Edinburgh in 1875 and 1877 (they were only 18 months apart in age), and joined the family firm, still known as D. & T. Stevenson until after Thomas's death in 1887. They each gave papers before the Society, but by now it was important for civil engineers to reach their professional colleagues beyond the locally-based Edinburgh audience, and the brothers tended to publish their papers elsewhere.[127] Charles Stevenson presented a paper 'On a New Form of Refractor for Dioptric Apparatus' in December 1888, and this won a Society prize.[128]

Others members of the firm, including Alan Brebner (1826-1889), played their part in the Society's activities. Brebner was elected in 1848, and became both a long-standing member of Council, and a Life-member (for which one paid ten guineas). Brebner's father, Alexander Brebner (c.1775-1859) had worked as a builder in the construction of the Bell Rock lighthouse.[129] Alan Brebner served initially as a pupil of D. & T. Stevenson, and rejoined the firm in 1850, from which time 'he was identified with the firm, first as resident engineer in the erection of harbours, lighthouses and other works; then as assistant, and latterly until his death, as a member of the firm'.[130] He became a partner of D. & T. Stevenson in 1878, and was responsible for the lighthouses at Muckle Flugga and Dubh Artach, as we shall see below. Although he appears not to have published many papers with the Society, he was clearly important behind the scenes, where he worked hard on committees.[131]

James Milne of Milton House, who was among the Stevensons' contractors, was based in Edinburgh's Canongate and came from a long dynasty of brass-founders, one of whom (also James Milne) was an original member of the Society back in 1821. He succeeded his brother John Milne in their business in about 1825, and was joined by his son, also John, to become James Milne & Sons in 1837. After the younger John's death in 1886, the firm was acknowledged: 'Mr [John] Milne carried out many contracts, both at home and abroad, for the construction and erection of lanterns, mechanical apparatus, and beacons for the lighthouse service, principally to the designs and under the superintendence of Messrs. D. and T. Stevensons, engineers to the Northern Lighthouse Commissioners.'[132]

Figures from the Adie instrument-making dynasty also featured in the lighthouse work discussed by the Royal Scottish Society of Arts, among them Alexander Adie (1775-1858), founder member, who had assisted Thomas Smith to work out the dimensions of the curves of his plaster-of-Paris mirror-faceted reflectors, and his son John Adie (1805-57), elected in May 1838, who produced the optics for Thomas Stevenson's hemispherical reflector as used at Peterhead and then at the Horsburgh lighthouse. Many of the telescopes used by keepers in the service of the Northern Lighthouse Board were supplied by their firm, as were the sundials which were used at a number of the sites. The firm also produced instruments designed to help with the installation and setting of French optics, including a metre scale.[133]

Alexander Cuningham, Secretary to the Commissioners of Northern Lighthouses, read two medal-winning papers before the Society on the subject of fog-signals. Trials and experiments were to follow, as not everyone was convinced that lighthouses were the correct location for such devices, and until this date there were fog-bells at only the Bell Rock and Skerryvore in Scotland.[134] Another member of the Society was noted at his death in 1855 by the then President, David Rhind FRSE. Despite feeling that it would be invidious to name any of the recently-deceased, long-serving, knowledgeable members:

> I cannot resist making an exception, and that is Mr Slight. We are all well aware how much service this gentleman rendered in our committees, how ready he was with his valuable assistance in many delicate and difficult investigations as to the merits of supposed inventions, and how much on all occasions we profited by his varied acquaintance with scientific subjects, and his accurate knowledge of everything that had been done in the Society since its commencement. I believe that Mr Slight began life as a country wright in Tranent, where he was born, and came to Edinburgh to be employed by the late Mr Stevenson, engineer, as his assistant in carrying on the Bell Rock Lighthouse. He remained for some time in this employment, where he had become known for his useful and varied information.[135]

Horizontal sundial engraved for 'Lamlash lighthouse' by Adie & Son, Edinburgh, c.1850.
(NMS T.1984.32)

James Slight (1792-1854) was father to George Henry Slight (b.1822), who at about this time submitted a number of papers to the Society. As we shall see in chapter 6, young Mr Slight was to move to London, where he worked as a workshop attendant, Trinity Wharf, Blackwall.[136] His son, also George Henry Slight (1859-1934), subsequently became a famous builder of lighthouses in Chile. Another original artificer on the Bell Rock was James Clark, an eminent clockmaker who built a turret clock with four dials for the Tron Church on Edinburgh's High Street. He was awarded the Society's gold medal in June 1820, for his 'Description of a Method of Cutting Screws', and also provided for the Northern Lighthouse Board a series of twelve skeleton mantle clocks, individually devised and dated, between 1812 and 1828, ten of which remain at 84 George Street.[137]

John Turnbull Thomson (1821-1884), whom we shall encounter in chapter 6 as responsible for building the 'First Pharos of the East' in 1850, was forced afterwards through ill-health to return to Britain, and, while spending time in Edinburgh, became a Fellow of the

Royal Scottish Society of Arts, and presented a paper before the Society on a 'Description of a Semi-Revolving Light', looking at a final proposed use of the parabolic reflector before he left for New Zealand. Thomson later described his first impressions there, but did not mention lighthouses, despite the New Zealand Lighthouse Service's long connection with the Stevenson firm.[138]

### D. & T. Stevenson, rock lighthouses and their optics

After Alan's retirement in 1853, his younger brothers David (1815-86) and Thomas (1818-87) acted jointly from 1855 to 1884 as Engineers to the Northern Lighthouse Board, as part of their business of D. & T. Stevenson. Together they designed and built about 29 beacons and lighthouses before they died within a year or so of each other in the later 1880s. The brothers were challenged by three new difficult rock lighthouses – at Muckle Flugga (then known as North Unst) on the northernmost tip of the Shetland Isles; at Dubh Artach (then spelled 'Dhu Heartach') adjacent to Skerryvore; and at Chicken Rock, off the southern tip of the Isle of Man. All the while, Thomas – the lighthouse engineer who, according to his son, apparently lacked the mathematical skill to understand optical science – improved the performance of lighthouse optics until all the available light was efficiently directed. He is perhaps better known today for his meteorological device, the Stevenson screen devised in about 1864 and used for protecting thermometers taking temperature readings.

Changes in the legislation – notably the Merchant Shipping Act of 1853 – continued and strengthened the power given to Trinity House in 1836 to approve or disapprove of improvements proposed by the Northern Lighthouse Board; and in addition it could now direct what lights should be built or discontinued, with the agreement of the Board of Trade. David Stevenson, already working on three new Scottish lights, came up with a wish-list of a further 45 sites, giving eight as a priority; these were agreed, with one further addition. However, the Board of Trade's emphasis on economy resulted in the first group of Scottish lighthouses being constructed in brick rather than the more traditional stone, while the roofs of the keepers' houses were now covered with slate.[139]

These long-term plans were, however, put on the back-burner by European conflict. The Crimean War of 1853 to 1856 was one of a series of hostilities between Russia and the 'sick old man of Europe', the Ottoman Empire, but on this occasion both France and Britain were involved. The route from the White Sea on Russia's northern coastline was to be blockaded by the Royal Navy to prevent the Russian fleet from sailing for the Mediterranean from the ports of Murmansk and Arkangel; navigational aids were required for this, at a time when there were only a total of three lighthouses in the dangerous waters surrounding the entire Orkney and Shetland Islands. Advised by the Admiralty, the Board of Trade required two further beacons to become operational in the Shetland Islands by October 1854.

Two sites were identified: on the island of Whalsay, just east of Shetland mainland; and somewhere close to the island of Unst in the far north. David Stevenson went north immediately, if reluctantly, in February 1854:

> When surveying the several sites on which we landed I had a very favourable opportunity of witnessing the effects of the storms during the recent severe winter which had left their traces in unmistakeable distinctness on every headland. ... they were particularly observable at North Unst where the deep water comes close to the rocks also at Lambaness and Balta where stones of half a ton were thrown up on the green sward at elevations of 80 to 85 feet above high water and I came to the conclusion that what I had formerly considered as *abnormal* seas occurring at certain peculiar places such as Whalsey [*sic*] were in point of fact normal in this country being common to the whole of the North and East coast of Shetland and indeed in all other places where similar physical circumstances prevail there being deep water close in. ... I reported that no buildings could be considered safe on any part of that coast which were not very considerably elevated above high water level.[140]

Unfortunately, a committee of Elder Brethren from Trinity House paid a visit to Muckle Flugga – the name means 'great precipice', an appropriate description of an enormous, almost perpendicular, stack of conical rock that rises straight out of the Atlantic Ocean to a height of 200 feet – on a quiet June afternoon, and decided that building a lighthouse there would be quite feasible for an experienced engineer like David Stevenson.[141] Even in the more measured tones of his popular article written for Norman Macleod's family magazine *Good Words*, David Stevenson was to write that

> ... the *Pharos* steamer left Glasgow, with the workmen and temporary lighthouse and dwellings on the 31st July, and the light was exhibited on the 11th August; and when it is considered that the whole of the materials and stores (consisting of water, cement, lime, coal, iron-work, glass, and provisions, and weighing upwards of 120 tons) had to be landed on an exposed rock, and carried up to the top in small quantities on the backs of the labourers, it will be seen that the exertions of Mr

Brebner, who acted as the resident engineer, and of Mr Watt, who took charge of the landing, were in the highest degree praiseworthy.[142]

A modern author comments that one must bear in mind that absolutely everything necessary for lighthouse construction had to be manhandled up the sheer precipice of the cliff face. Twenty stonemasons and various labourers lived on a barrack on Muckle Flugga, while a further 16 workmen were landed daily from the mainland base.[143]

It took them just 26 days to build the temporary light, 21 feet high, with a cast-iron lantern on top: this was lit on 11 October 1854. The following year, agreement was given for making this a permanent lighthouse, which in turn was completed and lit on 1 January 1858.

This was a 64-foot tower, with ten-foot foundations to anchor it into the rock summit, in the most exposed situation at the tip of the British Isles and in the path of the whole of the force of the Atlantic Ocean. During the 1856 season, over a hundred men laboured at the new lighthouse between April and November. A ten horse-power engine worked an inclined plane on the rock and saved the work of an estimated 16 men; bricks were brought over in small boats and thrown across to the rock when adverse weather prevented the landing of a larger vessel, so that the work was faster than if the more traditional stone had been used.[144] The artist Sam Bough was commissioned by David Stevenson to produce a painting. On a visit to the artist's studio, Robert Louis Stevenson commented:

Watercolour of North Unst lighthouse by Sam Bough RSA, *c*.1860.
(© The Trustees of D. Alan Stevenson)

I have seen one of these sketches in particular, a night-piece on a head-land, where the atmosphere of tempest, the darkness and the mingled spray and rain, are conveyed with remarkable truth and force. It was painted to hang near a Turner; and in answer to some words of praise – 'Yes, lad', said he, 'I wasn't going to look like a fool beside the old man.'[145]

Thomas Stevenson had in the meantime – as well as improving harbours around Scotland – been developing practical lighthouse optics. In 1849 he had built on his brother Alan's work, and a fixed light with prisms in front of the light source, with a reflecting hemisphere behind it, had been put up successfully in Peterhead Harbour. This was adapted into a revolving frame the following year and installed in the new Horsburgh lighthouse at Singapore (see chapter 6 below).[146] Julia Elton, in a recent paper on the development of lighthouse optics during this period, effectively demolishes both of these priority claims by Alan and Thomas Stevenson. In fact, the contemporary literature is confusing, but she feels that just as Alan Stevenson had praised the importance of the Skerryvore optic beyond its real position, so Thomas Stevenson praised the Horsburgh; and on the same grounds: highlighting priority underlines the significance of these improvements.[147]

That is not to say that Thomas Stevenson's innovations were insignificant. Elton believes that the first true modern revolving optic, the result of all of Thomas Stevenson's work, was the impressive first order light at North Ronaldsay, in Orkney.[148] In 1851 this first order (i.e. largest size) revolving eight-panel Fresnel optic, including Alan Stevenson's improved belt of focussing prisms above and below, was installed at North Ronaldsay, and a one-fifth scale model – as well as the full-size optic – was made by the French optical firm of Letourneau.[149] Thomas Stevenson went on to develop what he called the 'holophotal' system of lighthouse illumination, by which he meant 'the use of

Model of a first order revolving light with eight Fresnel lenses, for lighthouses, one-fifth scale, for North Ronaldsay, by T. Letourneau, Paris, 1851. Presented by the Northern Lighthouse Board.

(NMS T.1993.135)

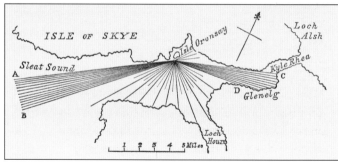

Fixed condensing light with sectors of unequal range, for sounds and narrow seas, by Chance Brothers & Company, Birmingham, designed by Thomas Stevenson, as used at Ornsay, 1857 (NMS T.1993.140). Presented by the Northern Lighthouse Board. Shown with a diagram showing how it works (© The Trustees of D. Alan Stevenson).

the entire light source'. He devised an 'apparent' light, which used prisms to project a beam from the shore-based lighthouse onto a beacon. This was first used at Stornoway in 1851.[150] He also developed an azimuthal condensing system, which reduced the available light in some sectors of azimuth and optimised it in others: this 'condensing' system was used to great effect at the Isle of Ornsay lighthouse, Isle of Skye, when introduced in 1857, where it could shine with varying intensity up and down the Sound of Sleat. James Balfour was charged with its installation, and the devising of his optical protractor certainly

must have helped with the calculations. This new form of light was also introduced in 1857 at Rubha nan Gall in the Sound of Mull, and Kyleakin, also on Skye.[151]

By the later 1850s, Thomas Stevenson was working with James Timmins Chance (1814-1902), the gifted and energetic member of the Birmingham firm of Messrs Chance Brothers who turned their 'lighthouse department' into such an imperial asset. Stevenson's occupation with internally reflecting prisms included a turning dioptric mirror first mooted by Stevenson in 1850 into an efficient reality. The result was the first production model, shown at the 1862 Exhibition in London, and now in National Museums Scotland. Described as a 'dioptric holophote with hemispherical rear reflector of prisms', it proved difficult to construct and Chance had to modify it for use. This he did, constructing a 'dioptric mirror', and in 1863 two were manufactured by Chance for D. & T. Stevenson, for two fixed sea-lights in New Zealand – one at Cape Saunders, the other at Taiaroa Head.[152]

The pinnacle of Thomas's optical labours was achieved in the Tay leading light which was constructed by Chance Brothers. As James Chance wrote: 'Mr Stevenson has added some ingenious arrangements. … A full-sized model of this instrument is now at the Paris Exhibition. It is especially interesting, as combining every existing dioptric method employed in lighthouses.'[153] It was first described before the Royal Scottish Society of Arts in December 1867, and installed in the lighthouses at Buddonness that year, while the 'exhibition optic' was returned to be displayed in the Museum in Edinburgh.[154] In a touching obituary notice for his cousin, William Swan testified to Thomas Stevenson's optical ability: '… it was in this work that Thomas achieved the well-earned and world-wide reputation of being the first in his time in the improvement of lighthouse apparatus.'[155] Alan Brebner's optical protractor, a very different instrument to that devised by Balfour, was used to calculate the shapes of the back prisms in the 1862 'dioptric holophote' mentioned above, and also for the Tay leading light.[156]

Two further rock lighthouse sites were to challenge the Northern Lighthouse Board and the partnership of D. & T. Stevenson before the end of the 1870s. These were Dubh Artach, designed by Thomas Stevenson and built between 1867 and 1871; and Chicken Rock, designed by David and Thomas Stevenson and

built between 1869 and 1874. Dubh Artach – the words are probably a corruption of the Gaelic for 'Black Rock' – is an isolated plug of black basalt rising 35 feet at high water, a precursor of the dangerous Torran reef that extends between the Ross of Mull and the Isle of Colonsay.[157] A shore station was set up at Earraid, a tidal island off the south of Mull, and, as before, a workmen's barrack was constructed for the site, only this time it was made of iron rather than the wood that had served on the Bell Rock and at Skerryvore. Alan Brebner was appointed resident engineer, as he had been at Muckle Flugga. Robert Louis Stevenson was still involved at this time in his attempts to become an engineer, and has left a number of vivid pen-pictures of the place:

Combined front Fresnel lens and rear reflecting prisms, which collects all the light of the lamp into one beam of parallel rays; designed by Thomas Stevenson in 1850. On roller-bearing rotation apparatus, made by Chance Brothers & Co., Birmingham, 1862. Presented by the Northern Lighthouse Board.

(NMS T.1993.138)

For it was no accident that had brought the lighthouse steamer to anchor in the Bay of Earraid. Fifteen miles away to seaward, a certain black rock stood environed by the Atlantic rollers, the outpost of the Torran reefs. Here was a tower to be built, and a star lighted, for the conduct of seamen. But as the rock was small, and hard of access, and far from land, the work would be one of years; and my father was now looking for a shore station, where the stones might be quarried and dressed, the men live, and the tender, with some degree of safety, lie at anchor.[158]

In a later essay destined to remain unpublished during Louis's lifetime, he points out that 34 wrecks had taken place between 1800 and 1865; and there had been enormous casualties, with 24 vessels lost, during the storms of December 1865 and January 1866.[159] The Board of Trade gave the Northern Lighthouse Board the go-ahead to build in October 1866, and the preliminary surveys began. The particular circumstance of this reef was that the 'oval nodule of black-trap', as Louis put it, lies at the head of a deep submarine valley, 80 miles long and stretching away into the open Atlantic.[160] David A. Stevenson realised that it was 'impossible to doubt that a funnel-shaped deep track, receiving directly the seas and currents of the Atlantic Ocean, must have some effect in concentrating the waves on the lighthouse rock at the head of this submerged valley, and may therefore account for the seemingly abnormal seas to which the tower is subjected'.[161] As his writer cousin atmospherically stated:

> No other life was there but that of sea-birds, and of the sea itself, that here ran like a mill-race, and growled about the outer reef for ever, and ever and again, in the calmest weather, roared and spouted on the rock itself. Times were different upon Dhu-Heartach when it blew, and the night fell dark, and the neighbour lights of Skerryvore and Rhu-val were quenched in fog, and the men sat prisoned high up in their iron drum, that then resounded with the lashing of the sprays. Fear sat with them in their sea-beleaguered dwelling; and the colour changed in anxious faces when some greater billow struck the barrack, and its pillars quivered and sprang under the blow.[162]

Louis went on to use his memories of this ghastly place as copy for his story 'The Merry Men' (1882), and of course, for his famous novel, *Kidnapped* (1886). But the weather conditions were in fact very different when he had gone with the artist Sam Bough RSA to visit the rock, when the lighthouse tender '... lay-to at last where the rock clapped its black head above the swell, with the tall iron barrack on its spider legs, and the truncated tower, and the cranes waving their arms, and the smoke of the engine-fire rising in the mid sea. ... it was in sunshine only that I saw Dhu Heartach'.[163]

The experience of the severity of the weather during the first three seasons of building the tower led to a revision of the original plans by the engineers: they decided to increase the height of the solid base by 11½ feet, from 52 feet 10 inches on the 18th course to the 21st course at 64 feet 4 inches above the highest tide. Dubh Artach had the most substantial solid base of any lighthouse built to date, and the masonry structure of 77 courses was completed by the end of 1871, the fifth season. The lantern and internal fixtures were put in place in 1872, in time for an inspection by the Commissioners in July, and the lamp was lit on 1 November of that year.

The final rock lighthouse to challenge David and Thomas Stevenson at this period was that of Chicken Rock, off the Isle of Man. The reason for this prosaic name is that the sea-bird which inhabits this rock is the storm petrel (*Hydrobates pelagicus*), also known as 'Mother Carey's Chickens' (Mother Carey was a quasi-mythological figure, who personified the cruel sea for nineteenth-century sailors).[164] The Northern Lighthouse Board had found that the two earlier aligned Calf of Man lights, built by Robert Stevenson in 1818, were frequently obscured by fog, and so began construction of the replacement lighthouse on Chicken Rock itself in 1869. Work was completed on the tower in June 1873, and it was lit on 1 January 1875. The 123-foot high lighthouse was built of white granite brought from Dalbeattie in Scotland to Port St Mary, where each block was carefully shaped before being shipped over to the rock to be assembled. No barrack was used, as the base at Port St Mary was only just over four miles away. However, the rock was under water twice every 24-hour period, and the tower took five years to complete.[165] Thomas's obituary in the professional journal of civil engineering stated that between them the brothers had designed and constructed 28 Scottish and Manx lighthouses, 'Dhu Heartach and Chickens [*sic*] Rock being of no ordinary difficulty. [The] firm's advice was taken by the Governments of India, Newfoundland, New Zealand and Japan, and schemes for lighting the whole coasts of the last two countries were devised by them, and are now being carried out.'[166] It is to this overseas activity that we now turn.

Within the firm of D. & T. Stevenson there were inbuilt stresses as to how the partnership allocated shares, and while the brothers David and Thomas were growing older and progressively unwell, Alan Brebner was taken on as a partner from 1878. These stresses threatened the survival of the family business, particularly as Thomas Stevenson remained so bitter at having no son to succeed him in the business.[167] However, at this point these were more or less resolved. David and Thomas Stevenson died within a year of each other in the late 1880s, and David's sons – David A. and Charles – working for the firm, were already in place to carry on the family tradition of engineering lighthouses.

## Notes to Chapter 5

1   'Shipwrecks' (1811).
2   Munro (1979), 82-83, citing 54 Geo III c 136.
3   Gifford (1988), 321.
4   Allan (2002), 41.
5   Eggeling (1960), 40-41; Gifford (1988), 320.
6   Ibid., 41. The original light, an array of reflectors, was sent to Newfoundland in 1837, where it can still be seen at Cape Bonavista, to where it was moved in 1892.
7   Munro (1979), 84-85.
8   See: http://www.isle-of-man.com/manxnotebook/maritime/lighthse/intro.htm
9   Stevenson (1946), 15.
10  55 Geo III c67.
11  Robertson (1971); Hellowell (1998a), 23-27.
12  Munro (1979), 85.
13  Paxton (2004); Leslie and Paxton (1999), 56, 181.
14  Bathurst (1999), 154-55.
15  Munro (1979), 275.
16  Stevenson (1848), 13-14.
17  Munro (1979), 85.
18  Stevenson (1848), 14.
19  Ibid., 14.
20  Simpson (1994), 17, quoting National Library of Scotland [NLS] MS Acc. 10706/12, 539. It is not known where these are now.
21  Simpson (1994), 16.
22  Brewster (1831), 43.
23  Ibid., 44.
24  Simpson (1994), 18.
25  Morrison-Low (2007), 183-86.
26  Stevenson (1835a), 2-3.
27  Ibid., 12-13.
28  Ibid., 16-17.
29  [Brewster] (1833), 172-73.
30  Stevenson (1833); Munro (1979), 100-102; Bathurst (1999), 140-44.
31  6 & 7 Wm IV c 79; Munro (1979), 106-108.
32  Stevenson (1835b), 1-2 and 6.
33  J. D. F. (1837), 176.
34  Oppenheim (1968), 103; Barrett (2006), 14-19.
35  Elton (2009), 206-209.
36  Catalogue …(1851), I, 319, item 99.
37  Chance ([1892]), 53-55; Chance (1919),137.
38  Strauss (1864), 186.
39  Kenward (1866), 157-58.
40  Brenni (1994); Brenni (1996); Tag (2005a) and (2005b); and Elton (2009), 194. Thomas Tag's articles are available at: http://hyper-radial.blogspot.com
41  Kenward (1866), 157.
42  Munro (1979), 121.
43  Stevenson (1848), 19.
44  Ibid., 20-21, quoting Lockhart (1878), 286.

45  Stevenson (1893), 499.
46  Stevenson (1848), 37-44.
47  Ibid., 103.
48  Ibid., 47.
49  Stevenson (1845); and Stevenson (1848), plate IV. There appears to be no example of this in a public collection.
50  Stevenson (1848), 67-69.
51  Ibid., 94-95.
52  Ibid., 95.
53  Ibid., 103-104.
54  http://www.buildingconservation.com/articles/rockofages/rockofages.htm
55  Stevenson (1848), 119, 125.
56  Ibid., 127.
57  Ibid., 131.
58  Ibid., 148-50.
59  Ibid., 167.
60  Ibid., 175.
61  Ibid., 176.
62  Ibid., 177.
63  Simpson (1994), 17.
64  Elton (2009), 201-202.
65  Stevenson (1881), 68.
66  Stevenson (1848), 177.
67  Catalogue … (1851), I, 319, item 99: Mair (1978), 166. An unfortunate association of ideas, as museums prefer that the public thinks of their collections as treasure rather than rubbish.
68  Stevenson (1848), 295.
69  Ibid., 295-96; see Morrison-Low (2006a).
70  Anon. (1867), 576.
71  Watkin and Hewat-Jaboor (2008), 386-87.
72  Stevenson (1848), 266-67.
73  Hague and Christie (1975), 227.
74  Grant (1988), 236-37.
75  Ibid., 239.
76  Ibid., 242-44; Curl (2005), 273-75.
77  Brück (2000), 91; Brück and Brück (1988), 95-134. Alan Stevenson was ill from 1852.
78  Stevenson (1824), 131-34 and 379.
79  Stevenson (1848), 56-57, quoting Sir J. Gardner Wilkinson, A Second Series of the Manners and Customs of the Ancient Egyptians … 3 vols (London: John Murray, 1841), 253.
80  Stevenson (1848), 181-89.
81  Stevenson (1865), vii.
82  Hague and Christie (1975), 183-84.
83  Munro (1979), 124.
84  It has been reassembled in the nearby Visitor Centre: http://www.ardnamurchanlighthouse.com/
85  Simpson (1996), 14; we are grateful to Tom Farmer for the generous gift of this important piece, NMS T.1986.591.

86  Bathurst (1999), 196.
87  Discussed by Emerson (1979), (1981), (1985) and (1988).
88  Brock (1984), 38-40.
89  Stevenson (1851), 195.
90  Ibid., 207.
91  See also Leslie and Paxton (1999), 176-80.
92  Sang (1838), and Stevenson (1848), 330 note.
93  Leslie and Paxton (1999), 74.
94  Stevenson (1844a) and (1844b).
95  Stevenson (1856b), 183-84.
96  Shapin (1984), 20.
97  Stevenson (1856b), 184.
98  See, for instance, Anderson and Gowenlock (1998).
99  Stevenson (1856b), 185.
100 See the Royal Scottish Society of Arts' website: http://www.rssa.org.uk/
101 Stevenson (1856b), 185-86.
102 Ibid., 186-87.
103 Simpson (1991), 67, n.115; this instrument remains in a private collection.
104 Published as Stevenson (1856a).
105 Stevenson (1856b), 187.
106 Leslie and Paxton (1999), 181, lists his published works; see also Paxton (2004).
107 Stevenson (1887a), 137-38.
108 Mair (1978), 185 and 214 gives this total as '98 learned papers', others list less than this: Leslie and Paxton (1999), 185-87 reckon 56; Townson (1980-81), 26-28, a total of 55.
109 Swan (1895), lxiii.
110 Bruce Peebles (1891), 88.
111 Clarke et al. (1989), 44-45.
112 Galbraith (1910), 4.
113 Swan (1844); Swan (1856b).
114 Knott (1900); Swan (1856a); Swan (1868a); Swan (1868b).
115 Balfour (1861a), 95; Balfour (1861b), 149.
116 'Proceedings', Transactions of the Royal Scottish Society of Arts, 5 (1861), 58.
117 Balfour (1864), 211.
118 Harman (2006), 33-34.
119 Leslie and Paxton (1999), 99.
120 Stevenson (1912b), 234-35. For a corrective view of Jenkin, and a discussion of RLS's failures as a biographer of a scientist, see Cookson and Hempstead (2000).
121 Leslie and Paxton (1999), 99.
122 Stevenson (1873).
123 Harman (2006), 67.
124 Quoted by Leslie and Paxton (1999), 109.
125 Quoted by Harman (2006), 10.
126 Quoted by Bathurst (1999), 215.
127 Stevenson (1883a) and (1883b).
128 Stevenson (1891). For a bibliography of both brothers, see Leslie and Paxton (1999), 188-89.
129 http://www.brebner.com/uploads/bre23949.pdf
130 'Obituary' (1890), 288.
131 Brebner (1891).
132 D. Bruce Peebles (1887), 391-93; also Connor and Simpson (2004), 809-810.
133 Connor and Simpson (2004), 454-55; Morrison-Low (2006a).
134 Munro (1979), 150-51; Cuningham (1864) and (1868).
135 Rhind (1856), 224.
136 Transactions of the Royal Scottish Society of Arts, 4 (1856), Appendix, 97 and 257; and Slight (1878).
137 Clark (1830); the eleventh clock is in a private collection; and the twelfth, dated 1828, is in National Museums Scotland (T.1990.89).
138 Thomson (1856) and (1883).
139 Munro (1979), 127-30.
140 Quoted in Leslie and Paxton (1999), 75.
141 Nicholson (1995), 130.
142 Stevenson (1865), 20-21.
143 Nicholson (1995), 130; see also Munro (1979), 133.
144 Munro (1979), 135-36.
145 Stevenson (1925), 173.
146 Stevenson (1881), 82 and 89.
147 Elton (2009), 208, quote p. 215.
148 Ibid., 215.
149 Stevenson (1881), 89.
150 Ibid., 156-60.
151 Stevenson (1861); Balfour (1861a); Stevenson (1881), 112-16; Munro (1979), 139.
152 Chance (1866), 497-99; Chance (1902), 73-82; Elton (2009), 221-23.
153 Chance (1866), 501.
154 Stevenson (1868a); Stevenson (1881), 108-11; Elton (2009), 219-21.
155 Swan (1895), lxiv.
156 Stevenson (1868a); Brebner (1869); Stevenson (1881), 242-44.
157 Munro (1979), 160.
158 Stevenson (1887a), 124.
159 Stevenson (1995), 1-5; see also Swearingen (1995).
160 Nicholson (1995), 147-48.
161 Stevenson (1876), 8.
162 Stevenson (1887a), 127.
163 Ibid., 126-28.
164 She appears as a figure in Charles Kingsley's The Water Babies (1863).
165 Nicholson (1995), 158-67; Hellowell (1998b).
166 'Obituary' (1888), 425.
167 Mair (1978), 212, 214-15, 221.

**ABOVE**

Oil painting of Dhu Heartach (Dubh Artach) lighthouse, 1871, by Sam Bough RSA.

(© The Trustees of D. Alan Stevenson)

**LEFT**

Building the Chicken Rock lighthouse, Isle of Man, photograph by Marshall Wane, c.1870. Presented by Dr J. D. Allan Gray. This photograph was among papers belonging to his paternal grandfather, Andrew Gray, Clerk of Works for the building of the Chicken Rock lighthouse under D. & T. Stevenson.

(NMS T.1981.143)

185

# CHAPTER 6

# Stevenson Exports
# and Later Work

BY THE LATTER part of the nineteenth century, contemporary light-house technology was derived from a multi-national approach: no single nation has ever had an exclusive claim to the invention of an entire technology, and lighthouses, with their mixture of applied optics, civil engineering and drive towards fuel efficiency, are no exception. How-ever, the success of the Scottish adaptation of building and lighting their extremely dangerous home coasts during their age of construction encouraged other nations to look to them and their experience for assistance. Of course, it helped that Scotland was a part of one of the great imperial nations, one which had experienced the first industrial revolution, and one in which the maritime imperative was a great driver. However, it is important to remember that capital costs increased after the introduction of steam-powered shipping in the 1840s, and iron ships, brought in from the 1850s, meant even more capital investment per vessel. Both the Northern Lighthouse Board and the Stevenson firm seized the advantage of showcasing their achievements in the shop-window provided by the international exhibitions of the later nine-teenth century, beginning with the Great Exhibition of 1851 in London's Crystal Palace.[1] This helped to advertise their solutions to various technical problems, so that nations beginning from scratch knew where experience could be found.

Between them David and Thomas Stevenson designed and built 28 lighthouses for the Northern Lighthouse Board, and from the 1860s, in response to requests from foreign Governments, they designed light-houses (and trained the appropriate supervisors) for India, Japan, New-foundland, China and New Zealand.[2] It was not only the Stevensons and the Northern Lighthouse Board who exported this technology: Scots engineers with the appropriate experience were recruited by foreign Governments, and the example of Chile at the end of the nineteenth century is outlined here. Although the first request for assistance from abroad came earlier than this, during Alan Stevenson's working life, we shall examine the circumstances here.

187

## The Stevensons abroad: export of a technology to Newfoundland

Well before the 1851 Great Exhibition was even a glimmer in the mind of its creator, Prince Albert of Saxe Coburg, the Stevensons had been contacted by newly-created lighthouse authorities overseas for advice and the benefit of their experience. In the Canadian Province of Newfoundland, local merchants, keen to safeguard their livelihoods and cargoes, had paid for a lighthouse at Fort Amherst, at the entrance to St John's Harbour, immediately after the cessation of hostilities in the War of 1812. This was a stone tower that marked the harbour entrance, with a simple mechanism of three reflectors using three whale oil lamps. Maintained by the garrison in which it was placed, it was paid for by the merchants using the harbour between 1813 and 1835.[3]

Newfoundland had to wait until it obtained representative government before it could set up a public lighthouse system, and the first general election was held there in 1832, with the first session of the House of Assembly opening on 1 January 1833. The Governor's address included – among other trappings of civilisation – the promise of a system of navigational aids around Newfoundland's hazardous coastline. Imitating the British systems (both that of the Northern Lighthouse Board and Trinity House) of collecting lighthouse dues in the harbours from users of sea-marks, the Government of Lower Canada had established a similar system in 1805, named Quebec Trinity House; by the middle of the nineteenth century their mandate covered the entire Gulf of St Lawrence. The new Government in St John's, Newfoundland, also chose to emulate this approach. The Newfoundland Lighthouse Board was established in 1834, and the Commissioners immediately ordered the construction of a lighthouse at Cape Spear to mark the entrance to St John's Bay.[4]

The Newfoundland Board contacted Robert Stevenson & Sons for advice about the structure and the lights, and in 1836 ordered a second lighthouse, similar to that on Cape Spear, to be constructed on Harbour Grace Island. A third lighthouse was built at Cape Bonavista in 1842.[5] Learning from Stevensons that new lighting apparatus was to be installed at the Bell Rock lighthouse later that year, they arranged for the original array to be sent to the new lighthouse then under construction at Cape Bonavista. This consisted of 16 Argand lamps, using whale oil burners, and the original 1811 silver-copper reflectors arranged in an iron frame rotating every 90 seconds, producing alternating red and white lights.[6]

These original lamps from the Bell Rock were replaced at Cape Bonavista in 1892 by reflectors only marginally less old. Installed new in the Isle of May lighthouse when the 1816 building was completed by Robert Stevenson, these were subsequently sent out to Harbour Grace Island, also in Newfoundland. Altogether, three sets of Argand burners and parabolic reflectors were transported to Canada from Scotland in the 1830s and 1840s: those from Inchkeith (1804) to Cape Spear (1836); those from the Isle of May (1819) to Harbour Grace Island (1837); and those from the Bell Rock (1811) to Cape Bonavista (1843). At this period the infant Newfoundland lighthouse service, strapped for cash, found second-hand apparatus perfectly adequate for their needs, especially as it was relatively simple to install and run. Neither the original Bell Rock lights, nor those from Inchkeith, survive today, but those from the Isle of May which replaced them in 1892 can still be seen at the restored Cape Bonavista lighthouse.[7]

The Stevensons' connection with Newfoundland did not end there. David Molloy has pointed out that the Point Amour stone lighthouse, built by the Canadian Board of Works and lit in 1857, was based on the Stevensons' experience of building lighthouses for the Northern Lighthouse Board.[8] Robert Oke, who had operated the Harbour Grace Island lighthouse for a decade, became Chief Inspector for the Newfoundland Lighthouse Service in 1860, and under his superintendence commissioned some of the most important lights on that dangerous coast. These included that at Cape St Mary's, which was first lit in 1860, with a revolving array by D. & T. Stevenson consisting of twelve Argand lamps, giving off flashing red and white lights.[9] The 1858 lighting apparatus at Baccalieu Island used Thomas Stevenson's hemispherical reflectors and front prisms, and the lighthouse at Ferryland Head

had a fixed white light, designed by D. & T. Stevenson, made by Chance Brothers, Birmingham, and installed in 1871.[10]

## The Horsburgh lighthouse, Singapore

In his account of lighthouses published in 1815 for David Brewster's *Edinburgh Encyclopaedia*, Robert Stevenson surveyed such structures that he knew about internationally at this date at

> the more remote quarters of the globe, [where] we shall find the shores in general in a very naked state with regard to this most necessary appendage to the navigation of the seas. We have occasion to know something of the consideration which is given to the marine surveys of the Indian seas by the indefatigable labours of Mr Horsburgh, hydrographer to the East India Company. But as yet, in so far as we know, nothing has been done in the lighthouse department in these seas, if perhaps we except the erection of a lighthouse at Old Woman's Island, at the entrance of Bombay harbour; and another on the island of Jauper, at the entrance of the Hoogly. ... On many of the headlands of the eastern straits and shores, lighthouses seem to be much wanted. ...[11]

Some 35 years later, his son Alan Stevenson received a request in 1850 from the Government Surveyor of Singapore, John Turnbull Thomson (1821-84), asking for a lighthouse design for the Pedra Branca Rock. Portuguese for 'white rock' after the guano-staining by the sea-birds that lived there, Pedra Branca is part of a dangerous reef ten miles from the nearest land, and 34 miles off the mainland of Singapore, the nearest point for supply. It had sustained many losses through shipwreck since the arrival of the empire-building Portuguese in the early sixteenth century. Singapore had been established by Sir Stamford Raffles in 1819 with the agreement of local rulers, and had rapidly become an important trading station for international merchant navies. Scots-born James Horsburgh (1762-1836) had been an eminent hydrographer and map-maker along this coastline, working for the East India Company from 1810. After his death, a subscription was opened in Canton to raise a memorial in his honour, resulting in the lighthouse which still bears his name providing safety to shipping arriving from China at the eastern entrance to the Strait of Singapore.[12] Despite a lack of first-hand experience of local conditions, Thomas Stevenson put the specification together from available data, and the lantern and lighting parts were dispatched and successfully assembled.[13]

Thomson had to work under difficult conditions; although it had taken the bureaucracy 13 years to decide to build the lighthouse, it took him a mere two years to achieve its completion, with a building force of 46 men – Malays, Indian convicts (a number had the word 'murder' tattooed on their foreheads), and Chinese.[14] The conditions of heavy seas during the monsoon season limited the period for building in a very restricted area to about seven months each year; there was the constant threat of pirates; and the granite blocks had to be quarried and dressed, and then transported some 25 miles away by sea.[15] Thomson wrote an account of the building of the lighthouse and its preparations, beginning with organising the acquisition of parts from Europe: 'These consisted of the lantern, lamps and machinery, with a lightning conductor. For this purpose, Mr Alan Stevenson, the eminent Engineer to the Northern Lighthouse Board, was addressed by letter, accompanied by charts of the Straits, remarks on climate, and other information, necessary to be made known for his consideration and from which he was requested to decide on the most proper kind of light adapted to the position, make the requisite plans and then execute them under his supervision.'[16]

In a paper given in 1850 (though not published until 1856), Thomas Stevenson wrote about the lighting system which maximised the light beam produced by

> … ordinary reflectors which are still much used in lighthouses … substituting a portion of a spherical mirror behind [the flame], and adding a lens with three distinct diacatoptric lenticular rings. The Horsburgh lighthouse, now being constructed on the Pedro Branca rock, near Singapore, according to plans by Mr J. T. Thomson, Government Surveyor, was lately fitted up with apparatus on this principle, under the direction of Mr A. Stevenson. It consists of a frame having nine holophotal reflectors of this kind.[17]

The prototype device was constructed by John Adie, the prominent Edinburgh scientific instrument maker, and the device was exhibited at the Great Exhibition. It was first used at Peterhead, in the harbour light there in 1849, but the Horsburgh Lighthouse was the first to use it in a revolving frame of nine elements.[18] Julia Elton comments that Thomas Stevenson's remarks are not particularly straightforward, and that in fact the new light at North Ronaldsay should be considered the first true modern revolving optic. The only illustration of the Horsburgh optic shows a traditional and unsophisticated device: but all of this emphasis was to the prove priority of invention.[19]

Pavitt comments that it seems very unusual that the laying of the foundation stone at the Horsburgh lighthouse was according to Masonic rites, despite the same ceremonial being observed at Raffles lighthouse four years later. He knew of no other lighthouse worldwide that had been founded with a similar ritual.[20] In fact, we have already seen that Robert Stevenson presided over such a ritual at the Bell Rock lighthouse, and it is possible that such observances were more the norm than not.[21] The Horsburgh lighthouse, still standing today, was described by a 'rambling naturalist' a few years later:

> I was able to land at some steps cut in the almost perpendicular side of the rock upon which the lighthouse is built. Although the rock, however, is naturally very inaccessible, a sort of moveable pier is constructed, by means of which a landing can be effected at almost any

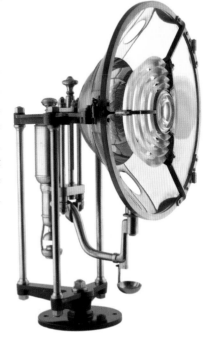

Parabolic reflector and lamp, with front glass prisms, designed by Thomas Stevenson and John Adie. First used at Peterhead Harbour in 1849, then in the Horsburgh lighthouse, Singapore, 1850, in an array of nine elements. Presented by the Northern Lighthouse Board.

(NMS T.1993.150)

ebb tide. The lighthouse, a testimonial to the invaluable services of the author of *The Directory* [sailing directions first compiled by James Horsburgh in 1816-17, which came to be known in editions after 1841 as the *East India Directory*] is a cylindrical building, with a basement and six stories, which are ascended by narrow ladders, to the light-room at the top. This contains nine cata-dioptric lights, arranged in sets of three, movable by clock-work, so that the angle between each set shows dark. The light is visible once in a minute, and is seen 15 miles. The rock upon which the lighthouse is built, is an irregular, much broken, rounded mass of grey and compact granite, extending out northward in a reef, but with only a few rolled stones at the south. It was commenced in 1850 and finished in 1851, and in many respects closely resembles the Bell Rock Lighthouse, 11 miles east of Arbroath. The chief light-keeper is an Englishman, who is assisted by Malays.[22]

Unfortunately, the combination of the climate and hard work appears to have wrecked Thomson's health. He returned to Britain on sick leave in May 1853, and enrolled at the University of Edinburgh to undertake further studies. He emigrated to New Zealand in 1856, still aged only 34. There he used his many skills in helping the development of the colony's infrastructure until his death in 1884.[23]

### Lighthouses in India and Burma

After a brief visit in 1853, the Governor-General of India, the Marquess of Dalhousie, noted that the Alguada Reef, a 'dangerous and dreaded line of rocks … renders a divergence from the direct course between Calcutta and the Irrawaddy so necessary', that half a day's passage was added on to the journey.[24] This hazardous rock is located off the mouth of the Bassein River, 22 miles out in the Bay of Bengal, off Cape Negrais. Lieutenant Alexander Fraser (1824-98) of the Bengal Engineers was dispatched back to Britain to consult 'experts' about lighthouse building:

> … of the Light houses I so inspected, those most analogous to the one proposed for the Alguada Reef, were the Eddystone built by Smeaton, the Bell Rock by Robert Stevenson, and the Skerryvore by his son, Alan Stevenson … I … had the benefit of constant communication with Messrs Thomas and David Stevenson, Engineers to the Board of Commissioners of Northern Light Houses, the former of whom is now, I believe, considered the best English [*sic*] authority on Light House illumination.[25]

Although the notorious Alguada Reef is situated off the south-western tip of Burma, at this time Burma was run by the British through her Indian administration. A recent article paints a bigger picture, in which lighthouses are seen as both symbols and structures of power and imperialism, an integral part of European colonial expansion in the area. In 1860 the Dutch and the British had discovered a labyrinth of unlit islets in a darkened sea that by 1910 had been dramatically altered into an illuminated night-time seascape, so that their Western rulers could both supervise and regulate the entire region. Although the lighthouses allowed for greater navigational safety, they were also emblematic of the hidden strength of their distant masters.[26]

Acting according to instructions, Fraser surveyed the reef and made careful soundings around it in 1856, taking into consideration the possibilities of the structure in terms of 'its facility of erection and economy'. Guided by Alan Stevenson's principles, he decided that the tower should be constructed of stone along the lines of the Skerryvore, to enable it to withstand the elements 'in so exposed and dangerous a situation as the Alguada Reef'.[27] Fraser recommended the installation of a fixed catadioptric light, and planned for building to take

place between November and the end of April, avoiding the monsoon season. He also suggested the use of Chinese stonemasons from Hong Kong, as so much time was lost in sickness by British workmen who found adjustment to the searing heat and driving spray impossible. Fraser located possible sites for a nearby quarry, a position for a stores depot, and a source for limestone.[28] Memoranda were exchanged amongst the Indian civil servants, discussing his proposals, while Fraser went to Britain in the summer of 1857. From London he wrote to the Secretary of the East India Company that he had visited both the Eddystone and the Bishop Rock lighthouses, noting that 'it would be convenient for me to visit the Light Houses on the Coasts of Scotland during next month'.[29]

Besides the Eddystone and Bishop Rock, Fraser also visited the Breakwater Light at Plymouth, the Bell Rock, Cromarty Harbour light, Tarbetness, Pentland Skerries (both towers), Sumburgh Head, Bressay Sound, Whalsay, Out Skerries, North Unst (or Muckle Flugga), North Ronaldsay, Hoy Sound High and Low lighthouses, Skerryvore and Ardna-

The Alguada Reef lighthouse, Burma, first lit in April 1865. Modelled on Skerryvore, and slightly larger. Image from the *Illustrated London News*, 21 October 1865.

murchan – a real case of 'if it's Tuesday, it must be Ardnamurchan'.[30] His experience thus rapidly acquired, led him to report 'on the measures that should be adopted for erection of a Light House on the Alguada Reef', together with details of costs for assembly and maintenance. In his visit to the Scottish lights, Fraser accompanied Thomas Stevenson, and had 'many opportunities of obtaining information on the subject of the several systems of optical illumination, and he gave me to read a report prepared by Messrs D. and T. Stevenson on the comparative merits of the catoptric and dioptric systems'. Fraser was convinced by this report that 'the system of catoptric illumination must be considered obsolete and useless as compared with the dioptric'.[31] He went on to quote the proposal that the United States Lighthouse Establishment, rapidly trying to modernise after 32 years inertia under Treasury Auditor Stephen Pleasonton, 'recommend that the Fresnel or lens system, modified, in special cases, by the holophotal apparatus of Mr Thomas Stevenson, be adopted as the illuminating apparatus system for the lights of the United States, to embrace all new lights now or hereafter authorized, and all lights requiring to be renovated, either by reason of deficient power or defective apparatus'.[32]

Modelled on Alan Stevenson's successful tower at Skerryvore, the lighthouse completed on the Alguada Reef in 1865 was some six feet higher than its prototype, partly to be seen further out to sea, but also to accommodate at least six months' worth of stores and provisions for the monsoon season, when it was effectively cut off by the weather. It was regarded as a triumph by the *Illustrated London News*, which published a view of the structure 'on a spot most dangerous and difficult of access. … Except in the very calmest of weather, the sea is always breaking over these rocks, and it is certain destruction for a vessel to be cast upon them'. In 1856, indeed, an emigrant ship with 300 passengers was lost, with the exception of 14 who were saved.

The building of the Alguada Reef lighthouse was delayed by the Indian Mutiny in 1857, and work did not start until the end of 1859. There were difficulties in working the stone, and eventually this was brought 1200 miles from Singapore; locating skilled workman also proved to be expensive, as they had to be brought from China and Madras. The foundations were begun in January 1860; the first stone laid in February 1861; and in April 1865 a 'first-class revolving holophotal light' designed by D. & T. Stevenson was lit, 'visible, in clear weather, from a distance of twenty nautical miles'.[33]

In an assessment of the role of the military engineer in India, E. W. C. Sandes comments that, despite civil engineers flocking to the subcontinent, it was military engineers who were most closely concerned with lighthouse construction there. He explains that this was due to the personality of Lieutenant Colonel Alexander Fraser CB, Royal (Bengal) Engineers, who committed himself in particular to the lighting of the Burmese coast, and who was succeeded in this task by other fellow officers. After serving in the Sikh Wars and the Second Burma War of 1852, he constructed the Alguada Lighthouse; afterwards he continued to work in this area. In 1862, while still engaged in this work, he submitted a comprehensive report on the lighting of the Burma coast. By 1870 Fraser and his staff had also designed and built lighthouses on the Oyster Reef between Akyaba and Alguada, at the Krishna Shoal and China Bakir between Alguada and the Rangoon River, and at Easter Grove at the Rangoon River estuary in Burma, and they had begun the remodelling of the Great Savage Rock Lighthouses.[34]

A modern biography of his son, Admiral Sir Bruce Fraser (1888-1981), says of his father that Alexander Fraser's principal monument is the Indian railway system, but this is closely followed by the lighthouses just enumerated.[35] Curiously, Alexander Fraser had no contemporary biography, though he appears to have been a more than capable engineer in the service of the Empire. A genealogical website provides a possible answer: that his private life did not stand up to the intense glare of Victorian scrutiny.[36]

The first lighthouse constructed in India appears to have been one at Bombay Harbour, as noted by Robert Stevenson in 1815. The natural harbour there, combined with land reclamation over the years, made the area tricky for increasing shipping to find its way through to a safe berth. Sandes states that for about a hundred years after the establishment of British rule, the only markers at the harbour entrance were a couple of tombs and a whitewashed house. By 1766 these had been exchanged for two signal-houses, one on Old Woman's Island and the other at Malabar Point, the first of these being replaced by the first proper lighthouse in India, whose construction was begun in 1768 and finished three years later.[37] It is unclear who was responsible for this lighthouse, known as the Colaba lighthouse, but Sandes believed that it was the work of the Bengal Engineers. It used reflectors and oil lamps, and was repaired in 1828 and 1853, but was superseded when a new light was completed at Prongs in 1874.[38]

Clearly delighted with what proved to be the tallest lighthouse in the world at that time, the Indian Government placed further orders, totalling some seven more built under the supervision of Fraser. Designs from D. & T. Stevenson were produced for Bombay, Cochin, the Hooghly River near Calcutta, and also for other British colonial outposts at Aden and the Cocas Islands, south of Sumatra. The firm was also asked to assess the lights on Mauritius for the French Government, and in 1871 a request came from China, asking for two suitably-trained Scottish engineers, who were in due course sent to Shanghai, followed by an order for ten buoys. This international aspect of the business continued well into the early twentieth century.[39]

## Japan

In the late nineteenth-century, Japan was a land long closed to Westerners since 1640, apart from a small island off the city of Nagasaki where Dutch traders lived. This is, of course, a gross oversimplification, and some small inroads by Europeans into Japan had been made over the years. The British East India Company had tried hard to gain a foot in the door, but famously it was the Americans who, in the person of Commodore Matthew Perry, sailed into Edo Bay in July 1853 with four heavily-armed battleships demanding trading rights. Perry obtained the initial 'treaty of peace and amity' for the United States in 1854, and something similar was achieved for Britain.[40] Further treaties in 1858 allowed increased commercial development and the establishment of a number of treaty ports where foreign merchants could reside, in effect providing extra-territorial rights to foreign governments. A supplementary convention concluded in 1866 stipulated that the Japanese Government was to provide efficient navigation lights in the apparatus to these treaty ports – the most important of these in the 1860s being Yokohama, although others included Nagasaki and one on Hokkaido, and later, Kobe and Niigata.[41]

By the 1860s the United States was distracted by concerns at home, namely the Civil War, so that Britain became the leading foreign power involved with Japan. By this time, however, Japan was also involved in a tremendous internal political upheaval, which was often bloody and violent, as the prevailing

Rock Island (Mikomoto) lighthouse, Japan, built by R. H. Brunton.

(© The Trustees of the National Library of Scotland)

Tokugawa shogunate's power over feudal magnates was undermined by (among other things) an inability to adjust to the presence of the foreigners. It is an immensely complicated period but essential background to understanding the convulsion that pulled Japan from being a predominantly feudal and inward-looking country to one that was hastily industrialised. Comparisons can be made with the Stalinist Soviet Union, or even modern China. By 1867 the anti-Tokugawa forces had gained the ascendancy and the Tokugawa troops surrendered: by the end of 1868 the civil war was all but over. The new regime, in which samurai from the Satsuma and Choshu regions were dominant, restored nominal power to the Emperor, and moved the imperial capital from Kyoto to Edo, which was renamed Tokyo: this event marks the start of the Meiji (meaning 'enlightened government') Restoration.[42]

The new, and particularly the younger, rulers wanted to make Japan a significant power in the Far East, and they especially wished to avoid the fate of China, where Western powers were grabbing concessions: for example, the British annexation of Hong Kong. As Japan's own resources were seen as being limited – although literacy rates were comparatively high by standards of the time – foreign experts were brought in to assist. Western technological know-how was transferred by showing and teaching. Thus technical experts and teachers were brought in from Europe and the United States, and among them was Richard Henry Brunton (1841-1901).[43]

Brunton was born in 1841, the son of a coastguard at Muchalls, just south of Aberdeen, on the north-east coast of Scotland. Interestingly, he only recently received an entry in the *Oxford Dictionary of National Biography*, despite having been the first lighthouse engineer in Japan, based in Yokohama for almost eight years.[44] In a telling article, Olive Checkland characterises Brunton as 'a brilliant and abrasive engineer'.[45] What comes across in both her paper and Brunton's own account of his time in Japan, is his lack of managerial skills – principally in his failure to avoid confrontation, want of diplomatic language and a complete inability to empathise with a foreign culture. Brunton was trained by and worked for John Willett, a railway and general engineer, in Aberdeen. In 1864 he moved to London where he worked for the London and South Western Railway – at this period there was little theoretical training for British engineers, who were apprenticed to professionals and 'learned on the job' in a 'hands-on' practical fashion. As Checkland remarks, regular British university engineering courses at this time were rare, but the University of Glasgow and University College London were turning out exceptional graduates, some of whom, like Henry Dyer and William Ayrton, were recruited for Japan.[46] Both

Dyer and Ayrton taught engineering at the Imperial College of Engineering in Tokyo, and were, and still are, held in high regard by the Japanese.

In 1867 the Japanese Government approached the Scottish engineering firm of D. & T. Stevenson through the British Board of Trade, with a proposal that they should establish a network of lights around what was then a very poorly marked coast. As Craig Mair has recounted, supplying lighthouse parts to Japan was a completely different commercial arrangement to sending lights to, say, Aden or India, where at least local difficulties with language or custom could be overcome by the fact that these were British colonies. Doing business with Japan meant that D. & T. Stevenson had to learn about Japanese elaborate formalities of procedure and etiquette, and, additionally, information or dimensions delivered by the Japanese could not be completely relied upon. It rapidly became clear that the answer was to train up a team of engineers, builders and mechanics, and to send them out to put together the skeleton of a lighthouse service from scratch.[47]

By this time, D. & T. Stevenson of Edinburgh had become principal contractors for lighthouse construction in Scotland: they would choose and survey the site, select the appropriate materials required, compose the specifications, provide the plans, and order custom-built gear from specialist suppliers. The Stevensons advertised the supervisory post for a lighthouse engineer in Japan, and Richard Henry Brunton was appointed in February 1868. Immediately, he and two assistants, Blundell and MacVean, were given a 'crash course' of training on the more specialist work of a lighthouse as opposed to that of a general engineer. The new recruits also spent time at St Abbs Head and Girdleness lighthouses, in order to understand the routine work of lighthouse-keepers. They were then despatched from Southampton in June, arriving at Yokohama in early August 1868.[48]

On arrival, Brunton reported to the British diplomat Sir Harry Parkes (1828-85), whose Royal Navy contacts enabled Brunton to circumnavigate Japan. Until 1883 the Royal Navy was undertaking an extensive hydrographic survey of Japanese waters for military and economic purposes. As Brunton wrote in his memoir: 'Admiral Keppel … detached HMS *Manilla* under Captain Johnson, and my first visit around the coast was made in this ship.' Between November 1868 and January 1869, a preliminary tour was made. Brunton observed that

> … the sites for fourteen lighthouses were visited and surveyed,
> their height above the sea measured; notes were taken of the building
> materials and labour obtainable at each, and other information

procured, all of which was embodied in a report afterwards presented to the Imperial Government and to the British Minister [Sir Harry Parkes]. ... The preliminary work being thus accomplished, decisions as to which points on the coast were most urgently in need of illumination, and the order in which the lighthouses were to be erected, were quickly made. The Lighthouse Establishment, consisting of dwellings, offices, stores, workshops, etc., was to be located at Yokohama.[49]

In a paper which he later gave before the Institution of Civil Engineers in London after his return from the Far East, Brunton explained the situation more graphically:

On arriving in Japan, the author examined the sites of the lighthouses which had been decided on; ... they were spread over 1500 miles of coast [including the Inland Sea]. The Inland Sea, separating the main island from Kiusiu and Shikoku, is about 250 miles long, and, at some places, it is 50 miles wide; it is filled with several thousand small islands, and navigation is carried on through recognised channels between them. It may be judged, therefore that to place a light on every point in the Inland Sea requisite to render navigation through it practicable, on dark nights, would be a work of magnitude and of doubtful utility.[50]

Revealingly, Brunton stated in his memoir that: 'The Japanese by themselves were at that time unable to carry out any large building operations. Indeed their skill in these was apparently the weakest of their accomplishments. It was therefore decided to obtain from England representative artisans in the different building trades, such as masons, plumbers, machinists, etc., besides several light keepers.'[51] This was all at Japanese expense. In his 1876 paper he was more circumspect:

At the time of [the author's] arrival no artisans were acquainted with anything beyond the slight and unimportant work customary in the country. Carpenters were skilful in the use of their tools, but masons, bricklayers, and blacksmiths were almost unknown. Men had therefore to be taught each of those trades, and the works had to be carefully watched during their progress. The staff of Europeans employed has been extremely small, but notwithstanding the difficulties surrounding the prosecution of the works, each lighthouse is well finished.[52]

The headquarters of the Lighthouse Department was at Yokohama, and as Brunton described it,

... the workshops, store-rooms, etc., are erected on a space of about four acres of ground and form a complete establishment, where the whole work required in the construction and maintenance of the

199

Satanomisaki (Chickakoff) lighthouse, Japan, built by R. H. Brunton.

lighthouses, lightships, and buoys, has been carried on. The yard is on the seashore, and is provided with a stone jetty, alongside of which boats can lie. ... In the yard there is an experimental lighthouse, a brick building, 20 feet square and 40 feet high. ... The principal object of the lighthouse is to afford means for furnishing a preparatory training to young Japanese lightkeepers previous to their being sent to the regular lighthouse stations. It is also used for examining apparatus, which during its voyage from England may have got shaken out of adjustment, or have been otherwise damaged.[53]

As main contractors, the Stevenson firm had a well tried and tested network of specialist subcontractors working to their designs. As Craig Mair has observed, the cast metal frames and machinery were made by Milne's of Edinburgh, Chance Brothers of Birmingham cast the optical glass for the lenses, and Smith's of Blair Street (still run by descendants of Thomas Smith) produced lamp wicks and

burners for the lighting. James Dove of Edinburgh usually made the lantern glass. Mair goes on to comment how extraordinary it was that time after time these same businesses won the Stevensons' tenders, but nonetheless, everything came successfully together at its remote destination.[54] However, this did not prevent French optical firms (Barbier & Fenestre, and L. Sautter Lemonnier & Cie) from enquiring of Stevensons whether their services might not be used for the Japanese service. Brunton argued that it was wiser 'on national grounds to keep the orders in England [*sic*]'.[55]

Since his arrival, Brunton had sent D. & T. Stevenson copious reports of the proposed lighthouse sites: earthquakes in particular being among the local conditions not hitherto encountered. David Stevenson immediately turned his fertile imagination to devising an 'aseismatic joint', which he presented in a paper before the Royal Scottish Society of Arts in 1868. In this he pointed to the devastating earthquake experienced in Naples in 1857;

and alluded to the fact that in Japan tremors could be felt 'as frequently as once a fortnight for a series of months together'. Indeed, Japan had experienced substantial earthquake damage in both 1854 and 1855. Stevenson's plan was to incorporate spherical balls of bell metal in cups of the same material placed between two platforms, the lower cups being fixed to beams forming the foundation, and the upper cups being fixed to the lowest beams of the superstructure, 'thus admitting', he wrote, 'within a limited range, free motion of the upper over the lower part of the building'. A prototype eight feet in diameter was constructed and tested at Milne's works, with some success, and Stevenson stated that 'for the towers, it is proposed to adopt plate-iron ... and place the whole on balls in the manner already described. ... The apparatus which has been recommended is the holophotal reflector, which affords certain advantages in its being less easily injured than the ordinary dioptric apparatus illuminated by one metal lamp.'[56] Brunton was extremely critical about the aseismatic joint, finding that in high winds the superstructure would 'give rise to a motion equally as distressing as a severe earthquake. In the same way a person stepping on one of the aseismatic tables, for the purpose of trimming or cleaning the lamps, causes the upper part to roll to such an extent that the lamps become deranged, and in the case of revolving lights the regular motion of the clockwork machinery is destroyed.'[57] Brunton preferred what he saw as 'the only alternative that seemed feasible [which] was to give the lighthouses great weight and solidity, thereby adding to their inertia and checking their oscillation'.[58] In a letter to the Stevensons in August 1872, he explained in some depth his reasons for discontinuing its use in Japanese lighthouse construction, with the agreement of the Japanese Government.[59]

Brunton gave details of the constructions of the lighthouses: they 'were constructed of stone or brick, wood or iron, as found most suitable for the locality'. Because all iron in Japan had to be imported from Europe, only three were made of iron, for particularly inaccessible sites. The lighting system in his earliest lighthouses used metallic reflectors because of the risk of earthquake, although Brunton later persuaded the Stevensons that the standard dioptric lights as used in Europe would be cheaper, more efficient in the use of oil and easier to maintain, and so these were fitted to the later lights. Letters from Brunton to the Stevensons are full of lively detail, and (sadly) the occasional failings of lightkeepers:

I am sorry to have to inform you that McIntosh sent out by you has lately given way to drink and other misbehaviour. I enclose your copy of a letter from the Japanese officials complaining of this. On my next visit to Kobe, where he now is, I will have this matter gone into and I will let you know what is done.[60]

More happily, while in Japan, Brunton completed some 34 lighthouses, two lightships, 13 buoys and three beacons, and was instrumental in various other successful engineering projects in Yokohama, including railways, drainage, bridge-building and telegraphy.[61] Yet, thanks to his inflexible attitude to the Japanese, his contract was not renewed. In 1876, at the age of 35, Brunton was obliged to return to London, his career effectively over.

To sum up, as Ian Inkster has pointed out, by an enormous assortment of authoritarian and promotional policies, Japan's centralised establishment ensured that dealings were maintained between Europeans and Japanese throughout the industrialisation process. Between 1870 and 1885 the Ministry of Engineering devoted an average of 42 per cent of its total expenditure on official foreign experts, with these costs hitting a pinnacle of 66 per cent in 1877. The Kobusho (Ministry of Information) ran its foreign employment programme not to increase Japan's manufacturing skills, as seemed apparent, but actually to create a strategic infrastructure. By 1872, 80 per cent of its 800 European workforce was engaged in telegraph, mining, railway and lighthouse developments.[62] In this the Northern Lighthouse Board, Messrs D. & T. Stevenson and Richard Henry Brunton, had all played their part. Today's Japanese Lighthouse Association (TOKOKAI) is considered to be one of the world's leaders, but it all began with some assistance from Edinburgh.

### New Zealand

We have already encountered Edinburgh-born James Melville Balfour (1831-69), Thomas Stevenson's brother-in-law, who served his apprenticeship with the engineers D. & T. Stevenson after spending time in Scottish and German workshops, particularly studying optics in the latter. Scottish emigrants in Otago, in New Zealand's South Island, sought the advice of D. & T. Stevenson about lighthouse provision. Balfour was recommended, and he designed and brought out with him lamp equipment for the Cape Saunders and Taiaroa Head lighthouses. He arrived to take up his appointment as Marine Engineer to the Otago Provincial Government in September 1863.[63] At the end of two years, this appointment ended and he became Marine Engineer to the Colonial Government of New Zealand, and immediately became involved in marine engineering plans and particularly that of 'establishing the lighthouse system after the Scotch model. … He also designed and had executed under his immediate superintendence various lighthouses, among others those at Tairoashead [*sic*], Nugget Point, Dog Island, Cape Campbell, and Farewell Spit, the lanterns and apparatus for which were sent from Edinburgh.'[64]

Helen Beaglehole has recently produced an authoritative and a detailed account of the history of the New Zealand lighthouse system, which grew fairly rapidly in the new colony as the colonists had to rely on the sea for both their own journeys and for imports and exports. As with Scotland, some of New Zealand's offshore hazards are amongst the most dangerous maritime perils in the world: the Cook Strait, for example, may be named after the superlative navigator of the eighteenth century, but it is still characterised as one of the most treacherous sections of water in the world.[65] Balfour's work in the South Island of New Zealand got off to a good start, but his relationship with the Otago Provincial Government faltered over the building of the Cape Saunders light. This was resolved, and Balfour, now employed by the newly-established Marine Department, started work on lighting the New Zealand coastline. Farewell Spit was lit in June 1870, followed by Nugget Point in July and Cape Campbell in August. A pair of matching towers was put up to mark Waitemata Harbour, the entrance to Auckland's main anchorage and port. One was lit in July 1870, the other a year later.[66]

Tragically, on 18 December 1869, Balfour's life was cut short at the age of 38. As *The Times* recorded:

It is my painful duty to record the death by drowning of two of our most public men, both in the prime of life, each at the head of his profession in New Zealand – Mr Thomas Patterson, C.E., and Mr James Balfour, marine engineer, the former was drowned crossing in Cobb's coach over the Kakanui river, Otago; the latter by upsetting of a boat in the roadstead of Timaru, on his way to attend the funeral of his friend and colleague. Both men of colonial reputation, their untimely death has cast a gloom over the whole community, and the loss of their professional services will be severely felt, as they were both engaged in several important undertakings.[67]

Balfour left a widow and seven-year-old daughter. As Helen Beaglehole recounts, professionally his death formed an interruption. Captain Robert Johnson, a man with much maritime experience and acting secretary of the Marine Department after Balfour's death, collaborated with Captain R. A. Edwin to draw up a scheme to light New Zealand's as-yet dark and dangerous coastline. In 1874 the colony's new Marine Engineer John Blackett and Johnson together made a series of voyages to identify where the lights should most advantageously be placed.[68]

The New Zealand Government continued to authorise the business of D. & T. Stevenson in Edinburgh to supply the lanterns and lighting systems for their lighthouse service, though the structures themselves were built by local firms. The same group of subcontractors – Milne's the brass and iron-founders and James Dove for lantern machinery – were involved in assembling individual optics with its machinery, having it tested and inspected by a member of the Stevenson firm, before dispatching it by steamer through the London-based New Zealand agent general to whatever port was closest to the eventual site in New Zealand. Unlike the case of the Japanese lighthouse service, where Brunton's nationalism had apparently prevailed, the Parisian optical glassworks of Barbier & Fenestre supplied Milne's Edinburgh workshop with the first order flashing light for Moko-Hinau for £1080, and also that for Tory Island, both at the end of 1875.[69] The subcontractors were organised through Stevensons, and everything was assembled in Milne's workshop – and there are photographs of these assemblies for a number of lighthouse optics. By 1884 the firm had been involved in some aspect of at least 25 New Zealand lights.[70] The optic and machinery were then dismantled and dispatched, and in due course reassembled on site. The Stephens Island optic, a first order dioptric group white light, was supplied by Barbier & Fenestre, with machinery by Milne & Son, and first lit 29 January 1894.[71]

## Chile

George Slight (1859-1934) was an Edinburgh-born engineer who moved from London to Chile in 1892, and eventually became the head of the Chilean Maritime Signalling Service. In all, he designed and supervised the construction of more than 70 lights. Southern Chile has one of the world's longest and most hazardous coastlines, being over 2500 miles long and containing over 5000 rocky islands. The Chilean Navy currently runs the Servizio de Señalización Marítima, and is still building new lighthouses in the southern part of the country: the Cape Horn light, southernmost lighthouse in the world, was inaugurated as recently as 1991.[72]

Photograph by Alexander Inglis, Edinburgh, annotated 'Stephens Island New Zealand Stevenson design' assembled in Milne's workshop, c.1894.

(© The Trustees of the National Library of Scotland)

204

Slight's grandfather, James Slight, was the joiner who, along with his brother Alexander, had worked on the patterns for the blocks of masonry for the Bell Rock lighthouse at the Arbroath workyard between 1807 and 1810. Robert Stevenson named part of the Inchcape Reef in their honour – Slights' Reach. The brothers also 'fitted up the interior of the [light] house, and the permanent railways on the rock; and made a complete model of the Light-House'.[73] It is not clear which model this is, but it is possible that it was the one made in 1822 'under the direction of Robert Stevenson', which is now in National Museums Scotland (see page 130). Engineers, as graphically described by John Smeaton, think through their models (especially in the days before three-dimensional computer modelling), and in 1822 Robert Stevenson was still struggling to complete his magnum opus on the Bell Rock light-house.[74] Perhaps the model helped him finish it. A more up-to-date example is that of the late Enric Miralles' use of models in the designing of the Scottish Parliament in Edinburgh.

George Henry Slight – confusingly the same name as his father, who was born in Edinburgh in 1822 – was living in London at the age of 21 according to the 1881 Census, where he is recorded along with his parents, two sisters and a brother, living in East India Dock Road. His father, aged 58, was listed as 'Superintendent Engineering Work', while the younger George Henry Slight was a 'fitter'. After training as a mechanical engineer, he served his apprenticeship on steamships running between England and India, and then spent time working for Trinity House.

Slight was invited to go to Chile during the presidency of Admiral Jorge Montt, who was keen to promote safe navigation in the treacherous seas around the southern part of the country. He was asked to design and build the Evangelista lighthouse on the west coast of the Magellan Straits. So difficult and remote was this building that it took four years to complete, the lamp being first lit on 19 December 1896.[75] Slight was appointed head of the Central Lighthouse Bureau, a post he held for about twenty years, and he stayed on in Chile to build further lighthouses. Today there is a George Slight Lighthouse Museum at Punta Angles. According to various sources, he met and married Charlotte Leigh Bunster, a member of an English family living in Valparaiso. Their descendants still live in Chile and the Chilean Navy currently has a vessel named *Ingeniero George Slight Marshall* in his honour. He helped to modernise the lighthouse system by introducing the Swedish flashing method of illumination using acetylene, and the English inscription on his gravestone in Santiago reads: 'His lights still shine over the waters of the Pacific Ocean.'[76]

David A. Stevenson.
(© The Trustees of D. Alan Stevenson)

Charles A. Stevenson.
(© The Trustees of D. Alan Stevenson)

## The Work of David A., Charles and D. Alan Stevenson

David A. Stevenson (1854-1938) and his business partner Charles A. Stevenson (1855-1950), sons of David Stevenson, had a rigorous training as engineers in the offices of D. & T. Stevenson. During the 1880s the firm developed different forms of buoys for the Northern Lighthouse Board, and experimented with oil, gas and electricity as illuminants. The firm became D. & C. Stevenson in 1890, and along with other engineering work, it built at least 18 Scottish lighthouses, several lightships and developed fog-horns. The younger David Stevenson became sole Engineer to the Board after his uncle Thomas died in 1887, a post he held until 1938. The introduction of Sir James Chance's incandescent burners to Scottish lighthouses in 1903, and the wireless activation of equipment in 1914 were significant innovations; Charles devised equiangular prisms that condensed the light into a narrower and more brilliant beam than had been achieved previously. By the end of the century, both David and Charles were held as leading authorities in their field, and were consulted as such by several colonial and foreign lighthouse services.[77] Among their significant achievements were the lighthouses at Rattray Head (1895), at Sule Skerry (1895), and at Flannan Isles (1899); and they made the first steps in automation with the 'unattended' *Otter Rock* lightship off Islay, the development of the lighthouse at Oxcars in the Forth, the 'unattended' lighthouse on Platte Fougère off Guernsey, and progress in the fog-signal gun.[78]

Charles Stevenson was involved in early experiments in the development of wireless communication. He also invented the 'leader cable' for guiding vessels through minefields safely into port, and this was used during the First World War off Harwich. With his son, D. Alan Stevenson (1891-1971), he developed a precursor of radar known as the 'talking beacon'. In this, ships in fog could plot their position from synchronised radio and fog-signals: the system was installed at the Cumbrae (1929) and Cloch (1939) lighthouses. In 1926-27, D. Alan Stevenson toured over one hundred lighthouses for the Indian Government, and advised on a centralised service, but he is perhaps best remembered as the foremost

206

historian of lighthouses of the mid-twentieth century. With the retirement of D. Alan Stevenson in 1951, over a century and half of lighthouse service by the Stevenson family came to an end.[79]

### New fuels: paraffin oil, gas and electricity

From about the end of the eighteenth century, the main illuminant used in Scottish lighthouses was whale oil, but this was gradually displaced by refined rape seed or colza oil, which was less expensive, and gave a better quality light.[80] However, it did have some disadvantages: in cold weather it became extremely viscous to the point of becoming unusable, but more worryingly, it gave off suffocating fumes, so that lighthouse lanterns had to be well-ventilated. However, the Glasgow-educated industrial chemist, James Young (1811-83), after experimenting with chemical production between 1847 and 1850, was led to the large scale manufacture of paraffin oil and solid paraffin. Paraffin was first produced at a commercial level in Scotland from the shale oil deposits found especially in West Lothian, along with other products, from the early 1850s. At about the same time, industrial chemists in the United States were undertaking similar experiments, producing a by-product of petroleum that they called 'kerosene'. Used with a wick, kerosene or paraffin produces a flame some ten times brighter than one used with colza oil, and, comparatively speaking, its sources were more plentiful and it was cheaper to produce. After its successful introduction into lighthouses, paraffin became the standard fuel for most British lighthouses until after the Second World War.[81]

Initially, however, the colza oil-burners were unsuitable for use with paraffin, which required more air to produce a satisfactory flame. In the United States, there were difficulties in using the new fuel, which led to resistance to its adoption there. A ship's captain from Norfolk, Virginia, named Henry Harrison Doty, felt that he could solve the problems, and in due course he filed a United States Patent for his lamp in November 1870. He had approached D. & T. Stevensons earlier that year, and they were interested enough to submit the Doty burner and

D. Alan Stevenson.
(© The Trustees of D. Alan Stevenson)

their own colza oil-burning lamps to a month's trials at Girdleness, the lighthouse outside Aberdeen. The new fuel and new burner were installed shortly afterwards at Pentland Skerries and at Pladda.[82] In 1872 Dubh Artach became the first rock lighthouse to adopt this fuel, leading the way for its adoption in all Scottish lighthouses. R. W. Munro comments that over £250 a year was saved in oil costs alone, although the increase in power varied considerably, depending on the type of lamp, from between 10 per cent to over 100 per cent. Paraffin proved satisfactory for many years, being dependable, giving focal compactness and concentrated brightness. In 1870, when it was only half the price of colza oil, the cost dropped from 1s 4d a gallon. By 1894 it had reached a low point of 4d a gallon. With 76,000 gallons a year being used to light the coasts, there was a saving of over £10,000.[83] Thomas Stevenson remarked that the 'burners have also been introduced, under the direction of Messrs Stevenson, into the lighthouse services of China, Japan, New Zealand, and Newfoundland, and experience has fully justified their claim to efficiency, durability, and simplicity'.[84]

In the nineteenth century it was felt that coal gas might be used as a fuel source for lighthouses, and it was used successfully in Ireland in a number of lighthouses. However, the Stevensons seemed to believe that the sites of Scottish lighthouses in general mitigated against its use (Thomas Stevenson worried about its reliability when connected to a town gas system, and the possibility of extinction by sea-water), and although bottled town gas began to be used towards the end of the nineteenth century in smaller beacons, it was not generally used in the lighthouses of the Northern Lighthouse Board.[85] The exception to this was the light and the twin foghorns at the base of Ailsa Craig in the Firth of Clyde, fuelled by gas made by heating mineral oil with coal in a retort house on the island, and to supply compressed air to the foghorns.[86]

Electricity was another matter, however. In 1831 Michael Faraday (1791-1867) of London's Royal Institution had discovered the electro-magnetic principle, leading to the construction of the electric generator. As scientific adviser to Trinity House during the 1850s and

Example of the first mineral oil burner invented by the donor. The first permanent installation of the use of mineral oil for lighthouses took place under the direction of Messrs D. & T. Stevenson, C.E., Edinburgh, at Pentland Skerries lighthouse, 17 January 1871. Presented by Captain H. H. Doty, Norfolk, Virginia. (NMS T.1886.46)

208

the 1860s, he became closely involved with various schemes to electrify lighthouses.[87] Faraday did not develop systems of electrical light, but was asked to investigate those proposed by others: and one reasonably-successful system was proposed in the late 1850s by Frederick Hale Holmes (c.1811-70). This used a carbon arc lamp, with its power generated from an electro-magnetic machine driven by a steam engine. Earlier attempts had been fuelled by batteries, which were quickly drained.[88] After much testing by Faraday, Holmes's system was installed in the South Foreland lighthouse and first shone on 8 December 1858. Although it was not continuously used over the next few years, it was modified so as to ensure its effectiveness. In 1871 a new alternating current machine devised by Holmes was installed. Faraday undertook much of the monitoring of the light, visiting South Foreland in all weathers and frequently going out to sea to observe the light. Although electric lights were installed in other lighthouses, the programme was deemed a failure due to the expense involved. In 1880, electricity at South Foreland was abandoned.[89]

Further north, however, the Commissioners of Northern Lights were impressed by this new form of illuminant and, advised by the Stevensons, keen to press ahead. Michael Schiffer suggests that this can be seen as a desultory gesture to keep up with the French programme, which had, paradoxically, been begun under the mistaken illusion that the British were about to take the technological lead by electrifying their lighthouses.[90] In 1883, the Board of Trade agreed to the capital outlay, suggesting that the Isle of May might be an appropriate place as it was the most significant Scottish landfall on the east coast, providing guidance for coastal trade, and showing the way into the shelter of the Forth.[91] An unsigned, although fairly comprehensive, report appeared in the weekly journal *Engineering*, and it is worth quoting at some length:

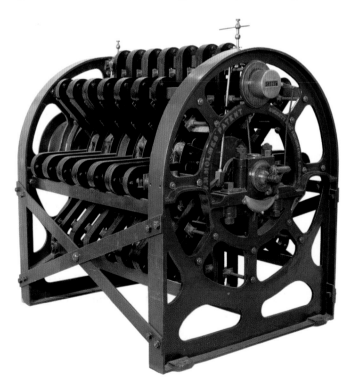

Lighthouse alternating current generator designed by Frederick H. Holmes, built by Buckett Brothers, London, and used at South Foreland lighthouse near Dover, 1872. Presented by Trinity House, Tower Hill, London.

(NMS T.1927.45)

The buildings, the dipotric apparatus, the steam engines, and other appliances in connection with the introduction of the electric light on the 'May', have all been constructed according to the design and under the supervision of Messrs. Stevenson, Edinburgh, engineers to the northern lights Commissioners. ...

A gulley which intersects the island crosswise, at some distance from the light tower, has been chosen as the site for the new dwellings and the engine-house. There is a small lake at the northern end of this gulley, which has been converted into a reservoir, the water of which is to be used for condensation purposes. Two steam engines, each of 16 horse-power, and made by Messrs. Umpherston, Leith, have been placed in the engine-house for driving two dynamos, which were supplied by De Meritens, of Paris. As a rule, only one engine and one dynamo will be used at a time, the spare engine and dynamo being provided to guard against accident; and unless when very foggy weather occurs it will not be necessary to use the full power of both engines and dynamo machines.

The dynamos are of the alternate current type, and of the largest size hitherto made by M. de Meritens, having sixty permanent horse-shoe magnets arranged around a centre, in twelve sets of five each, all with their poles directed towards the centre. ... The currents are conveyed to the lighthouse tower, situated at a distance of 880 feet, by means of copper rods 1 inch in diameter. ... Communication between the engine-house and the tower is also obtained by means of a telephone. The conductors are led up the tower to the lamps inside the dioptric apparatus.

As might be expected, the electric lamps are of the most improved kind. One of them is always in place inside the dioptric apparatus, while another is ready, with the carbons adjusted to the correct height, to be shunted into the focus of the apparatus when required. The carbons, which are fully 1½ inches in diameter, have a small core of pure graphite running through the centre. These improved carbons are found to burn with great steadiness and regularity.

The dipotric apparatus is of a novel description, being on the condensing principle so successfully introduced into the Scottish lighthouses by Messrs Stevenson thirty years ago, and since then largely adopted in other lighthouses. In this case the apparatus is so designed as to give a group of four flashes in quick succession, with intervals of darkness for thirty seconds, and it condenses the light which would spread over 45 degrees into 3 degrees or fifteen times. The apparatus has also been arranged to admit of the beams of light being dipped to show near the lighthouse during dense fog, instead of being sent around the horizon. The condensing prisms circulate round the central apparatus by means of a machine driven by a falling weight. Messrs Chance Brothers, of Birmingham, made the dioptric apparatus, and Messrs Milne, of Edinburgh, made the revolving machine.[92]

This plant cost almost £16,000 and maintaining the electrical system required more specially-trained staff, thus seven keepers were resident on the island. This increased rate, estimated at more than £1000 a year, meant a rise in light dues. Despite the excellence, reliability and quality of the light, by 1924 it was recognised that this form of illuminant was just too expensive to continue. The carbon arc lamp was exchanged for a single incandescent mantle burning vaporised paraffin oil, using the 1886 lens.[93] As Schiffer's paper shows, despite arc-lighting systems being produced specifically for the lighthouse market, the expense for its purchase and putting in place far exceeded that of an oil lamp arrangement.[94] A vacuum electric light was used at Cumbrae in 1900, but this too proved difficult to maintain in reliable order, and the system was discontinued in 1906.[95] Electricity did not become a prevalent form of power for lighthouses until after the establishment of the National Grid, and even then only for some mainland lights; paraffin, and then acetylene became the more usual form of illuminant.

### The hyper-radiant lens

As early as 1869 Thomas Stevenson had recognised that larger lamps using paraffin and coal gas, which might use as many as five, or six, or even seven concentric wicks, would become too powerful even for a first order Fresnel lens, and larger lenses, which he designated as 'hyper-radiant', would become necessary. Towards the end of his career, in January 1886, he reported to the Royal Society of Edinburgh about the conclusion of lighthouse trials undertaken by Trinity House (at the suggestion of the Board of Trade), regarding the relative merits of various illuminants for lighthouses – electricity, gas and oil. Both the Engineer to the Irish Board, John Richardson Wigham (1829-1906), and the Engineer to the Northern Lighthouse Board, Stevenson himself, were invited to attend. Trinity House built three experimental towers in a row alongside the South Foreland lighthouse near Dover, and a number of tests were carried out over a twelve-month period. Various conclusions were drawn about the merits of rival systems of electric light, gas-burners or oil-burners. Stevenson pointed out that Wigham's large diameter gas-burner was at a

Electric arc lamp of the Serrin type used in the Isle of May lighthouse, between 1886 and 1924, made by A. de Meritens & Cie, Paris. Presented by the Northern Lighthouse Board. (NMS T.1993.158)

211

disadvantage because the optical array into which it was placed was too small.

At the suggestion of Alan Brebner, Stevenson continued, it was decided to trial some Fresnel lenses with various burners:

> An experimental lens in that proportion, suited for a 6-wick burner, was constructed and tried at the South Foreland, the focal distance of the lens being increased, while the holophotal system which I proposed in 1850, with totally reflecting prisms concentric with the refracting portion of the apparatus, was also adopted. The lens as designed has a focal distance of 1330 mm, and has two reflecting prisms above and below the refracting portion, the whole subtending an angle of 60° horizontally and of 70° vertically.[96]

The design proved the most efficient in the trials, and 'would avoid all the disadvantages … including excessive heat in the lightroom, difficulty of management of the burners, and obstruction of light by the necessary ventilating tubes'.[97] This experimental panel was made by Barbier & Fenestre of Paris. Chance Brothers of Birmingham made their first hyperradiant lens in 1887, renamed 'hyper-radial' by James Kenward of that company. He com-

mented in 1897 that 'the hyper-radial lens of 1330 millimetres focal distance first suggested (as Professor Tyndall declared) by Mr John Wigham, and concurrently at least by Mr Thomas Stevenson, who less fitly termed it hyper-radiant … has quite justified the expectation of lighthouse engineers as a convenient and powerful instrument admirably adapted to the large burners now employed'.[98]

Charles Stevenson improved on this with his spherical and his equiangular refractors, which remedied a loss of emergent light in the Fresnel refractors; two years later he improved on this design, and as Kenward reported, 'the improved refractors have been adopted with success in several of the Scottish lighthouses'.[99] R. W. Munro explains that at this time – after the successful building of Dubh Artach and Chicken Rock – the Commissioners' attention was directed to the increasing importance of the 'north-about' route. By the 1880s maritime steam traffic had grown, and in reasonable weather many captains between Europe and North America preferred the less congested route between Orkney and Shetland – avoiding the crowded English Channel and the hazardous Pentland Firth. This resulted in two new lights on Fair Isle, North and South (1892), Fair Isle North using the Stevensons'

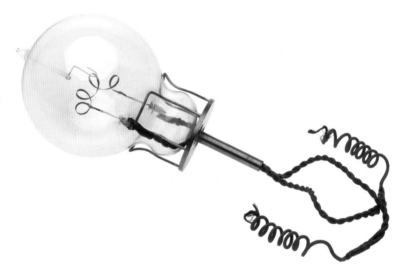

Vacuum bulb made for use at Cumbrae lighthouse. The electrical system was expensive and difficult to maintain and was discontinued in 1906. Presented by D. Alan Stevenson

(NMS T.1958.46)

212

first hyper-radiant lens made by Barbier & Benard; and a further six well-placed lights – Sule Skerry (1895), with a group-flashing hyper-radiant lens by the same French firm, Rattray Head (1895), Flannan Islands (1899), Stroma (1896), Helliar Holm (1893), and Noup Head (1899) in Orkney. The younger Stevenson brothers – David A. and Charles – tackled these problems, which a modern author maintains were only different in scale from those surmounted by the three previous generations of the family.[100]

Sule Skerry is the most remote lighthouse in Scotland, being 40 miles west of Orkney, and a similar distance north off the coast of Sutherland, yet directly in the path of vessels making their way through the Pentland Firth to or from the Iceland seas. It was built over two years, because the length of the days at such a northerly latitude meant that darkness fell early, and the winter weather was extremely stormy. The enormous lantern, 16 feet in diameter, was placed on top of an 88-foot tower, and the new light could be seen at Cape Wrath, 35 miles away, on 60 nights during its first three months of operation. The families of keepers based here were housed in Stromness from 1895 until full automation in December 1982. The hyper-radiant lens was removed and presented to National Museums Scotland in 1978, having been replaced by an automatic gas-light with a fourth order lens.[101]

The lighthouse at Rattray Head marked a dangerous reef off the sand dunes of the Buchan coast, and the design was a radical departure from previous practice. Stevensons built a rock tower in two parts, the lower section containing a foghorn and engine-room, the upper portion for the light-keepers' room and the lantern. This was the first time a first-class siren fog-signal had been installed in a rock lighthouse. Work began in 1892, and the masonry of both portions of the tower was completed in 16 months, spread over three seasons. The lower section was 46 feet high, the entrance door reached by a 32-foot external ladder. At high water, the base is covered to a depth of about eight feet, but it is possible to walk ashore when the tide is out. The upper section brings it to a total height of 120 feet above the rock. When first lit in 1895, the five-wick paraffin lamp had a candle-power of 44,000, compared with 6500 at neighbouring Buchan Ness.[102]

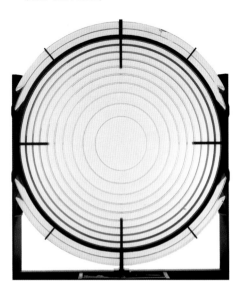

Prototype hyper-radiant lens panel for a lighthouse, by Barbier & Fenestre, Paris, 1885, used at South Foreland Trials, 1885.

Presented by the Northern Lighthouse Board. (NMS T.1993.156)

213

Twenty miles west of the Island of Lewis in the Outer Hebrides lies a small island group known as the Flannan Islands. For some 40 years they had been discussed as a possible lighthouse site, as the islands had become increasingly important as a landfall for Atlantic shipping. Designed by David A. Stevenson, the 75-foot tower was constructed for the Northern Lighthouse Board between 1895 and 1899 and is located near the highest point on Eilean Mòr. Construction was undertaken by George Lawson of Rutherglen at a cost of £6914 inclusive of the building of the landing places, stairs and railway tracks. All the materials used had to be hauled up the 150-foot cliffs directly from supply boats, no trivial task in the ever-churning Atlantic. This included an unfortunate horse, slung ashore on a crane. The light was first lit on 7 December 1899, and other than its relative isolation and the difficulties in its construction, it would be a fairly unremarkable light, were it not for the events which took place just over a year after it was commissioned.[103]

In late December 1900, it became clear that no light had shone from the new lighthouse for ten days; at the shore station, where the lightkeepers' families were based, at Breasclete in Loch Roag, there had been no news. The *Hesperus,* making the ordinary relief, found the station to be deserted, with the lamp trimmed and ready, lens and machinery cleaned, the kitchen tidied, and two sets of outdoor clothing missing:

Group flashing hyper-radiant lighthouse optic of 2660 mm diameter in nine panels, which showed three flashes in quick succession every 40 seconds, designed by David A. Stevenson, 1893, constructed by Barbier & Benard, Paris, and Steven & Struthers, Glasgow, for Sule Skerry, the most remote manned lighthouse in Scotland from 1895 until 1978. The apparatus made one revolution in one and a half minutes, but only the Fresnel optical panels are present. Presented by the Northern Lighthouse Board.

(NMS T.1978.95)

The last written entries in the log were for 13 December, but particulars for 14 December, and of the time of extinguishing the light on 15 December, along with barometer and thermometer readings and state of the wind taken at 9am on 15 December, were noted on the slate for transference later to the log.

… Everything was in order, the lamp was ready to be lit, and it was evident that the work of the forenoon of the 15th had completed, indicating that the men disappeared on the afternoon of Saturday, 15 December.[104]

This dreadful accident caught the public imagination, possibly most vividly in the poem 'Flannan Isle' by Wilfrid Wilson Gibson (1878-1962). The last verse runs:

We seemed to stand for an endless while,
Though still no word was said
Three men alive on Flannan Isle,
Who thought on three men dead.

1   *Catalogue ...* (1851), I, 319-20 and 320-21.
2   Thompson (1986), 93.
3   Molloy (1994), 7 and 42.
4   Ibid., 11-12.
5   Ibid., 13 and 52.
6   Ibid., 68-69; see: http://www.lighthousedepot.com/
    lite_digest.asp?action=get_article&sk=2217
    I would like to thank Donald Johnson, Site
    Supervisor, Provincial Historic Sites, Bonavista, NL,
    for this information.
7   Tulloch (1983), 49; Molloy (1994), 53.
8   Molloy (1994), 90.
9   Ibid., 14, 120; National Library of Scotland [NLS]
    Acc. 10706/167/12 is an illustration of the lighting
    array before it left Edinburgh.
10  Molloy (1994), 14, 135-36.
11  Stevenson (1818), 5.
12  Pavitt (1966), 1-4; Tarling (1994), 4; Cook (2004b).
13  Mair (1978), 172.
14  Thomson (1852), 414.
15  Hall-Jones and Hooi (1979), 11; Pavitt (1966), 5.
16  Pavitt (1966), 11, quoting from Thomson (1852),
    403.
17  Stevenson (1856a), 10 and plate 1, fig. 2;
    *Catalogue ...* (1851), I, 320, item 100.
18  Stevenson (1881), 89.
19  Elton (2009), 215.
20  Pavitt (1966), 23, quoting the *Singapore Free Press*,
    24 May 1850.
21  Stevenson (1824), 131-34 and 379.
22  Collingwood (1868), 287.
23  Hall-Jones and Hooi (1979), 25-30.
24  *Selection ...* (1858), 1.
25  Ibid., i-ii.
26  Tagliacozzo (2005), 308, 328.
27  *Selection ...* (1858), 8 and 9.
28  Ibid., 12-21.
29  Ibid., 36.
30  Ibid., 41.
31  Ibid., 48.
32  Ibid., 56, quoting Corwin (1852), 328.
33  *Illustrated London News*, 21 October 1865,
    390.
34  Sandes (1935), 168-69, 183.
35  Humble (1983), 4-5.
36  http://www.clanfraser.ca/admiral_fraser.htm
    reprinting Fraser (2008).
37  Sandes (1935), 178.
38  Ibid., 178-79.
39  Chance (1902), 56, 63; Mair (1978), 189, 205-206.
40  This section draws on Morrison-Low (2006b);
    Buruma (2005), 1-15.
41  'Introduction' to Brunton (1991), 4-5.
42  Buruma (2005), 15-47.

43  Checkland (1992).
44  Waswo (2004).
45  Checkland (1992).
46  Ibid., 218.
47  Talbot (1913), 9-10; Mair (1978), 190.
48  Stevenson (1868b), 559-60; Brunton (1991), 23-
    26.
49  Brunton (1991), 27, 66-67.
50  Brunton (1877), 3.
51  Brunton (1991), 27-28.
52  Brunton (1877), 20-21.
53  Ibid., 18.
54  Mair (1978), 191.
55  NLS Acc. 10706/581/290, R. H. Brunton to D. & T.
    Stevenson, 8 November 1872.
56  Stevenson (1868b), 564.
57  Brunton (1991), 24-25; Brunton (1877), 7.
58  Brunton (1877), 8.
59  NLS Acc. 10706/581/229, letter R. H. Brunton to
    D. & T. Stevenson, 20 August 1872.
60  NLS Acc.10706/581/158, letter R. H. Brunton to
    D. & T. Stevenson, 14 July 1871.
61  Brunton (1876); Checkland (1992); Waswo
    (2004).
62  Inkster (1991), 191.
63  Aspden (2008), 43.
64  'Memoir' (1871), 201.
65  Beaglehole (2006), 22.
66  Ibid., 63.
67  *The Times*, 23 February 1870.
68  Beaglehole (2006), 63.
69  NLS Acc.10706/85/43 and 46.
70  Mair (1978), 211.
71  Beaglehole (2006), 289.
72  http://www.unc.edu/~rowlett/lighthouse/chls.htm
    (and) http://www.directemar.cl/senmar/ingles/
    default.htm
73  Stevenson (1824), 497; mentioned also 391, 397,
    414 and 420.
74  NMS T.1867.22.1; for Smeaton's remarks, see
    Smeaton (1793), 70 para. 121; the other contem-
    porary model (made from rock taken from the
    Inchcape Reef) of the Bell Rock lighthouse is known
    to have been made by William Kennedy as it has
    his initials under the base. This is now held by Angus
    Museums, inventory no. A2008.1.
75  Garcés (2003), 21.
76  http://tribalpages.com/family-tree/geoslight;
    Garcés (2003), 23.
77  Mair (1978), 217-39; Leslie and Paxton (1999),
    110-43.
78  Talbot (1913), 9.
79  Mair (1978), 240-60; Leslie and Paxton (1999),
    144-49.

80  Macadam (1883), 56; Stevenson (1959), 278.
81  Boyle (1996a), 13.
82  Macadam (1883); Munro (1979), 147; Tag (2001), 23.
83  Munro (1979), 147.
84  Stevenson (1881), 208.
85  Stevenson (1881), 117, 150; Munro (1979), 149.
86  Stevenson (1887b); Munro (1979), 153-54. The 1886 Ailsa Craig optic is now at the Museum of Scottish Lighthouses, inv. no. SLM.2007.12.
87  James (1999); James (2000). Faraday's successor in this role was his successor at the Royal Institution, John Tyndall, for whom see MacLeod (1969).
88  Schiffer (2005), 282-83.
89  Major (2000), 24-26. Schiffer (2005). A Holmes lighthouse generator, used at Souter Point, 1867, is in the Science Museum. London, inv. no. 1915-295; an arc lamp used at South Foreland is at National Museums Scotland T.1927.37; another in the Science Museum. London, inv. no. 1923-169.
90  Schiffer (2005), 298.
91  Quoted in Munro (1979), 148.
92  'Electric Light' (1886). The 1886 Isle of May first order lens remained in use until the light was automated in 1989. It is now on display in the Museum of Scottish Lighthouses, Fraserburgh, inv. no. SLM.2005.11394.
93  Eggeling (1960), 42; Munro (1979), 148-50.
94  Schiffer (2005), 291.
95  Munro (1979), 150
96  Stevenson (1886), 498, quotation 495.
97  Ibid., 498, 499.
98  Kenward (1897), 283; see also Tag (2009-10).
99  Stevenson (1892); Kenward (1897), 284.
100 Munro (1979), 165.
101 Ibid., 165-67; http://www.nlb.org.uk/Lighthouse Library/Lighthouse/Sule-Skerry/
102 Munro (1979), 168.
103 Ibid., 168-71; Nicholson (1995), 168-79; Muirhead (2000).
104 http://www.nlb.org.uk/HistoricalInformation/ FlannanIsles/Background-Report/

Isle of May reflector array at Cape Bonavista, Newfoundland.

(Photograph by Don Johnson)

# CHAPTER 7

# Modern Times

THE EXTRAORDINARY TECHNOLOGICAL advances of the past hundred years, most of them applied in other areas first and then adapted for use in the special case of lighthouses, have transformed the lighthouse service in Scotland and in other services worldwide. The builders of the Bell Rock lighthouse, from the Commissioners to the artificers, would not recognise most of the tools now at the navigator's disposal, but there is something reassuring in the unchanging nature of a light, marked on a chart, shining out from the top of tower, even with the knowledge that today there is nobody actually present and looking after its friendly beam. Navigation itself, along with all other branches of applied science, has not remained static, and safety around the coastline has similarly changed beyond all recognition. Amongst twentieth-century innovations are radar, solar panels, Global Navigation Satellite Systems (GNSS) and automatic monitoring systems, such as AIS or Automatic Identification System. It would take an entire book to cover these changes in any depth, and so this chapter will look at the more evident and long-term alterations, particularly those which affect the Northern Lighthouse Board's service provisions. Along with other General Lighthouse Authorities (GLAs) for Great Britain and Ireland – Trinity House and the Commissioners of Irish Lights – the technological changes now taken almost for granted at the Northern Lighthouse Board would have been undreamed of in the days of Thomas Smith and Robert Stevenson. Perhaps the most obvious difference to a lightkeeper returning, Rip van Winkle-like, from the turn of the twentieth century to today's lighthouse service, would be the loss of the keepers themselves – automation.

## Automation

It may come as a surprise to discover that the Northern Lighthouse Board considers that its programme of automation began as long ago as 1894,

OPPOSITE PAGE

Lighthouse service visit: gas being delivered by helicopter at Dubh Artach, 1985.

(© Photographer Keith Allardyce, copyright The Museum of Scottish Lighthouses)

Control clock for lighting and extinguishing an unattended gas beacon by clockwork, made by James Ritchie, Edinburgh. This type of mechanism was used by the Northern Lighthouse Board from 1894, when the light at Oxcars Rock, in the Firth of Forth, was automated. Presented by the Northern Lighthouse Board.

(NMS T.1993.159)

when Oxcars lighthouse (1886) in the Forth had its two lightkeepers withdrawn. The light was then operated by bottled gas delivered weekly from the gasworks at the Granton Depot, and controlled by a clockwork timer. In England, Trinity House reckons that automation came to its lighthouses from 1910 with Gustaf Dalen's invention of the sun valve; this was fitted to a number of lights powered by acetylene gas. The sun valve was sensitive to daylight, turning the gas on as darkness fell, and switching it off with the appearance of daylight.

The second immediately discernible difference in the way lighthouses operate today from their counterparts a century ago is the nature of the light itself: most of those huge arrays of prisms, turning inexorably either on powerful clockwork, or on rollers over a large bath of mercury, have been replaced by smaller, yet still more powerful lamps. Many have what is known as a sealed headlamp array, which was first tested on the island of Fidra in the Firth of Forth. This went automatic in October 1970 – the power being supplied by an underwater electric cable connected to the electricity mains (although a backup generator was on hand) – and monitored from nearby St Abb's Head. This proved a success.[1] Sealed headlamp arrays have been installed in a number of forms, emitting different light characteristics in various stations since then. Only now, after some 40 years of successful use, and with further changes in technology, are they being superseded by light-emitting diodes (LEDs). The LED is one of the technologies which was developed outside the marine environment, but has proved to be a powerful innovation when applied there. Some substances emit electroluminescence under particular circumstances, and the British scientist, H. J. Round, working for Marconi, is credited with this discovery in 1907. However, the electric light-bulb was cheap and also efficient, and further development had to wait until 1961, when two experimenters at Texas Instruments found that if they passed an electric current through particular semiconductor alloys they emitted infrared radiation. Since then, the technology has developed rapidly, moving into the visible spectrum and becoming markedly cheaper. The advantages of LED technology for use in the lighthouse service include its low-energy consumption and maintenance, small size, long life, fast switching times, and the fact that, unlike conventional light sources, the LED does not become hot. This makes it ideal for use in buoys and minor lights.

James Park – the first lightkeeper – was appointed to Kinnaird Head in 1787. Lightkeeping evolved from the early days, when only one keeper was appointed to each lighthouse. The first assistant lightkeeper was later appointed in 1815, and in due course most lights had a complement of three – one principal keeper and two assistants. Further roles were developed when the need arose. Wives and families were accommodated in nearby houses. During the nineteenth century the Northern Lighthouse Board – and their staff of keepers, engineers and boat crews – had evolved into a well-oiled machine (both literally and metaphorically) supplying about 150 lighthouses. A way of service had emerged where – in some instances – generations of the same family might enter the lighthouse service. It was a very disciplined life, with a strict hierarchy.

As the overriding purpose of the keeper was to show the light in hours of darkness, a shift system was implemented, similar to that on board ship. Other duties, such as keeping the lens and lantern clean, or trimming the lamp, could be done in daylight hours, and records were kept of weather conditions, fuel consumption, and shipwrecks, which were sent back to the headquarters at 84 George Street in due course. On rock stations the men were on their own for many weeks, until the relief arrived. Often, with bad weather, such

221

relief could be seriously delayed. By the end of the nineteenth century, families were housed at shore stations, usually within existing communities, so that the children could go to school.

During both World Wars the lights were blacked out, but the lighthouses continued to be manned. The lights could be turned on if an Allied convoy passed the hazard, although keepers were not supposed to report enemy movements in order to remain 'neutral'. Nevertheless, a number of lighthouses were attacked by enemy aircraft. These included, as we have seen, Bell Rock, as well as Kinnaird Head, Stroma, Out Skerries, Auskerry, Pentland Skerries, Corsewall, Holburn Head, Fair Isle North and Fair Isle South.[2] Monach in the Outer Hebrides was abandoned as being too remote and dangerous for the keepers. The service was tightly governed by a series of rules, and lights – and keepers – were constantly inspected, often with little warning. The men who ran and serviced the lights were admirable and dedicated professionals, made redundant only by advances in technology.

Rock lights, as we have seen, were not necessarily connected by any ready means of communication to the shore; pigeon post, for example, was used to connect the lightkeepers on Ailsa Craig with the mainland, with considerable success at the end of the nineteenth century. On the other hand, attempts to use a heliograph on Sule Skerry were hindered by lack of sunlight.[3] The new inventions of radio and telephone were pursued with some success by Charles Stevenson; and by 1925 the Flannans, Barra Head, Sule Skerry and Monach were in regular contact with the shore. Inchkeith was chosen as an experimental 'wireless fog signal' in the 1920s. The first permanent radio beacon in Scotland was installed at Kinnaird Head in 1929, and one followed soon after at Sule Skerry. We have already seen in chapter 6 how Charles Stevenson developed a 'talking beacon' for the Clyde Lighthouse Trustees in 1931. He also devised wireless-controlled acetylene fog-guns, remotely controlled from further up-river.[4] Radio-telephones continued to be used in increasing numbers, especially after the Second World War.

The way of life of the lighthouse-keeper came to an end as remote control, radio and radar all combined to make the profession redundant. In the 1980s it became apparent that landing all fuel and provisions at rock stations by boat could be done in other ways. However, bringing essential supplies in to the lighthouse by helicopter was

'Sailor' radio-telephone, Type RT 144, made by S. P. Radio A/S, Denmark, 1976. Presented by the Northern Lighthouse Board.

(NMS.T.2011.44)

becoming increasingly expensive. It was also apparent that moving growing families disrupted the children's education. The Northern Lighthouse Board stopped recruiting career keepers in the mid-1970s, and automation came in gradually but relentlessly, first to the land lights, then to the rock lights, and finally to the more remote stations.

Maintenance of the lights had changed: in an illuminating article written in 2004, Mike Wright, Maintenance Engineer, looked back as far as the 1950s to examine the changes. Major lights, he commented, were of course manned.

'At these stations large clockwork mechanisms turned lenses round a fixed optic, often a paraffin vapour burner.' At automation, National Museums Scotland obtained its second large optic from Inchkeith, made by the company Chance Brothers of Birmingham. Turned by a clockwork mechanism by James Dove of Edinburgh, the entire design was by David A. Stevenson. The optic dates from 1889 when it replaced the 1835 Fresnel array, which first came to National Museums Scotland in 1890. Wright continued:

> Fog signals were air powered with the compressors driven by Kelvin engines. Minor lights were essentially powered by either

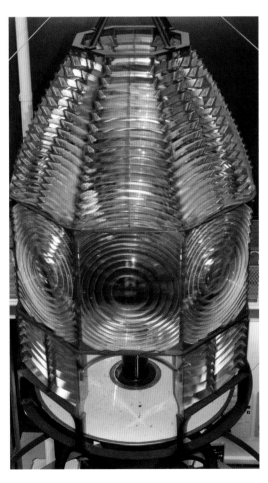

ABOVE: Paraffin burner by Chance Brothers, Birmingham. Presented by Chance Brothers, Birmingham.

(NMS T.2001.226)

RIGHT: First order dioptric holophotal revolving light, showing a flash every half minute and making one complete revolution in four minutes. Designed by David A. Stevenson, manufactured by Chance Brothers, Birmingham, and James Dove & Co., Edinburgh, for Inchkeith lighthouse between 1889 and 1985. Presented by the Northern Lighthouse Board

(NMS T.1985.84)

propane or acetylene. When radio beacons were first installed they were powered by dedicated generator sets.[5]

Essentially, the Maintenance Team would spend the summer months progressing around the lighthouses and sharing accommodation with the lightkeepers' families. As automation began to gather pace, more effective use was made of the time of the technical staff, and considerable restructuring of the entire service – not without some pain – was required.

By 1995 it could be seen that a slimmed-down service would mean the closure of the Granton Depot, the reduction in the number of part-time attendant lightkeepers, and, after the completion of automation, the reduction of numbers of engineers.[6] In 1997 Bill Paterson, Director of Engineering, was able to report that 'for the last thirty years, the Northern Lighthouse Board has been automating its lighthouses, working towards a totally automated service. In March 1998, this programme will come to an end and all Scottish lighthouses will be automated.'[7] He continued with an account of the final five manned lights: Butt of Lewis, designed to become the location of one of the Northern Lighthouse Board Differential GPS (dGPS) stations, was also going to be the final family station to be demanned, with no changes to the light character or range; temporary engineering works altering Cape Wrath, North Ronaldsay, and Rinns of Islay were progressing well; while Fair Isle South was destined to be the 'last Scottish manned Lighthouse to be automated', and all were ready for complete automation the following March.[8]

The ceremony marking the end of the profession of lighthouse-keeping was 'a quiet, dignified way to say goodbye and thank you to those who gave their working life to the safety of mariners'.[9] On 31 March 1998, as planned, a ceremony was held by HRH The Princess Royal, as Patron of the Northern Lighthouse Board, at Fair Isle South. There were memories of the past shared that day, including the tragedy of the bombing of that lighthouse, and that at neighbouring Fair Isle North, during the Second World War.[10] Since then, there have been a number of books of reminiscences published about a way of life that was hard, but one that certainly had its moments.[11]

Automation did not mean leaving the lights to themselves. An article in the Northern Lighthouse Board's *Journal* in 1997 enquired: 'Some of you may be wondering how we keep our eye on lighthouses when they are not manned. What about all the ones that never were manned? How do we know if they are working? What do we do if they are not?' – all good questions that mariners, who had come to rely on the lights and sea-marks of the Northern Lighthouse Board might well have asked. The 'Monitor Centre' at 84 George Street, Edinburgh, is manned continuously, and in 1997 two personal computers gave information on the status of 64 major lights, four minor lights and one buoy.[12] If there was a problem, the watch-keeper would telephone one of the operations management staff, who was permanently on call.[13] As in 1786, it is imperative that the lights continue to shine, for the safety of the mariner.

An enlightening article appeared in the Board's *Journal* in 2001, updating the state of play of the 'two PCs' in use at the Monitor Centre four years previously. Roddy MacKay noted that (discounting the Signal Tower at Arbroath's arrangement of flags visible to the Bell Rock lighthouse) an early monitoring and remote control system had been organised from the late 1960s to 1974 which ran from the Inchkeith fog-signal:

> The lightkeepers at Inchkeith operated the fog signal and a VHF radio link allowed them to turn on and off the fog signal and generators. Their operation was monitored using a microphone and an open VHF channel back to Inchkeith. Diesel generators were used to charge the fog signal and monitor system batteries.[14]

Even before the automation of major lighthouses in the 1970s, a number of acetylene gas-operated Dalen lights had been installed at offshore positions, such as Auskerry, Start Point and Out Skerries during the 1960s. Attendants or Observers, employed by the Northern Lighthouse Board for various tasks from the nineteenth century, were now charged with overseeing such installations. 'The first monitored light was by UHF radio from Fidra,' reported MacKay, 'where mains power was available, to Barns Ness which was at that time still manned.' This was followed by low-power direct current electrical installations at Ushenish (to Neist Point), Dubh Artach (to Ruvaal and later Rinns of Islay) and Flannan Isles (to Butt of Lewis). Using UHF radio equipment, these operated for three minutes every two hours while the light was shining, sending digital messages by means of tones; and the system was successful enough to encourage another high power link between Holy Island and Corsewall in 1977. Telephone devices ('RADLE' and 'RADAC') were used for about 20 years, but it was the microchip revolution which allowed computer technology to become rapid and cheap. At the Northern Lighthouse Board

> ... the driving force ... was the construction of the new lighthouse at North Rona commissioned in 1984, which would require an UHF link

to Butt of Lewis. If anyone has ever wondered why Fair Isle South, Rinns of Islay, Butt of Lewis and Cape Wrath were amongst the last automated sites, it was due to their selection as regional monitor centres along with Kinnaird Head and St Abbs Head to be manned with lightkeepers. The sophistication of the technology quickly rendered this idea redundant with a common Headquarters Monitor Centre being the obvious choice.[15]

By careful updating, the Monitor Centre worked efficiently for over a decade, connected to some 72 stations. Just as the software needed a comprehensive replacement in time for the threatened Y2K Millennium Bug, a new system was installed which could bypass this, and 'it was simultaneously decided to monitor all previously unmonitored Aids to Navigation (AtoNs), including all buoys and minor lights', extending the structure from 80 locations to over 350 sites. The new Depot at Oban has become the site of a backup Monitor Centre.[16]

The Depot at Oban, first established in 1904, was fully modernised, and in late 2001 the Engineering Storage and Testing Facility (ESTF) was moved from Granton to the west coast. The lease of the buildings on the Forth had expired. Granton Harbour had been built by David Stevenson (between lighthouses) for the Duke of Buccleuch in 1835, and in 1852 the Northern Lighthouse Board leased some land there, transferring its Edinburgh store from Leith, where it had been based for the previous 50 years. In 1868 a store and buoy shed were constructed, and in 1874 the experimental light tower, still a local landmark, was added. A gasworks was installed for the production of coal gas in 1892, used for lighting buoys and beacons; and, in due course, for supplying the Oxcars lighthouse from 1894.

A barge towed by the *Pharos* was used to transport the gas cylinders to their point of use in the Forth area. In 1907, the premises were improved and extended; a new buoy store was equipped with a railway siding and a travelling crane. During the 1930s, coal gas as an illuminant was replaced by dissolved acetylene gas and the original gasworks was demolished. From 1955 the *Pharos* vessel was stationed at Granton, moving to Leith in the early 1970s; and in 1988, with the decommissioning of that particular vessel, no more tenders were berthed on the east coast. Further buildings were provided at the Granton site, with another buoy store in 1969, and additional engineering stores and garages in 1990; but six years later the depot function was entirely based at Stromness, and ESTF moved to Oban. Granton returned to the Buccleuch estates, and is currently used as a variety of artists' workshops.[17] In December 2001, the new and modernised depot at Oban was opened.[18] By the end of the following year, the Commissioners decided that the base at Stromness should be closed, while facilities should be concentrated at Oban; Stromness was closed on 24 October 2003, after more than one hundred years of service.[19]

### Technological change: navigation positioning

In November of 1995 the three UK GLAs launched a consultation paper for users entitled 'Marine Aids to Navigation into the 21st century', envisioning an increasing use of radio navigational aids, while retaining the more traditional ones, such as lighthouses, buoys and beacons. It covered GNSS in the form of United States Navstar Satellite Global Positioning System (with an accuracy ± 100 metres) and dGPS, differential GPS (accuracy ± 10 metres), the turning-off of the Decca system and its replacement by a Europe-wide system, known as the Loran-C radio navigation system.[20]

Decca was developed from 1939 in Britain and first used on 6 June 1944 to guide ships leading the D-Day invasion fleet through the mine-fields off the northern coast of France. The first chain of transmitters was established on the south coast of England, and began broadcasting the day before the invasion. Had such a system not been in place, it is widely believed that the ultimately successful Normandy landings could not have taken place. Decca was a radio navigation position fixing system, based on continuous low-frequency wave signals. Transmitting stations at known locations provided hyperbolic lines of position to a receiver on board a ship. The receiver displayed the position lines either as numerical readings that could be plotted on a chart, or – in later years – as the ship's position in longitude and latitude. The system worked by measuring the differences between the signals received from the transmitters, allowing the users to establish their positions with a reasonable degree of accuracy and consistency.

At the peak of its service, Decca chains operated in all the major shipping areas of the world, with an estimated 200,000 users in Europe. The Decca company derived its income from the hire of the Decca receivers to the system's users. By the early 1970s, however, commer-cial competitors were producing and selling cheaper receivers to users, and the Decca company made huge financial losses. In 1979 the company was bought by the Racal Electronics Group. Now named Racal-Decca Marine Navigation Ltd, the company could no longer sustain the Decca system, thanks to this loss of revenue, and after prolonged negotiations the three UK GLAs assumed responsibility for the Decca system from February 1987, financing this from the General Lighthouse Fund. The system was modernised and automated by the end of 1995.

There was a downside to the Decca sys-tem, however: it had a comparatively short range, and was not so effective after dark, thanks to skywave interference. Other land-based systems – e.g. Loran-C, another low-frequency land-based radio navigation – had a much longer range (the name stands for LOng RAnge Navigation). The GLAs ceased to use the Decca system, saving around £3.5 million each year, after 31 March 2000. In the meantime it had been overtaken, technologically speaking, by

Decca Navigator Mk 51 receiver, serial number 1035, type 80322A, used on the fishing boat *St Adrian II* out of Pitten-weem, Fife, made by Racal-Decca, England, c.1985. Presented by David Tod.

(NMS T.2007.47)

more accurate and reliable satellite positioning systems, and after GPS differential corrections became available, Decca systems were withdrawn at about the same time around the globe.[21]

In 1973 the United States military was looking for a foolproof method of satellite navigation. A brainstorming session at the Pentagon produced the concept of GPS on the basis of the participants' experience with all its satellite predecessors. The essential components of GPS are the 24 Navstar satellites built by Rockwell International, each the size of a large car and weighing 1900 pounds. All 24 satellites orbit the earth every twelve hours in a formation that ensures that every point on the planet will always be in radio contact with at least four satellites. The first operational GPS satellite was launched in 1978, and the system reached full 24 satellite capability in 1993. Considering how extraordinarily sophisticated the technology is, the operating principle of GPS is remarkably simple. Each satellite continuously broadcasts a digital radio signal that includes both its own position and the time, exact to a billionth of a second. A GPS receiver takes this information – from four satellites – and uses it to calculate its position on the planet to within a few hundred feet. The receiver compares its own time with the time sent by a satellite and uses the difference between the two times to calculate its distance from the satellite. (Light travels at 186,000 miles per second: if the satellite time happened to be, for example, one-thousandth of a second behind the GPS receiver's time, then the receiver would calculate that it was 186 miles from that satellite.) By checking its time against the time of three satellites whose positions are known, a receiver can pinpoint its longitude, latitude and altitude. However, this arrangement is run by the US military and has in-built errors (which can be changed by those who run it); or, indeed, it can be turned off without warning. The receiver's clock, if not set by its American controllers, will be imprecise and thus not synchronised with the satellite clocks; therefore the measured transmission time will be (however slightly) incorrect, and therefore inaccurate. As Bill Paterson explained in an article in 1997, GPS then operated in two modes, one being the Standard Positioning Service (SPS), which was made available to civilian users and provided an accuracy of nominally 100 metres; however, even greater accuracies could be achieved with particular receivers. Some military users, on the other hand, had access to the second mode, the Precise Positioning Service (PPS), which gave considerably more pin-point correctness.[22]

The solution to this very real 'inaccuracy' was the development for civilians of Differential GPS (dGPS):

In Differential GPS, a GPS navigator receiver is placed at a precisely known surveyed position, for example, a lighthouse. Signals are received from the satellites and the position determined. The position as given by the satellites is then compared with the known position and the error calculated ... with dGPS the accuracy for the maritime application is expected to be better than ± 10 metres.[23]

In fact a year later, Peter Christmas was able to report that on 31 July 1998 the UK GLAs' dGPS 'came on line to provide, at the moment only on a trial basis, a radio-navigation system accurate to "better than 10 metres" (but most often more accurate than that) all around the coast of the British Isles. The Board now runs three [now four] of the twelve stations – at the Butt of Lewis, Sumburgh Head and Girdleness [also Earl's Hill, Stirling]. Thus, now almost the whole of the coast of north-west Europe is covered by similar, highly-accurate systems.'[24] This was done by upgrading existing radio beacon sites, and installing monitoring equipment at Duncansby Head and in the George Street Monitor Centre. The power supply systems were upgraded at each site, with a standby generator being installed at Girdleness.

The Board has decided to close the traditional marine beacon service in February 1999, and so the introduction of differential GPS adds an essential component to the service provided to the mariner by Northern Lighthouse Board. This dGPS service will be unencrypted and free at the point of use to the user with the correct receiving equipment, and will allow satellite navigation users to obtain a more accurate repeatable position of very high integrity.[25]

Although some of the in-built inaccuracies to GPS were removed by the Americans in 2000, dGPS remains much more accurate.

Along with other Government bodies, the GLAs remain concerned by the reliance of mariners solely on satellite systems, and the vulnerability of the transmissions from satellites to interference by, for instance, car thieves. There needs to be the safety-net of a back-up system, should those overhead satellites fail, or be jammed, or even switched off. This is where their backing of Loran and, subsequently eLoran comes in. Global Navigation Satellite Systems (GNSS), of which GPS is one, are vulnerable to 'both intentional and unintentional interference, as well as occasional undetected failures. This renders total dependence on GNSS unwise,' wrote Peter Douglas in 2005. From June of that year, the GLAs began a trial period of transmission of a Loran-C – the acronym means LOng RAnge Navigation, as described earlier – radio navigation signal from BT Rugby. As Douglas explained:

Loran-C is a low frequency electronic position-fixing system using pulsed transmissions at 100kHz, operating in a similar manner to the former Decca service, but with fewer masts spaced several hundred miles apart. ... the Rugby signal will be synchronised with similar signals from stations in France and Germany.

Its lower frequency than GNSS made it less vulnerable to interference. Research at that time was moving towards an enhanced Loran, or eLoran: '... the accuracy attainable with eLoran is likely to be of the order of 20 metres.'[26]

By early 2007 the GLAs had produced their first Radio Navigation Plan and it is worth quoting from Peter Douglas's report:

A key part of the Plan is the provision of a terrestrial position fixing system, to provide an alternative to GPS with different potential failure modes. The only suitable system for this role is enhanced Loran (eLoran), and accordingly the GLAs have procured the transmission of eLoran services from a site on the Solway Firth for the next 15 years, to be part of the reborn European Loran service. The announcement of this contract, signifying the DfT/GLA [Department for Transport/General Lighthouse Authority] commitment to eLoran, has had a major impact on governments in both Europe and North America.[27]

Even so, changes continue, sometimes in an unexpected direction: in 1996 the Northern Lighthouse Board received approval for four new lights, one close to Kyle of Lochalsh, and three on the west coast of the Outer Hebrides, in response to the recommendation of the Donaldson Report into the loss of the MV *Braer*, an oil-tanker carrying a cargo of 85,000 tonnes of crude oil from Bergen to Quebec, wrecked off the Shetland coast in January 1993. (Fortunately, Shetland's harsh weather helped break up the oil slicks, and such environmental damage as was done was not as lasting or as catastrophic as initially feared.) These plans included a new major light at Haskeir, off North Uist, the first of its kind, having a hybrid solar/wind power renewable energy source, monitored from 84 George Street. The minor lights at Gasker off North Harris, and on the Monach Isles, were identical to the example recently and successfully established at Mull of Easwick. It was thought at this point that re-using the abandoned tower at Monach (first lit in 1864, closed in 1942, and abandoned in 1948) with a minor light would be too expensive.[28] The three minor lights were completed in 200 days between April and October 1997. Then, after a review in 2005, it was decided to increase the range of the light from Monach from 10 miles to 18 miles, for which the most economic option was to move back into the old tower. As Andrew Mulhern summed up:

As a result of the combination of exposed off-shore location, natural heritage value (seals and sea birds), cultural heritage value (Grade B Listed Buildings), contemporary health and safety demands and financial constraints, the project to re-light the Monach Isles lighthouse provides an excellent example of the type of work we do in the Projects Section of the Engineers Department. … It is heartening to see that, despite the passage of almost 150 years and advances in navigation technology, the original Stevenson-designed Monach Isles lighthouse still has a vital role in the provision of a major aid to navigation.[29]

ABOVE: Syncrostat lamp changer for use in marine signal lanterns, by Tideland Signal Ltd, Surrey. It can be monitored and controlled remotely in order to see how many bulbs are remaining and to adjust the sun switch settings. Presented by the Northern Lighthouse Board.

(NMS.T.2011.40)

RIGHT: Solar panel, made by Solarex, United States, and designed specifically for use in extreme marine environments. Presented by the Northern Lighthouse Board.

(NMS.T.2011.43)

Hand-in-hand with automation went the 'greening' of lighthouses. For example, in 1999 it was reported that Flannan Isles lighthouse had been converted in March from acetylene gas to solar electric power, with wind generators; Chicken Rock Minor Light had been converted from propane gas to solar electric power; Helliar Holm Minor Light to solar electric power, where 'each lantern contains a lamp changer with 6 lamps each'. Other conversions included Start Point, Ushenish, Rona, Noup Head, Auskerry, Out Skerries, Foula and Rubha nan Gall – all from 'acetylene gas to solar/wind hybrid electric conversion, using the existing small 4th Order lens suitably modified to accommodate 35 watt metal halide lamps in a 3 position lamp changer'.[30] The use of solar panels for energy at all sites has become commonplace since then. The Northern Lighthouse Board has more recently made care of the environment much more central to its actions, for ethical, economic, legal and commercial reasons.[31]

By 2002 Automatic Identification System (AIS), a broadcast system operating in the VHF maritime mobile band, had become imminent,

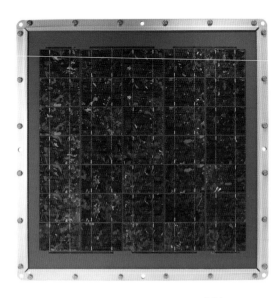

with implications for the Northern Lighthouse Board. An article in the *Journal* explained some of the potential:

> AIS is capable of sending ship information such as identification, position, course, speed, ship type, cargo information and more to other ships (and aircraft) and to shore. It can handle multiple reports at rapid update rates and ensures reliable and robust ship to ship and ship to shore operations. ... The potential of AIS as an anti-collision device cannot be under estimated.

The Northern Lighthouse Board participated in trials at the start of 2003, by housing AIS equipment in three east coast lighthouses at Barns Ness, Elie Ness and Fife Ness, with a second phase beginning in March on the west coast, as well as AIS units being installed on two buoys. The article ends with the prescient words: 'It can clearly be seen that, within a relatively short period of time, the vast majority of vessels, whether commercial or leisure, will be fitted with this equipment.'[32] By 2005, the system was a mandatory fitting in the majority of commercial shipping, known as Class A. It was agreed that a small-craft version, known as Class B should be developed, and this was tested by the Northern Lighthouse Board on the west coast. This navigational application can be viewed in action in Scotland's busiest shipping lanes, in real time, online. Work continues to mark hazards in the waters in which the Northern Lighthouse Board has legal responsibility with these systems.

### Scotland's lighthouses into the twenty-first century

The coasts around Scotland are still some of the most dangerous in the world, and as part of an island, we are dependent on the GLAs to keep our waters as safe as feasibly possible – for commerce, for security, for food, for the maintenance of the environment, and even for leisure. The Merchant Shipping Act of 1995 ensures that the Northern Lighthouse Board keeps Scottish and Isle of Man seas safe. Despite over a decade of devolution, the Board itself has not been devolved and comes under the remit of the Department for Transport in London. There has perhaps been some friction in the past, but today the Board works closely and well with Trinity House, and both authorities co-operate directly with the Commissioners of Irish Lights. There remain, however, good reasons for keeping three authorities, rather than running them as one. Like the other GLAs, the Northern Lighthouse Board is an active member of the global association, the International Association of Marine Aids to Navigation and Lighthouse Authorities (IALA). The

Board currently runs two ships: the *Pole Star* for working with buoys, and the *Pharos*, at 3600 tonnes, a multifunctional tender with a helipad. These two vessels maintain the hardware that keeps Scotland's lighthouses, buoys and beacons in prime condition. The present *Pharos*, commissioned in May 2007, is the tenth to bear this name.[33]

All foghorns have now been turned off: the bridge of today's merchant ship is enclosed and no one can hear the warning; and if they can, it would be too late to stop such enormous leviathans. This turning-off began with the deactivation of those foghorns at Cape Wrath, Copinsay, Fair Isle North and Rattray Head in 2001. The first foghorn – after experiments with bells, gunfire, horns and gongs – was that installed at St Abbs Head as late as 1876. We saw in chapter 6 how those at Ailsa Craig (1886) were worked by compressed air operated by gas engines, while the foghorn at Rattray Head (1895) influenced the design of the lighthouse itself. That mournful wail, particularly through an east coast 'haar', could send shivers up the spines of those who lived close to the sea; but in 1899, when the Inchkeith foghorn sounded more or less continuously for 130 hours, those who lived on the Fife coastline were less than amused. A few years earlier, in 1885, the Commissioners had used their powers of compulsory purchase on the island of Fidra to acquire land for a lighthouse, and the Dirleton Estate made a claim for compensation for damages through possible foghorn use. However, the Court of Session found that protection of life at sea was more important than the possibility of 'harsh or disagreeable sounds occurring now and then'.[34] By 2005 the Northern Lighthouse Board reviewed all its Aids to Navigation (AtoNs), including

Compressed air siren foghorn in three parts, for Inchkeith Island. Presented by the Northern Lighthouse Board.

(NMS T.1985.113)

foghorns. 'The conclusion was that audible fog-signals had a significantly reduced role in the modern marine environment, as a result of the widespread use of electronic position finding aids and radar, and the adoption of enclosed bridges on many vessels.' The very last Scottish foghorn was switched off on 4 October 2005 at Skerryvore lighthouse.

However, not all lights will be turned off: they are still needed, as an essential back-up to satellite navigation, and lighthouses often house more than the light, especially with the coming of electronics. The Northern Lighthouse Board has moved with the times: all buoys are now solar-powered, and many minor lights and lighthouses. The Board has a statutory duty to inspect the lights on oil-rigs, and all harbour lights. They make sure that wrecks are marked (although these do not last long in Scottish waters); and that off-shore wind farms are similarly indicated for the safety of passing ships. The Engineering Department has provided a new design of aluminium lattice modular lighthouses, with glass-reinforced plastic (GRP) day-mark panels, which can be rapidly assembled on site, rather like a famous furniture store's 'flat-pack' kits. This was first used at Sandaig in 2002, and these have gone on to be used with great success elsewhere.[35]

The coming of electronics to navigation has meant that the mariner – and the Board – has a number of systems to turn to for safe passage at sea. Working with a global network of other lighthouse services and the International Association of Marine Aids to Navigation and Lighthouse Authorities, the Northern Lighthouse Board endeavours to make the Scottish seas a safer environment. Today[36] the Northern Lighthouse Board looks after 206 lighthouses, 163 buoys, 29 beacons, 29 Racons, four dGPS stations and one GLA-shared eLoran station around Scotland's 6200-mile coastline, which has at least 790 islands in its beautiful and dangerous waters.

Some may look back to the arduous and hierarchical life of the lightkeeper, and see romance and nostalgia in what was essentially a hard, uncomfortable and, at times, lonely life. Those who have run the Northern Lighthouse Board since those early days in the 1780s have endeavoured, even before the inbuilt structures we take for granted today in the public service – such as pensions, sick-pay, or health and safety – to ensure that the backbone of the workforce was always looked after, in the best ways possible for their time. The family feeling the Stevensons endeavoured to engender is still there in today's fit and capable staff, facing whatever the future may bring. As Bella Bathurst commented at the close of her book about the Lighthouse Stevensons, 'at the tail end of the twentieth century it does not require three grown men to keep a light bulb', and this had been foreseen by the Commissioners meeting at 84 George Street, who had taken care to ensure that the Northern Lighthouse Board was fit for purpose once technology had overtaken the lightkeeper.[37]

There are still people in the Northern Lighthouse Board, actively ensuring the delivery of 'a reliable, efficient and cost-effective network of Aids to Navigation for the benefit and safety of all Mariners' – in fact, living up to their motto. This truly continues to be an age of Scottish lighthouses.

### Notes to Chapter 7

1   Munro (1979), 257-58.
2   '100 Years' (1999).
3   Munro (1979), 223-24.
4   Ibid., 190.
5   Wright (2004), 20.
6   Taylor (1995).
7   Paterson (1997b), 8.
8   Ibid., 9.
9   Grundon (1998).
10  Eunson (1998); Craigie (1998).
11  Cassells (1994); Robertson (1997); Lane (1998); and Hill (2003).
12  'Lightkeepers' (1997).
13  Ibid.
14  MacKay (2001), 18.
15  Ibid., 18.
16  Ibid., 20.
17  Waddell (2001a).
18  Waddell (2001b).
19  'Farewell to Stromness' (2003).
20  'Marine Aids' (1995).
21  'Demise of Decca' (2000-2001).
22  Paterson (1997a), 21.
23  Ibid.
24  Christmas (1998), 8.
25  'dGPS Update' (1998).
26  Douglas (2005).
27  Douglas (2007).
28  'New Lights' (1996), 16; McIntosh (1997); also Donaldson (1994), 384-85.
29  Mulhern (2007), 18.
30  Paterson (1999).
31  Petrie (2001).
32  'AIS' (2002).
33  'MV Pharos' (2005); 'NLV Pharos' (2007).
34  Munro (1979), 151-152; Renton (2001); 'The Last Blast ...' (2005). Besides the Inchkeith foghorn: NMS T.1985.113, other examples in the collection are: the 1933 Buchan Ness foghorn (NMS T.1978.32); an air siren, sectioned to show the inner fan (NMS T.1956.38); and an air raid siren, electrically operated (NMS T.1984.240).
35  Watt (2005).
36  At December 2013. See http://www.nlb.org.uk/ourlights/responsibility.htm 'What We Deliver'.
37  Bathurst (1999), 236.

# Glossary

AIS: Automatic Identification System.

ARGAND LAMP: Improved oil lamp invented and patented in 1780 by Swiss Aime Argand (1750-1803).

ASEISMATIC JOINT: Device designed by David Stevenson for mitigating the effects of shocks on lighthouses in countries subject to earthquakes.

AtoNs: Aids to Navigation.

BALANCE CRANE: Lifting device containing a horizontal beam (the lever) pivoted about a point called the fulcrum. The principle of the lever allows a heavy load attached to the shorter end of the beam to be lifted by a smaller force applied in the opposite direction to the longer end of the beam. The ratio of the load's weight to the applied force is equal to the ratio of the lengths of the longer arm and the shorter arm, and is called the mechanical advantage.

CATADIOPTRIC: See OPTICAL TERMS (below).

CATOPTRIC: See OPTICAL TERMS (below).

CLINOMETER: Instrument for measuring angles of slope, or tilt.

COLZA OIL: Vegetable oil, usually made from one of the brassica genus.

DAVIS QUADRANT: Navigation instrument, invented by John Davis in 1734; also known as a backstaff.

DECCA SYSTEM: Low frequency radio navigation system, British.

DfT: Department for Transport (UK).

dGPS: Differential Global Positioning System.

DIOPTRIC: See optical terms (below).

DOTY BURNER: Efficient paraffin-fuelled lamp, with stepped concentric wicks, devised by Captain H. H. Doty of Virginia, in 1870.

ELORAN: Enhanced Loran (LOng RAnge Navigation): see Loran-C (below); accuracy of ±8 meters.

EQUIANGULAR PRISMS: Prisms with equal angles.

ESTF: Engineering Storage and Testing Facility.

FLOATING-LIGHT: A temporary warning light on a moored light vessel, usually while a lighthouse is under construction.

FRESNEL LENS: Devised by the French physicist Augustin Fresnel, this lens reduces the amount of material and weight required compared to a conventional spherical lens by breaking the lens into a set of concentric annular sections or prisms.

FRESNEL OPTIC: Lighthouse lens using Fresnel lenses.

GLAZING BARS: Window struts, or astragals.

GLA: General Lighthouse Authority, defined as being a dedicated government agency of a country or nation tasked with and responsible for the provision and maintenance of lighthouses, light vessels, navigational aids and any other equipment or facilities which ensure the safety of mariners and sailors navigating the country's territorial waters, seas or oceans.

GNSS: Global Navigation Satellite Systems.

GPS: Global Positioning System.

GRP: Day-mark panels; glass-reinforced plastic day-mark panels.

HYDRAULIC LIME: Used to make lime mortar, a cement which sets under water.

IALA: International Association of Marine Aids to Navigation and Lighthouse Authorities.

JAG-BOLTS: A metal bolt with a nicked or barbed shank which resists retraction, as when leaded into stone.

LEADER CABLE: An electric submarine cable laid on the ocean bed, devised by Charles Stevenson, used for guiding ships into port during the First World War.

LEADING LIGHTS: A pair of beacons separated in distance and elevation, so that when their lights are aligned, with one above the other, they provide a bearing for a vessel.

LIGHT-ROOM: Glazed lantern on top of a lighthouse, from where the light source shines through the optic.

Loran-C: Terrestrial radio navigation system using low frequency radio transmitters in multiple deployment to determine the location and speed of the receiver.

POLYZONAL LENSES: David Brewster's name for his form of the 'Fresnel' lens: a lens built up in a series of zones or rings.

PPS: Precise Positioning Service (a military component of GPS).

RACON: Radar beacon.

RADAC: Automated telephone system, using 8-track tape and recorded synthesised voice warnings, obsolete by the mid-1980s.

RADLE: Automated telephone system, using 8-track tape and recorded verbal warnings, obsolete by the mid-1980s.

REFLECTOR: Device to enhance the light source placed in front of it, usually made of metal, in the shape of a parabola or a hemisphere.

RUTTER: Early set of sailing instructions (French: *routier*)

SANDGLASS: Double-ended time-measuring device made of glass in which sand trickles through a narrow gap into the lower half during a specified amount of time.

SPS: Standard Positioning Service.

SOUND TOLL REGISTERS: Sound Toll Registers (STR) are one of the great serial sources of early modern history of western Europe. They are kept by the Danish National Archives (Rigsarkivet) Copenhagen. The STR are the records of the toll the king of Denmark levied on the passage of ships through the Sound, the strait between Denmark and Sweden. They have been preserved for about 300 of the 360 years from 1497 till 1857, when the Sound Toll was abolished, and include a practically uninterrupted series from 1574 to 1857. See: http://www.soundtoll.nl/www/index.php?option=com_content&view=article&id=69&Itemid=70&lang=en

UHF RADIO: Radio using an Ultra High Frequency, between 300 MHz and 3000 MHz.

VHF RADIO: Radio using a Very High Frequency, 30 MHz to 300 MHz.

Optical terms, as they evolved during the nineteenth century:

OPTIC: Instrument for concentrating or diffusing light rays.

CATOPTRIC: Reflecting, using metal parabolic reflectors and lamps.

DIOPTRIC: Refracting, using glass lenses and prisms.

CATADIOPTRIC: Combination of reflecting and refracting elements, usually, but not always, taken to mean all-glass optics incorporating internally reflecting prisms.

HOLOPHOTAL : 'Light of maximum intensity'. Thomas Stevenson's own term meaning an optical device by which the whole sphere of diverging light is made to form a single parallel beam. It came to be applied particularly to Stevenson's improved form of annular lens panel. The French called these lights, '*les phares à éclipses*'.

DIA-CATOPTRIC: Refracting and reflecting. Alan Stevenson used the term to describe the early Fresnel system combining a revolving lens with small subsidiary lenses and silvered mirrors (though Fresnel himself used the word catadioptric to describe the system). Thomas Stevenson later used it to describe Horsburgh Light which had a catadioptric lens combined with a metal parabola.

## Orders

A method of classification devised by Augustin Fresnel to describe the power and range of dioptric lights. Fifth and sixth order lights have not been included.

- FIRST ORDER:
  Focal length 920 mm
  Range of 20–30 nautical miles
- SECOND ORDER:
  Focal length 700 mm
  Range of 16–20 nautical miles
- THIRD ORDER (large size):
  Focal length 500 mm
  Range of 15–20 nautical miles
- THIRD ORDER (small size):
  Focal length 350 mm
  Range of 12–14 nautical miles
- FOURTH ORDER:
  Focal length 250 mm
  Range of 9–12 nautical miles
- HYPER-RADIANT
  Focal length 1330 mm
  Range of 30-plus nautical miles

(From Elton [2009], pp. 238-39)

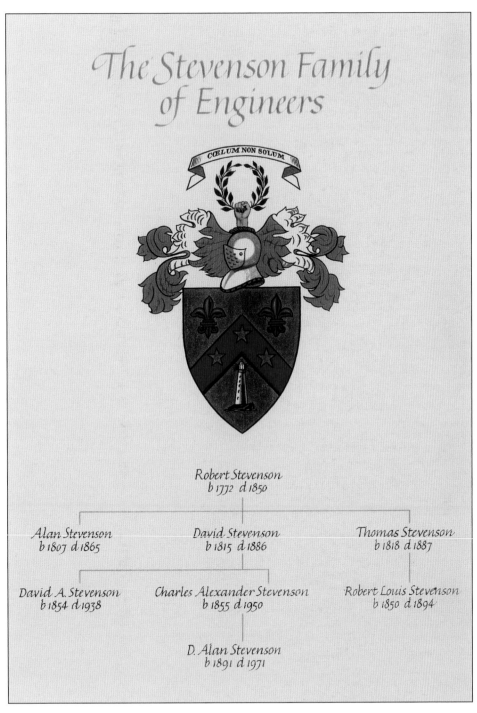

The Stevenson Family of Engineers

COELUM NON SOLUM

Robert Stevenson
b 1772 d 1850

Alan Stevenson
b 1807 d 1865

David Stevenson
b 1815 d 1886

Thomas Stevenson
b 1818 d 1887

David A. Stevenson
b 1854 d 1938

Charles Alexander Stevenson
b 1855 d 1950

Robert Louis Stevenson
b 1850 d 1894

D. Alan Stevenson
b 1891 d 1971

THE STEVENSON FAMILY TREE
(© The Trustees of D. Alan Stevenson)

239

# Bibliography and References

**Manuscript sources**

Guildhall Library, London:
    Corporation of Trinity House Archives
        Court Minutes, 1661-2000 Ms 30004
        Board Minutes, 1685-2000 Ms 30010
        Letter Books, 1685-1747 Ms 30048
        Eddystone Lighthouse 1708-1824, Mss 30127-31

National Library of Scotland, Edinburgh:
    Acc. 4215 Records of Robert Stevenson & Sons,
        Civil Engineers
    Acc. 10706 Records of Robert Stevenson & Sons,
        Civil Engineers

**Published sources**

'100 YEARS' (1999) – 'Looking Back over 100 Years',
    *Northern Lighthouse Board Journal* (Christmas
    1999), 12-13.
ADAIR (1703) – John Adair, *The Description of the Sea-
    Coast and Islands of Scotland* (Edinburgh: [the
    author], 1703).
'AIS' (2002) – 'Automatic Identification System (AIS)',
    *Northern Lighthouse Board Journal* (Christmas
    2002), 4-5.
ALLAN (2002) – James Allen, *General Guide to the Isle
    of May, Fife's own Island of Mystery and History,
    Sea Cliffs, Sea Birds and Seals*, 2nd edition
    (Anstruther: Tervor, 2002).
ALLARDYCE (1998) – Keith Allardyce, *Scotland's Edge
    Revisited* (Glasgow: HarperCollins, 1998).
ALLARDYCE and HOOD (1986) – Keith Allardyce and
    Evelyn Hood, *Scotland's Edge: A Celebration of
    Two Hundred Years of the Lighthouse Service
    in Scotland and the Isle of Man* (Glasgow and
    London: Collins, 1986).
ALTICK (1968) – Richard Altick, *The Shows of London
    – A Panoramic History of Exhibitions, 1600-1862*
    (Cambridge, MA: Harvard University Press,
    Belknap Press, 1968).
ANDERSON (1989) – R. G. W. Anderson, 'Museums in

the Making: the Origins and Development of the
    National Collections', in CALDER (1989), 1-17.
ANDERSON and GOWENLOCK (1998) – Alex Anderson
    and Brian G. Gowenlock, *Chemistry in Heriot-Watt
    1821-1991* (Edinburgh: Heriot-Watt University,
    1998).
ANON. (1801) – Article 'Reflector' in *Supplement to the
    Third Edition of the Encyclopaedia Britannica,* 3rd
    edition, 2 vols (Edinburgh: Thomson Bonar, 1801),
    395-96.
ANON. (1811) – Anon., 'Bell Rock Light-house', *The
    Edinburgh Annual Register for 1809,* part second
    (Edinburgh: John Ballantyne & Co., 1811), 542-48.
ANON. (1823) – Anon., Article 'Reflector' in *Encyclo-
    paedia Britannica,* 6th edition, 20 vols (Edinburgh:
    Archibald Constable and Company, 1823), XVII,
    671.
ANON. (1836) – 'Papers relating to John Adair', *Ban-
    natyne Miscellany,* 2 (Edinburgh: The Bannatyne
    Club, 1836), 311-44.
ANON. (1867) – Anon., 'Alan Stevenson', *Minutes of
    Proceedings of the Institution of Civil Engineers,*
    26 (1867), 575-77.
ANSON (1930) – Peter F. Anson, *Fishing Boats and Fisher
    Folk on the East Coast of Scotland* (London: J. M.
    Dent and Sons Ltd, 1930).
ARAGO (1859) – François Arago [trans. W. H. Smyth,
    Baden Powell, and R. Grant], *Biographies of
    Distinguished Scientific Men,* 2nd series (Boston,
    1859).
ARAGO et FRESNEL (1821) – [F.] Arago et [A.] Fresnel,
    'Note sur les becs à plusieurs mèches appliqués
    aux lampes d'Argant ou à double courant d'air',
    *Annales de chimie et de physique,* 16 (1821), 377-
    83.
ARAGO and FRESNEL (1822) – [F.] Arago and [A.] Fresnel,
    'On Argand Lamps with Concentric Wicks', *Reper-
    tory of Arts, Manufactures, and Agriculture …,* 2nd
    series, 40 (1822), 307-11.
ASIN and OTERO (1933) – Miguel Asin and M. Lopez
    Otero, 'The Pharos of Alexandria', *Proceedings of
    the British Academy,* 19 (1933), 277-92.

ASPDEN (2008) – R. J. Aspden, 'Balfour, James Melville', in Michael Chrimes, et al. (ed.), *Biographical Dictionary of Civil Engineers in Great Britain and Ireland, vol. 2: 1830 to 1890* (London: Thomas Telford Publishing on behalf of The Institution of Civil Engineers, 2008), 43-44.

BAIGENT (2004) – Elizabeth Baigent, 'Collins, Greenvile', *Oxford Dictionary of National Biography* (Oxford: Oxford University Press, 2004) [available online at http://www.oxforddnb.com/].

BALFOUR (1861a) – James M. Balfour, 'Description and Drawing of a "Refraction Protractor" and of its application to the designing of the Prisms employed in Lighthouse Apparatus', *Transactions of the Royal Scottish Society of Arts*, 5 (1861), 95-102.

BALFOUR (1861b) – James M. Balfour, 'Description of an Instrument for Dividing Circles on Paper', *Transactions of the Royal Scottish Society of Arts*, cf. 5 (1861), 149-51.

BALFOUR (1864) – James M. Balfour, 'Description of a Simple Improvement on Reflectors for Lighthouses', *Transactions of the Royal Scottish Society of Arts*, 6 (1864), 211-14.

BALFOUR (1868) – James M. Balfour, 'Description of a Combined Optical Square and "Line Finder"', *Transactions of the Royal Scottish Society of Arts*, 7 (1868), 319-20.

BALFOUR PAUL (1877-1978) – Sir James Balfour Paul, et al. (eds), *Accounts of the Lord High Treasurer of Scotland*, 14 vols (Edinburgh: H. M. General Register House, 1877-1978).

BALL (1793) – Andrew Ball, 'Parish of Crail', in SINCLAIR (1791-99), IX, (1793), 439-58.

BALLANTYNE (1865) – R. M. Ballantyne, *The Lighthouse: being the Story of Great Fight between Man and the Sea* (London: James Nisbet and Co., 1865).

BARBER (1992) – Peter Barber, 'England I: Pageantry, Defense, and Government: Maps at Court to 1550', in BUISSERET (1992), 26-56.

BARBER (1998a) – Peter M. Barber, 'The British Isles', in Marcel Watelet (ed.), *The Mercator Atlas of Europe* (Pleasant Hill, Oregon: Walking Tree Press, 1998), 43-77.

BARBER (1998b) – Peter M. Barber, 'Mapping Britain from Afar', *Mercator's World*, 3 (July/August 1998), 20-27.

BARNES (2003) – Alison Barnes, *Henry Winstanley: Artist, Inventor and Lighthouse-builder*, 1644-1703 (Saffron Walden and Plymouth: Tourist Information Service and Saffron Walden Museum, Uttlesford District Council, and Plymouth City Museum & Art Gallery, 2003).

BARNES (2005a) – Alison Barnes (ed.), *Frederic G. Kitton, 'A Visit to the Eddystone Lighthouse', reprinted from 'The Strand Magazine', October 1892* (Plymouth: City Museum & Art Gallery, 2005).

BARNES (2005b) – Alison Barnes, 'Architect Hunt: Letter', *Country Life* (24 February 2005), 70.

BARNES (2005c) – Alison Barnes, 'New Light on Eddystone', *History Today*, 55, no. 9 (September 2005), 2-3.

BARNES (2008a) – Alison Barnes, 'Henry Winstanley and the Rose & Crown', *Lamp 75: Quarterly Journal of the Association of Lighthouse Keepers* (January 2008), 10-11.

BARNES (2008b) – Alison Barnes, 'Mathematical Water Magic', *History Today*, 58, no. 10 (October 2008), 8-9.

BARRETT (2006) – Roger Barrett, *Start Point and its Lighthouse: History Map and Guide* (Chudleigh: Orchard Publications, 2006).

BATHURST (1999) – Bella Bathurst, *The Lighthouse Stevensons: the extraordinary Story of the Building of the Scottish Lighthouses by the Ancestors of Robert Louis Stevenson* (Glasgow: HarperCollins, 1999).

BEAGLEHOLE (2006) – Helen Beaglehole, *Lighting the Coast: A History of New Zealand's Coastal Lighthouse System* (Canterbury, NZ: Canterbury University Press, 2006).

BEILBY (1992) – Alec Beilby, *Heroes All! The Story of the RNLI* (Sparkford: Patrick Stephens, 1992).

BELL (1981) – A. S. Bell (ed.), *The Scottish Antiquarian Tradition: Essays to mark the Bicentenary of the Society of Antiquaries of Scotland and Its Museum 1789-1980* (Edinburgh: John Donald, 1981).

BETTS (2003-07) – Jonathan Betts, 'John Hyacinth de Magellan (1722-1790) Part 1: Horological and Scientific Agent', *Antiquarian Horology*, 27 (2003), 509-17; 'Part 2: The Early Clocks', ibid., 28 (2004), 173-83; 'Part 3: The Later Clocks and Watches', ibid., 30 (2007), 25-44; 'Part 4: The Precision Pioneers', ibid. 365-75.

BINDING (2003) – Paul Binding, *Imagined Corners: Exploring the World's First Atlas* (London: Headline Review, 2003).

BLAKE (1956) – George Blake, *Clyde Lighthouses: A Short History of the Clyde Lighthouse Trust 1756-1956* (Glasgow: Jackson Son and Co., 1956).

BOYLE (1996a) – Martin Boyle, *Lighthouses: To Light Their Way* (Southampton: B. & T. Publications, 1996).

BOYLE (1996b) – Martin Boyle, *Lighthouses: Four Countries – One Aim* (Southampton: B. & T. Publications, 1996).

BOYLE (1997) – Martin Boyle, *Lighthouses of England and Wales: Eddystone* (B. & T. Publications, 1997).

BRAY (1879) – William Bray (ed.), *Diary of John Evelyn, FRS*, 4 vols (London: G. Bell and Sons, 1879).

BREBNER (1869) – Alan Brebner, 'Description of Mr Alan Brebner's Refraction Protractor, for Glass with Refractive Index of 1.51', *Minutes of the Proceedings of the Institution of Civil Engineers*, 26 (1869), 34 and pl. 7.

BREBNER (1891) – Alan Brebner, 'Modern Harbour Construction', *Transactions of the Royal Scottish Society of Arts*, 12 (1891), 1-29.

BRENNI (1994) – Paolo Brenni, 'Soleil-Duboscq-Pellin: a Dynasty of Scientific Instrument Makers', in Giorgio Dragoni, Anita McConnell and Gerard L'E. Turner (eds), *Proceedings of the Eleventh International Scientific Instrument Symposium* (Bologna: Grafis, 1994), 107-11.

BRENNI (1996) – Paolo Brenni, '19th Century French Scientific Instrument Makers: XIII: Soleil, Duboscq, and their Successors', *Bulletin of the Scientific Instrument Society*, no. 51 (1996), 7-16.

BREWSTER (1808-30) – David Brewster (ed.), *Edinburgh Encyclopaedia*, 20 vols (Edinburgh: William Blackwood and John Waugh, 1808-30).

BREWSTER (1812) – David Brewster, 'Burning Instruments', in the *Edinburgh Encyclopaedia*, V (1812), 130-44.

BREWSTER (1813) – David Brewster, *Treatise on New Philosophical Instruments* (Edinburgh: William Blackwood; London: John Murray, 1813).

BREWSTER (1823) – David Brewster, 'On the Construction of Polyzonal Lenses and Mirrors of great magnitude, for Light-Houses ...', *Edinburgh Philosophical Journal*, 8 (1823), 160-69.

BREWSTER (1831) – David Brewster, 'Construction of Polyzonal Lenses and their Combination with plain Mirrors for Illumination in Lighthouses' (read 7 May 1827), *Transactions of the Royal Society of Edinburgh*, 9 (1831), 33-72.

[BREWSTER] (1833) – [David Brewster], 'British Lighthouse System', *Edinburgh Review*, 57 (1833), 169-93.

[BREWSTER] (1835) – [David Brewster], 'Report from the Select Committee on Lighthouses, with the Minutes of Evidence', *Edinburgh Review*, 59 (1835), 221-41.

[BREWSTER] (1859) – [David Brewster], 'Life-Boats – Lightening Conductors – Lighthouses', *North British Review*, 31 (1859), 492-529.

[BREWSTER] (1860) – [David Brewster], 'British Lighthouses', *North British Review*, 32 (1860), 487-519.

BROCK (1984) – W. H. Brock, 'Brewster as a Scientific Journalist', in A. D. Morrison-Low and J. R. R. Christie (eds), *'Martyr of Science': Sir David Brewster 1781-1868* (Edinburgh: Royal Scottish Museum, 1984), 37-42.

BROWN (1980) – I. G. Brown, *The Hobby-Horsical Antiquary: A Scottish Character, 1640-1830* (Edinburgh: National Library of Scotland, 1980).

BROWN (1982) – Cynthia Gaskell Brown, *The Eddystone Lighthouses* (Plymouth: City Museum & Art Gallery, 1982).

BRUCE PEEBLES (1887) – D. Bruce Peebles, 'President's Address', *Transactions of the Royal Scottish Society of Arts*, 11 (1887), 390-418.

BRUCE PEEBLES (1891) – D. Bruce Peebles, 'President's Address', *Transactions of the Royal Scottish Society of Arts*, 12 (1891), 83-120.

BRÜCK (2000) – Mary Brück, 'Bue Island 1851: A Clouded-out but Unique Eclipse Expedition', *Irish Astronomical Journal*, 27 (2000), 91-94.

BRÜCK and BRÜCK (1988) – H. A. Brück and M. T. Brück, *The Peripatetic Astronomer: the Life of Charles Piazzi Smyth* (Bristol and Philadelphia: Adam Hilger, 1998).

BRUNTON (1887) – R. H. Brunton, 'The Japan Lights', *Minutes of the Proceedings of the Institution of Civil Engineers*, 47 (1877), 1-42.

BRUNTON (1991) – R. H. Brunton, ed. by H. Cortazzi, *Building Japan 1868-1876* (Sandgate, Kent: Japan Library Limited, 1991).

BRYCE (1845) – John Bryce, 'Parish of Ardrossan', *The New Statistical Account of Scotland*, 15 vols (Edinburgh: William Blackwood and Sons, 1845), V, 191-210.

[BRYDEN] (1989) – [D. J. Bryden], 'Lighthouses', in CALDER (1989), 107-108.

BRYDEN (1998-99) – D. J. Bryden, '"Mr Clerk the Graver"; a Biographical Study in the Cultural Infra-Structure of Early Modern Scotland', *Review of Scottish Culture*, 11 (1998-99), 13-31.

BUISSERET (1992) – David Buisseret (ed.), *Monarchs, Ministers and Maps: The Emergence of Cartography as a Tool of Government in Early Modern Europe* (Chicago and London: University of Chicago Press, 1992).

BUISSERET (2003) – David Buisseret, *The Mapmakers' Quest: Depicting New Worlds in Renaissance Europe* (Oxford: Oxford University Press, 2003).

BURUMA (2005) – Ian Buruma, *Inventing Japan: from Empire to Economic Miracle* (London: Phoenix, 2005).

CADBURY (2003) – Deborah Cadbury, *Seven Wonders of the Industrial World* (London: HarperCollins Publishers Limited, 2003).

CALDER (1986) – Jenni Calder (ed.), *The Enterprising Scot: Scottish Adventure and Achievement* (Edinburgh: HMSO, 1986).

CALDER (1989) – Jenni Calder (ed.), *The Wealth of a Nation in the National Museums of Scotland* (Edinburgh: National Museums of Scotland; Glasgow: Richard Drew Publishing Ltd, 1989).

CAMERON (1996) – J. S. Cameron, 'James V (1513-42)', in Peter G. B. McNeill and Hector L. MacQueen (eds), *Atlas of Scottish History to 1707* (Edinburgh: Scottish Medievalists and Department of Geography, University of Edinburgh, 1996), 122-23.

CAMERON (1998) – Jamie Cameron, *James V: the Personal Rule, 1528-1542* (East Linton: Tuckwell Press, 1998).

CAMPBELL (1904) – J. M. Campbell, *Notes on the Natural History of the Bell Rock* (Edinburgh: David Douglas, 1904).

CAMPBELL (1999) – Mungo Campbell, *A Complete Catalogue of Works by Turner in the National Gallery of Scotland* (Edinburgh: National Galleries of Scotland, 1999).

CASSELLS (1994) – Ian Cassells, *No More Paraffin-Oilers* (Latheronwheel, Caithness: Whittles Pub., 1994).

*Catalogue ... (1851) – Illustrated Catalogue of the*

*Exhibition of all Nations*, 3 vols (London: Spicer Brothers & W. Clowes and Son, 1851).

*Catalogue ... (1855)* – *Paris Universal Exhibition 1855: Catalogue of the Works exhibited in the British Section of the Exhibition ...* (London: Chapman and Hall, 1855).

*Catalogue ... (1877)* – *Catalogue of the Special Loan Collection of Scientific Apparatus at the South Kensington Museum, MDCCCLXXVI*, 3rd edition (London: HMSO, 1877).

*Catalogue ... (1882)* – *Official Catalogue of the Exhibition of Naval Architecture, Marine Engineering, Fisheries, Life-Saving, Coast-Lighting, and Submarine Engineering, &c. Tynemouth, September, 1882*, 3rd edition (Newcastle-upon-Tyne: North East Coast Exhibition Committee, 1882).

*Catalogue ... (1891)* – *Royal Naval Exhibition 1891. Official Catalogue & Guide*, 3rd edition (London: W. P. Griffiths & Sons, 1891).

CHAMBERS (1835) – Robert Chambers, *A Biographical Dictionary of Eminent Scotsmen*, 4 vols (Glasgow: Blackie and Son, 1835).

CHAMBERS (1844) – Robert and William Chambers, *The Gazetteer of Scotland*, 2 vols (Edinburgh: Andrew Jack for the Proprietors, 1844).

CHANCE ([1892]) – James Frederick Chance, *Chance of Bromsgrove and Birmingham ...* (London: Spottiswoode, Ballantyne, n.d. [1892]).

CHANCE (1919) – James Frederick Chance, *A History of the Firm of Chance Brothers & Co. Glass and Alkali Manufacturers* (London: Spottiswoode, Ballantyne, 1919).

CHANCE (1866) – James T. Chance, 'On Optical Apparatus used in Lighthouses', *Proceedings of the Minutes of the Institution of Civil Engineers*, 26 (1866).

CHANCE (1902) – James Frederick Chance, *The Lighthouse Work of Sir James Chance, Baronet* (London: Smith, Elder & Co., 1902).

CHANCE and WILLIAMS (2008) – Toby Chance and Peter Williams, *Lighthouses: the Race to Illuminate the World* (London: New Holland Publishers Ltd, 2008).

CHECKLAND (1992) – Olive Checkland, 'Richard Henry Brunton and the Japan Lights 1868-1876, a brilliant and abrasive engineer', *Transactions of the Newcomen Society*, 63 (1992), 217-28.

CHITNIS (1976) – Anand Chitnis, *The Scottish Enlightenment: a Social History* (Croom Helm, 1976).

CHRISTMAS (1998) – Peter Christmas, 'Operations Department', *Northern Lighthouse Board Journal* (Christmas 1998), 8.

CLARK (1830) – James Clark, 'Description of a Method of Cutting Screws, with drawings of the apparatus employed', *Edinburgh Journal of Science*, new series, 2 (1830), 273-76.

CLARKE, et al. (1989) – T. N. Clarke, A. D. Morrison-Low and A. D. C. Simpson, *Brass & Glass: Scientific Instrument Making Workshops in Scotland* (Edinburgh: National Museums of Scotland, 1989).

CLAYTON and RICE (1988) – Peter Clayton and Martin Rice (eds), *The Seven Wonders of the Ancient World* (London: Routledge, 1988).

CLIFTON (1995) – Gloria Clifton, *Directory of British Scientific Instrument Makers 1550-1850* (London: Zwemmer in association with the National Maritime Museum, 1995).

CLOSE (1868) – Captain M. C. Close, 'Report on Lighthouses and Coast Illuminators (Class 66)', *Reports on the Paris Universal Exhibition, 1867*, 6 vols (London: HMSO, 1868), IV, 665-98.

COASE (1974) – R. H. Coase, 'The Lighthouse in Economics', *Journal of Law and Economics*, 17 (1974), 357-76.

COLLINGWOOD (1868) – Cuthbert Collingwood, *Rambles of a Naturalist on the Shores and Waters of the China Sea* (London: John Murray, 1868).

COLLINS (1776) – Greenvile Collins, *Great Britain's Coasting Pilot* (London: J. Mount, T. Page, and W. Mount, 1776).

CONNOR and SIMPSON (2004) – R. D. Connor and A. D. C. Simpson, ed. by A. D. Morrison-Low, *Weights and Measures in Scotland: A European Perspective* (Edinburgh: National Museums of Scotland, 2004).

COOK (2004a) – Andrew S. Cook, 'Dalrymple, Alexander', *Oxford Dictionary of National Biography* (Oxford: Oxford University Press, 2004) [available online at http://www.oxforddnb.com/].

COOK (2004b) – Andrew S. Cook, 'Horsburgh [Horsbrough], James', *Oxford Dictionary of National Biography* (Oxford: Oxford University Press, 2004) [available online at http://www.oxforddnb.com/].

COOKSON and HEMPSTEAD (2000) – Gillian Cookson and Colin A. Hempstead, *A Victorian Scientists and Engineer: Fleeming Jenkin and the Birth of Electrical Engineering* (Aldershot: Ashgate, 2000).

COOMBS (2004) – Katherine Coombs, 'Lens [Laus] Family', *Oxford Dictionary of National Biography* (Oxford: Oxford University Press, 2004) [available online at http://www.oxforddnb.com/].

CORWIN (1852) – Thomas Corwin, 'Extract from the Report of officers convened under the direction of Hon. Thomas Corwin, Secretary of the Treasury, on the Light House System of the United States coast', *American Journal of Science and Arts*, 13 (1852), 318-36.

CRAIGIE (1998) – Stella Craigie, 'Tragedy at Fair Isle South', *Northern Lighthouse Board Journal* (Summer 1998), 20-21.

CRANE (2002) – Nicholas Crane, *Mercator: The Man who Mapped the Planet* (London: Weidenfeld & Nicolson, 2002).

CUNINGHAM (1864) – Alexander Cuningham, 'On Fogs and Sea and Fog-Signals on Shore', *Transactions of the Royal Scottish Society of Arts*, 6 (1864), 214-33.

CUNINGHAM (1868) – Alexander Cuningham, 'Suggestions for a Proposed Uniform System of Fog Signals', *Transactions of the Royal Scottish Society of Arts*, 7 (1868), 174-86.

CUNNINGHAM (1885) – David Cunningham, 'Account of Shifting one of the Lighthouses at Buddonness, near Dundee Harbour', *Minutes of Proceedings of the Institution of Civil Engineers*, 79 (1885), 347-50.

CURL (2005) – James Stevens Curl, *The Egyptian Revival: Ancient Egypt as the Inspiration for Design Motifs in the West* (London: Routledge, 2005).

DAICHES, JONES and JONES (1986) – D. Daiches, P. Jones, and J. Jones (eds), *A Hotbed of Genius: The Scottish Enlightenment, 1730-90* (Edinburgh: Edinburgh University Press, 1986).

DEFOE (1971) – Daniel Defoe, *A Tour through the Whole Island of Great Britain* (London: Penguin Books, 1971; first published 1724-26).

DEFOE (2005) – Daniel Defoe, *The Storm* (London: Penguin Books, 2005; first published 1704).

'DEMISE OF DECCA' (2000-01) – 'Demise of Decca', *Beam: the Journal of the Irish Lighthouse Service* (2000-01) [www.commissionersofirishlights.com].

'dGPS UPDATE' (1998) – 'dGPS Update', *Northern Lighthouse Board Journal* (Summer 1998), 10.

DITCHBURN (1990) – David Ditchburn, 'A Note on Scandinavian Trade with Scotland in the Later Middle Ages', in Grant G. Simpson (ed.), *Scotland and Scandinavia 800-1800* (Edinburgh: John Donald, 1990), 70-89.

DONALDSON (1994) – The Rt Hon The Lord Donaldson of Lymington, *Safer Ships, Cleaner Seas: Report of Lord Donaldson's Inquiry into the Prevention of Pollution from Merchant Shipping* (HMSO, 1994).

DOUGLAS (2005) – Peter Douglas, 'Introducing Loran-C', *Northern Lighthouse Board Journal* (Summer 2005), 14-15.

DOUGLAS (2007) – Peter Douglas, 'Navigation News', *Northern Lighthouse Board Journal* (Summer 2007), 22-23.

DREYER and FICHOU (2005) – Francis Dreyer and Jean-Christophe Fichou, *L'histoire de tous les phares de France* (Rennes: Éditions Ouest-France, 2005).

DRURY (1980) – P. J. Drury, 'No Other Palace in the Kingdom Will Compare with It: The Evolution of Audley End, 1605-1745', *Architectural History*, 23 (1980), 1-171.

DRURY and GOW (1984) – P. J. Drury and I. R. Gow, *Audley End*, Essex (London: HMSO, 1984).

[DUNCAN] (1835) – [William Duncan], *Description of the Coast between Aberdeen and Leith* (Aberdeen: John Davidson, 1835).

EGGELING (1960) – W. J. Eggeling, *The Isle of May: A Scottish Nature Reserve* (Edinburgh and London: Oliver and Boyd, 1960).

'ELECTRIC LIGHT' (1886) – 'The Electric Light at the Firth of Forth', *Engineering*, 42 (1886), 638.

ELTON (2009) – Julia Elton, 'A Light to Lighten our Darkness: Lighthouse Optics and the Later Development of Fresnel's Revolutionary Refracting lens 1780-1900', *International Journal for the History of Engineering and Technology* [prev. *Transactions of the Newcomen Society*], 76 (2009), 183-244.

EMERSON (1979) – R. L. Emerson, 'The Philosophical Society of Edinburgh, 1738-1747', *British Journal for the History of Science*, 12 (1979), 154-91.

EMERSON (1981) – R. L. Emerson, 'The Philosophical Society of Edinburgh, 1748-1768', *British Journal for the History of Science*, 14 (1981), 133-76.

EMERSON (1985) – R. L. Emerson, 'The Philosophical Society of Edinburgh, 1768-1783', *British Journal for the History of Science*, 18 (1985), 255-303.

EMERSON (1988) – Roger L. Emerson, 'Science and the Origins and Concerns of the Scottish Enlightenment', *History of Science*, 26 (1988), 333-66.

EMERSON (1992) – Roger L. Emerson, *Professors, Patronage and Politics: the Aberdeen Universities in the Eighteenth Century* (Aberdeen: Aberdeen University Press, 1992).

EMPEREUR (1998) – Jean-Yves Empereur, *Le Phare d'Alexandrie: La Merveille retrouvée* (Paris: Gallimard, 1998).

EUNSON (1998) – Christina Eunson, 'Some Reminiscences on the Bombing of Fair Isle North in 1939', *Northern Lighthouse Board Journal* (Summer 1998), 19-20.

EVANS (2005) – John Evans, *The Gentleman Usher: the Life and Times of George Dempster 1732-1818* (Barnsley: Pen & Sword Military, 2005).

EVERETT (2006) – Martyn Everett, 'The Prints of Henry Winstanley', *Newport News*, 28 May 2006 [see online at: http://sites.google.com/site/martyneverett/theprintsofhenrywinstanley].

EWAN (1990) – Elizabeth Ewan, *Townlife in Fourteenth-Century Scotland* (Edinburgh: EUP, 1990).

'FAREWELL TO STROMNESS' (2003) – 'Farewell to Stromness', *Northern Lighthouse Board Journal* (Christmas 2003), 14-15.

FERGUSON (1991) – David M. Ferguson, *Shipwrecks of North East Scotland 1444-1990* (Aberdeen: Aberdeen University Press, 1991).

FIENNES (1947) – Christopher Morris (ed.), *The Journeys of Celia Fiennes* (London: The Cresset Press, 1947).

FORRESTER (1792) – James Forrester, 'Parish of Anstruther-Wester', in SINCLAIR (1791-99), III, (1792), 77-88.

FRASER (2008) – Marie Fraser, 'Admiral Bruce Fraser (1888-1981)', *Canadian Explorer* (March 2008) [see http://www.clanfraser.ca/admiral_fraser.htm].

FROST (1975) – Honor Frost, 'The Pharos Site, Alexandria, Egypt', *International Journal of Nautical Archaeology*, 4 (1975), 126-30.

GALBRAITH (1910) – J. L. Galbraith, *A Scotch Professor of the Old School: a Sketch of the Life of William Swan, LL.D.* (James MacLehose & Sons, 1910).

GARCÉS (2003) – Nelson Garcés, *Faros de Chile: Lighthouses of Chile* (Chile: Editorial Sipimex, 2003).

GIFFORD (1988) – John Gifford, *The Buildings of Scotland: Fife* (London: Penguin Books, 1988).

GILKES (1991) – Michael Gilkes, 'Lead Kindly Light', *[Royal Cruising Club] Roving Commissions*, 31 (1991), 102-105.

244

Gordon (1869) – [Margaret Maria] Gordon, *The Home Life of Sir David Brewster by his daughter* (Edinburgh: Edmonston and Douglas, 1869).

Grant (1988) – Eric Grant, 'The Sphinx in the North: Egyptian Influences on Landscape, Architecture and Interior Design in Eighteenth and Nineteenth Century Scotland', in Denis Crosgrove and Stephen Daniels (eds), *The Iconography of Landscape: Essays on the Symbolic Representation, Design and use of Past Environments* (Cambridge: Cambridge University Press, 1988), 236-53.

Greenhill and Morrison (1995) – Basil Greenhill and J. S. Morrison, *The Archaeology of Boats and Ships: An Introduction* (London: Conway Maritime Press, 1995).

Griffiths (1998) – Antony Griffiths, *The Print in Stuart Britain 1603-1689* (London: British Museum Press, 1998).

Groome (1894) – F. H. Groome, *Ordnance Gazetteer of Scotland: a Survey of Scottish Topography, Statistical, Biographical and Historical*, 6 vols (London: W. Mackenzie, 1894).

Grundon (1998) – Mike Grundon, 'Quiet and Dignified Farewell', *Northern Lighthouse Board Journal* (Summer 1998), 16-18, article from the *Shetland Times*.

Guichard and Tretheway (2002) – Jean Guichard and Ken Tretheway, *North Atlantic Lighthouses* (Paris: Flammarion, 2002).

Hackmann (1994) – Willem Hackmann, 'Jan van der Straet (Stradanus) and the Origins of the Mariner's Compass', in W. D. Hackmann and A. J. Turner, (eds), *Learning, Language and Invention: Essays presented to Francis Maddison* (Aldershot: Variorum, 1994), 148-79.

Hague (1965) – Douglas Hague, 'Lighthouses of a Scottish Island', *Country Life*, 19 August 1965, 465-69.

Hague (1977) – Douglas Hague, 'Scottish Lights', in Lisbeth M. Thoms (ed.), *The Archaeology of Industrial Scotland: Scottish Archaeological Forum*, 8 (1977), 75-90.

Hague and Christie (1975) – Douglas B. Hague and Rosemary Christie, *Lighthouses: their Architecture, History and Archaeology* (Llandysul, Dyfed: Gomer Press, 1975).

Hakluyt (1889) – Richard Hakluyt, *Discovery of Muscovy: from the Collections of Richard Hakluyt* (London: Cassel & Co. Ltd., 1889).

Hall-Jones and Hooi (1979) – John Hall-Jones and Christopher Hooi, *An Early Surveyor in Singapore: John Turnbull Thomson in Singapore, 1841-1853* (Singapore: National Museum, 1979).

Hamilton (1793) – John Hamilton, 'Parish of Kilmory', in Sinclair (1791-99), IX (1793), 165-71.

Hamilton (1998) – James Hamilton, *Turner and the Scientists* (London: Tate Gallery Publishing Ltd., 1998).

Harrison-Wallace (2004) – Charles Harrison-Wallace, website relating to Peter Monamy, Isaac Sailmaker, and all four lighthouses at the Eddystone Reef [see online at http://www.cichw.net/pmlight.html].

Hardwick (1977) – Nora Hardwick (ed.), *A Diary of the Journey through the North of England made by William and John Blathwayt of Dyrham Park in 1703* (Dursley, Gloucestershire: [n.p.], 1977).

Harman (2006) – Claire Harman, *Robert Louis Stevenson: A Biography* (Harper Perennial, 2006).

Hart-Davis and Troscianko (2002) – Adam Hart-Davis and Emily Troscianko, *Henry Winstanley and the Eddystone Lighthouse* (Sutton Publishing, 2002).

Harvey (1993) – P. D. A. Harvey, *Maps in Tudor England* (London/Chicago: University of Chicago Press, 1993).

Hellowell (1998a) – John Hellowell, *A Tour of Manx Lighthouses* (Milford Haven: Peter Williams Associates, 1998).

Hellowell (1998b) – John Hellowell, 'Chicken Rock Lighthouse 1875', *Northern Lighthouse Board Journal* (Summer 1998), 22-23.

Hill (2003) – Peter Hill, *Stargazing: Memoirs of a Young Lighthouse Keeper* (Edinburgh: Canongate, 2003).

Hodge [1988] – James Hodge, 'Four Cornishmen: their contribution to science and engineering', typescript of the University of Exeter, second Kemp Lecture, delivered at the Royal Institution of Cornwall, Truro (23 March 1988).

Holloway (1989) – James Holloway, *Patrons and Painters: Art in Scotland 1650-1760* (Edinburgh: National Galleries of Scotland, 1989).

Home (2004) – Rod Home, 'Magellan, John Hyacinth', *Oxford Dictionary of National Biography* (Oxford: Oxford University Press, 2004) [available online at: http://www.oxforddnb.com/].

Hook and Sher (1995) – Andrew Hook and Richard B. Sher (eds), *The Glasgow Enlightenment* (East Linton: Tuckwell Press, in association with the Eighteenth-Century Scottish Studies 1, 1995).

Hope (1807) – Thomas Hope, *Household Furniture and Interior Decoration* (London: Longman, Hurst, Rees and Orme, 1807).

Humble (1983) – Richard Humble, *Fraser of North Cape: the Life of Admiral of the Fleet Lord Fraser (1888-1981)* (Routledge and Kegan Paul, 1983).

Hume (1977) – John R. Hume, *The Industrial Archaeology of Scotland 2. The Highlands and Islands* (London: B. T. Batsford, 1977).

Hume (1997) – John R. Hume, *Harbour Lights in Scotland* (Edinburgh: Scottish Vernacular Buildings Working Group, 1997).

Hutchinson (1777) – William Hutchinson, *A Treatise on Practical Seamanship* (London: Printed [by Cowburne] and sold for the author at all the principle seaports, 1777).

Hutchinson (1791) – William Hutchinson, *A Treatise founded upon Philosophical and Rational Principles … for … Practical Seamanship* (Liverpool: Printed by Thomas Billinge, 1791).

HUTCHINSON (1994) – Gillian Hutchinson, *Medieval Ships and Shipping* (London: Leicester University Press, 1994).

INKSTER (1991) – Ian Inkster, *Science and Technology in History: An Approach to Industrial Development* (London: Macmillan, 1991).

J. D. F. (1837) – J. D. F[orbes], 'Report by a Committee of the Royal Society (of Edinburgh) regarding the New Dioptric Light of the Isle of May', *London and Edinburgh Philosophical Magazine and Journal of Science*, 10 (1837), 176-77.

JAMES (1999) – Frank A. J. L. James, '"the civil-engineer's talent": Michael Faraday, science, engineering and the English lighthouse service, 1836-1865', *Transactions of the Newcomen Society*, 70 (1999), 153-60.

JAMES (2000) – Frank A. J. L. James, 'Michael Faraday and Lighthouses', in Ian Inkster, et al. (eds), *The Golden Age: Essays in British Social and Economic History 1850-1870* (Aldershot: Ashgate, 2000), 92-104.

JARDINE (1845) – Fergus Jardine, 'Parish of Kinghorn', *The New Statistical Account of Scotland* (Edinburgh: William Blackwood & Sons, 1845), IX, 800-21.

JONKERS (2003) – A. R. T. Jonkers, *Earth's Magnetism in the Age of Sail* (Baltimore and London: The Johns Hopkins University Press, 2003).

KENWARD (1866) – James Kenward, 'Lighthouse Illumination and the Dioptric Apparatus', in Samuel Timmins (ed.), *The Resources, Products, and Industrial History of Birmingham and the Midland Hardware District ...* (Robert Hardwicke, 1866), 153-62.

KENWARD (1897) – James Kenward, 'Lighthouse Progress, 1887-1897', *Nature*, 56 (1897), 282-85.

KIDD (1845) – Alexander Kidd, 'Parish of Moonzie', *The New Statistical Account of Scotland* (Edinburgh: William Blackwood and Sons, 1845), IX, 786-98.

KITTON (1892) – Frederic G. Kitton, 'A Visit to the Eddystone Lighthouse', *The Strand Magazine* (October 1892), 340-51.

KNOTT (1900) – C. G. Knott, 'On Swan's Prism Photometer, commonly called Lummer and Brodhun's Photometer', *The London, Edinburgh and Dublin Philosophical Magazine and Journal of Science*, 5th series, 49 (1900), 118-20.

LAING (2002) – William Laing, 'John Marr – "an injenious mariner of Dundee"', *Cairt: Newsletter of the Scottish Maps Forum*, Issue 1 (April 2002), 3-6.

LAMB and FRYDENDAHL (1991) – Hubert Lamb and Knud Frydendahl, *Historic Storms of the North Sea, British Isles and Northwest Europe* (Cambridge: Cambridge University Press, 1991).

LANDSTRÖM (1978) – Björn Landström, *Sailing Ships* (London: George Allen & Unwin, 1978).

LANE (1998) – A. J. Lane, *It Was Fun While It Lasted* (Latheronwheel, Caithness: Whittles Pub., 1998).

LESLIE and PAXTON (1999) – Jean Leslie and Roland Paxton, *Bright Lights: the Stevenson Engineers 1752-1971* (Edinburgh: pub. by authors, 1999).

LEWER (1918) – H. W. Lewer, 'Henry Winstanley, Engraver', *Essex Review*, 27 (1918), 160-71.

'LIGHTKEEPERS' (1997) – 'When there are no more Lightkeepers ...', *Northern Lighthouse Board Journal* (Christmas 1997), 19-20.

[LIVINGSTON] (1894) – [Josiah Livingston], *Some Edinburgh Shops* (Edinburgh: James Thin, 1894).

LOCKHART (1878) – J. G. Lockhart, *The Life of Sir Walter Scott, Bart.* (London: Adam and Charles Black, 1878).

LOVETT (1941) – E. Neville Lovett, 'Mr Lovett out of Iorland', *Dublin Historical Record* 3 (1941), 54-66, 79-80.

LUTTRELL (1857) – Narcissus Luttrell, *A Brief Historical Relation of State Affairs from September 1678 to April 1714* (Oxford University Press, 1857).

LYELL (1867) – Charles Lyell, *Principles of Geology, or the Modern Changes of the Earth and its Inhabitants considered as Illustrative of Geology*, 10th edition, 2 vols (London: John Murray, 1867).

MACADAM (1883) – Stevenson Macadam, 'On Recent Improvements in Lighthouse Illumination, with special reference to the employment of Paraffin Oil', *Transactions of the Royal Scottish Society of Arts*, 10 (1883), 56-72.

MCCONNELL (1994) – Anita McConnell, 'Bankruptcy Proceedings against William Harris, Optician, of Cornhill, 1830', *Annals of Science*, 51 (1994), 273-79.

MCCONNELL (2004) – Anita McConnell, 'Hutchinson, William', *Oxford Dictionary of National Biography* (Oxford: Oxford University Press, 2004) [available online: http://www.oxforddnb.com/].

MACDOUGALL (1991a) – Norman Macdougall, 'The Kingship of James IV of Scotland: "The Glory of All Princely Governing"?', in Jenny Wormald (ed.), *Scotland Revisited* (London: Collins and Brown, 1991), 25-35.

MACDOUGALL (1991b) – Norman Macdougall, '"The Greattest Scheip that ewer Saillit in Ingland or France": James IV's "Great Michael"', in Norman Macdougall (ed.), *Scotland and War, AD 79-1918* (Edinburgh: John Donald, 1991), 36-60.

MACDOUGALL (1997) – Norman Macdougall, *James IV* (East Linton: Tuckwell Press, 1997).

MACDOUGALL (2004) – Philip MacDougall, 'St Lo, George', *Oxford Dictionary of National Biography* (Oxford: Oxford University Press, 2004) [available online: http://www.oxforddnb.com/].

MCGOWAN (1981) – Alan McGowan, *The Ship. Tiller and Whipstaff: the Development of the Sailing Ship 1400-1700* (London: HMSO, 1981).

MCINTOSH (1997) – Bob McIntosh, 'New Lights for the West Coast Route', *Northern Lighthouse Board Journal* (Summer 1997), 6-9; ibid. (Christmas 1997), 21-23.

MACKAY (2001) – Roddy MacKay, 'Monitoring Scottish Lighthouses,' *Northern Lighthouse Board Journal* (Christmas 2001), 18-20.

MacKenzie (2006) – Hector MacKenzie, 'Clyde Light-houses Trust: A Short History of Innovation in a Lesser-known Lighthouse Service', *World Light-house Society Newsletter*, 4, no. 4 (fourth quarter, 2006), 5-8.

MacLeod (1969) – Roy M. MacLeod, 'Science and Government in Victorian England: Lighthouse Illumination and the Board of Trade, 1866-1886', *Isis*, 60 (1969), 5-38.

Mainstone (1981) – Rowland Mainstone, 'The Eddy-stone Lighthouse', in Skempton (1981), 9-14.

Mair (1978) – Craig Mair, *A Star for Seamen: the Stevenson Family of Engineers* (London: John Murray, 1978).

Majdalany (1959) – Fred Majdalany, *The Red Rocks of Eddystone* (Longmans, Green & Co. Ltd., 1959).

Major (2000) – Alan Major, *The Kentish Lights* (Sea-ford: S. B. Publications, 2000).

'Marine Aids' (1995) – 'Marine Aids to Navigation into the 21st century: a Consultation Paper', *Northern Lighthouse Journal* (Christmas 1995), 4-9.

Marshall (1983) – David A. Marshall, *L'île des Chevaux: the Story of Inchkeith* (Wemyss: David Marshall, 1983).

Marshall (2004) – Rosalind K. Marshall, 'Lesley, John', *Oxford Dictionary of National Biography* (Oxford: Oxford University Press, 2004) [available online: http://www.oxforddnb.com/].

Martin (1998) – Colin Martin, *Scotland's Historic Shipwrecks* (London: Batsford, 1998).

Martin (n.d.) – Paula Martin, *North Carr Lightship: a Maritime Experience* (Anstruther: North Carr Preservation Group, n.d.).

Marwick (1871) – Sir James Marwick, *Extracts from the Records of the Burgh of Edinburgh, 1528-1557* (Edinburgh: Scottish Records Society, 1871).

Mayer (2004) – T. F. Mayer, 'Lily, George', *Oxford Dictionary of National Biography* (Oxford Univer-sity Press, 2004) [http://www.oxforddnb.com/].

'Memoir' (1871) – 'Memoir – James Melville Balfour', *Minutes of Proceedings of the Institution of Civil Engineers*, 31 (1871), 200-202.

Merrett (1977) – L. H. Merrett, 'Smeaton's Tower', *Maritime History*, 5 (1977), 136-147, 164.

Merriman (1945) – R. D. Merriman, 'Captain George St Lo, RN, 1658-1718', *Mariner's Mirror*, 31 (1945), 13-22.

Merriman (2004) – Marcus Merriman, 'Elder, John', *Oxford Dictionary of National Biography* (Oxford University Press, 2004) [available online: http://www.oxforddnb.com/].

Millon (1999) – Henry A. Millon (ed.), *The Triumph of the Baroque: Architecture in Europe 1600-1750* (New York: Rizzoli Internat. Publications, 1999).

Moir (1973) – D. G. Moir, *The Early Maps of Scot-land to 1850*, 3rd edition, 2 vols (Edinburgh: The Royal Scottish Geological Society, 1973).

Molloy (1994) – David J. Molloy, *The First Land-fall: Historic Lighthouses of Newfoundland and Labrador* (St John's, Newfoundland: Breakwater, 1994).

Monipennie (1612) – John Monipennie, *Scots Chroni-cles* (London: Budge and Stafford, 1612; Glasgow: reprinted for Wylie & Co. by R. Chapman, 1820).

Moore (1985) – J. N. Moore, 'Scotland's First Sea Atlas', *Map Collector*, no. 30 (1985), 30-34.

Moore (1988) – J. N. Moore, *A Line of the Coast: The Development of Coastal Mapping and Hydrography in Scotland from 1540 to 1707* (Glasgow: Univer-sity of Glasgow, Department of Geography and Topographic Science, 1988).

Moore (1995) – John N. Moore, 'Prelude to Disaster: Hydrography in the late Seventeenth Century', abstract in *Charting the Scottish Seas 1500-2000* (Edinburgh: Royal Society of Edinburgh, 1995), 4.

Moore (2000) – J. N. Moore, 'John Adair's Contri-bution to the Charting of the Scottish Coasts: a Re-assessment', *Imago Mundi*, 52 (2000), 43-65.

Morgan (1878) – C. Octavius S. Morgan, 'Observa-tions upon a Model in Silver of the first Lighthouse erected on the Eddystone Rocks', *Archaeological Journal* 35 (1878), 120-25; reproduced as *The Eddystone Lighthouse Salt by Rowe of Plymouth circa* 1698 for the Antique Dealers' Fair, Grosvenor House [London], 1948.

Morrison-Low (1993) – A. D. Morrison-Low, 'Early Navigational Instruments in Scotland: Icons and Survivals', in R. G. W. Anderson, J. A. Bennett, and W. F. Ryan (eds) *Making Instruments Count: Essays on Historical Scientific Instruments presented to Gerard L'Estrange Turner* (Aldershot: Variorum, 1993), 218-31.

Morrison-Low (2002) – A. D. Morrison-Low, '"Feasting my eyes with the view of fine instru-ments": Scientific Instruments in Enlightenment Scotland, 1680-1820', in Withers and Wood (2002), 17-53.

Morrison-Low (2006a) – Alison Morrison-Low, '"It was a Dark and Stormy Night": Instrument Makers and the Northern Lights', in Bart Grob and Hans Hooijmaijers (eds), *Who Needs Scientific Instru-ments? Conference on Scientific Instruments and their Users* (Leiden: Museum Boerhaave, 2006), 89-97.

Morrison-Low (2006b) – Alison D. Morrison-Low, 'From West to East: Nineteenth-Century Scottish Lighthouse Technology in the Pacific Rim', in Ewa Wyka (ed.), *Proceedings of the XXV Scientific Instrument Symposium: East and West, the Com-mon European Heritage* (Krakow: Jagellonian University Museum, 2006), 47-52.

Morrison-Low (2007) – A. D. Morrison-Low, *Making Scientific Instruments in the Industrial Revolution* (Aldershot: Ashgate, 2007).

Morrison-Low and McDonald (2000) – Alison Morrison-Low and Stuart McDonald, 'Eilean Glas Optic Moves to London for Ten Years', *Northern Lighthouse Journal* (Christmas 2000), 22-24.

MUCKLEROY (1978) – Keith Muckleroy, *Maritime Archaeology* (Cambridge University Press, 1978).

MUDIE (1995) – Frances Mudie, *The Fraternity of Masters and Seamen, or, Trinity House in Dundee* ([Dundee: Dundee Public Library], 1995).

MUIRHEAD (2000) – Robert Muirhead, 'A dreadful accident happened on Flannan Isle ...', *Northern Lighthouse Board Journal* (Christmas 2000), 25-26.

MULHERN (2007) – Andrew Mulhern, 'The Monachs Lighthouse: an Evolving Story over 143 Years ...', *Northern Lighthouse Board Journal* (Christmas 2007), 14-18.

MUNK (1878) – William Munk (ed.), *Roll of the Royal College of Physicians of London*, 2nd enlarged edition, 10 vols (London: Longman, Green, Longman and Roberts, 1878-2004).

MUNRO (1979) – R. W. Munro, *Scottish Lighthouses* (Stornoway: Thule Press, 1979).

MUSEUM REPORTER (1991) – 'Robert Stevenson Restored', *Museum Reporter* [newsletter from National Museums Scotland], no. 22 (Nov. to Dec. 1991), [2].

'MV PHAROS' (2005) – 'MV Pharos, into its 206th year and beyond ...', *Northern Lighthouse Board Journal* (Summer 2005), 16-17.

NAISH (1985) – John Naish, *Seamarks: Their History and Development* (London: Stanford Maritime Limited, 1985).

'NAUTILUS' (1831) – 'Nautilus', 'Reflecting Lighthouses – Mr Ezekiel Walker', *Mechanics' Magazine*, 15 (1831), 90-91.

NEILSON (1795) – Edward Neilson, 'Parish of Kirkbean', in SINCLAIR (1791-99), XV, 119-33.

'NEW LIGHTS' (1996) – 'New Lights for the West Coast Route and for Kyle of Lochalsh', *Northern Lighthouse Journal* (Summer 1996), 16-19.

NICHOLSON (1995) – Christopher Nicholson, *Rock Lighthouses of Britain: the End of an Era?*, 2nd ed. (Latheronwheel, Caithness: Whittles Publishing, 1995).

'NLV PHAROS' (2007) – 'NLV Pharos: a truly versatile ship ...', *Northern Lighthouse Board Journal* (Summer 2007), 14-15.

NORIE (1846) – J. W. Norie, *New and Extensive Sailing Directions for the Navigation of the North Sea ...*, 7th edition (London: Charles Wilson, 1846), revised by J. S. Hobbs.

NORTH SEA PILOT ... (1868) – *North Sea Pilot. Part II: North and East Coasts of Scotland* (London: J. D. Potter, 1868).

OBITUARY (1815) – Death notice for Thomas Smith, *Scots Magazine*, 77 (1815), 718.

'OBITUARY' (1888) – 'Obituary' for Thomas Stevenson, *Minutes of the Proceedings of the Institution of Civil Engineers*, 91 (1888), 424-26.

'OBITUARY' (1890) – 'Obituary' for Alan Brebner, *Minutes of the Proceedings of the Institution of Civil Engineers*, 101 (1890), 287-89.

OPPENHEIM (1968) – M. M. Oppenheim, *The Maritime History of Devon* (Exeter: University of Exeter, 1968).

O'RIORDAN (1982) – Ian O'Riordan, *The Eddystone Silver Salt* (Plymouth: City Museum & Art Gallery, 1982).

OUSTON (1979) – Hugh Ouston, 'York in Edinburgh: James VII and the Patronage of Learning in Scotland, 1679-1688', in John Dwyer, Roger A. Mason, and Alexander Murdoch (eds), *New Perspectives on the Politics and Culture of Early Modern Scotland* (Edinburgh: John Donald, 1979), 133-55.

PAGE (1860) – F. R. Page, *A Concise History and Description of Newfoundland* (London: R. H. Laurie, 1860).

PALMER (1998) – Mike Palmer, *Eddystone 300: the Finger of Light* (Torpoint: Palmridge Publishing, 1998).

PALMER (2005) – Mike Palmer, *Eddystone: the Finger of Light*, 2nd edition (Woodbridge, Suffolk: Seafarer Books, 2005).

PARRY (1973) – J. H. Parry, *The Age of Reconnaissance: Discovery, Exploration and Settlement 1450-1650* (London: Sphere Books Limited, 1973).

PATERSON (1997a) – Bill Paterson, 'Differential Corrections to the Global Positioning System', *Northern Lighthouse Board Journal* (Summer 1997), 20-21.

PATERSON (1997b) – Bill Paterson, 'Automation of Last Five Manned Lighthouses', *Northern Lighthouse Board Journal* (Christmas 1997), 20-21.

PATERSON (1999) – Bill Paterson, 'Works in progress', *Northern Lighthouse Board Journal* (Summer 1999), 10-12.

PAVITT (1966) – J. A. L. Pavitt, *First Pharos of the Eastern Seas: Horsburgh Lighthouse* (Singapore: Donald Moore Press, 1966).

PAXTON (2004) – Roland Paxton, entries in the *Oxford Dictionary of National Biography* (Oxford, 2004) [online: http://www.oxforddnb.com/] for Thomas Smith, Alan, David, Charles, and Robert Stevenson.

PEARSON (1991) – Fiona Pearson, *Virtue and Vision: Sculpture in Scotland 1540-1990* (Edinburgh: National Galleries of Scotland, 1991).

PETRIE (2001) – Mike Petrie, 'Environmental Management and the Board', *Northern Lighthouse Board Journal* (Summer 2001), 10-11.

PHILLIPS (1964) – F. C. Phillips, 'Metamorphic rocks of the sea floor between Start Point and Dodman Point, S. W. England', *Journal of the Marine Biological Association of the United Kingdom*, 44 (1964), 655-63.

PHILLIPSON and MITCHISON (1970) – N. T. Phillipson and Rosalind Mitchison (eds), *Scotland in the Age of Improvement* (Edinburgh University Press, 1970).

PIGGOTT (1976) – Stuart Piggott, *Ruins in a Landscape: Essays in Antiquarianism* (Edinburgh: Edinburgh University Press, 1976).

PITTOCK and CARTER (1987) – Joan Pittock and Jennifer Carter (eds), *Aberdeen and the Enlightenment* (Aberdeen: Aberdeen University Press, 1987).

248

PLAβMEYER and SIEBEL (2001) – Peter Plaβmeyer and Sabine Siebel, *Ehrenfried Walther von Tischirnhaus (1651-1708): Experimente mit dem Sonnenfeuer* (Dresden: Staaliche Kunstsammlungen Dresden Mathematisch-Physikalischer Salon, 2001).

PLINY (1991) – John F. Healy (ed.), *Pliny the Elder, Natural History: a Selection* (Penguin Books, 1991).

RENNIE (1848) – Sir John Rennie, *An Historical, Practical and Theoretical Account of the Breakwater in Plymouth Sound* (London: Henry Bohn and John Weale, 1848).

RENTON (2001) – Alan Renton, *Lost Sounds: the Story of Coast Fog Signals* (Latheronwheel, Caithness: Whittles Publishing, 2001).

RHIND (1856) – David Rhind, 'Presidential Address, 12 November 1855', *Transactions of the Royal Scottish Society of Arts*, 4 (1856), Appendix, 219-25.

RIIS (1992) – Thomas Riis, 'Long Distance Trade or Tramping: Scottish Ships in the Baltic, Sixteenth and Seventeenth Centuries', in SMOUT (1992), 59-75.

ROBERTSON (1971) – W. A. Robertson, 'Manx Lighthouses and the Northern Lighthouse Board', *Journal of the Manx Museum*, 7 (1971), 164-67.

ROBERTSON (1997) – Martha Robertson, *A Quiet Life* (Caithness: Whittles Publishing, 1997).

ROBERTSON (2006) – Hamish Robertson, *Mariners of Dundee: Their City, Their River, Their Fraternity* (Dundee: PDQ Print Services, 2006).

ROBINSON (1958) – A. H. W. Robinson, 'The Charting of the Scottish Coasts', *Scottish Geographical Magazine*, 74 (1958), 116-27.

ROBINSON (1981) – Adrian Robinson, 'Murdoch Mackenzie and his Orcades Sea Atlas', *Map Collector*, no. 16 (1981), 24-27.

ROBINSON (2007) – John and Diane Robinson, *Lighthouses of Liverpool Bay* (Stroud: Tempus Publishing Limited, 2007).

ROBINSON and McKIE (1970) – Eric Robinson and Douglas McKie, *Partners in Science: Letters of James Watt and Joseph Black* (London: Constable, 1970).

ROSMORDUC and DUTOUR (2004) – J. and V. Rosmorduc and F. Dutour, *Les révolutions de l'optique et l'œuvre de Fresnel* (Paris: Vuibert, 2004).

ROWATT (1924-25) – Thomas Rowatt, 'Notes on Original Models of the Eddystone Lighthouses', *Transactions of the Newcomen Society* 5 (1924-25), 15-23.

RULE (1982) – Margaret Rule, *The Mary Rose: The Excavation and Raising of Henry VIII's Flagship* (London: Naval Institute Press, 1982).

SANDES (1935) – E. W. C. Sandes, *The Military Engineer in India*, 2 vols (Chatham: Institution of Royal Engineers, 1835), vol. II.

SANG (1838) – Edward Sang, 'Notice of a Dioptric Light erected at Kirkcaldy Harbour, with a Description of an Apparatus for Cutting the Annular Lens of a true optical figure', *Edinburgh New Philosophical Journal*, 25 (1838), 249-54.

SCHECHNER (2005) – Sara J. Schechner, 'Between Knowing and Doing: Mirrors and their Imperfections in the Renaissance', *Early Science and Medicine*, 10 (2005), 137-62.

SCHIFFER (2005) – Michael Brian Schiffer, 'The Electric Lighthouse in the Nineteenth Century: Aid to Navigation and Political Technology', *Technology and Culture*, 46 (2005), 275-305.

SCHRØDER (1969) – Michael Schrøder, *The Argand Lamp: Its Origins and Development in France and England 1780-1800* (Odense University Press, 1969).

*Selection ...* (1858) – *Selection of Papers regarding the Construction of a Light House on the Alguada Reef* (Calcutta: J. Gray, Bengal Hurkaru Press, 1858).

SEMMENS (1998) – Jason Semmens, *Eddystone: 300 Years* (Cornwall: Alexander Associates, 1998).

SHAPIN (1984) – Steven Shapin, 'Brewster and the Edinburgh Career in Science', in A. D. Morrison-Low and J. R. R. Christie (eds), *'Martyr of Science': Sir David Brewster 1781-1868* (Edinburgh: Royal Scottish Museum, 1984), 17-23.

SHERBORN (1937) – D. C. Sherborn, 'Brewster's Edinburgh Encyclopaedia', *Journal of the Society for the Bibliography of Natural History*, 1 (1937), 112.

'SHIPWRECKS' (1811) – [Anon.] 'Shipwrecks', *Scots Magazine*, 73 (1811), 70.

SHIRLEY (1995) – R. W. Shirley, 'The Maritime Maps and Atlases of Seller, Thornton, Mount & Page,' *Map Collector*, no. 73 (1995), 4-5.

SILLIMAN (1972) – Robert H. Silliman, 'Fresnel, Augustin Jean', in C. C. Gillispie (ed.), *Dictionary of Scientific Biography*, 18 vols (New York: Charles Scribner's Sons, 1970-90), V, 165-71.

SIM (1792) – David Sim, 'Parish of Barrie', in SINCLAIR (1791-99), IV, 236-47.

SIMPSON (1990) – A. D. C. Simpson, 'A Seventeenth Century Cross Staff', *Bulletin of the Scientific Instrument Society*, no. 27 (1990), 8-9.

SIMPSON (1991) – A. D. C. Simpson, 'Brewster's Society of Arts and the Pantograph Dispute', *Book of the Old Edinburgh Club*, new series, 1 (1991), 47-73.

SIMPSON (1993) – A. D. C. Simpson, 'John Adair, cartographer, and Sir Robert Sibbald's Scottish Atlas', *Map Collector*, no. 62 (1993), 32-36.

SIMPSON (1994) – Allen Simpson, 'François Soleil, Andrew Ross and William Cookson: the Fresnel Lens Applied', *Bulletin of the Scientific Instrument Society*, no. 41 (1994), 16-19.

SIMPSON (1996) – A. D. C. Simpson, 'The Lighthouse Collection of the National Museums of Scotland', *Northern Lighthouse Journal* (Christmas 1996), 9-14.

SINCLAIR (1791-99) – Sir John Sinclair (ed.), *The Statistical Account of Scotland*, 21 vols (Edinburgh: William Creech, 1791-99).

SKEMPTON (1981) – A. W. Skempton (ed.), *John Smeaton, FRS* (London: Thomas Telford Limited, 1981).

SKEMPTON (1992) – A. W. Skempton (ed.), *John Smeaton Civil Engineer 1724-1792* (exhibition catalogue) (London: Institution of Civil Engineers, 1992).

SLIGHT (1878) – George H. Slight, 'Description of an

Improved Centrifugal Governor for Regulating the Revolving Machines of Light-Vessels and Light-houses', *Transactions of the Royal Scottish Society of the Arts*, 9 (1878), 306-309.

SMAILES (1990) – Helen Smailes, *The Concise Catalogue of the Scottish National Portrait Gallery* (Edinburgh: National Galleries of Scotland, 1990).

SMEATON (1791) – John Smeaton, *A Narrative of the Building, and a Description of the Construction, of the Edystone Light-house with Stone ...* (London: G. Nicol, 1791).

SMEATON (1793) – John Smeaton, *A Narrative of the Building, and a Description of the Construction, of the Edystone Light-house with Stone ...*, The second edition, corrected (London: printed [by H. Hughes] for G. Nicol, 1793).

SMEATON (1987) – W. A. Smeaton, 'Some Large Burning Lenses and their Use by Eighteenth-Century French and British Chemists', *Annals of Science* 44 (1987), 265-76.

SMILES (1862) – Samuel Smiles, *Lives of the Engineers* II (London: John Murray, 1862).

SMITH (1987) – Diana C. F. Smith, 'The Progress of the *Orcades* Survey, with Biographical Notes on Murdoch Mackenzie Senior (1712-1797)', *Annals of Science*, 44 (1987), 277-88.

SMOUT (1992) – T. C. Smout (ed.), *Scotland and the Sea* (Edinburgh: John Donald, 1992).

SPRAGUE DE CAMP (1965) – L. Sprague de Camp, 'The "Darkhouse" of Alexandria', *Technology and Culture*, 6 (1965), 423-27.

SPRY (1756) – E. Spry, 'An Account of the Case of a Man who died of the Effects of the Fire at Eddystone Light-house', *Philosophical Transactions of the Royal Society of London*, 49 (1756), 477-79.

STAMP (2004) – Cordelia Stamp (ed.), *The Bell Rock Light: Robert Stevenson's Account of the Building of the Bell Rock Lighthouse told by his Grandson Robert Louis Stevenson* (Whitby: Caedmon of Whitby, 2004).

STEELE (1709) – Richard Steele, 'Letter from a Lover – Letter on the Tendency of Satirical Characters – Table of Fame – Continental Intelligence', *Tatler*, no. 74, Thursday 29 September, 1709.

STEELE (1711) – Richard Steele, 'Letter on the Severity of School-masters – On Impertinents – Poachers', *Spectator*, no. 168, Wednesday 12 September, 1711.

STELL (1984) – Geoffrey Stell, 'Southerness Lighthouses', *Trans. of the Dumfriesshire and Galloway Natural History and Antiquarian Society*, 59 (1984), 64-69.

STEVENSON (1833) – Alan Stevenson, *Letter to the Author of an Article on the 'British Lighthouse System' in Number CXV of the Edinburgh Review* (Edinburgh and London, 1833).

STEVENSON (1835a) – Alan Stevenson, *Report to the Committee of the Commissioners of Northern Lights, Appointed to take into Consideration the Subject of Illuminating Lighthouses by Means of Lenses* (Edinburgh: Neil and Company, 1835).

STEVENSON (1835b) – Alan Stevenson, *Extracts from Reports on the New Dioptric Light of Inchkeith ...* (Edinburgh: Neil and Company, 1835)

STEVENSON (1848) – Alan Stevenson, *Account of the Skerryvore Lighthouse, with Notes on the Illumination of Lighthouses* (Edinburgh and London: Adam and Charles Black, 1848).

STEVENSON (1850) – Alan Stevenson, *A Rudimentary Treatise on the History, Construction and Illumination of Lighthouses* (London: John Weale, 1850). Much of this derived from the 1848 *Account of Skerryvore*.

STEVENSON (1851) – Alan Stevenson, 'Biographical Sketch of the late Robert Stevenson, FRSE ...', *Edinburgh New Philosophical Journal*, 50 (1851), 193-209.

STEVENSON (1865) – Alan Stevenson, *The Ten Hymns of Synesius, Bishop of Cyrene AD 410 in English Verse, and Some Occasional Pieces* (Edinburgh: privately printed, 1865).

STEVENSON (1988) – Alexander Stevenson, 'Trade with the South, 1070-1513', in Michael Lynch, Michael Spearman and Geoffrey Stell (eds), *The Scottish Medieval Town* (Edinburgh: John Donald, 1988), 180-206.

STEVENSON (1883b) – Charles Stevenson, 'A New Form of Seismograph', *Transactions of the Royal Scottish Society of Arts*, 10 (1883), 546-49.

STEVENSON (1891) – Charles Stevenson, 'On a New Form of Refractor for Dioptric Apparatus', *Transactions of the Royal Scottish Society of Arts*, 12 (1891), 219-20.

STEVENSON (1892) – Charles A. Stevenson, 'Note on the Progress of the Dioptric Lens as used in Lighthouse Illumination', *Nature* 46 (1892), 514-16.

STEVENSON (1946) – D. Alan Stevenson (ed.), *English Lighthouse Tours, 1801, 1813, 1818, by Robert Stevenson* (London: Thomas Nelson and Sons Limited, 1946).

STEVENSON (1959) – D. Alan Stevenson, *The World's Lighthouses before 1820* (London: Oxford University Press, 1959); new Dover edition, re-titled *The World's Lighthouses from Ancient Times to 1820* (New York: Dover, 2002).

STEVENSON (1844b) – David Stevenson, 'Description of Portable Levelling Instruments', *Transactions of the Royal Scottish Society of Arts*, 2 (1844), 314.

STEVENSON (1856b) – David Stevenson, 'Presidential Address, 14 November 1853', *Transactions of the Royal Scottish Society of Arts*, 4 (1856), 183-90.

STEVENSON (1865) – David Stevenson, *Lighthouses* [from *Good Words*] (Edinburgh: Adam and Charles Black, 1865).

STEVENSON (1868b) – David Stevenson, 'Notice of Aseismatic Arrangements, adapted to Structures in Countries subject to Earthquake Shocks', *Transactions of the Royal Scottish Society of Arts*, 7 (1868), 557-66.

STEVENSON (1878) – David Stevenson, *Life of Robert*

*Stevenson, Civil Engineer* (Edinburgh: A. & C. Black, 1878).

STEVENSON (1876) – David A. Stevenson, 'The Dhu Heartach Lighthouse', *Minutes of the Proceedings of the Institution of Civil Engineers*, 46 (1876), 1-19.

STEVENSON (1883a) – David A. Stevenson, 'On Coast Fog Signals', *Transactions of the Royal Scottish Society of Arts*, 10 (1883), 490-506.

STEVENSON (1887b) – David A. Stevenson, 'Ailsa Craig Lighthouse and Fog Signals', *Minutes of the Proceedings of the Institution of Civil Engineers*, 89 (1887), 297-303.

STEVENSON (c.1810) – [Robert Stevenson], 'Bell Rock', in BREWSTER (1808-30), III (c.1810), 441-43.

STEVENSON (1813) – [Robert Stevenson], 'Appendix D. Account of the Bell Rock Lighthouse', in James Headrick (ed.), *General View of the Agriculture of the County of Angus, or Forfarshire …* (Edinburgh: Archibald Constable and Company, 1813), 65-72.

STEVENSON (1814) – [Robert Stevenson], 'Eddystone Rocks', in BREWSTER (1808-30), VIII (1814), 328.

STEVENSON (1816a) – Robert Stevenson, 'Observations upon the Alveus, or General Bed of the German Ocean and British Channel', *Annals of Philosophy*, 8 (1816), 173-82.

STEVENSON (1816b) – [Robert Stevenson], 'Bell Rock', in *Supplement to the Fourth, Fifth, and Sixth Editions of the Encyclopaedia Britannica*, 6 vols (Edinburgh: Archibald Constable & Company, 1824), II (1816), 253-58.

STEVENSON (1817) – Robert Stevenson, 'Inchkeith', in BREWSTER (1808-30), XII (1817), 9-12.

STEVENSON (1818) – Robert Stevenson, 'Lighthouse', in BREWSTER (1808-30), XIII (1818), 1-19.

STEVENSON (1824) – Robert Stevenson, *An Account of the Bell Rock Light-House* (Edinburgh: printed for A. Constable, 1824).

STEVENSON (1825) – Robert Stevenson, 'Account of the Erection of the Bell Rock Light-house', *Edinburgh Philosophical Journal*, 12 (1825), 18-38.

STEVENSON (1873) – Robert Louis Stevenson, 'On a New Form of Intermittent Light for Lighthouses', *Transactions of the Royal Scottish Society of Arts*, 8 (1873), 271-75.

STEVENSON (1887a) – Robert Louis Stevenson, *Memories and Portraits* (London: Chatto & Windus, 1887).

STEVENSON (1893) – Robert Louis Stevenson, 'Scott's Voyage in the Lighthouse Yacht: Introduction to Robert Stevenson's Reminiscences of Sir Walter Scott, Baronet', *Scribner's Magazine*, 14 (1893), 492-502.

STEVENSON (1912a) – Robert Louis Stevenson, *Records of a Family of Engineers* (Chatto and Windus, 1912).

STEVENSON (1912b) – Robert Louis Stevenson, *Memoir of Fleeming Jenkin* (London and Edinburgh: Chatto and Windus, 1912).

STEVENSON (1925) – Robert Louis Stevenson, *Essays Literary and Critical* (London: Heinemann, 1925).

STEVENSON (1995) – Robert Louis Stevenson, *The New Lighthouse on the Dhu Heartach Rock, Argyllshire*, edited with an introduction by Roger G. Swearingen (St Helena: Silverado Museum, 1995).

STEVENSON (1844a) – Thomas Stevenson, 'Some Account of Levelling Instruments, with Description of one in an Improved Form', *Transactions of the Royal Scottish Society of Arts*, 2 (1844), 307-13.

STEVENSON (1845) – Thomas Stevenson, 'Account of Experiments upon the force of the waves of the Atlantic and German Oceans', *Transactions of the Royal Society of Edinburgh*, 16 (1845), 23-32; also reprinted in STEVENSON (1848), 385-91.

STEVENSON (1856a) – Thomas Stevenson, 'Description of the Holophotal System of Illuminating Lighthouses', *Transactions of the Royal Scottish Society of Arts*, 4 (1856), 1-20.

STEVENSON (1861) – Thomas Stevenson, 'On Azimuthal Condensing Apparatus of Unequal Power, adapted for Fixed and Revolving Lighthouses placed on Islands near the Shore', *Edinburgh New Philosophical Journal*, 13 (1861), 273-79.

STEVENSON (1868a) – Thomas Stevenson, 'Some New Arrangements for Lighthouse Illumination, including those of the Tay Leading Lights', *Transactions of the Royal Scottish Society of Arts*, 7 (1856), 540-46.

STEVENSON (1881) – Thomas Stevenson, *Lighthouse Construction and Illumination* (London and New York: E. & F. N. Spon, 1881).

STEVENSON (1886) – Thomas Stevenson, 'Notes on Experiments for the Board of Trade, made at the South Foreland Lighthouse by the Trinity House of London, on Lighthouse Illuminants, &c.', *Proceedings of the Royal Society of Edinburgh*, 13 (1886), 494-500.

STRAUSS (1864) – G. L. M. Strauss, et al., *England's Workshops* (London; Groombridge and Sons, 1864).

STUART (1844) – John Stuart (ed.), *Extracts from the Council Register of the Burgh of Aberdeen, 1398-1570* (Aberdeen: Spalding Club Publications, 1844).

STUART (1848) – John Stuart (ed.), *Extracts from the Council Register of the Burgh of Aberdeen, 1570-1625* (Aberdeen: Spalding Club Publications, 1848).

STUART SHAW (1983) – John Stuart Shaw, *The Management of Scottish Society 1707-1764* (Edinburgh: John Donald, 1983).

STUART SHAW (1999) – John Stuart Shaw, *The Political History of Eighteenth-Century Scotland* (Basingstoke: Macmillan, 1999).

SUTHERLAND (1993) – Gavin Sutherland, *The Whaling Years: Peterhead 1788-1893* (Aberdeen: Centre for Scottish Studies, University of Aberdeen, 1993).

SWALLOW (1998) – Sarah Swallow, *Lighthouses of Scotland: Kinnaird Head* (Fraserburgh: B. & T. Publications, 1998).

SWAN (1844) – William Swan, 'On the Determination of the Index of Refraction by the Sextant, and also by means of an Instrument depending on a new Optical method of ascertaining the Angles of Prisms', *Transactions of the Royal Scottish Society of Arts,* 2 (1844), 287-98.

SWAN (1856a) – William Swan, 'Formulae for Constructing Mr Thomas Stevenson's Totally Reflecting Hemispherical Mirror', *Transactions of the Royal Scottish Society of Arts,* 4 (1856), 20-33.

SWAN (1856b) – William Swan, 'On a new method of observing the Spectra of Stars', *London, Edinburgh and Dublin Philosophical Magazine and Journal of Science,* 4th series, 11 (1856), 448-50.

SWAN (1868a) – William Swan, 'On New Forms of Lighthouse Apparatus: Part I', *Transactions of the Royal Scottish Society of Arts,* 7 (1868), 473-507.

SWAN (1868b) – William Swan, 'On New Forms of Lighthouse Apparatus: Part II', *Transactions of the Royal Scottish Society of Arts,* 7 (1868), 507-39.

SWAN (1895) – William Swan, 'Obituary Notice: Thomas Stevenson C.E.', *Proceedings of the Royal Society of Edinburgh* 20 (1895), lxi-lxxviii.

SWEARINGEN (1995) – Roger G. Swearingen, '*A New Lighthouse on the Dhu Heartach Rock, Argyllshire*: a previously unpublished essay by Robert Louis Stevenson', *Northern Lighthouse Journal* (Christmas 1995), 26-28.

TAG (2001) – Thomas Tag, 'The Doty Dilemma', *Leading Lights,* 3 (2001), 22-27.

TAG (2005a) – Thomas Tag, 'The Early Development of the Fresnel Lens, Part One', *U.S. Lighthouse Society's The Keeper's Log* (Spring 2005).

TAG (2005b) – Thomas Tag, 'The Sautter Lens Works, Producers of the Fresnel Lens, Part Two', *U.S. Lighthouse Society's The Keeper's Log* (Summer 2005).

TAG (2009-10) – Thomas Tag, 'Hyper-radial Lenses' [at http://hyper-radial.blogspot.com/].

TAGLIACOZZO (2005) – Eric Tagliacozzo, 'The Lit Archipelago: Coast Lighting and the Imperial Optic in Insular Southeast Asia, 1860-1910', *Technology and Culture,* 46 (2005), 306-28.

TALBOT (1913) – Frederick A. Talbot, *Lightships and Lighthouses* (London: Heinemann, 1913).

TARLING (1994) – Nicholas Tarling, '"This First Pharos of the Eastern Seas": the Construction of the Horsburgh Lighthouse on Pedra Branca', *Journal of the Malayan Branch of the Royal Asiatic Society,* 67 (1994), 1-8.

TAYLOR (1980) – A. B. Taylor, *Alexander Lindsay, A Rutter of the Scottish Seas, circa 1540: abridged version of a Manuscript* (London: National Maritime Museum, 1980).

TAYLOR (1954) – E. G. R. Taylor, *The Mathematical Practitioners of Tudor and Stuart England 1485-1714* (Cambridge: Cambridge University Press for the Institute of Navigation, 1954).

TAYLOR (1971) – E. G. R. Taylor, *The Haven-Finding Art: A History of Navigation from Odysseus to Captain Cook,* revised edition (London: Hollis and Carter, 1971).

TAYLOR (1995) – James Taylor, 'Foreword', *Northern Lighthouse Journal* (Christmas 1995), 2.

TAYLOR (2001) – James Taylor, 'Private Property, Public Interest, and the Role of the State in Nineteenth-Century Britain', *Historical Journal* 44 (2001), 749-71.

'THE LAST BLAST ...' (2005) – 'The Last Blast ... Farewell to the Scottish Fog Horn', *Northern Lighthouse Board Journal* (Christmas 2005), 26-27.

*THINGS TO SEE* (1969) – *Things to See in the Royal Scottish Museum,* 1st edition (Edinburgh: Royal Scottish Museum, 1969).

*THINGS TO SEE* (1980) – *Things to See in the Royal Scottish Museum,* 2nd edition (Edinburgh: Royal Scottish Museum, 1980).

THOMPSON (1986) – Christine Thomson, 'Engineers of Enterprise: the Stevenson family', in CALDER (1986), 89-94.

THOMSON (1852) – J. T. Thomson, 'Account of the Horsburgh Lighthouse', *Journal of the Indian Archipelago and Eastern Asia,* 6 (1852), 376-498.

THOMSON (1856) – J. T. Thomson, 'Description of a Semi-Revolving Light', *Transactions of the Royal Scottish Society of Arts,* 4 (1883), 306-12.

THOMSON (1883) – J. T. Thomson, 'Original Exploration in the Scottish Settlement of Otago, and Recent Travel in other Parts of New Zealand', *Transactions of the Royal Scottish Society of Arts,* 10 (1883), 73-115.

TOWNSON (1980-81) – John M. Townson, 'Thomas Stevenson 1818-1887', *Transactions of the Newcomen Society,* 52 (1980-81), 15-29.

TRETHEWEY (2004) – Ken Trethewey, *Lighthouses of Asia* (2004) [http://www.pharology.eu/Lighthouses/Asia/lighthouses_of_asia.htm]

TULLOCH (1983) – Judith Tulloch, 'Nineteenth Century Lighthouse Technology' in Richard Jarrell and A. E. Roos (eds), *Critical Issues in the History of Canadian Science and Technology* (Thornhill, Ontario: HSTC Publications, 1983), 47-58.

TURNER (1974) – Trevor Turner, 'John Smeaton (1724-1792)', *Endeavour,* 33 (1974), 29-33.

TURNER (2000) – Gerard L'E. Turner, *Elizabethan Instrument Makers: the origins of the London Trade in Precision Instrument Making* (Oxford: Oxford University Press, 2000).

UNGER (1980) – Richard Unger, *The Ship in the Medieval Economy 600-1600* (Croom Helm, 1980).

VAN DEN BROEKE, et al. (1996) – M. P. R. van den Broeke, P. C. J. van der Krogt and Peter Meurer, *Abraham Ortelius and the First Atlas: Essays commemorating the Quadricentennial of his Death 1598-1998* ('t Goy-Houten, Netherlands: HES, 1996).

VERNER (1978) – C. Verner, 'John Seller and the Chart Trade in Seventeenth Century England', in Norman W. J. Thrower (ed.), *The Complete Plattmaker* (Berkeley and Los Angeles: University of California Press, 1978), 127-57.

VERNEY (1930) – Margaret Maria, Lady Verney (ed.), *Verney Letters of the Eighteenth Century from the MSS. at Claydon House*, 2 vols (London: Ernest Benn, 1930).

WADDELL (2001a) – Moray Waddell, 'Engineering Storage and Test Facility (ESTF)', *Northern Lighthouse Board Journal* (Christmas 2001), 13.

WADDELL (2001b) – Moray Waddell, 'Oban Depot: the Official Opening Ceremony 10 December 2001', *Northern Lighthouse Board Journal* (Christmas 2001), 16-17.

WALKER (1801) – Ezekiel Walker, 'Letter to the Editor', *Monthly Magazine*, 12 (1801), 402.

WARD (2004) – R. M. Ward, 'Sailing Directions for James V of Scotland', *History Scotland*, 4 (March/April 2004), 26-32.

WARNICKE (2004) – Retha M. Warnicke, 'Nowell, Laurence', *Oxford Dictionary of National Biography* (Oxford: Oxford University Press, 2004) [available online: http://www.oxforddnb.com/].

WASWO (2004) – Ann Waswo, 'Brunton, (Richard) Henry', *Oxford Dictionary of National Biography* (Oxford: Oxford University Press, 2004) [available online: http://www.oxforddnb.com/].

WATERHOUSE and CHRIMES (2004) – Paul Waterhouse and Michael Chrimes, 'Winstanley, Henry', *Oxford Dictionary of National Biography* (Oxford: Oxford University Press, 2004) [available online: http://www.oxforddnb.com/].

WATERS (1955) – D. W. Waters, 'Early Time and Distance Measurement', *Journal of the Institute of Navigation*, 8 (1955), 153-73.

WATERS (1958) – David W. Waters, *The Art of Navigation in England in Elizabethan and early Stuart Times* (London: Hollis and Carter, 1958).

[WATERS, et al.] (1970) – [D. W. Waters, et al. (eds)], *An Inventory of the Navigation and Astronomy Collections in the National Maritime Museum*, 3 vols (London: National Maritime Museum 1970).

WATERSTON (1997) – Charles D. Waterston, *Collections in Context: the Museum of the Royal Society of Edinburgh and the Inception of a National Museum for Scotland* (Edinburgh: National Museums Scotland, 1997).

WATKIN and HEWAT-JABOOR (2008) – David Watkin and Philip Hewat-Jaboor (eds), *Thomas Hope, Regency Designer* (New Haven and London: Yale University Press, 2008).

WATSON (2003) – Norman Watson, *The Dundee Whalers 1750-1914* (East Linton: Tuckwell Press, 2003).

WATT (2005) – James Watt, 'The Old Sandaig Lighthouse now at 57° 13'44.4 N 5° 39'18.7 W', *Northern Lighthouse Board Journal* (Summer 2005), 26-27.

WAYLAND (1967) – Virginia Wayland, *The Winstanley Geographical Cards* (Pasedena, California: Virginia and Harold Wayland, 1967).

WEBSTER (1989) – Diana C. F. Webster, 'A Cartographic Controversy: in defence of Murdoch Mackenzie', in Finlay MacLeod (ed.), *Togail Tir Marking Time: the Map of the Western Isles* (Stornoway: Acair and An Lanntair Gallery, 1989), 33-42.

WEBSTER (2005) – Diana Webster, 'A haill universall see kart: evidence of a late 16th century sea chart', *Cairt: Newsletter of the Scottish Maps Forum*, 6 (January, 2005).

WESTON (1811) – Robert Harcourt Weston, *Letters and important documents relative to the Edystone lighthouse : selected chiefly from the correspondence of the late Robert Weston, Esq., and from other manuscripts to which is added a report made to the Lords of the Treasury in 1809 by the Trinity Corporation; with some observations upon that report* (London: Printed by C. Baldwin for G. & W. Nicol, 1811).

WILLSHER (1990) – Betty Willsher, *Understanding Scottish Graveyards* (Edinburgh: Council for Scottish Archaeology, 1990).

WILSON (1994) – Bryce Wilson, *The Lighthouses of Orkney*, 2nd ed. (Stromness: Stromness Museum, 1994).

WINSTANLEY (1686) – Henry Winstanley, *Ye Royall Pallace of Audley End*, 24 prints, 1686.

WINSTANLEY (1699) – Henry Winstanley, 'Edystone Light-house, A Narrative of the Building', contemporary engraving, 1699.

WITHERS (1996) – Charles W. J. Withers, 'Geography, Science and National Identity in Early Modern Scotland: the Case of Scotland and the Work of Sir Robert Sibbald', *Annals of Science* 53 (1996), 29-73.

WITHERS (1999) – Charles W. J. Withers, 'Reporting, Mapping, Trusting: Making Geographical Knowledge in the Late Seventeenth Century', *Isis*, 90 (1999), 497-521.

WITHERS (2004) – Charles W. J. Withers, 'Adair, John', *Oxford Dictionary of National Biography* (Oxford: Oxford University Press, 2004) [available online: http://www.oxforddnb.com/].

WITHERS and WOOD (2002) – Charles W. J. Withers and Paul Wood (eds), *Science and Medicine in the Scottish Enlightenment* (East Linton: Tuckwell Press, 2002).

WOLFE (1999) – John J. Wolfe, *Brandy, Balloons, & Lamps: Ami Argand, 1750-1803* (Carbondale and Edwardsville: Southern Illinois University Press, 1999).

WRIGHT (2004) – Mike Wright, 'The Changing Ways of Maintenance Management', *Northern Lighthouse Board Journal* (Summer 2004), 20-21.

# Selective Index

NB: References to illustrations or figures are denoted in italics at the end of each entry.

Aberdeen 4, 76, 87, 91, 104, 106, 163; *115*
– sea-mark at 103
– University of 85, 93 (*and see* LIGHTHOUSES)
*Account of the Bell Rock Lighthouse* (*see* BELL ROCK)
ACTS OF PARLIAMENT
– 1786 Act for erecting four lighthouses in the northern parts of Great Britain [26 Geo. III c101] 21, 106
– 1789 Act empowering Commissioners to erect further lighthouses [29 Geo. III c 52] 107
– 1806 Act for erecting lighthouse on the Bell or Cape Rock [46 Geo. III c 132] 119
– 1814 Act to purchase Isle of May and further lighthouses to be built [54 Geo. III c 136] 99, 143, 154
– 1853 Merchant Shipping Act 174
– 1995 Merchant Shipping Act 232
Adair, John 4, 90, 91, 92, 94, 96, 98, 115; *11, 92, 98*
– *Description of the Sea-Coast and Islands of Scotland* 4, 91-92, 98; *98*
Adam, Robert 161
Aden (*see* LIGHTHOUSES)
Adie, Alexander 166, 172
Adie & Son, Edinburgh 128, 159, 166, 167, 172; *128, 159, 173*
Adie, John 158, 169, 172, 191; *159, 191*

Admiralty 37, 38, 46, 57, 64, 65, 88, 95, 175
Aids to Navigation (AtoNs) 226, 233-34
Ailsa Craig (*see* LIGHTHOUSES)
Airth, Pool of 78
Albert of Saxe Coburg, Prince 188
Alexandria, port of 2, 3
Alguada Reef (*see* LIGHTHOUSES)
Anderson, George 8-9, 98
Anderson, Lucy 9; *9*
Angus Museums 139
Anne, HRH, Princess Royal 228
Anne, Queen 47, 81
Anson, Peter 80
Arago, François 19, 26, 27, 167
Arbroath (Aberbrothock) 115, 116, 120, 121, 126, 131, 135, 143, 205
– Abbot of Aberbrothock 115-16
– Signal Tower 131-32, 137, 225; *132*
Ardnamurchan (*see* LIGHTHOUSES)
Ardrossan Harbour 5
Argand, François-Pierre-Ami 16, 144, 145, 149, 163
– Argand's Patent Lamp & Co. 16
– brass gauge *128*
– lamp 5, 16-17, 18, 19, 24, 68, 136, 144, 145, 149, 163, 188, 189; *16, 19*
– Stevenson's frost-lamp for 18
Argyll 106
Arnish Point (*see* LIGHTHOUSES)

Arran, Isle of 22
Asin, Miguel and M. Lopez Otera 8
Audley End 33-34, 35
Auskerry (*see* LIGHTHOUSES)
Automatic Identification System (AIS) 219, 231-32
Ayrton, William 197-98

Baccalieu Island, Newfoundland (*see* LIGHTHOUSES)
Balfour, James Melville 170, 178, 179, 202-203; *170*
– refraction protractor 170, 178
Banks, Sir Joseph (President of the Royal Society) 122
Barber, Peter 84, 86, 87
Barbier & Bénard, Paris xxiii, 213, 214
Barbier & Fenestre, Paris 200, 204, 212; *213, 214*
Barclay, Dr John 133
Barnes, Alison ix, 33, 35, 38
Barns Ness 97, 98 (*see* LIGHTHOUSES)
Barra Head (*see* LIGHTHOUSES)
Barton, Andrew 78
Barton, John 78
Bassey 132-33; *132*
Baston, Thomas 38
Bathurst, Bella xix, 134, 164, 234
Baxter, Jean 15
Bay of Bengal 192
BEACONS 3-7, 33
– Aberdeen Harbour 4, 103-104
– Dunyvaig Castle 4

– Calf of Man 145
– Covesea Skerries 6-7; *7, 7*
– Horse Isle, Ardrossan 5
– Leith Harbour 4, 96; *96*
– Oxcars 6
– river Nith 5
– river Tay (Lucky Scaup) 4
– Scurdie Ness 5
– Start Point 5
Beaglehole, Helen 203
BELL ROCK 109, 115, 116, 117
– accommodation at 135
– *Account of the Bell Rock Lighthouse* 65, 115, 116, 117, 118, 129, 133, 135; *114, 132*
– Arbroath workyard for 123, 126, 132, 143, 205
– automation at 139
– balance-crane 125, 126
– barrack 120, 121, 124, 179; *121*
– boats used in construction: light-ship 119; *Sir Joseph Banks* (schooner) 122, 125; *Smeaton* (sloop) 120, 121, 133; *Tonge Gerrit* (becomes floating-light *Pharos*) 120, 124; *119*
– cement 129
– comparison with Eddystone 118-19, 123, 127, 129
– controversy over engineer 133-35
– costs of 118, 129
– enemy attack on 138
– final stone 127, 133
– fire 139
– first construction 129-33

- fog-warning bells 127, 131, 136, 139, 172; *139*
- foundations/foundation stone 122, 123, 129, 162, 191
- growth of tower 122, 125, 126, 127
- helicopter tragedy at 138
- internal construction 130
- lantern 129, 130, 136-37, 138
- in legend 115-16
- lighthouse at xviii, xxi, xxiv, 8, 31, 32, 75, 95, 101, 109, 115-141, 144, 153, 155, 158, 160, 163, 173, 192, 205, 219, 225; *xxvi, 114, 141*
- lighthouses after Bell Rock 143-85
- lighting at 25, 110, 125, 126, 127, 128, 130-31, 135, 136, 137-39, 188, 189; *131*
- media portrayals 118, 160
- model of 118-19, 120, 131; *xxii, 121, 130*
- 'Notice to Mariners' *119*
- original lamps at Cape Bonavista 136, 188
- praam-boats 121, 124
- quarries for: Craigleith, Edinburgh 120, 127; Mylnefield, near Dundee 120; Rubislaw, Aberdeenshire 120
- railway at 122, 124
- religious beliefs at 120, 162
- staffing 131
- stonemasons 123, 133
- as a stone structure 118, 123, 155, 156
- storms at 115, 122, 125, 127; 114
- visit by John Rennie 121
- visit by Walter Scott 135
- work (in 1807) 118-22; (in 1808) 122-23; (in 1809) 98, 124-25; (in 1810) 126-28
Bell-Pettigrew Museum 133
Bentinck, William,

Marquess of Titchfield (later 4th Duke of Portland) 23, 98, 99, 143
Bidston Hill (*see* LIGHTHOUSES)
Black Sea 3
Blackett, John 204
Blackheath 26
Blathwayt, John 40
Blathwayt, William 40
Bodmin 68
Bonnyman, John (lightkeeper) 128
Bough, Sam 176-77, 181, 185; *176, 185*
Boulogne (*see* LIGHTHOUSES)
Boulton, Matthew 17, 133
Boulton & Watt 126
Brebner, Alan 172, 175-76, 179, 182, 212
- optical protractor 179; *180*
Brebner, Alexander 172
Bressay Sound (*see* LIGHTHOUSES)
Brewster, Sir David Brewster xv, 1, 25, 26, 147, 148, 149, 151, 164-65, 166, 167, 169
- *Edinburgh Encyclopaedia* 102, 117, 190
- polyzonal lens 25; *25*
Broughty Ferry 13
Broun-Ramsay, James, 1st Marquess of Dalhousie 192
Brunton, Richard Henry 196, 197-202, 200, 204; *196, 200*
Bryce, Alexander 94, 95
BT Rugby 229-30
Buccleuch, Duke of 226
Buchan Ness (Buchanness) (*see* LIGHTHOUSES)
Buckett Brothers *209*
Buddon Ness (Buddonness, Buttonness, Bottanais, Buttness) (*see* LIGHTHOUSES)
Buffon, Georges 27
Bullock, William 161
Bunster, Charlotte Leigh 205
burning lens *147*
Bute 106

Caithness 84, 95, 106
Calcutta 192, 195
Calf of Man (*see* LIGHTHOUSES)

Campbell, James Maclean 136-37
Campbell, John, 7th Duke of Argyll 154, 156
Cape Bonavista, Newfoundland (*see* LIGHTHOUSES)
Cape Campbell, New Zealand (*see* LIGHTHOUSES)
Cape Horn, Chile (*see* LIGHTHOUSES)
Cape of Good Hope 32
Cape Saunders, New Zealand (*see* LIGHTHOUSES)
Cape Spear (*see* LIGHTHOUSES)
Cape St Mary's (*see* LIGHTHOUSES)
Cape Wrath (*see* LIGHTHOUSES)
Carron Iron Works, Falkirk 13, 163
Carse, Alexander *141*
Chance Brothers & Co., Birmingham xxiii, 148, 151-52, 179, 190, 200, 210, 212, 223; *xiii, 178, 179, 180, 223, 223*
- hyper-radiant lens 212
- paraffin burner *223*
Chance, Sir James Timmins 151, 178, 206
- dioptric holophotal revolving light *223*
Chancellor, Richard 77
Chanonry Point (*see* LIGHTHOUSES)
Charles I, King 97
Charles II, King 34, 88
charts and maps 74-113; *74, 81, 86, 89, 92, 94, 96, 98, 113* (*see* MAPPING and CHARTING)
Chatham 88
Checkland, Olive 197
Chicken Rock (*see* LIGHTHOUSES)
Chile 173, 187, 204-205
- Chilean Maritime Signalling Service 204
- lighthouses in 204-205
China xviii, 88, 187, 190, 194, 196, 208
China Bakir, Burma (*see* LIGHTHOUSES)
Christmas, Peter 229
Clark, James 127, 143, 173; *142*
Clark, James 91

Clerk, John 116
Cloch Point 23, 105; *23* (*see* LIGHTHOUSES)
Collins, Greenvile 88, 89, 90, 91, 92, 96, 97, 115; *113, 115*
- charts 115; *89, 115*
- *Great Britain's Coasting Pilot* 88, 90, 96, 101; *8, 90, 96*
Clyde, Firth of 10, 22, 79, 95, 104, 154
Clyde Lighthouse Trustees 5, 105, 222
Coase, R. H. 47
Cocas Islands (*see* LIGHTHOUSES)
Colaba, India (*see* LIGHTHOUSES)
Colonsay, Isle of 179
Commission des Phares, Paris 18, 27
Condorcet, Jean 27, 149
Cook Straight, New Zealand 203, 208
Cookson, Isaac xxiii, 148, 149, 150, 151, 152
Cooper, Richard 11, 94
Copeland (*see* LIGHTHOUSES)
Copinsay (*see* LIGHTHOUSES)
Corduan, Tour de (*see* LIGHTHOUSES)
Corsewall Point (*see* LIGHTHOUSES)
Corunna, great tower of (*see* LIGHTHOUSES)
Covesea Skerries (*see* LIGHTHOUSES)
Craighead 6
Crail, parish church of 4
Crane, Nicholas 87
Craw, James 132-33; *132*
Crimean War 174-75
Cromarty (*see* LIGHTHOUSES)
Cromer (*see* LIGHTHOUSES)
Cumbrae, Great 104
Cumbrae, Little (*see* LIGHTHOUSES)
Cuningham, Alexander 172
Cunningham, John 97, 98
Cunningham of Barns, Alexander 97, 98
Cunningham of Barns, David 103

Dalbeattie granite 68, 182

255

Dalen, Gustaf 220
– Dalen operated gas light 220, 225
Dalrymple, Alexander 95, 106; *95*
Daniell, William *106*
Davis quadrant 83
day-mark 2, 5
de Magalhães, João Jacinto (Jean Hyacinthe de Magellan) 17
de Meritens & Cie, A., Paris 210-11; *211*
de Nicolay d'Arfeville, Nicolas 80, 84, 91; *81, 92*
Decca system 226-28, 230; *227*
Dee, John 87
Defoe, Daniel 44-45
Dempster, George xvii, 106
dGPS 224, 226, 228-29
Dirleton Estate 233
Dog Island, New Zealand (*see* LIGHTHOUSES)
Donaldson Report 230
Dornoch Firth 109
Doty, Henry Harrison 207
– burner 137, 207; *208*
Douglas, George, 16th Earl of Morton xxi, 55
Douglas Head (*see* LIGHT-HOUSES)
Douglas, James, 13th Earl of Morton 68, 93, 94, 95
– Grand Master of Grand Masonic Lodge, England 94
Douglas, Peter 229-30
Douglass, Sir James (President, Royal Society of London) 94, 95
Dove, James xxiii, 127, 200, 204, 223; *xiii, 223*
Dover 3, 211
Dowie, Henry 9
Dubh Artach (Dhu Heartach) (*see* LIGHT-HOUSES)
Dumfries 5
– Town Council 5, 104
Dunbar 98, 143, 150
Duncansby Head (*see* LIGHTHOUSES)
Dundee 12, 13, 89
– Fraternity of Masters and Seamen of Dundee (Trinity House, Dundee) 8, 11, 12, 13, 101, 102; *180*

– Harbour 101
– Harbour Trust 103
– whale oil 101
– whaling fleet 12
Dunnet Head (*see* LIGHT-HOUSES)
Dyer, Henry 197-98

Earl's Hill 229
Earraid 179, 180
earthquakes 200-201
East India Company 190, 193, 196
East Lothian 139, 143, 161
Easter Grove, Burma (*see* LIGHTHOUSES)
EDDYSTONE ROCK xix-xx, xxiv, 7, 9, 24, 31-74, 116, 118, 153, 155, 156, 163, 192, 193; *xx; xxvi, 31*
– 1st lighthouse (Winstanley) 33-46; *39, 42*
– 2nd lighthouse (Rudyerd) 46-61; *48, 49, 49, 52, 56, 56, 58, 58*
– 3rd lighthouse (Smeaton) xxi, 31, 33, 61-70, 119, 123; *67, 67, 67*
– 4th lighthouse (Douglass) 68; *68, 69*
– cement 65; *66*
– documentation, lack of 32-33
– Eddystone lighthouse salt 40; *40*
– engravings of *69, 73*
– fire at 58-61, 62
– geology of rocks 32
– lead from keeper's stomach *60*
– lighting 40, 41, 43-44, 50, 51, 58-59, 68-69
– meaning of name 31
– models of 40, 44, 53, 54, 62, 64, 65, 66, 67; *30, 49, 55, 67*
– quarries for 63-64, 68
– receipt for lighthouse fees *50*
– representation on penny 70
– syndicate for the lease of 57, 61, 64
EDINBURGH 6, 13, 122, 125, 127, 133, 147, 167
– Baxter's Place 108
– Blair Street 14, 15, 16, 108, 200

– Bristo Street 14
– *Evening News* xxiii
– George Street 15, 21, 90, 93, 94, 96, 109, 170, 172, 221
– Greenside Lane 108
– High School 146
– High Street 172
– Hunter Square 14, 15
– Leith Walk 133
– Museum of Science and Art (*see* National Museums Scotland)
– New Town 13, 14, 15, 120
– Old Town 14
– Princes Street 161
– School of Arts 166, 167
– South Side 15
– street lighting 14, 15
– Town Council 14
– University of 17, 25, 93, 108, 146, 147, 157, 169, 170, 172
– Volunteers 99, 106
*Edinburgh Encyclopaedia* 1, 25, 26, 102, 117; *xxvi, 103*
*Edinburgh New Philosophical Journal* 165
*Edinburgh Philosophical Journal* 117
*Edinburgh Review* 149
Edo Bay 196
Edwin, Captain R. A. 203
Egypt/Egyptian art, influence of 20, 160-63
Eilean Glas (Scalpay) (*see* LIGHTHOUSES)
eidograph 167
Eilean Mòr 214
Elder, John 84, 85, 87
Elgin 6
Elie Ness (*see* LIGHT-HOUSES)
Elizabeth I, Queen 33, 47, 87, 88
e-Loran 229, 230
Elton, Julia 157, 177, 191
*Encyclopaedia Britannica* 21, 25, 118
Engineering Storage and Testing Facility (ESTF) 226
English Channel xix, xxi, 27, 31, 32, 37, 70, 95, 212
Evangelista, Chile (*see* LIGHTHOUSES)
Evelyn, John 53, 89
Ewing, James 105

EXHIBITIONS
– 1851 Great Exhibition, London xxii, 15, 19, 151, 157, 160, 163, 187, 188, 191
– 1862 International Exhibition, London xviii, xxii; *xvi, xix*
– 1867 Paris Universal Exhibition 6, 179
– 1901 Glasgow Exhibition 136

Fair Isle, North and South (*see* LIGHTHOUSES)
Falkirk 13
Faraday, Michael 208-209
Farewell Spit, New Zealand (*see* LIGHT-HOUSES)
Ferryland Head, Newfoundland (*see* LIGHT-HOUSES)
Ferryport-on-Craig 13
Fidra Island (*see* LIGHT-HOUSES)
Fiennes, Celia 35, 40
Fife 4, 24, 139
Fife Ness (Fifeness) (*see* LIGHTHOUSES)
First World War xxii, 138, 206, 222
Flamborough Head (*see* LIGHTHOUSES)
Flanders 82
Flannan Isles (*see* LIGHT-HOUSES)
floating-lights 65, 68, 119; *119*
fog-signals (*see* BELL ROCK) 208, 213, 223, 225, 233, 234; *233*
Forrest, John 127
Fort Amherst, Newfoundland (*see* LIGHTHOUSES)
Forth, Firth of 4, 6, 7, 18, 22, 23, 97, 98, 108, 125, 220-26; *11*
Fortune, Peter 128
Foula (*see* LIGHTHOUSES)
Fraser, Admiral Sir Bruce 195
Fraser, Alexander 162, 192-95, 211, 212, 219
Fraserburgh 77, 106
Fraternity of Masters and Seamen of Dundee (*see* DUNDEE)
Freemasonry 94, 123, 162, 191
Fresnel, Augustin 19, 26,

256

27, 144, 147, 148, 149, 150, 152, 157, 177, 194, 211, 212; *27*
– lens 27, 157, 160, 164; *150, 157, 158, 177, 179*
Fresnel, Léonor 18, 148, 152

Galbraith, William 166
Galloway, Mull of (*see* LIGHTHOUSES)
Gasker (*see* LIGHTHOUSES)
General Lighthouse Fund 227
GENERAL LIGHTHOUSE AUTHORITIES (GLAs)
– Commissioners of Irish Lights 211, 219, 232
– Northern Lighthouse Board (Northern Lights) xvii-xviii, xix, xxi-xxii, xxiii, xxiv, 5, 6, 7, 10, 18, 20, 21, 22, 23, 24, 75, 97, 98, 99, 104, 105-10, 116, 118, 119, 126, 127, 129, 131, 134, 136, 139, 143, 144, 145, 146, 147, 148, 150, 152, 153, 155, 156, 163, 164, 172, 173, 174, 179, 180, 181, 182, 187, 188, 189, 190; *220*
– Northern Lights, Commissioners of 5, 7, 22, 98, 99, 104, 107, 149
– Trinity House xvii, 17, 21, 24, 26, 32, 33, 36, 40, 41, 46, 47, 50, 51, 64, 65, 68, 88, 90, 99, 104, 145, 147, 151, 174, 175, 188, 205, 208, 211, 219, 220, 232
George III, King 123
George IV, King 15
Ghim, Walter 87
Gibson, Wilfrid Wilson 215
Gilbert of London, Messrs (opticians) 147
Girdleness (Girdle Ness) (*see* LIGHTHOUSES)
Gironde, River 3, 27
Glasgow 10, 22, 85, 95, 104, 106, 145, 175
– Town Council 104
– University of 85, 93, 108, 119
Glen, James 124
Global Navigation Satellite Systems (GNSS) 226, 229-30

Global Positioning System (GPS) xviii, 224, 228-30
Grant, Eric 161, 162
Granton Depot xxii, 220, 224, 226
Granton Harbour 226
*Great Michael* (later *La Grande Nef d'Eccosse*) 79, 84
Great Exhibition, London (*see* EXHIBITIONS)
Great Storm (1703) 44-46, 47
Greenside Company 13
GRP day-mark panels 234
Gullane 149

Hague, Douglas 3, 5, 10, 18, 98, 160
Hall, Henry (poss. Richard or William) 60-61
Halliman's Reef or Scars (*see* Covesea Skerries)
Harbour Grace Island, Newfoundland (*see* LIGHTHOUSES)
HARBOUR LIGHTS
– Aberdeen 104
– Dundee 102
– Kirkcaldy 166
– Leith 23
– Newport, Fife 102
– North Queensferry 5
– Peterhead 172, 177, 191; *191*
– Portpatrick 23, 108
Harris, Isle 106
Harvey, P. D. A. 85
Harwich 7, 90
Haskeir (*see* LIGHTHOUSES)
Helliar Holm (*see* LIGHTHOUSES)
Henry VIII, King xvii, 33, 79, 84, 87
Heriot-Watt College or University 167
Hill, D. O. and Adamson, Robert 80
Holburn Head (*see* LIGHTHOUSES)
Holland, John 57, 58; *58*
Holmes, Frederick Hale 209
– generator *209*
Hooghly (Hoogly) River 190, 195
Hope, Thomas 20, 160, 161, 163
Horner, Leonard 166
– School of Arts 167

Horsburgh, James 190
Horsburgh, John 117
Horsburgh, Singapore (*see* LIGHTHOUSES)
Horse Isle 5
Howard, James, 3rd Earl of Suffolk 33
Howard, Thomas, 1st Earl of Suffolk 34
Hoy Sound, High and Low (*see* LIGHTHOUSES)
Huddart, Joseph 133
Hulsbergh (Hulsberg), Henry 55; *56, 56*
Hume, John 5
Hume, Joseph 149
Hurter, Johann Heinrich 17
Hutchinson, William 20, 21, 22, 26
– *Treatise on Practical Seamanship* 21
Hynish 154, 155, 156
Hyskeir (*see* LIGHTHOUSES)

Ibn al-Shaikh 2
*Illustrated London News* 194; *193*
Inchcape Reef (*see* LIGHTHOUSES)
Inchkeith (*see* LIGHTHOUSES)
India 182, 187 (*and see* LIGHTHOUSES)
Indian Mutiny 194
Industrial Museum of Scotland (*see* National Museums Scotland)
Inkster, Ian 202
Institution of Civil Engineers 168, 199
International Association of Marine Aids to Navigation and Lighthouse Authorities (IALA) 232-33, 234
Inverness 106
Ireland 18, 208
Islay, Isle of 4
Isles of Scilly (*see under* Scilly Isles)

jag-bolts 53
James II, King 34, 91
James III, King 81
James IV, King 78, 79, 96
James V, King 79, 80, 84
James VI and I, King 34, 81, 88
Jameson, Robert 165

Japan 182, 187, 192, 196-202
– Japanese Lighthouse Association (TOKOKAI) 202
– Lighthouse Department 199-200, 208
– Meiji Restoration 196-97
– Yokohama 197 (and see LIGHTHOUSES)
Jauper, India (*see* LIGHTHOUSES)
Jenkin, Professor Fleeming 170-71
Jessop, Josiah 30, 57-58, 60-61, 63, 66; *58*
Johnson, Captain Robert 198, 203, 204
Johnston, Jaaziell 38, 39, 51; *39*
Joseph, Samuel 130

Kay, Mary 13
Kenward, James 152, 212
Kilwarlin (South Rock), Ireland (*see* LIGHTHOUSES)
Kinnaird Head (*see* LIGHTHOUSES)
Kirkcaldy Harbour 166
Körso, Sweden (*see* LIGHTHOUSES)
Krishna Shoal, Burma (*see* LIGHTHOUSES)
Kyleakin (*see* LIGHTHOUSES)
Kyoto 197

Lamb, Hubert 44
Lanark 106
Langness (*see* LIGHTHOUSES)
Lanterna of Genoa (*see* LIGHTHOUSES)
Lawson, George 214
Lawson's Agricultural Museum 15
Leask, Henry 128
Leith 96, 108, 119
– Harbour 4, 23
– Port 78, 82
Lens, Bernard 38, 49, 51, 52, 53; *52, 55*
Lepaute, Henry 137, 148, 152
Leslie, John 85
Leslie, Sir John 147
Letourneau, Theodore 152, 153, 177; *177*
Lewis, Isle of 95

– Butt of (see LIGHT-
HOUSES)
light dues 23, 33, 50, 52,
98, 99, 104, 106, 149,
129, 188
light-ships
– in Japan 202
– *North Carr* 5
– *Otter Rock* 206
– *Pharos* 119
lighthouse automation 70,
163, 219-26
lighthouse, definition of
1-2
lighthouse keepers and
families 7, 8-9, 24, 59-
61, 98, 99, 100, 128,
130-33, 136, 138, 139,
154, 156, 160, 172,
174, 192, 198, 199,
200, 201-202, 211, 213,
214-15, 219, 220, 221-
24, 225, 226, 234-35
LIGHTHOUSE LIGHTING
7, 11, 43-44, 50, 58, 68,
119; *158*
– acetylene gas 211, 220,
224, 225, 226, 231
– candles 7, 9,11-20, 41,
101
– coal 2, 8, 9 10, 21, 22,
23, 24, 97, 105, 226
– colour 125, 130-31,
135, 137
– colza oil 5-19, 20, 136,
208
– copper 5
– copper parabolic 18,
20, 24, 125, 126, 127,
128, 131; *131*
– distinguishing between
145, 148-49
– double 107, 108
– electricity 20, 137, 139,
206, 207-11, 220, 225;
*211, 212*
– equiangular prisms
136, 137, 212
– fixed 223
– gas 208, 211, 220, 226;
*220*
– gauge for 127, 128;
*128*
– glazing bars 163
– hemispherical 188,
189; *189*
– holophotal 167, 177-
78, 191, 201, 212; *189*
– hyper-radiant 136, 137,
211-215; 213, *214*
– lamp changer 231; *231*

– lanterns 22, 24, 138,
207, 221, 231; *xxiv, 163*
– leading 101, 102
– lenses (dioptrics) 8, 25-
27, 101, 137, 143, 147-
153, 157, 164; *xiii*
– LEDs (light emitting
diodes) 220; *221*
– mirrors 7, 20, 26, 157
– mirror-faceted 20-23,
100, 102, 104, 172
– oil lamps 9, 11-20, 22,
24, 99, 100, 101, 102,
104, 105, 108; *19, 23*
– optics apparatus *180*
– parabolic 21-25, 99,
100, 105, 136, 137,
145, 148, 189
– paraffin 20, 137, 207-
211; *223*
– reflectors (catoptrics)
23, 135, 144, 153, 163,
188; *217*
– revolving machinery
100, 137, 143, 148, 158,
210; *177, 223*
– sealed beam array 220;
*221*
– solar panels 231; *231*
– spherical 20, 21

LIGHTHOUSES
Aberdeen 4, 104, 115
Aden 195, 198
Ailsa Craig 208, 222, 233
Alguada Reef, Burma 160,
192-95; *193*
Ardnamurchan 156, 160,
163, 164; *163*
Arnish Point 164
Auskerry 222, 225, 231
Baccalieu Island, New-
foundland 189
Barns Ness 97, 98, 225,
232
Barra Head 146, 147, 222
Bell Rock lighthouse (see
BELL ROCK)
Bidston Hill 20, 21
Boulogne 3
Bressay Sound 193; *193*
Buchan Ness (Buchanness)
146, 213
Buddon Ness (see also Tay)
– High and Low 179; *180*
– lights xvii, 12, 23, 101,
102; *103*
Burma, lighthouses in
192-96
Butt of Lewis 224-26,
229

Calf of Man 145, 183
Cape Bonavista, New-
foundland 136, 188,
189; *217*
*Cape Campbell*, New
Zealand 203
Cape Horn, Chile 204
Cape St Mary's, New-
foundland 188, 189;
*189*
Cape Saunders, New
Zealand 178, 202-203
Cape Spear, Newfound-
land 136, 188, 189
Cape Wrath 213, 224,
226, 233, 143; *142*
Chanonry Point 160, 163
Chicken Rock 137, 145,
174, 179, 181, 182, 212,
231; *185*
Chile, lighthouses in 204-
205
China Bakir, Burma 195
Cloch Point 23, 105, 206;
*23*
Cocas Islands 195, 203
Colaba, India 195
Copeland, Irish coast 22
Copinsay 233
Corduan, Tour de 3, 19,
27, 118, 146, 163; *xxvi*
Corsewall 143, 222, 225
Corunna, great tower of
3
Covesea Skerries 6, 7, 164;
*6, 7*
Cromarty 160, 164, 193
Cromer 24-25
Cumbrae, Little xvii, 10,
22, 104, 105, 107, 206,
211; *10, 212*
Dog Island, New Zealand
203
Douglas Head 145, 146
Dover 3
Dubh Artach (Dhu
Heartach) 156, 172,
174, 179, 180, 181, 182,
208, 212, 218, 225; *185,
218*
– description by Robert
Louis Stevenson 179-81
Duncansby Head 229
Dunnet Head 146
Easter Grove, Burma 195
Eddystone (see EDDY-
STONE ROCK)
Eilean Glas (Scalpay) xxiii,
22, 106, 144, 160; *xiii,
106, 221*
Elie Ness 232

Evangelista, Chile 205
Fair Isle, North and South
212, 222, 224, 226, 233
Farewell Spit, New
Zealand 203
Ferryland Head, New-
foundland 189-90
Fidra Island 220, 225, 233
Fife Ness (Fifeness) 5, 12,
89, 115, 232
Flamborough Head 125
Flannan Isles 222, 225;
*186*
– building of 206, 213
– mystery of 214-15
– poem 215
– power conversion 231
Fort Amherst, Newfound-
land 188
Foula 231
Gasker 230
Girdleness (Girdle Ness)
xxiii, 146, 163, 198,
208; *164*
Great Savage Rock light-
houses 195
Halliman's Reef or Scars
(see Covesea Skerries)
Harbour Grace Island,
Newfoundland 136,
188, 189
Haskier 230
Helliar Holm 213, 231
Hokkaido, Japan 196
Holburn Head 222
Holy Island (see Lamlash)
Hooghly (Hoogly) River
190, 195
Horsburgh, Singapore
172, 177, 190-92; *191*
Hoy Sound High 164,
193
Hoy Sound Low 164, 193
Hyskier 156
Inchcape Reef 31, 103,
110, 115, 116, 118, 135,
133, 139, 143 205; *115*
Inchkeith xxiii, 6, 18, 23,
90-101, 125, 130, 136,
144, 150; *24, 236*
– fog signal 222, 225
– foghorn 233; *233*
– lenses at 150, 163, 189;
*150*
India, lighthouses in 192-
96
Isle of May xvii, 4, 7, 8,
10, 11, 12, 23, 96-99,
100, 116, 136, 143,
144, 150, 210-10; *8, 9,
11, 97, 144, 217*

258

– first Scottish lighthouse 97
– lights 98, 136
– lower 164
– reflectors at Cape Bonavista 136, 189
Isle of Ornsay 178; *178*
Japan, lighthouses in 196-202
Jauper, India 190
Kilwarlin (South Rock), Ireland 118; *xxvi, 119*
Kinnaird Head 21, 75, 106, 107, 144, 221, 222; *110*
– first radio beacon in Scotland 222, 226 231
Kobe, Japan 196
Körso, Sweden 20
Krishna Shoal, Burma 195
Kyle of Lochalsh 230
Kyleakin 178
Lamlash (Holy Island) 225; *173*
Langness 145
Lanterna of Genoa 3
Lismore 146
Little Ross 164
Loch Ryan 164
Malabar Point, India 195
Mauritius 196
Milford 25
Moko-Hinau, New Zealand 204
Monach 189, 222, 230-31
Muckle Flugga, North Unst 172, 174, 175, 176, 179, 193; *176*
Mull of Easwick 230
Mull of Galloway 107, 143, 146, 147
Mull of Kintyre 22, 106, 107, 144
Nagasaki, Japan 196
Niigata, Japan 196
Neist Point 225
North Rona 225, 231
North Ronaldsay (North Ranilsha) 21, 24, 106, 107, 144, 177, 191, 193, 224; *107, 177*
Noss Head 160, 163, 164
Noup Head 231
Nugget Point, New Zealand 203
Old Woman's Island (Bombay Harbour), India 190, 195
*Otter Rock* light-ship 206
Out Skerries 222, 225, 231

Oxcars Rock 6, 206, 220, 226, 230; *220*
Oyster Reef, Burma 195
Pentland Skerries 22, 107, 108, 144, 193, 208, 222; *144, 208*
Peterhead 12, 172; *191*
– Harbour light 177
Pharos
– Alexandria 2-3 8, 162
– (*see also* light-ships)
– meaning of 2, 117
Pladda 22, 144, 208; *67, 107*
Platte Fougère, Guernsey 206
Point Amour, Newfoundland 189
Point of Ayre 145
Portland 18, 26, 64, 65; *29*
Prongs, India 195
Rattray Head 206, 233
Rinns of Islay 146, 224, 225, 226
Rock Island (Mikomoto), Japan *196*
Rubha nan Gall 178, 231
Ruvaal (Rhu-val) 181, 225
St Abbs Head 97, 198, 220, 226, 233
St Agnes, Scilly Isles 9, 10, 24, 25
– cresset *10*
St Catherine's, Isle of Wight 3
St John's Harbour, Newfoundland 188
Sanda Island 164
Satanomisaki (Chickakoff), Japan *200*
signalling from lighthouses
– carrier pigeons 132
– copper signal ball 132
– heliograph
Skerryvore (*see under* SKERRYVORE)
South Foreland 209, 211, 212; *209, 213*
Southerness xvii, 104; *105*
Start Point, Devon 151
Start Point, Orkney 24, 144, 225, 231
Stephens Island, New Zealand 204; *204*
Stroma 213, 222
Sule Skerry xxiii, 206, 213
– heliograph on 222
– hyper-radiant optic *214*
Sumburgh Head 193, 229

Taiaroa Head, New Zealand 178, 202, 203
Tarbat Ness (Tarbetness) 109, 143, 147, 193
Tay, River 4, 11, 12, 89, 101, 102
– Firth (of) 89, 103, 115
– 'Leading Lights of Tay' *103, 103*
– River and Firth 11
– River 12
Tory Island, New Zealand 204
Tynemouth 3
Ushenish 225, 231
Waitemata Harbour, New Zealand 203
Whalsay 175
Yokohama, Japan 196

Lily, George 85, 87
Lindsay, Alexander xiii, 80, 82, 84, 91, 97, 115
Lismore (*see* LIGHT-HOUSES)
Little Ross (*see* LIGHT-HOUSES)
Littlebury 34, 35, 38, 40, 41, 44, 46
Liverpool 20 21, 95, 106, 145
Loch Ryan (*see* LIGHT-HOUSES)
Lockhart, J. G. 135
London 16, 17
– Museum, William Bullock's 161
– Royal Institution 208
– University College London 197
Loran 229
Loran-C radio-navigation 227, 229-30
Lossiemouth 6
Lovett, Col. John 46, 47, 48, 49, 50, 55, 57
Lovett (née Verney), Mary 47, 55
Low Countries 11, 77
Luttrell, Narcissus 37
Lyell, Charles 102

Macdonald, A. (*cover image*)
Macdougall, Norman 78
MacKay, Roddy 225
Mackenzie, Hector 104
Mackenzie, Murdoch 95; *94*
Maclaurin, Colin 93, 94, 95

Macleod, Norman 175
Magellan Straits 205
Mainstone, Rowland 62
Mair, Craig 13, 109, 134, 200
Malabar Point (*see* LIGHT-HOUSES)
Man, Isle of xix, 145, 174, 181, 232; *185*
MAPPING and CHARTING
– 16th century 84-88; *81, 87, 92*
– 17th century 88-92; *113, 115*
– 18th century 92-95; *89*
– Admiralty Hydrographic Office 95
– 'De kuften van Schotland' *74*
Marr, John 89, 97, 101; *89*
Mauritius (*see* LIGHT-HOUSES)
May, Isle of (*see* LIGHT-HOUSES)
Maxwell, James 97
Meirs & Son, Thomas, London 127; *139*
Meiji Restoration 197
Mercator, Gerard 86, 87
Merchant Shipping Act of 1995 (*see* ACTS OF PARLIAMENT)
Mersey 154
Milford (*see* LIGHT-HOUSES)
Mill Bay 63, 65
Milne & Son, Edinburgh 6, 19, 153, 163, 200, 201, 204, 210; *189, 204*
Milne, James 172; *158*
Milne, John 157, 172
Minch 107
Moir, D. G. 87
Moko-Hinau, New Zealand (*see* LIGHT-HOUSES)
Molloy, David 189
Monach (*see* LIGHT-HOUSES)
Monitor Centre (George Street, Edinburgh) 225, 226, 229, 230, 235
Montgolfier brothers 16
Montgomerie, Hugh, 12th Earl of Eglinton 5
Montrose Harbour 5
Montt, Admiral Jorge 205
Moore, John 89, 90, 91
Moray Firth 6, 109

Morton, 13th Earl of (*see* Douglas)
Morton, Susan, Countess of xix
Moxon, James 91
Muckle Flugga, North Unst (*see* LIGHTHOUSES)
Mulhern, Andrew 230-31
Mull of Easwick (*see* LIGHTHOUSES)
Mull of Galloway (*see* LIGHTHOUSES)
Mull of Kintyre (*see* LIGHTHOUSES)
Munro, Jean xxi
Munro, R. W. 'Billy' xxi, 5, 12, 75, 106, 139, 143, 208, 212
Murray, John, 4th Duke of Atholl 145
Museum of Scotland (*see* National Museums Scotland)
Museum of Scottish Lighthouses xxii
Musgrave, Sir William 33

Nagasaki, Japan (*see* LIGHTHOUSES)
National Heritage Memorial Fund *114*
National Lifeboat Service 77
National Maritime Museum 83
National Museums Scotland x, xviii-xix, xxi, xxii, xxiii, 31, 41, 45, 128, 151, 157, 166, 179, 205, 213, 223
navigation instruments 81-83; *83, 83*
navigation positioning 226-32
Navstar (US Satellite GPS) 226, 228
Navy
– Merchant xviii, 77-78, 80-2, 95, 118, 180
– Royal xviii, 37, 49, 50, 51, 88, 98, 138, 143
– Scots 78-80, 83
New Zealand 170, 174, 179, 182, 187,
– lighthouses in 174, 182, 187, 202-204
Newcastle 40
Newhaven 78; *80*
Newfoundland 136; *189*
– Lighthouse Board 188, 189, 208

– lighthouse service 182, 187, 188-90; *186*
– lighthouses in 136, 188-90
– and Robert Stevenson & Sons 188
Nith, River 5
– Nith Navigation Commission 104
Norberg, Jonas 20
Norfolk 21
North Carr Rocks 5
Northern Lighthouse Board (Northern Lights) (*see* General Lighthouse Authorities)
North Queensferry 5
North Rona (*see* LIGHTHOUSES)
North Ronaldsay (North Ranilsha) (*see* LIGHTHOUSES)
North Sea 11, 22, 75, 77, 86, 106, 109, 115, 124
*North Sea Pilot* 5
Northumberland coast 3
North Unst (*see* Muckle Flugga)
Noss Head (*see* LIGHTHOUSES)
Noup Head (*see* LIGHTHOUSES)
Nowell, Laurence 85, 87
Noyes, Richard 57
Nugget Point, New Zealand (*see* LIGHTHOUSES)

Oban
– Depot in 226
Oke, Robert 189
Old Woman's Island (Bombay Island), India (*see* LIGHTHOUSES)
Oppenheim, Michael 35
Orkney Islands 22, 24, 84, 89, 90, 91, 95, 106, 107, 175, 177, 212, 213; *94*
– Start Point, Sanday 5, 108
Ornsay, Isle of (*see* LIGHTHOUSES)
Ortelius, Abraham 86, 87; *86*
Otago, New Zealand 202, 203
*Otter Rock* (*see* LIGHT-SHIPS)
Out Skerries (*see* LIGHTHOUSES)
Oxcars Rock (*see* LIGHTHOUSES)

Oyster Reef, Burma (*see* LIGHTHOUSES)

Palmer, Mike 48
Paris 6, 16, 19
Park, James 221
Parker, George, 2nd Earl of Macclesfield 62
Parker, William 16, 17
Parkes, Sir Harry 198, 199
Paterson, Bill 224, 228
Patterson, Thomas 203
Pavitt, J. A. L. 191
Paxton, Roland 117, 134, 171
Pedra Branca Rock 190, 191
Peebles, David Bruce 169
Pentland
– Firth 22, 94, 108, 212, 213
– Skerries (*see* LIGHTHOUSES)
Pepys, Samuel 89
Perronet de Granvelle, Antoine 87
Perry, Commodore Matthew 196
Perth 4, 101
Peterhead (*see* LIGHTHOUSES)
– Harbour light 177
Pharos (*see* LIGHTHOUSES)
– (*see also* LIGHT-SHIPS)
Philosophical Society of Edinburgh 93, 94
Pilgrim Trust, The 40; *114*
Pitt, Moses 90
– *Great Atlas* 90
Pladda (*see* LIGHTHOUSES)
Playfair, William 167
Pleasonton, Stephen 194
Pliny the Elder (Gaius Plinius Secundus)
– *Natural History* 2, 3
Plymouth 31, 32, 36, 37, 38, 40, 43, 45, 49, 50, 51, 58, 59, 60, 63, 64
– Breakwater 134, 193
– City Museum & Art Gallery 40, 43
– Dockyard 35, 37, 57
– Hoe 68
– Sound 35, 41, 60
– Standing Salt 40; *40*
Point Amour, Newfoundland (*see* LIGHTHOUSES)
Point of Ayre (*see* LIGHTHOUSES)
Point of Scalpa 22
Pole, Reginald 87

Pont, Timothy 89
Ponui Passage, New Zealand (*see* LIGHTHOUSES)
Portland (*see* LIGHTHOUSES)
– limestone 64, 67
Portland, Duke of (*see* Bentinck)
Portpatrick Harbour 23, 108
Precise Positioning Service (PPS) 228
Prongs, India (*see* LIGHTHOUSES)
Racal-Decca Marine Navigation Ltd 227
racon (radar beacon) 139, 222
RADAC 225
RADLE 225
RAF Leuchars 138, 139
Raffles, Sir Stamford 190
Rattray Head (*see* LIGHTHOUSES)
Reid, John 128
Reid-Head (Red Head) 12, 115
Rennie, George 121, 115
Rennie, James 134
Rennie, John 119, 121, 133-34
Rennie, Sir John 134
Rhind, David 172
Rhinns of Galloway 145
Riis, Thomas 81
Rinns of Islay (*see* LIGHTHOUSES)
Ritchie, James *220*
Rockwell International 228
Robert Stevenson & Sons, Civil Engineers (*see* STEVENSON FAMILY)
Roberts, David 161
Roberts, Henry 40, 44
Robison, Professor John 17
Rock Island (Mikomoto), Japan (*see* LIGHTHOUSES)
Rogers, Thomas 26, 29
Ronaldsay, island of (North Ranilsha) 21, 144
Ross
– Bishop of 85
– Sheriff of 106
Rosyth 138
Rowatt, Thomas 54-55
Rowe, Peter 40

Royal Institution (now Royal Scottish Academy) 161

Royal Scottish Museum (*see* National Museums Scotland)

Royal Scottish Society of Arts (RSSA) (formerly Society for Promoting the Useful Arts in Scotland) xv, 164-74, 200; *xv*
– foundation 164
– Keith Medal 167
– proceedings 165
– Royal Charter 165, 167
– and Stevensons 165-72

Royal Society of Edinburgh xix, xxi, 150, 164, 165, 168, 211

Royal Society of London 60, 62, 94

Rubha nan Gall (*see* LIGHTHOUSES)

Rudyard (Rudyerd), John xx, 48, 49, 50, 51, 53, 54, 57, 62, 63; *46, 48, 49, 55, 58*
– Eddystone, Rudyard's plan for (*see* EDDY-STONE LIGHTHOUSE)

Ruvaal (Rhu-val) (*see* LIGHTHOUSES)

St Abbs Head (*see* LIGHT-HOUSES)

St Agnes, Scilly Isles (*see* LIGHTHOUSES)

St Andrews
– Castle 80
– University of 85, 93, 133

St Catherine's, Isle of Wight (*see* LIGHT-HOUSES)

St John's Harbour, New-foundland 188

St Lo, Captain George 37, 38

Saffron Waldon 33

Sailmaker, Isaac 55, 57

Saltoun, Lord 107

Sandaig 234

Sanda Island (*see* LIGHTHOUSES)

Sandes, E. W. C. 194-95

Sang, Edward 166

Satanomisaki (Chickakoff), Japan (*see* LIGHT-HOUSES)

Sautter Lemonnier & Cie, L. 200

Scalpay 106

Schiffer, Michael 209, 211

Scilly Isles 9, 10, 24, 25, 50

*Scotiae Tabula* 86; *86*

Scotstarvit 9, 23, 98

Scott, Miss Henrietta (later Duchess of Portland) 9, 98

Scott, (Sir) Walter 99, 135, 144, 153, 154

*Scottish Atlas* 90

Scottish Parliament 205

SCOTLAND 75
– coastline 76-76, 90, 91, 105, 109, 143, 145
– Enlightenment 93, 161
– map-making of 84-95
– Parliament, 91, 92-93
– Privy Council of 11, 90, 91, 101
– shipbuilding 77-81
– trade 75, 77, 80, 95, 105
– weather 76-77, 81-82

Scurdie Ness 5

sea-marks/sea-marking xix, xxi, 1, 3-7, 31, 75, 95, 96, 103, 104, 188

Second World War xxii, 99, 109, 138, 207, 222, 224, 227

Seller, John 88
– *English Pilot* 88

Servizio de Señalización Marítima 204

Seton, John Thomas 95

Seven Wonders of the Ancient World 2

Shapin, Steven 166, 167

Shetland Islands 76, 82, 84, 88, 89, 90, 91, 143, 173, 175, 212, 230

SHIPS and SHIPWRECKS
– *Aberdeen* 24, 99
– *Adelaar* 76
– *Dartmouth* 76
– *Edward Bonaventure* 77
– *El Gran Grifón* 76
– *Great Michael* 79, 84
– HMS *Argyll* 138
– HMS *Manilla* 198
– HMS *Nymph* 98, 143
– HMS *Pallas* 98, 143
– HMS *York* 109
– *Kennemerland* 76, 82
– *Lastdrager* 82
– *Mary Rose* 82
– MV *Braer* 230
– *Oceanic* 76
– *Oscar* 76, 104

– *Pole Star* 233
– *Sir Joseph Banks* 122, 125
– *Smeaton* 120, 121, 133
– *Swan* 76, 82
– *Tonge Gerrit* (later floating-light *Pharos*) 119, 120, 121, 124, 133, 175, 226, 233
– *Travencore* 4
– *Winchelsea* 46

Short, James 94

Sibbald, Sir Robert 91, 93
– *Scottish Atlas* 90

signalling from lighthouses (*see* LIGHTHOUSES)

Simpson, Dr Allen vii, xxii-xxiii

SKERRYVORE 9, 158, 172, 193
– and Alan Stevenson 153-160 (*see also* STEVENSON FAMILY)
– beauty of 160
– cement 156
– description of 156-57
– difficulties of landing at 153-4
– fog signals 172, 174, 234
– Hynish workyard 154
– instruments for designing optics at 158; *159*
– lantern 156
– lighting 19, 157, 158, 163; *158*
– masonry 155, 156, 158
– meaning of name 154
– models *156*
– oil lamp 143, 151; *19*
– optics 177, 192, 193, 194
– quarries for 155-6

Skye, Isle of 178

Slezer, John
– *Theatrum Scotiae* 90, 91

Slight, Alexander 205

Slight, George Henry (father) 172, 205

Slight, George Henry (son) 172, 204-205
– George Henry Slight Lighthouse Museum (Chile) 205
– *Ingeniero George Slight Marshall* 205

Slight, James 123, 172, 205

Slights' Reach 205

SMEATON, JOHN xx-xxi 7, 31, 32, 33, 35, 36, 40, 41, 46, 47, 49, 53, 54, 55, 57, 58, 59, 60, 61, 62, 63, 64, 65, 66, 68, 70, 116, 127, 155, 156, 192, 205; *62*
– and Eddystone Light-house 30
– third Eddystone light-house 61-70; *67, 67, 67*
– *A Narrative of the Building …* 31, 44, 54, 58, 65, 116, 131; *31*

Smiles, Samuel 70, 134

Smith, Diana 95, 133-34

Smith, James 15-16, 108; *16*

Smith, Janet 169

Smith, Thomas ('Leerie Smith') xxi, 10, 13-15, 20, 21, 22, 102, 105, 107, 108, 126, 172

Smith, Thomas (grandson) 15

Smiths & Co., Edinburgh 14, 15, 200

Smyth, Charles Piazzi 162

Society for Promoting the Useful Arts in Scotland (*see* Royal Scottish Society of Arts)

Soleil, François 147
– burning lens 147, 148, 152, 157; *147, 157, 158, 161*

Soleil, François, *jeune* 151, 152, 153

Solway 95
– Firth 4, 104, 230

Sound of Mull 76, 82

Sound of Sleat 178

Sound Toll Registers, Copenhagen 81

South Foreland (*see* LIGHT-HOUSES)

Southerness (*see* LIGHT-HOUSES)

Southey, Robert 115

*Spieghel der Zeevaerdt* 87

Spragge, Edward 56

Spry, Dr 60, 61

Standard Positioning Service (SPS) 228

Stanley, William, 9th Earl of Derby 145

Start Point, Devon (*see* LIGHTHOUSES)

Start Point, Orkney (*see* LIGHTHOUSES)

Steele, Richard 35

261

Stephens Island, New
Zealand 204; *204*
Steven & Struthers,
Messrs, Glasgow xxiii,
137, *214*
Stevenson, Alexander 77

STEVENSON FAMILY
Stevenson, Alan 6, 7, 8,
16, 18, 19, 20, 25, 128,
134, 135, 190, 191,
193; *156, 158, 168*
– *Account of the Skerry-
vore Lighthouse* 146,
147, 155, 163, 166, 167;
*128, 161*
– early lighthouse work
146-53
– lighthouse work after
Skerryvore 160-64
– retirement of 174, 177,
187, 192, 193, 194
– *Rudimentary Treatise ...
on Lighthouses* 18
– and Skerryvore light-
house 153-60
Stevenson business xxiv,
109, 174
– D. & C. Stevenson 137,
187, 188, 206
– D. & T. Stevenson 102,
108, 136, 167, 170,
172, 174-82, 187, 188,
192, 194; *208*
work in India 195;
work in Japan 198-200,
202; work in New
Zealand 203, 207
– Robert Stevenson &
Sons, Civil Engineers:
rock lighthouses and
optics 174-82, 187, 189,
190; wireless communi-
cation 206-207
– work abroad 188-205
Stevenson, Charles
– 'On a New Form of
Refractor' 172, 182,
212, 213; *206*
– 'talking beacon' 222
Stevenson, D. Alan xxi, 3,
8, 9, 10, 12, 17, 18, 45,
133, 134, 136, 207; *207*
Stevenson, David 134,
153, 166, 167, 168, 171,
174, 175, 175, 182; *166*
– aseismatic joint 200-
201
Stevenson, David A. xxiii,
137, 171, 181, 182,
213; *xxii, 206, 214*

– and Flannan Islands
lighthouse 223
Stevenson family xxi, 25,
160, 165, 234-35
– family tree 239
Stevenson, Robert xxi,
xxiii, 1, 5, 18, 19, 20,
22, 24, 25, 26, 31, 32,
70, 98, 99, 101, 102,
105, 107, 108, 109, 116,
117-41, 145, 146, 147,
148, 149, 153, 154, 162,
165, 167, 169, 182, 189,
190; *xxiv, 97, 116, 166*
– *Account of the Bell
Rock Lighthouse* 65,
115, 116, 117, 118, 129,
133, 135; *114, 132*
– in *Edinburgh Encyclo-
paedia* 1, 190, 192,
195, 205, 219
– and Portland High
Lighthouse 26, 29
Stevenson, Robert Louis
13, 15, 116, 117, 135,
170-171, 181; *170*
– as author and writer
13, 15 171, 176, 179-81
– 'On a New Form of
Intermittent Light' 171
Stevenson, Thomas 153,
154, 157, 164, 166, 167,
168, 169, 170, 172, 174;
*168, 191*
– and Alexander Fraser
194, 211, 212, 219
– azimuthal condensing
system 178
– combined front Fresnel
lens 179; *179*
– fixed condensing light
180, 182, 189
– lighting systems of 178,
179, 180, 182, 189; *178*
– and Ornsay lighthouse
178; *178*
– and Stevenson screen
174, 177
– and Tay leading light
179

Stirlingshire 13, 78
Stornoway 178
Stroma (*see* LIGHT-
HOUSES)
Stromness 213, 226
Strout, Thomas 61
Sturt, John (I.) 38, 49, 51,
*52*
– and Rudyerd's light-
house 39

Sule Skerry (*see* LIGHT-
HOUSES)
Sumburgh Head (*see*
LIGHTHOUSES)
sundials 82
– at Lamlash *173*
Swan, Professor William
13, 166, 168, 169-170,
179; *169*
Sweden 20
Swinburne & Co., R. W.
151
Syme, John *116; 166*

Taiaroa Head, New
Zealand (*see* LIGHT-
HOUSES)
Tait, Peter Guthrie 168
Tarbat Ness (Tarbetness)
(*see* LIGHTHOUSES)
Tay
– Firth of 11, 89, 98,
103, 115
– 'Leading Lights of Tay'
103
– River 4, 11, 12, 89, 198,
101, 102; *103* (*see* Bud-
don Ness *under* LIGHT-
HOUSES)
Taylor, A. B. 80, 84
Taylor, E. G. R. 1
telephone/radio-telephone
210, 222, 225; *222*
Telford, Thomas 134
Thomson, John Turnbull
173-74, 190-92
Tiree, Isle of 151, 153,
154
Tolcher, Mr *59, 60*
Tolcher, Joseph 60
Torran reef 179, 180
Tory Island, New Zealand
(*see* LIGHTHOUSES)
Toward Point 22
traverse board 83; *83*
Tresco Abbey Gardens 10
Trinity House (*see*
GENERAL LIGHTHOUSE
AUTHORITIES)
Trinity House, Dundee
(*see* Dundee)
Turner, J. M. W. 115,
117, 177; *xx, 114*
Tynemouth (*see* LIGHT-
HOUSES)

UHF radio 225
Umpherston, Messrs 210
Unst (*see* Muckle Flugga)
United States Lighthouse
Establishment 194

University College, London
197
Ushenish 225, 231

Valparaiso 205
Verney, Sir John, Viscount
Fermanagh and Baron
Belturbet of Fermanagh
47, 48
VHF radio 231, 225

Waghenaer, Lucas Jansz
87, 88
Waitemata Harbour, New
Zealand (*see* LIGHT-
HOUSES)
Walker, Ezekiel 21, 22
Wallace, William 167
Wane, Marshall *185*
Watchet limestone 66
Waterston, Charles xix
Watt, James 17
Weston, Robert xx, 47,
55, 57, 60, 61-63, 66
Weston, Robert Harcourt
xx-xxi, 55, 60
Weymouth 64
Whalsay
– Out Skerries 175 (*see*
LIGHTHOUSES)
Whitehaven 145
Whitfield, Walter 35, 36
Wigham, John Richardson
211-12
Wight, Isle of 3
Willett, John 197
William III, King 34, 35,
40, 44
Winstanley, Elizabeth 45,
46
Winstanley, Henry 33-46,
47, 51, 54, 62, 63
– engraving of Eddystone
Lighthouse 39
– Winstanley's Water-
works (Piccadilly Water
Theatre) 35
Wirral 20
Wood, Sir Andrew 78
Wright, Mike 223

Yarmouth 24
Yokohama (*see* LIGHT-
HOUSES)
Young, James
– paraffin 207

The Scottish coastline remains one of the most dangerous in the world. The story of how her margins were lit is one of determined engineering endeavour and heroic struggle against the elements. The Northern Lighthouse Board, formed in 1786, continues to assist mariners and live up to its motto *'In Salutem Omnium'*, for the safety of all.

The story begins in Egypt, with one of the Seven Wonders of the Ancient World, for all lighthouse builders have learned from their predecessors. Using the collections of National Museums Scotland, this account shows how the world's first rock lighthouse in the dangerous English Channel at the Eddystone Reef off Plymouth was first destroyed by storm and then by fire, before being made in stone, and outlasting the rock itself. The lessons learned there were absorbed by the young Robert Stevenson, whose apprenticeship with his step-father Thomas Smith allowed him to experience at first hand the darkness and the dangers of Scotland's perilous coastline. Stevenson's building of a light-house on the dangerous Inchcape Reef, or Bell Rock, 11 miles from Arbroath, would prove to be his most important engineering success.

Robert Stevenson's family was associated with lighthouse construction for a further three generations, not only in Scotland, but in Newfoundland, Burma, Japan and New Zealand. This account, drawn from their writings and illustrated by the unmatched collection of lighthouse artefacts, often made for exhibition at the nineteenth century international trade fairs in London and Paris, now held by National Museums Scotland, is brought up to date with how the Northern Lighthouse Board operates today.

National Museums Scotland

RRP £17.99
ISBN: 978-1-905267-47-7

9 781905 267477

www.nms.ac.uk/books